EXHIBIT
of
APPLIED PHOTOGRAPHY

Prepared by
WILLIAM F. WINTER
of Schenectady, N. Y.

✤

Under the auspices of the
LENOX LIBRARY ASSOCIATION
Sedgwick Hall, Lenox, Mass.
August 23 — September 8
1934

SHAKER HANDICRAFTS

NOVEMBER 12 TO DECEMBER 12, 1935

WHITNEY MUSEUM OF AMERICAN ART

TEN WEST EIGHTH STREET · NEW YORK

THE
SHA

Opening Reception
Monday, October 10th, 3 to 6 P. M.
Continuing until October 30th

FURNITURE, INDUSTRIAL MATERIAL AND TEXTILES
OF THE SHAKERS OF NEW ENGLAND
AND NEW YORK
Lent by EDWARD D. ANDREWS, Ph.D.
and FAITH ANDREWS, of Pittsfield, Mass.

CAMERA STUDIES OF THE SHAKER COMMUNITIES
OF HANCOCK, MASS., AND MOUNT LEBANON, N. Y.
Made and Lent by William F. Winter
of Schenectady, N. Y.

THE TRUSTEES OF THE

WORCESTER ART MUSEUM

REQUEST THE HONOR OF YOUR PRESENCE

AT A PRIVATE VIEW OF AN

EXHIBITION OF
SHAKER ARTS AND CRAFTS

ASSEMBLED BY

MR. AND MRS. EDWARD DEMING ANDREWS

ON WEDNESDAY EVENING, DECEMBER THE SEVENTH

NINETEEN HUNDRED AND THIRTY-EIGHT

AT EIGHT-THIRTY O'CLOCK

MR. ANDREWS WILL SPEAK BRIEFLY

IN THE GALLERIES

EXHIBIT
of
SHAKER FURNITURE

Under the auspices of the
LENOX LIBRARY ASSOCIATION
LENOX, MASSACHUSETTS
August 23 — September 8

Shaker Art and Craftsmanship

An Exhibition at the Berkshire Museum,
Pittsfield, Massachusetts. Opening July the
Thirtieth, Nineteen Hundred and Forty.

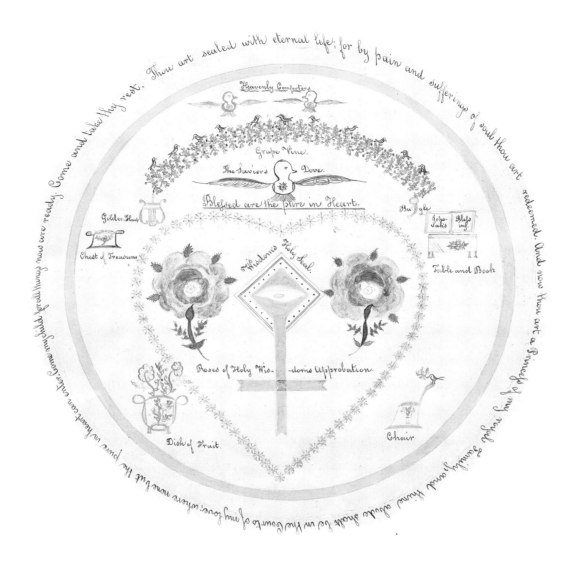

GATHER UP THE FRAGMENTS:

The Andrews Shaker Collection

Mario S. De Pillis and Christian Goodwillie

Distributed by Yale University Press
New Haven and London

Title Page:
From Holy Mother Wisdom . . . To Eldress Dana or Mother (detail)
Miranda Barber, Mount Lebanon, N.Y. 1848
Ink and watercolor; 9 3/4" x 7 5/8"
(pages 248-249)

© 2008 Hancock Shaker Village, Inc.
Published by Hancock Shaker Village, Inc.
Distributed by Yale University Press
Photography by Michael Fredericks
Design by Laura Rogers, Dandelion Design, Inc.

Support for the exhibition and catalog provided by

Country Curtains.   **TD Banknorth**

Library of Congress Control Number: 2008924518

ISBN: 978-0-300-13760-6

Printed in Italy by L.E.G.O., Vicenza.

Table of Contents

Acknowledgments

Mario S. De Pillis: When asked to tell the story of the Andrewses as collectors, scholars, and persons, I felt that the task might be impossible. For helping me make it possible my profound thanks go to: Edward Deming Andrews II, Paul S. Boyer, Alexander F. De Pillis, Vincent B. De Pillis, John Demos, Harry Fiss, Heidi Fritschel, Alex Kent, Stephen J. Paterwic, Margo Miller, Ellen Spear, Darryl Thompson, and above all my friend and co-author, Christian Goodwillie. E. Richard McKinstry and Jeanne Solensky of the Winterthur Library were wonderfully responsive. Our copyeditor, Debby Smith, tactfully probed the soft spots. In retrieving the obscure but crucial local history of Shirley, Massachusetts Robert Adam of the Shirley Historical Society and Hugh Davis of Leverett, Massachusetts were indispensable. Tapping his vast knowledge of Shaker literature, manuscripts, and objects as well as his experience as an early staff member at Hancock, David D. Newell inspired me to redirect a primitive early draft. With lawyerly balance and precision, my son, Vincent B. De Pillis, critiqued my initial disorganization and enriched some overly direct passages with nuance. Christian Goodwillie, a joy to work with, was amazingly patient with my aged and persnickety views.

But I could not really have completed or even begun the work without the friendship and enthusiastic cooperation of the Andrewses' daughter, Ann E. Andrews Kane, and her husband, Thomas Kane.

Christian Goodwillie: Working on this book has been an incredible experience for me. My initial research was conducted at the Winterthur Library, and was supported by a Faith Andrews Fellowship administered and coordinated by Kasey Grier and Kay Collins. Librarians E. Richard McKinstry, Jeanne Solensky, and Emily Guthrie were patient and extremely helpful as I explored the Andrews Archives. At the Winterthur Museum Beth Parker Miller and Lisa Minardi showed me many, if not all, of the Shaker objects given by the Andrewses. The late John Sweeney was kind enough to consent to an interview about his friendship with the Andrewses. Sandra Barghini, Laura Beresford, Kate Hebert, Stuart Ross and Roger Chivers at the American Museum in Britain were exceptional hosts when I traveled to see the extraordinary Shaker objects in their collection. Stuart Ross's beautiful photographs of many of those objects grace the pages of this book. Julie Zeftel and Deanna Cross from the Image Library of The Metropolitan Museum of Art helpfully managed my requests for new photography of Shaker furniture at The Met. Kristen Leipert of the Frances Mulhall Achilles Library and Archives at the Whitney Museum of American Art brought many excellent documents and photographs to my attention. Craig Williams and Robyn Gibson of the New York State Museum provided access to Charles Adams's notebooks and also valuable historic photographs in that collection. Richard Brooker kindly allowed us to use a stereoview of the Shaker school at Mount Lebanon, New York. David Schorsch, and Willis and Karel Henry all cheerfully allowed us to use photographs they had commissioned. Ray Lavoie deserves recognition for the wonderful photographs he made of objects in the collection of Dr. Ribic and Dr. Kingsley. Finally, the late Alison Ledes of The Magazine *Antiques* provided access and permission to the historic photographs from that magazine which are reproduced herein.

This book could not possibly be considered comprehensive without the cheerful participation of the many private collectors who have objects formerly belonging to the Andrewses in their collections. I wish to sincerely thank Thomas R. and Ann Andrews Kane, Phyllis Andrews, Edward Deming Andrews II, J.J. Gerald and Miriam McCue, M. Stephen and Miriam R. Miller, Thomas and Jan Pavlovic, Bob and Aileen Hamilton, Andrew Epstein, John Ribic and Carla Kingsley, J. Richard and E. Barbara Pierce, William and Sandra Soule, David and Virginia Newell, and Gene and Karen Faul. Special additional thanks must go to David Newell, Edward Deming Andrews II, M. Stephen Miller, and Tom Queen, who each made extraordinary efforts in connecting me with people who had objects or history relevant to this project. Thank you to Garrett V. Andrews for his touching remembrance of his grandparents. Conservator Alex Carlisle undertook careful and expert repairs on some of the objects depicted. Jane Crosthwaite and Glendyne Wergland provided very helpful and close readings of the essay texts—on very short notice—this was most appreciated! Thanks to Frank and Cornelia Frisbee Houde, and Robert Adam, for helping flesh out the story of Ted Andrews's time in Shirley, and providing excellent historic photographs. This book would not bear the imprimatur of Yale University Press without the guidance of John Demos, for which we heartily thank him. Chris Rogers, Chris Coffin, and Laura Davulis at Yale University Press have all been patient shepherds of this book as it has slowly evolved, we are thrilled to have worked with them.

Finally, I must thank the people most central to this project. Ellen Spear deserves generous thanks for recognizing the need to meet the obligations of Hancock Shaker Village, Inc. to the Andrews family. I am privileged to have been given the opportunity to have compiled and co-authored this work. My co-workers and friends Michael Vogt, Jessica Kuhnen, Adriana De la Cuadra, Anita Orosz, Paul Lange, and Maria Biajoli all deserve my thanks for their careful attention to detail in helping me understand the true extent of the Andrews Collection at Hancock Shaker Village. Debby Smith has once again done an outstanding job of copy-editing a book I have been involved in. Special thanks goes to Magda Gabor-Hotchkiss for her enthusiasm in indexing this volume. Brother Arnold Hadd provided important information, otherwise unavailable, on the Andrewses' forays into Maine. Additionally, he, Stephen Paterwic and Timothy D. Rieman provided thoughtful criticism of my writing. Big thanks to Todd Burdick for being Todd. Mary Rentz is the main reason I've had this excellent opportunity, I won't forget that, thank you. I must also extend great thanks to Michael Fredericks, whose stunning photographs reveal the inherent beauty of these Shaker objects as never before, and who was also an excellent traveling companion. The talented Laura Rogers of Dandelion Design deserves tremendous credit for putting up with me through all the twists and turns of assembling this book. She has done a beautiful job in designing it and has my eternal gratitude. Most of all I thank my co-author, friend, sometime houseguest, and mentor, Mario S. De Pillis, for grounding me in his experiences with the Andrewses as living human beings who I will never know. Working with Mario has been an outstanding experience. Lastly, I wish to recognize my parents Gretchen and Douglas Goodwillie, and my wife Erika (and Creetchio, Clover, and Hipolito for stepping on my papers as often as possible), for all the love and support they have given me over the years. Thank you all!

Foreword

We are honored to present this publication to accompany our major exhibition of the Andrews Collection. This book fulfils a forty-five year-old promise. The fulfillment of this promise goes far beyond tidying up a contractual obligation. This catalogue, documenting the extraordinary collecting foresight of Faith and Edward Deming Andrews, is a testament to their unwavering devotion to the Shakers and equally to the vision and passion of Amy Bess Miller. Indeed, we who are the current stewards of the "City of Peace" each day must fulfill a promise to the founding board of the Village and to all of the people over the past forty-five years who have nurtured this special place.

You will read in Mario S. De Pillis's essay, of a letter written by the great Trappist monk, Thomas Merton, who wrote, in describing the importance of studying Shaker culture, "There can be so much meaning to a study of this kind: meaning for twentieth century America which has lost so much in the last hundred years – lost while seeming to gain."

But what of us in the twenty-first century? Ted Andrews set down "twelve precepts" which were his dream for the use of his collection in interpreting Shaker culture. They still ring true for us today, as does Amy Bess Miller's notion that making the Shakers accessible can kindle interest and passion for their culture and beliefs.

Drawing on wisdom from both the Andrewses and Amy Bess Miller, HSV continues to bring the Shaker story to life today by exploring and emphasizing those aspects of Shaker life (some of the 12 precepts) that have special relevance to our lives in this moment. In 2008, they are sustainable agriculture, renewable energy and historic preservation. No doubt in the future, other aspects of Shaker culture—other precepts—will be more important to the public and the future stewards of Hancock will emphasize them accordingly. Each generation's ability to draw from the Shaker culture that which is most important will make their experience timeless and worthy of preservation, interpretation and emulation.

Despite events that led to a disaffection between the Andrewses and Hancock, the ability of the Village to be true both to the Andrewses' ideals and to Amy Bess Miller's practical vision will be the enduring legacy of these figures and the ultimate reason for Hancock Shaker Village's permanence.

Our special thanks to the current Board of Trustees of Hancock Shaker Village, whose belief in our mission and support of this endeavor make this publication possible, to TDBankNorth and Country Curtains for their financial support of the exhibition and catalog, to the Andrews family for their encouragement and access to important records, and to the Miller family for their continued interest in the Village and their commitment to public life in the Berkshires.

We are honored to fulfill the promise to the Andrewses that this catalog represents, and to acknowledge the international importance of Hancock Shaker Village's collections and of its establishment by Amy Bess Miller almost 50 years ago. One without the other would have left us with only half the story.

Ellen Spear, *President & CEO*
May 2008

A Family Remembrance

Edward Deming Andrews ca. 1940
Collection of the Family of David V. and Phyllis C. Andrews

My paternal grandfather, Edward Deming Andrews, died in 1964 when I was eleven. He was survived by his wife, Faith, for twenty-five years. Edward knew of the Shakers prior to 1923. Looking back, however, Faith would always characterize hers and Edward's initial encounters with the Hancock Shakers in 1923 as having been fateful. Edward would very likely agree, but his early death makes knowing impossible. This, however, I *do* know, and largely from my own pre-teenage personal experience of him: Edward Deming Andrews— in all his aspects, including his communicative skills, demeanor, education, values, et al.— was ideally suited for what became his life's work.

Early on in life my grandfather demonstrated a natural propensity for introspection, language and the written word. By age thirty-six he would have a Ph.D., but as a twelve-year-old boy in 1906 he initiated a diary, an ambitious project at any age. Diary entries are numerous, regular and detailed through 1914, the product of an unusual discipline, order and insight. Leafing through this diary recently, I found its preface to be emblematic of its author. After giving his name and address and asking the diary's finder to return it, Edward states: "Ye Reader will please excuse egotisme expressed hereine—". Anyone who knew my grandfather might describe him as an observant, always active intellect or as a man with an outwardly quiet depth, but never as one whose ego seemed dominant. Albeit ironically, Edward's self-mocking apology to the reader of his youthful diary is more indicative of his desire for ego not to appear than it is of anything else.

Faith shared with me that once, before I was born, when they were driving down a dirt road in the Berkshires, my grandfather accidentally hit a rabbit. When you hit something like this you know it, but how many of us would immediately stop, turn around, find the mortally wounded rabbit, and end its misery?

Many years later, and from a grandson's perspective, Edward's persona would manifest itself differently. Except when he was surprised once to find a woodchuck in his vegetable garden, I have no recollection at all of my grandfather being animated or agitated. He always appeared even-tempered, deliberate, considered, ruled much more by intellect than emotion—serene. I remember that my grandfather would participate in but would not dominate a conversation among adults. On the rare occasion I ever saw him dressed with any form of necktie, it would always be a bow tie, but his typical garb would be a plain white cotton buttoned long sleeved shirt tucked into equally plain khaki trousers. Dressed thusly, if at home he would be sitting in his wing chair, pipe nearby, actively listening to his only son or my mother or maybe Faith.

I was just getting to know my grandfather, Edward Deming Andrews, when he died. But I am certain he died fulfilled, a gentle, peaceful man whose calling, having matured and ripened over time, came to fruition as soon as he and Faith alighted from their Model T and first smelled Hancock's baking bread.

Garrett V. Andrews
May 2008

Introduction

"Gather up the fragments that remain, that nothing be lost." John 6:12

The United Society of Believers in Christ's Second Appearing, commonly called Shakers, used the above quotation on their "Table Monitor," a broadside poem posted in Shaker dining rooms. For the Shakers the verse from John was a reminder to eat everything on their plates, to waste nothing.

The pioneering Shaker scholars and collectors Edward Deming Andrews and Faith Young Andrews quoted this same verse in their classic 1937 book *Shaker Furniture* (p. 68) in a descriptive caption written for a photo of a communal dining table. This simple example of the Andrewses' awareness of how the material and spiritual worlds were combined in Shaker culture is a kind of metaphor for their life's mission and work. The Andrewses, beginning in 1923, and continuing until the death of Faith Andrews in 1990, worked to "gather up the fragments" of Shaker culture. They energetically collected objects, studied sources, mounted exhibitions, and published books on Shaker culture. Simultaneously, they engaged in deep friendships with the Shakers, and also important figures in the New York City art-world of the 1930s. The Andrewses, as Mario S. De Pillis points out in his essay, were proselytizers for Shaker culture. It was through the efforts of Edward Deming and Faith Andrews that Shaker furniture has come into the American vernacular. It is also due to their efforts that large collections of Shaker materials exist at Hancock Shaker Village, The Metropolitan Museum of Art, The Winterthur Museum, and The American Museum in Britain. The Andrewses collected all objects great and small—gift drawings, manuscripts, printed works, furniture, boxes, kitchenware, metalware, textiles, tools—in short, anything touched by the Shakers. Through careful documentation and scholarship the Andrewses illuminated these materials, and their work and their collection have bequeathed to future generations the most comprehensive body of evidence on the culture of the United Society of Believers.

This book fulfills an important obligation to the Andrews family on the part of Hancock Shaker Village, Inc. In an unpublished manuscript written in 1983 entitled "The Hancock Story" Faith Andrews wrote the following: "This treatise is submitted in the hope that history will eventually have access to the true Hancock story, the story of our efforts to establish the museum through our knowledge and collection. Only when this is accomplished can the full meaning of Hancock's spiritual name 'The City of Peace' be restored." With this volume we have attempted to "gather up the fragments" of the Andrewses' legacy—both material and scholarly. It is our sincere hope that the essays, catalog, and illustrations contained herein will finally and amply recognize and honor the tremendous contributions of Edward Deming and Faith Andrews, not only to Hancock Shaker Village, Inc., but to the understanding and preservation of Shaker culture as a whole.

Mario S. De Pillis and Christian Goodwillie
May 2008

Edward Deming Andrews ca. 1920.

Collection of Thomas R. and Ann Andrews Kane

The Edward Deming Andrews Shaker Collection: Saving a Culture

By Mario S. De Pillis

Three somewhat shadowy go-betweens intervene between works of art and the gallery goer:
the dealer, the collector, and the museum curator.
  —John Updike, "The Artful Clarks"

Blessed be nothing.
  —Sadie Neale, Shaker sister, Mount Lebanon, N.Y.

The storied collection of Shaker materials bearing the name of Edward Deming Andrews has entered the mainstream of American social and cultural history. From its inception in the 1920s to its final disposition in the 1960s, the collection also generated a history of its own that helped alter conceptions of American art and expand our understanding of American religion and culture.

The Shakers, formally known as the United Society of Believers in Christ's Second Appearing, began dying out in the late nineteenth century. With a passion rivaling that of the original early Shakers, Edward "Ted" Deming Andrews (1894–1964) and his wife, Faith Young Andrews (1896–1990), believed that the Shakers had created a unique culture, lofty in its principles and matchless in the design of every object they crafted. Accordingly, the Andrewses devoted their lives to collecting every conceivable product of Shaker hands, as well as the manuscripts and books that showed forth the mind and spirit of the Believers. Between the early 1920s, when they started, and 1937, when their book on Shaker furniture brought them national recognition, they had changed from collectors to proselytizers, with a mission to save a culture in terminal decay, and they pursued their mission with unrelenting zeal.[1]

They had sore need of zeal. At that time, influential proponents of "high" art who considered Shaker objects "rural" or "primitive" controlled the museums and the art markets. The Andrewses had to persuade the tastemakers and custodians of art and culture that Shaker craftsmanship and design and even Shaker religion were things of unique beauty that must be rescued for posterity. Not until the late 1930s did the Andrewses find success. But neither their mission nor their collection was complete until the 1960s, and so they labored on (to use a Shaker expression) to the end of their lives.

The history of the Andrews Collection from the 1920s to the 1960s illuminates the conflicts of class and ideology in the life of museums and among the collectors who supply them; it also illustrates the changing attitudes of museums and art historians toward "folk" art and "high" art. Through their writings and their collection the Andrewses introduced the history and culture of the Shakers to an international audience.

Inseparable from the history of the collection is the story of the Andrewses' increasingly desperate attempts to find a permanent home for their huge accumulation of Shaker materials, a tale full of betrayals, disappointments, broken friendships, and unappreciated donations. The collection came to rest in three ideal homes: the American Museum of Bath, England, the Winterthur Museum and Library in Winterthur, Delaware, and Hancock Shaker Village, Inc. on the edge of Pittsfield, Massachusetts.

The history of the Andrews Collection is intertwined with the biography of the Andrewses themselves and with the great cultural ferment in the city of New York in the 1920s and 1930s. The Andrewses' mission transported them from their small-town origins to a much larger world, where they were able to wield enormous influence. They came to know and interact with various aspects of American culture from the luminaries of the art world of New York City to cultural bureaucrats of Washington, D.C., and the Trappists of the Abbey of Gethsemani (the Trappist spelling) in Kentucky.

The life and works of the Andrewses have sparked curious hostilities, mostly since the late 1980s. The storied jealousies of the academic and museum worlds make the petty contentions over the Andrewses understandable, if not edifying. In the disposition of great art, the usual elements have long wielded their influence: the desire for fame, the drive for prestige among various institutions, the corrosion of sexual politics, the tyranny of anecdote—and the power of money. Biography can then become susceptible, more than intellectual or institutional history, to the self-promotion of the biographer at the expense of the subject. Janet Malcolm has brilliantly illuminated the problem in her study of the "world" of Gertrude Stein that arose after that figure's death.[2] The history of Gertrude Stein's art collection belongs on the world stage; the history of the Andrews Collection, while less grand, exhibits a similar dynamic. Every *Nachlass* presents problems for the historian.[3]

As a participant observer, even an actor, in the crucial part of that history from 1956 to the death of Ted Andrews in 1964, I cannot entirely avoid the dangers of *parti pris*. In the essay that follows, I tell the story of the Andrewses as impartially as I can—however, it will soon become apparent to the reader that I have a deep respect for the Andrewses' achievement, and that I fundamentally disagree with those who in recent years have portrayed the Andrewses as self-seeking antique dealers and shallow scholars. Finally, with regard to their formidable opponent, Amy Bess Miller, I must emphasize that though she must appear unsympathetic at times, she was a person of enormous talent and significant achievement. There would have been no restoration of Hancock Shaker Village without her.

My own friendship with the Andrewses began in 1956. Ted Andrews inscribed a copy of his book *The People Called Shakers* to me as his "favorite student at Yale," where I was a doctoral candidate in American history from 1955 to 1958. Actually, I was never his student, just a helper during his two-year tenure as a Yale Fellow in the Department of American Studies. He took a shine to me because of my research interest in the Shakers, and we discussed our common interest frequently. I could see the nobility of his intentions in trying to preserve for posterity the principles and art of an entire culture.

The earliest thoughts of Ted Andrews about the Shakers had nothing to do with educational theories or any heroic effort to save the remains of Shaker culture. Rather, the Andrews Collection had its origins in the mind of an idealistic young soldier who dreamed of greatness as a poet or novelist and conceived the idea of writing the great American novel on the subject of the Shakers. His literary activities and debates in 1918–19 in a remarkable salon in Shirley, Massachusetts, a short distance from his barracks, earned him the sobriquet "the Poet-Sergeant."

The Poet-Sergeant of Camp Devens

On June 22, 1919, just two months before his discharge, Ted Andrews made an entry in his journal that illuminates the entire history of the Andrews Collection and puts to rest the oft-repeated canard that his interest in the Shakers was a later outgrowth of antique collecting.

Edward Deming Andrews
at Camp Devens.
Collection of Thomas R. and Ann Andrews Kane

As I was walking to work yesterday morning, I thought how bold and adventurous a scheme it would be to live this fall and winter and next spring with the Shakers of West Pittsfield or Lebanon, studying and amassing notes on their ways and customs, endeavoring to analyze their characters and their religion—and then, out alone, away from it all, to weave a romance into that background of somberness and quaint decadence.

For the Shakers are passing away, I thought to myself. They have left Shirley, a pitiful remanant [*sic*]. They will not be long in the Berkshire Hills, in the country I know best of all. My romance would have there more truth, more beauty a greater reality.[4]

In four additional entries for that day the twenty-five-year-old Andrews reflected on what the future held for him, on his desire for recognition in some field (he was thinking of literature), and on his feeling that he must confront evil in the world and, while seeking success, that he must avoid the sin of pride. He had a deep Christian sense of sin. In the poems and late-night entries in his Camp Devens journal he expressed his hopes and self-doubts with naked honesty. He yearned for spiritual fulfillment, for a great vocation, which he ultimately found in the study and preservation of Shaker culture.

This true wellspring of Ted's fascination with the Shakers is far removed from the folkloric version, recounted many years later, of how the Andrewses' life with the Shakers began. That account, widely repeated, might be called the Shaker Loaf of Bread story.

One September afternoon in 1923, so the story goes, a young schoolteacher and his wife were driving their Model T Ford east from the New York state line to their hometown of Pittsfield, Massachusetts. They had been visiting antique shops, looking for old china and pewter. As they came down the mountain toward Hancock Shaker Village—known to them from early youth—they decided to stop and buy a loaf of the Shakers' fine bread. As they looked around the Shaker kitchen, the beauty of every visible object struck them: "We decided that this was it. We were taken with it at once. Of course, all we could see were kitchen bowls [and chairs] but they were beautiful things." They had tasted, they wrote, quoting the Shakers, "the crums of heaven."[5]

Thus did the couple explain, over half a century later, how they started collecting Shaker materials. In fact, the Andrewses' collecting had begun earlier and what Faith remembered was their second Hancock visit. Even their daughter thought the story a bit "romanticized."[6] Though the folkloric version jumbled the chronology a bit, there is no doubt that some kind of renewed enthusiasm did emerge around 1923.[7]

Anti-Andrews writers repeat the Loaf of Bread story to prove how the Andrewses (particularly Ted) romanticized the Shakers. Recent examples may be found in the work of Stephen Bowe and Peter Richmond and of Stephen J. Stein, who portrays Edward Deming Andrews as a self-seeking operator, as a man who "sentimentalized" and "spiritualized" the Shakers (as though the Shakers had nothing to do with spiritual matters), as a naïf who deceived himself and compromised his work by identifying with the Shakers, and as a propagandist who sought to make the Shakers "highly marketable."[8] Stein also follows the traditional dating of the Andrewses' first interest in the Shakers from the bread incident of 1923.

The fiery young idealist of Camp Devens was indeed a romantic, but in the best sense of the word.[9] The Andrews Collection began neither in the hobby or business of collecting antiques nor in the chance purchase of a loaf of bread but in the aspirations of a young man in his twenties. Ted's youthful diary supplies an eloquent rebuttal to the anti-Andrews critics of the past fifteen years for whom Andrews was not a scholar or idealist but an antique dealer. Most notably, it frees the record of the folkloric version that they themselves came to believe.

The Sergeant Poet more than fulfilled his dream. Surely Ted's diary entry shows that he was moved by the idea of the dying Shakers. He intended to live among the Shakers and then go away, alone, and "weave a romance into that background of somberness and quaint decadence"—a thought reminiscent of the mentality of the many white writers, painters, and photographers who, in the same era, visited the Indians of the trans-Mississippi West to record them before they disappeared.

But instead this "decadent" culture converted Ted Andrews himself to an idealistic way of life loosely based on Shaker principles sometimes called "the Shaker Way." What the young soldier originally viewed as a somber and quaint culture, he came to see as a uniquely humane, joyful, and admirable way of life.

Within a few years, the Shaker "remnant" that the young idealist of Camp Devens had hoped to memorialize in literature in fact proved strong enough to co-opt Ted Andrews, the mature scholar, with a vision of Shaker purity.

Frank and Shirley Lawton: A Salon for Soldiers

In June 1919, when Ted Andrews made his diary entry about his "bold and adventurous scheme" to live with the Shakers, he was already having a bold and adventurous experience as a member of a discussion group devoted to literature, philosophy, politics, and high culture—a salon hosted by Frank Lawton and his daughter, Shirley. Most participants were soldiers from nearby Camp Devens, who had an easy walk to the Lawton home from their barracks. Also nearby were the two recently defunct Shaker villages of Shirley and Harvard, where Lawton had some connections. The building of Camp Devens and its use in World War I pushed the population of the Shirley area from three thousand to a "floating population" of thirty thousand between 1917 and 1920.[10]

Oil portraits of Frank Jephthah Lawton and his daughter Shirley Lawton Houde circa 1917.

All images on this page are from the Collection of Frank L. & Cornelia H. Frisbee Houde.

Frank Lawton was a native of the town, with roots going back to the eighteenth century.[11] Although he dabbled in antiques, running a small business on the side, a modest family inheritance allowed him ample time to express his cultivated tastes and to entertain soldiers. His daughter, who married Billie Houde, one of the soldiers, later wrote a memoir of those exciting times in her family. Her title, "Water for Soldiers," is an allusion to the locally famous sign that Frank Lawton posted in front of his house, inviting passing soldiers (whether drilling or away from camp on breaks) to stop and drink cold, pure well-water. Hundreds did so in summer, even those who came on horseback.

Ted Andrews appears twice in Shirley Lawton Houde's memoir—though not by name. In describing dozens of individuals (not all soldiers) she used monikers: the Persian, the Italian, the Hebrew, the Saint (a Mormon), the Poet. She elevated Ted above the ethnic and religious stereotypes, calling him "the Poet Sergeant," and proudly noted his visit around 1939 to the Lawtons, some twenty years later: "The Poet Sergeant and his loyal wife are experts on all matters of the vanishing Shaker sect. Their son [David Volk] and daughter [Ann E.] are almost grown."[12] Billie Houde and Shirley Lawton Houde often talked about the Andrewses and remembered that Frank Lawton showed the Andrews children the Shaker "record books" he had found at the local dump. The Houdes remained close friends of the Andrewses for fifty years.[13]

The discussion group (Frank Lawton's daughter called it "a gathering of literary people") was a special part of a vast civilian effort to help keep up the morale of the thousands of soldiers who came to Camp Devens in 1917. Frank Lawton was the local leader of the War Camp Community Service, analogous to the USO (United Service Organizations) of World War II, entertaining as many as 250 soldiers on his grounds. From 1917 to about 1921 over a thousand solders signed his Soldier Books, many calling him Daddy. His dedication to the discussion group went far beyond his formal obligations to the War Camp Community Service.

The wide-ranging discussions shook Ted Andrews to his core, leading him to question his values, search his conscience, think about his goals, and plan for some kind of literary future. His inner turmoil reached a peak on June 22, 1919, when he made the longest entry in his journal—on the same date that included the passage on devoting his life to the study of the Shakers. The Lawton Salon analyzed everything from the ideas of Walt Whitman to the future of America and the world and challenged his religious and ethical beliefs. Although he attended the meetings faithfully, Ted also felt intimidated by the "intellectual giants" who aggressively and cleverly argued their radical positions.

This sign, nailed to the corner of the Lawton's house, advertised "Water for Soldiers."

Ted and Faith Andrews signed Frank Lawton's Soldier Book on a post-army visit to his mentor in 1921.

There was I, a mortal, being pounded upon from all sides. I longed for freedom, for the power to impose, or at least intrude my own personality and thought, on the circle around me. I begged my heart to be another self. Hearing argument and wisdom displayed everywhere, and bound myself by a natural shyness—just like Bobby MacKaye's [another member of the circle]—I felt to the point of a profound unhappiness that I was inexcusably deficient in those qualities; doubted whether shyness was to blame.

Yes, I wanted to escape from the intellectual giants who surrounded me and who seemed to have possessed themselves of what I hoped were unfair advantages, I craved an occasion where I could justify myself, where I might be sincerely represented, where I would not appear by tiny bits, reflections, repetitions, falsely-colored, torn misshapen qualities.

O Pride what wounds you bear!

Beneath the tone of self-mockery at his own pretensions lay his self-searching and his concern for his future. One finds the same honest self-examination in Ted's earliest teenage journals, albeit in a more childlike style.[14]

The repeated poundings were undermining his beliefs: "Slowly I am becoming emancipated from the religious oppression of my adolescent years; and in the motives of my life desire and aspiration are taking the place once occupied by duty and fear." His reverence for the generous and nonjudgmental Lawtons helped soften the pain of transition.

Mr. Lawton and Shirley Lawton are incapable of partiality and prejudice. They are like ethereal beings. They witness the good and evil in the people who pass before them; they welcome them all in, and showing them all favors, show none, no matter how well they may be known. . . . Every soul, in their minds, has equal rights and privileges, is a manifestation of a Life kindled by divinity and warped by unequal fates far beyond control. Can there be a greater wisdom than such understanding, with withholding of all judgments? Theirs is a love for Man.[15]

It is perhaps not surprising that the discussions were so influential. The Lawtons were highly cultivated people, Unitarians connected with some of the important dissenting strands of nineteenth-century American thought. Their Quaker neighbor Edward Mott Davis (1889–1942), scion of a distinguished family and owner of a large farm adjacent to the Shirley Shakers, was a close friend. Davis's great-grandmother was the abolitionist Lucretia Mott, and his father, William Morris Davis (1850–1934), was a professor of geology and geography at Harvard who was credited with being the "father of American geography." Like many others in the Shirley area, the Davis family invited scores of soldiers to dinner in 1917–18; and in the next world war, Edward Mott Davis Jr. (1917–1997), later a prominent professor of anthropology, gave dinners and conducted discussion groups for soldiers from Camp Devens.[16]

Shirley Center was a magnet for the local intelligentsia and well-to-do summer residents, together with a changing roster of writers and artists. Prominent in the Lawton salon was Percy MacKaye (1875–1956), a close friend of Ted Andrews. Percy was a poet and playwright, and one of the four sons of Steele MacKaye (1842–1894), a major figure in the history of the American theater. Local residents of Shirley Center and environs referred to Percy as The Poet. Percy's brother, Benton (1879–1975), who became a leader of the U.S. Forest Service and the "Father of the Appalachian Trail," attended the discussions as well. Benton ("Bobby" to Andrews) was an avid socialist.

The history and fate of the local Shakers attracted Frank Lawton as a native, as an amateur historian, and as a neighbor. Like Clara Endicott Sears (who received some Shaker manuscripts from Lawton), and a few others in that first generation of students of Shakerism, he must have sensed that the Shakers were more than a minor footnote in American history. Known for "picking the dump," Lawton treasured some Shaker manuscripts he had found at the local dump or collected from other sources, and he regularly brought them to the discussion group, where participants "would pore over the Shaker manuscript [a Shaker journal from the 1840s] and read passages aloud to the company."[17] The group read from Shaker manuscripts on at least three occasions when Ted Andrews was present.

This sign advertised the antique business run by Frank and Shirley Lawton.
Collection of Frank L. and Cornelia H. Frisbee Houde.

It is clear from his diary entries that Ted found his vocation as a writer and Shaker scholar in the stimulating atmosphere of Lawton's salon and was drawn to the topic of the Shakers in part as a result of Frank Lawton's serious interest in Shaker history. Ted's diaries from the time of his military career and immediately thereafter reveal idealism, sensitivity to beauty, and a skepticism about the materialism that, as he saw it, dominated American cultural life. I believe that these characteristics go far in explaining why Andrews saw, with singular clarity, the beauty of Shaker culture, and why he fought with such devotion to preserve that culture.

Before leaving the army, Ted had already begun to study the early nineteenth-century history of the Shirley area, spending his spare time in the "wee town library of Ayer."[18] At this early date his interest in the history of New England competed with his dedication to literary, "democratic" art. He reserved space at the back of his Camp Devens journal for long quotations from Carl Sandburg, Rupert Brooke, English literary critics, Hindu philosophers, and others, as well as many of his own commentaries on social justice, immigration, and the weakness of men in resisting sexual sins. He copied many of his own somewhat stilted but honest poems into the diaries. A typical lyric went like this:

> We were too
> To love the places where the laurel grew;
> And all we knew
> Was just fear of thunder.
> But now our childhood
> Whispers from them all . . .
> Return, old fear of thunder.[19]

Other poems speak of stars and roses, autumn melancholy and love, and "steel in the air" (death): he did well with basic themes, sensitive to his surroundings. He was immensely pleased when Frank Lawton suggested that he send some poems to the *Atlantic Monthly*, but he soon decided that he did not have the talent for a purely literary career.

Other diary entries show that Ted could rise above parochial Pittsfield and appreciate the urban beauty and harshness of New York City, especially in its hard-working "people from all parts of the world [who] daily pierce the oppression, the unrelenting weariness of toil . . . leading lives of simple beauty and devotion" (July 11, 1919)—this from the mind of a small-town New Englander at the height of the red scares and resurgent anti-immigrant nativism. His son-in-law, himself an immigrant of the late 1930s, wrote of him:

> To me, Ted and Faith seemed to be cast from the same mold as my own parents, a music professor and his all around helpmate. He was almost totally preoccupied by artistic concerns, and she taking care of all practical and social matters. Like my father (a classical composer), Ted struck me as being a quintessentially self-directed person, drawing upon extensive inner resources, and minimally concerned with what, I believe, the Shakers called The World. Faith, on the other hand, understood The World, and dealt with it effectively, first and foremost to make it possible for Ted to do "his thing," which was, in fact, also "her thing."[20]

ON LEAVE

I have come home awhile
To see the folks and friends and fields
I knew so well, and loved,
Before I went away.
The welcome and the gentle talk
Of old acquaintance on the street,
The shop-lined street of yesterday,
Were just the same—almost,
Today.

I have come home awhile
To seek what has been lost so long.
I hear the long, low drone of trade
At dawn today, the huckster's cry,
While I was still but half awake;
And in the kitchen, kettles rattling
Mid the merry hum of song.

'Twas mother singing; and I dressed,
And soon
Her song and mine were one,
We were so glad.

I have come home awhile
Half-sentient of the mighty change
Which all my being thrills
With its immensity . . .
But these will ever be unchanged:
The lingering walks beneath the elms
When the supper dishes are laid away;
The sweet return, the chamber's hush;
A friendly book, an idle talk or song;
And in the hall, the high clock on the landing,
Ticking slow, and the green lamp's glow
In the evening.

I have come home awhile
To live.

—*Edward D. Andrews*, Camp Devens

Ted Andrews was clearly dedicated, insightful, well educated, and literary, but he sharply questioned his own artistic abilities. Inspired and excited by the Lawton salon, he thought that he might write "the Great American Play" (he added the quotation marks, taking a lesser, ironic measure of himself), but in March 1918 he put the idea aside forever.[21] At this point he wrote about his quandary in a poem titled "Irresolute." Ted's soul-searching continued through the summer of 1919 and included ruminations over sexual sin and "loftier desires" (July 11, 1919). His strong, controlling mother was not always encouraging: his short journal entry for July 12, 1920, points toward a less literary ambition: "I feel that Ken [Ken Bates, a close friend] and even mother have no deep grounded faith in my artistic or literary possibilities, but I myself have felt glowing within me a fiery faith."

While he loved poetry and wrote a good deal of it, Ted quickly concluded that prose is superior to poetry: "Prose, follow prose!" begins an entry for July 17, 1920, written on his return from a stimulating Lawton salon. "You know now," he continued, "that all is not beauty; you know that the rhythm and music of poetry will never express the naked musicless truth of life." After two years of discussion and much interior dialogue, his new "fiery faith" had burned away his indecision.

In the end, all but two or three of the intellectual giants at the Lawton salon are forgotten, while Edward Deming Andrews ultimately achieved eminence—with the indispensable help of his wife, Faith. His idealism shone forth during the Lawton years and he worked diligently on writing. He developed a clear and serviceable prose, honoring his vow to favor the "musicless" prose of truth. In Frank Lawton's salon Ted Andrews found his own kind of music.

Edward Deming Andrews and Faith Young Andrews: Collector-Scholars

Born in Pittsfield in 1896, Faith Young came from a family of modest means and conservative Episcopalian piety. Faith repeatedly mentioned her bland childhood and her mother's harsh and narrow-minded religious restrictions. "I don't think there was very much excitement in my life as a child," she told an interviewer in 1972. "I was brought up in a very strict New England atmosphere, never allowed to do very much, except go to church." Her mother was interested in the peculiarities of the Shakers and told Faith of her visits to the Shakers and of seeing them dance in their services. Her mother respected the Shakers and told Faith never to stare at them when they came to town.[22]

"I had two hobbies, as I became a teenager," Faith recalled, "both of them hard to achieve. One was dancing and the other was hiking, but I acted according to the rules of the home." She met Ted Andrews at a dance in 1919. Her family was dubious about marriage to a Congregationalist, but the diplomacy of an uncle saved the day. For the wedding ceremony of 1921, Faith petitioned her bishop to allow them to omit the words "obey," "until death do us part," and "in sickness and in health."[23]

Faith wrote that her marriage came as a joyous release. "It seemed," she said in a 1987 interview, "like the beginning of my life. I think it was. We had a wonderful marriage."[24] It was indeed close, so much so that when I visited her one afternoon at her Pittsfield home a few weeks after Ted's death in 1964, she assured me that she had seen him repeatedly since his death, usually at the head of the stairs to the second floor.

Faith had graduated from the Berkshire Business College when she met Ted and was working for a local insurance company. She used her proficiency in typing, shorthand, and proofreading to help support the family during the Depression; and her skills became indispensable to Ted in preparing his manuscripts and managing their vast collection.

Two years older than Faith, Ted was the son of Carrie (Caroline) Volk Andrews (1864–1926) and Seldon Deming Andrews (1864–1950), the prominent owner of a Pittsfield hardware store. Seldon and

Faith Young Andrews at the time of her wedding in 1921.
Collection of Thomas R. and Ann Andrews Kane

Edward Deming and Faith Andrews ca. 1922.
Collection of the Family of David V. and Phyllis C. Andrews

Carrie were staunch Congregationalists, and Carrie was extremely religious. Seldon was born in Richmond, Massachusetts, abutting the town of Hancock, of a family that first settled in that town in 1789,[25] a year before the Shakers started their Hancock community.

Ted Andrews graduated from Pittsfield High School and attended Amherst College, earning his degree in 1916. He worked briefly as a reporter for the *Springfield Republican* (then still a newspaper of national repute). When the United States joined World War I, Ted entered the army, on August 25, 1917, and served for two years.[26]

After his discharge Ted taught English and social studies at several high schools, including the Fessenden School in Newton, Massachusetts, for two years.[27] In 1923 the Andrewses moved to Yale University, where Ted worked for seven years on a Ph.D. in education, supported by a Sterling Fellowship. While he revered education, he had little respect for the School of Education with its courses on how to be a high school principal. His dissertation director permitted him to do a historical study of schools in Vermont.

In 1919, even before their marriage, Ted and Faith had begun collecting antiques. But as Faith noted in later interviews and in their co-authored memoir, *Fruits of the Shaker Tree of Life*, they had sought "colonial pieces," she said, "because we hadn't heard that the Shakers had any furniture. We had heard very little about the Shakers then."[28] Their main interest continued to be early American materials, especially the Queen Anne style of furniture. They spent much of their time documenting the materials and doing library research. The Model T Ford they received as a wedding present in 1921 was a great help. Since they had both grown up at the end of the era of rural transportation by horse and wagon, they were keenly appreciative of this new aid as they combed the area for early American materials.

At first they made little distinction between early American or "colonial" and Shaker objects and were not even clear why they started their collection. By 1925 they were concentrating on finding only Shaker materials and over the next twenty-five years acquired most of their collection. The Crash of 1929 briefly slowed their collecting. After receiving a doctorate in education in 1930, Ted, who now had two children to support, could not find a teaching job. He and Faith managed to scrape by, however, from 1930 to 1933 on Ted's small salary as temporary curator of history at the New York State Museum in Albany, saving rent by living with the recently widowed "Dad" Seldon in his large Victorian house on Clinton Avenue in Pittsfield. Not until Ted received a Guggenheim grant for 1937–38 did they feel solvent.

Despite the Depression, they were able to round out the main body of their collection. Faith noted in an interview:

During the Depression we did the major part of our collecting and a great deal of research. We laid the foundation for the books, because we were not teaching. We were in the Victorian house with Dad. It was a very happy situation and every day we went to Hancock, or New Lebanon, or/and Watervliet and then we followed to other New England communities.[29]

Mere collecting gradually came to be overshadowed by their grand mission to save Shaker culture for posterity.

Looking back in 1957, toward the end of their careers, Ted Andrews wrote, with the help of Faith, the most complete statement of their aim to save Shaker culture:

Our initial aim was the acquisition of all types of household furniture and accessories made by the Shakers, in the pursuit of which we gradually extended activity to the New York State communities at New Lebanon and Watervliet, and then to the societies in Connecticut, Maine, and New Hampshire. Interest broadened in time to include the furnishings and products of the varied Shaker shops, most of them long disused but filled with the paraphernalia of industry. Meanwhile we began to collect communitarian literature. The followers of Mother Ann Lee were assiduous publicists and keepers of journals and records, and their buildings held a wealth of printed and written documents. The search was irresistible, the lure ever-expanding.

As time passed and the material accumulated, we became more and more concerned about its eventual disposition. The alternatives of whether, and how, to preserve, or whether to disperse and thereby create opportunity for future collecting, have been faced by others, but for us there was a complicating factor. Our collection told the complex story of a productive culture that constituted a rich strain in American historical experience, and in scope, authenticity, and documentation could probably never be duplicated. To consider it as an exclusively personal possession became increasingly difficult. More or less consciously, we came to the view that had been held by the Shakers themselves, that property was a trust, a heritage to be used and "improved" under responsible stewardship.[30]

In this general statement Ted Andrews covers the three main aspects of their careers: the collecting, the sense of mission (fully developed by the 1930s), and the completion of the mission by finding a proper home. Writing for connoisseurs and historians in the magazine *Antiques*, Ted omits the unique characteristic of the collection, one that distinguishes it from all others: the Andrewses collected not just documents and furniture but also pews, books, stoves, stools, shovels, hymnals, baskets, drawings, textiles, hand tools, pots and pans, giant ledgers, massive shop tools, decaying Shaker seed packages, and every other concrete aspect of Shaker life. Eventually, they even saved some buildings—with the help of others. They were after the entire culture, not just the history or the furniture.

The Andrewses' initial dealings with the Shakers were not as easy as the Loaf of Bread story implies. In the 1920s Shaker resistance to selling any objects varied according to the community and the person in charge. In their first efforts, the Andrewses had to learn how to overcome the initial wariness of the Shakers (mostly elderly women at this time). By the 1930s, the Andrewses had gradually established warm relations with key contacts, such as Sister Sadie Neale of the former headquarters community of "Mount Lebanon" in New Lebanon, New York. Indeed no other outsiders had established so intimate a friendship, and it was for this reason that Charles Adams, founder of the Shaker Collection at the New York State Museum, sought out the Andrewses as a go-between.[31] Some Shakers did not like collectors, including the Andrewses, and it took a lot of tact and perseverance to maintain a connection.

Shaker sisters were frequent visitors at the Andrewses' eighteenth-century farmhouse in Richmond, Massachusetts, just down the road from Hancock Shaker Village, and the continual visiting back and forth with the Shakers energized them in their ongoing campaign to persuade the arts and museum worlds of the esthetic value of Shaker artifacts.[32] They treasured these visits and remembered them warmly.

While the Andrewses enjoyed a special relationship with many individual sisters and a few surviving brothers, the United Society of Believers, which had always maintained a strict boundary with the world, continued to do so well into the 1930s.[33] The Andrewses remarked that in the 1920s the Shakers still held themselves aloof.

[They] were suspicious of strangers whose visits were often motivated by mere curiosity. But once assured of the sincerity of motive, no people could be more friendly. Our objective was nothing less than the documentation and interpretation of an incomparably rich native culture. And when Sadie [Neale] was once convinced on this score, she gave without stint of herself and her great knowledge.[34]

By dint of their tact, sincerity, and perseverance, and the gradual and organic development of personal friendships with individual Shakers, the Andrewses eventually gained access to unusual items that were not for sale to the "world's people." Their first purchase directly from the Shakers was a wooden bowl they obtained from Sister Alice Smith at Hancock.

There was surprisingly little social communication between Shaker communities or even between families (semi-independent subunits) within each community—and not a little jealousy. The Andrewses later became an additional source of information on the outside world for individual Believers like Sister Alice.[35] Seldon Andrews was greatly respected by the Shakers, who traded at his hardware store in Pittsfield. Later, in the 1930s, Ted and Faith became uniquely privileged visitors, often taking dinner with the Shakers, though seated apart from them.

Sister Alice Smith hoeing in the garden at Hancock, Mass. circa 1930.
Courtesy, The Winterthur Library: The Edward Deming Andrews
Memorial Shaker Collection, No. SA 60

Faith recalled that the two Shakers who impressed her most were Sister Sadie Neale (1849–1948) of the Mount Lebanon community and Sister Alice Smith (1884–1935) of Hancock, both pivotal figures in the history of the Andrews Shaker collection. One historian has suggested that Sister Sadie Neale was hostile to the Andrewses, but his only evidence consists of two one-line diary entries before 1929 expressing annoyance that the Andrewses were taking up "considerable of my time."[36] A full reading of the primary sources tells a very different story. Sadie Neale actually made twenty-one diary references to the Andrewses between 1929 and 1943—none of them hostile. Chary of her time, Sadie used the phrase "use up considerable of my time" twice, and only in 1929, when the Andrewses first began buying furniture from her. She was a person of great self-discipline.

After 1930 as Sadie and other Shaker sisters got to know the Andrewses, they became friends and were regular visitors at the Andrewses' Richmond farmhouse. Always warm and cordial to Faith Andrews, her friend of many years, Sadie wrote in April 1932: "I have thought of you many times and will be glad to see you and learn how you have progressed in your latest enterprise. I will not write all I want to say to you as it will be more comprehensive to talk it out."[37] Her last letter to the Andrewses, written in 1945, when she was ninety-six years old, closed with these sentences: "I am nearing the end of my journey and shall not miss these things much longer. . . . I hope to see you once more. . . . I will love you and leave you in peace."[38]

The Andrewses had close friends at other communities. In 1932 Eldress Prudence A. Stickney of Sabbathday Lake, Maine, expressed similar love and trust: "I am so thankful we have such loyal friends in you, who defend our cause. . . . You seem more like Shakers, than many who have worn the garb, and made outward profession."[39] Ted was a pallbearer at Sister Alice Smith's funeral,[40] a role emblematic of his love of the Shakers and of their trust in him. In 1932 Sadie Neale was pleased to introduce the Andrewses at the first major exhibition of the Andrews Collection.[41] It is clear that several highly respected Shakers were, in fact, quite close to the Andrewses, and the Andrewses could not have made their vast acquisitions without their friendly cooperation—despite the competition and jealousies between individual Shakers, as well as between Shaker families over the visits of the world's people and sales to them.[42]

Sister Alice, who came to Hancock before 1893 from Norwich, Connecticut, possibly as an orphan, was much younger than Sadie Neale; and as the remaining very elderly leaders passed away, Sister Alice became relatively prominent.[43] "She was the most exciting person we ever met," Faith reported in an interview in 1982.[44] Sister Alice was also instrumental in the Andrewses' acquisition of Shaker gift drawings. The Shakers received these drawings during the Era of Spirit Manifestations or "Mother's Work" (1837–50), the last and most intense of the Shaker revivals. The spiritual manifestations of the time included phenomena, such as trances, gyrations, glossalalia, falling down, and singing strange songs, that had become almost traditional in the generation following the Great Awakening. Peculiarly Shaker, however, were descriptions of "gifts" (seen in the mind's eye) of gold, silk, beautiful vases, and the like, usually received from the other world by Believers in a trance state. The gift-receivers sometimes transmitted messages from historical figures like George Washington or Napoleon and often told of receiving gifts from Mother Ann Lee herself. Members receiving such gifts would describe them or would act out their visits to the spirit world to converse with Mother Ann or other deceased leaders. Uniquely Shaker among the spiritual gifts were those that took the form of drawings. These "gift drawings" depicted visions the artists received. Scores of gift drawings have survived and today are counted among the most precious of all Shaker artifacts. Thus, for the spiritually inclined Ted Andrews, Sister Alice represented a kind of medium, transmitting these exceptional gifts to posterity, and she held a very special place in the Andrewses' minds.

As they gained the confidence of the Shakers at Hancock, at Mount Lebanon, and, soon after, at the Canterbury Community in New Hampshire, the Andrewses were able to buy more furniture and other artifacts. At first they did most of their early collecting at Mount Lebanon. Faith noted that "buildings were unoccupied, rooms had been closed up for forty or fifty years, numbers diminishing."[45]

The Andrewses' initial, 1923 encounter with the Shakers was more than an esthetic epiphany; it challenged them ideologically and psychologically. The Shakers seem to have distilled an essence of the Andrewses' Puritan New England heritage and transmuted it into something that to them was beautiful and strange. In particular, the deeply restrictive tenets of Shaker doctrine must have resonated with Ted, and perhaps more so with Faith, who had suffered deeply under her mother's joyless moralism. When an interviewer asked Faith what stood out most in her childhood, she said, "the New Englandism that I was exposed to."[46]

Despite Faith's rebellion against the "New Englandism" of her childhood, she and Ted cared deeply about this culture and its people. It is perhaps not too much to characterize their profound love of their New England heritage as an ethnic identity that they shared with the Shakers. This emotional identification was one source of their drive to scour the Northeast to retrieve the richest diversity of Shaker materials ever assembled, including many objects of no conceivable monetary value at the time, such as bits of Shaker cloth, samples of ribbons, and curious tools.

Beginning in the late nineteenth century many artifacts and manuscripts were disappearing in fires and trash bins. To be sure, before the rescue work of the Andrewses, a few collectors, scholars, and dealers recognized the importance of Shaker manuscripts and artifacts, most notably Wallace H. Cathcart of the Western Reserve Historical Society; Edward Brockway Wight (whose collection became the Wight Shaker Collection at Williams College); H. H. Ballard, librarian of the Berkshire Atheneum in Pittsfield, Massachusetts; John Patterson MacLean, a book dealer and collector in Ohio whose collection went to the Library of Congress; and Clara Endicott Sears, who restored Fruitlands in Massachusetts.

Through the publication in 1905 of his pioneering work *A Bibliography of Shaker Literature*, John Patterson MacLean (1848–1939) helped raise awareness among acquisition librarians of the importance of collecting Shaker imprints and manuscripts. But, like the Andrewses after him, MacLean had a hard time convincing scholars of the importance of studying the Shakers and their culture; and, like the Andrewses, he understood the need to preserve the disappearing materials of Shaker history. Unlike the Andrewses, however, he was interested only in books and manuscripts. One curious experience he had in common with the Andrewses: he felt compelled to withdraw his large Shaker collection from a major museum because it did not meet his expectations.[47] Though Ted Andrews and John MacLean never met, MacLean, "the grand old man of Shaker research in the West," as he became known, wrote to congratulate Ted on his first books and sent an inscribed copy of his old but still valuable *Bibliography of Shaker Literature*. MacLean was then in his nineties.

Another important early collector, Clara Endicott Sears (1863–1960), thought of herself as a competitor of the Andrewses. Like them, she was partly motivated by a strong regard for her New England heritage, but from an upper-class point of view. She was a Boston Brahmin—a descendant of John Winthrop, the first governor of Massachusetts, and six other colonial governors—whose preservationist and collecting activities focused not just on the Shakers but also on members of the New England intellectual aristocracy from Bronson Alcott to Henry Wadsworth Longfellow. Her wealth allowed her to establish the Fruitlands Museum in Harvard, Massachusetts, in 1914. "I am the very essence of New England," she once boasted in a private letter. She had that essence in common with the Andrewses, but she also shared Ted's educational view of restoration, asserting of Fruitlands:

"This place is not meant for recreation. It is meant for inspiration."[48] Though long acquainted with Sears and sharing some aspects of their New England heritage, the Andrewses were never close to Sears, and Faith remarked in a 1972 interview, "She was a difficult woman," a phrase frequently used against Faith herself.[49]

Sears did not concern herself with public criticism of her work, which she considered above "vulgarization." But the Andrewses felt the sting of criticism. When they first began collecting, about twenty years after MacLean started and some ten years after Sears, their neighbors and some contemporaries outside of Pittsfield ridiculed them as "junk dealers." More recently, Stephen J. Stein misleadingly quoted the phrase "Antique Pilgrims" as the Shakers' pejorative for the Andrewses.[50] Actually, the phrase was used in a very positive sense and by only one Shaker, Sadie Neale, who meant it as a term of endearment in a warm and loving letter written October 13, 1942. "Where? Oh where are our Antique Pilgrims?" she began and went on to say how much she missed seeing them. She signed the letter, "With much love yours ignorantly, Sadie A. Neale."[51] Neale looked upon the Andrewses as dear friends who understood the culture of the Believers. In the 1920s and 1930s, when the Andrewses began collecting, some Shakers were suspicious of self-seeking antiquers. Many Shakers, however, soon realized that the Andrewses were different: though separated from the world, the Shakers did not lack worldly insight.

"People couldn't understand," Faith recalled of their neighbors in the 1920s, "why Ted, who showed such promise as a historian and writer, would be devoting himself to bringing this trash into the house and into the barn or what we were doing, what we were going to do with it—and we didn't know."[52] Faith's admission—"we didn't know"—confirms their nonmercenary, open-ended view of the future of the collection. Faith repeatedly alluded to their local reputation for being the "queer Andrews" for collecting the "rural" furniture of the Shakers, the "primitive" art of eighteenth-century limners, and similar "junk."[53]

In the early 1920s the worlds of historical scholarship, religious studies, art museums, and other arbiters of cultural history and art were oblivious to what later became so fashionable as to be called (without the need of the definite article) "Shaker." Since the 1980s the history and culture of "Shaker" has become the subject of scores of plays, books, articles, newspaper reports (including perennial tourist feature stories on "the last Shakers" still living in Maine), and musical adaptations of Shaker hymns. Shaker artifacts appear regularly at leading auction houses. The Andrewses' advocacy of Shaker music and their transcriptions of Shaker hymns enabled the dean of American classical composers in the 1940s, Aaron Copland, to use Shaker themes in his most popular work, *Appalachian Spring*. Largely because of the proselytizing of the Andrewses, educated Americans are no longer disinterested in the Shakers and their culture.

And thus it was that instead of writing the literary masterpiece about Shaker life that he first dreamed of at Camp Devens, Ted Andrews ended up as a scholar and collector seeking to preserve the Shakers' historical and material culture. Faith almost matched his missionary zeal to convert the world to a love of Shaker principles and Shaker esthetic achievements. They found themselves trying to save a whole culture and they succeeded beyond their dreams.

But to complete their work they had to reach two goals: persuade the world of the spiritual worth of the Shaker way and find a suitable home for their collection. They never reached the first and found homes only after much pain.

The Andrewses' Dream of Purity and Its Critics

By the late 1930s the Andrewses began to view their collection not as another group of museum items but as the deposit of a culture to be jealously guarded, a culture so pure that it is easily profaned by those who do not understand spiritual things.

This attitude, somewhat overstated here, explains why the Andrewses (especially Ted) engaged in a deeply personal way with the religious and ethical dimension of Shakerism. In the process of rescuing Shaker materials, they were moved to study Shaker doctrines, hymnody, and art, gradually reaching a point of deep empathy with the religious spirit of the Shakers—what Ted Andrews liked to call their "divine afflatus," a term he borrowed from a Shaker publication of Shirley, Massachusetts.[54] The Andrewses conceived of the Shaker communities (or "societies," as they were sometimes called in the nineteenth century) as harmoniously integrated, socio-religious entities, a view many later critics considered a "romanticizing" of the

Shakers. They were moving toward a new view of the United Society of Believers as a cultural whole, as an admirable spiritual and ethical entity and not merely as a group of great designers, inventors, craftsmen, and folk artists. For the Andrewses, Shaker society was a separate, self-contained world of art, culture, and spiritual yearning, which they hoped to save. As Faith put it in speaking of their attitude around the mid-1930s, "[We] wanted to explain to the world, give them the whole culture from beginning to end, the industries, the furniture making, the life, the architecture, everything."[55] Ted expressed the same attitude in his 1939 "Prospectus for a Museum of the American Shakers,"[56] emphasizing that their collection was a unit and was not to be broken up.

The Andrewses' motives for burdening themselves with so great a mission are complex: certainly they included Ted's dreams in Camp Devens; Ted and Faith's conversion in the late 1920s to the Shaker esthetic; their dismay—even horror—at the accidental and sometime willful destruction of Shaker buildings, artifacts, books, and manuscripts; their later friendship with museum leaders and curators; and even a childhood awareness of their Shaker neighbors.

From conversations with the Andrewses about the religious life of New England and the "Puritan" heritage that shaped it, I also sensed that their admiration for all things Shaker was bound up with their pride in their heritage. One example of this pride was their purchase of a dilapidated eighteenth-century saltbox in Richmond, about three miles from the Shaker Village in Hancock, to use as a summer home. They restored the house with great care, dubbing it "Shaker Farm," though it was neither Shaker nor a farm. After the purchase they were delighted to discover that Ted's great uncle Truman Bishop Andrews was the second owner of the 1795 house. He had brought his new wife there in 1837, exactly one hundred years earlier. The Andrewses never installed electricity or running water, and they used a wood-fired stove until the late 1950s.[57] In Emily Dickinson's phrase, they saw "New Englandly." In saving Shaker culture they were, in a sense, saving their own culture.

The Andrewses thought that their ascetic way of living connected them spiritually with the Shakers. But not until they began their friendship with the Trappist writer, peace activist, and spiritual adviser to his abbey Thomas Merton (1915–1968) did they find a sympathetic ear for their promotion of Shaker spirituality and purity. They came to venerate the Catholic monk and devoted an entire chapter of their memoir, *Fruits of the Shaker Tree of Life*, to him. With some exaggeration they called Merton "a spiritual mentor and intimate friend."[58] They felt that the contemplative monk, more than any other person they encountered in their entire careers, understood the true nature of Shaker perfectionism and purity and how those qualities came to be expressed in artifacts of Shaker culture. Merton, for his part, deeply respected his worldly friends and their scholarly mission and showed remarkable understanding of their work.[59]

Merton's interest in the Shakers was long-standing. He loved the simplicity of Shaker design, which he saw as a reflection of their spiritual simplicity. He studied their doctrines, compared their spiritual life with that of the Cistercians (unfavorably to the Cistercians at one point), photographed their architecture, and, until he met the Andrewses, had even planned to write a book about the Believers. In his small writing room at the Abbey of Our Lady of Gethsemane in Kentucky he treasured the plain Shaker school desk on which he did much of his writing; sometimes, when he was alone, he would sing the Shaker hymn "Decisive Work."[60] No other person is as important for understanding the motivation and ideals of the Andrewses and hence the history of the Andrews Collection.

The Andrewses' "Shaker Farm" at Richmond.
Collection of Thomas R. and Ann Andrews Kane

Merton's oft-quoted trope about the Shaker chair appears in his introduction to the Andrewses' *Religion in Wood*: "The peculiar grace of a Shaker chair is due to the fact that it was made by someone capable of believing that an angel might come and sit on it."[61]

Others recognized the special dedication of the Andrewses, expressing amazement at their integrity and their mastery of all things Shaker. Mark Van Doren (1894–1972), the critic, poet, and scholar, summed up Ted Andrews's life and work as "scholarship so dedicated that it stands alone in our time. He knew the Shakers in this way because he loved them: not sentimentally, not nostalgically, but with an abiding respect for the ideas their entire life expressed."[62] Particularly cogent for the reputation of Ted Andrews and the collection is Van Doren's emphasis on Ted's lack of "sentimentality" and "nostalgia." Van Doren was the influential teacher of Thomas Merton, John Berryman, Allen Ginsberg, Jack Kerouac, and other literary figures, some of whom were part of the Andrewses' circle of friends in New York.

Another friend, Homer Eaton Keyes (1875–1938), editor of *Antiques* magazine and the foremost scholar of early American furniture, ceramics, and painting, reflected on the work of persuading the public of the importance of the Shakers in his preface to the Andrewses' *Shaker Furniture* in 1937. He noted that the Andrewses' years of research on Shaker culture and craftsmanship must make the great achievement of the Shakers "obvious to any reader of this book who is sensitive to the impact of convincing evidence carefully marshaled and clearly presented." He pointed out that the Andrewses "never for a moment forgot their obligation to shun all sentimentality in their effort both to demonstrate the actuality of Shaker accomplishment and to reveal its underlying motives in behalf of the worldlings of today."[63]

After the first large-scale exhibition of the Andrews Collection at the Berkshire Museum in Pittsfield, from October 10 to October 30, 1932, the "worldlings" began to recognize the preeminence of the Andrewses, and from about that date the Andrewses gradually shifted their goal from memorializing the culture to saving it. They did everything they could to bring the virtues and achievements of the Shakers to the attention of the rich and the learned. In their zeal to convert others they did tend to "romanticize" Shaker history and life, particularly in the period before 1865. By concentrating on this early "classic" period (1820–60), which they saw as a time of pure Shakerism, they overlooked the disharmonies present in that community, as in every long-lasting religious commune. Contention and compromise were especially prominent among the Shakers in the period of decline after the Civil War, but conflicts based on gender and other aspects of community life appeared almost from the beginning.[64] There is little doubt that the Andrewses exaggerated the Shakers' social consensus, their lack of coercion, and the homogeneity of Shaker style. If this was romanticism, it was scholarly and salutary for the 1920s and 1930s, when very few Americans had a high opinion of Shaker life and Shaker style. A healthy corrective to consensus history finally appeared in with the "New History" of the 1970s and the establishment of gender studies and quantitative methods.[65]

It was during the classic period, according to the Andrewses' understanding, that the Believers created their distinctive style—expressed in superbly designed artifacts ranging from manure shovels and chairs to window units—produced all their major doctrinal works, organized their communal economy and institutional structures, and made dance part of their worship. The first two generations of Shakers created these unique features of their polity, doctrine, and daily life. The Andrewses did exaggerate the purity and simplicity, or union and order, of the Shaker "people," but their emphasis on the period before 1865 cannot be dismissed as a "frozen view of the Believers" or a "fossilized concretion."[66]

While Ted Andrews's periodization has a strong rationale, he did reflect his time, as all historians do. As late as the 1950s the leading cultural institutions memorializing New England, such as Sturbridge Village, Old Deerfield, the American Antiquarian Society, and the Massachusetts Historical Society, focused their collecting activities on the products of the colonial and early Federal periods—a periodization that may reflect a New England ethnic identity rather than a unified "colonial" style and ideology. But this ethnocentric whiff of Puritan filiopietism—still powerful in the 1950s—was unavoidable.

A typical criticism is that in the mid-1930s, when the Andrewses hired William F. Winter to photograph outstanding items in their collection, they "staged" the pieces to emphasize their own view of Shaker life.[67] (The photographs appeared in the Andrews-Winter book *Shaker Furniture*.) But the Andrewses were simply trying to provide a helpful context for related Shaker objects, and they explicitly stated that in arranging the furniture and choosing backgrounds they made "sometimes arbitrary" decisions in trying to give some idea of "both the atmosphere and practical economy of the Shaker home." In other words, the context was the Andrewses' conception of Shaker purity and order "as we imagined it must be." They also felt limited by "the ordinary rules of pictorial [photographic] technique" in the placement of objects.[68] But aside from their intentions, it is now clearly understood that "reality" as represented in a photograph is not a simple true-or-false statement—as recent cultural critics have noted. The discourse of meaning includes the viewer as well as the photographer.[69]

While the photographs carry the Andrewses' message, perhaps even a distorted one, the extenuating factor was the need to persuade the public; the case for the beauty of Shaker furniture and artifacts still had to be argued. The Andrewses had to draw on all their influence among the Shakers to borrow Shaker rooms, which turned out to be less than ideal. Winter had to compromise, making the best use of daylight in exposing the slow films available in the 1930s; and because he could not include actual Shaker figures, his photographs inevitably distorted whatever might be defined as "reality."

Winter's documentation of the Andrews Collection illustrates the depth of concern and the wealth of experience the Andrewses brought to bear in their efforts to document their collection and make it known. While William F. Winter never achieved a national reputation, he had the great respect of a small circle of cognoscenti in photography, such as Juliana Force, director of the Whitney Museum of American Art, who paid Winter for part of the project. Winter was sympathetic to the Shakers and lived at Hancock to study their locale while taking pictures; his understanding and empathy appealed to the Shakers.

William F. Winter Jr. ca. 1930
Courtesy of the New York State Museum, Albany, N.Y.

Another common criticism asserts that the Andrewses were marketing mavens and proponents of old conservative American values. The author of the most widely accepted general history of the Shakers, Stephen J. Stein, dismisses any spiritual approach to Shaker culture in the very first sentence of his book, quoting the famous Merton passage about the angel-ready chair and immediately following it with a quotation, the equally clichéd complaint from one of the last of the Shakers, Sister Mildred Barker: "I almost expect to be remembered as a chair or a table."[70] Sister Mildred did not know Merton and spoke not in response to him but in response to Ken Burns, the filmmaker, in his 1984 documentary about the Shakers.[71] She was probably reacting to the 1980s rage for collecting "Shaker." Stein's opening sentences assert the irrelevance of both Ted Andrews and Merton to the study of Shaker history.

Stein also takes Ted Andrews to task for praising the Shakers for "qualities that many Americans admire—a solid work ethic, inventiveness, sincerity, honesty, commitment to religion, practicality. He showed their heroic side in their willingness to suffer persecution for what they believed. . . . Andrews created a good feeling about the Shakers. In a word, he made them highly marketable."[72]

Stein portrays Ted Andrews as insincere and calculating, reducing the Andrewses' praise of the Shakers to a mere marketing ploy. This judgment is incomprehensible in the light of the Andrewses' fifty-five-year journey through Shaker spirituality, history, and culture.

A post-Marxist "exposé" of the commodification of Shaker style and design in the recent book by the British authors Stephen Bowe and Peter Richmond also begins with a quotation from Merton—without identifying him in the text and clearly borrowing Stein's gambit. Unbeknownst to the authors, Merton (a former Marxist) had already commented on the commodification of religion in 1966. Bowe and Richmond, upset at the popularity and commercialization of Shaker design in the United Kingdom, have, without the benefit of research, painted the couple as scoundrels who "schmoozed Shaker sisters" in order to grab their furniture "for a couple of dollars, only to sell it for much more, . . . thousands of dollars more."[73] Like most critics of the Andrewses since the 1990s, the authors had no knowledge of the Andrews family history, no direct acquaintance with them as human personalities, and no knowledge of the history of the collection.

Another attack (American in origin) has it that "the Andrews were also antiques dealers in search of product and opportunities to market it. Their motives in studying the Shakers, as scholarly as they were, were by today's standards, at least, deeply compromised by their commercial mission."[74]

Actually, the Andrewses had no interest whatsoever in selling "product" even though the increasingly large market prices for "Shaker" were tempting to a modest couple who valued frugality. Though the Andrewses did run a tiny antiques business in their home for a couple of years in the early 1920s, they were not serious dealers, and at the beginning they were as much interested in colonial pieces as in Shaker. In an interview of October 2006, their daughter, Ann E. Andrews Kane, remembered the dabbling in sales as avocational and short-lived. Faith Andrews stated that before Ted had any steady teaching job they supported themselves "by a summer antique business which we conducted in [Ted's parents'] home in Pittsfield." It faded after Ted started graduate studies at Yale in 1923.[75] They sometimes sold a piece to get a finer one. They were uncomfortable with the business of selling and had a hard time putting a sale price on the items in their collection. Thus, in a revealing letter of 1958 to one of the founders of the American Museum in Bath, England, Faith wrote, "We wish that the disagreeable task of putting on prices might be eliminated and that we might adopt the Shaker policy of 'possessing as though we possessed not.'"[76]

As part of their proselytizing on the museum-quality beauty of Shaker artifacts, the Andrewses sometimes sold pieces to or acted as agents for influential tastemakers, including Juliana Force; Dorothy Canning Miller, curator of the Museum of Modern Art and the Andrewses' close friend; and various members of the Rockefeller family. Most such purchasers were in New York City in the 1930s. In 1937, with the appearance of *Shaker Furniture*, the book that made the Andrewses' reputation, requests for them to act as agents and advisers for purchase became more frequent. When Homer Eaton Keyes heard that a well-to-do woman with the "good" Manhattan address of Sutton Place had just purchased the book, he wrote to Faith Andrews about her: "I surmise that she wants to get some chairs such as you have in your dining room, and that sounds like a good opportunity to move some of the stuff that is in Hancock. If you will quote me some prices I shall whisper in her ear."[77] Keyes also lived at Sutton Place.

Compared with Keyes, and indeed most of the New York power elite, with whom they had to deal, the Andrewses lived abstemiously. Their daily life reflected their spiritual, somewhat ascetic, view of the Shakers. Never seduced by their years among the big-city sophisticates (except perhaps in shifting their cuisine from beans and apple tapioca to a more cosmopolitan fare), they loved spareness, associating it with the Shakers, even to the point of using candles at Shaker Farm in Richmond. They wanted to emulate the Shaker spirit and live "sparsely."[78] They were lucky (and persistent enough) to get jobs during the Depression. They sometimes could not afford gasoline and used bicycles in summer to get from Richmond to Pittsfield (ten miles) or Lenox (six miles).[79] They scrimped and saved to buy items for their collection and to subsidize the work of publication. In the mid-1930s Faith had a "family nest egg" that she refused to spend, saving it for a planned publication. When they achieved renown in the 1950s, no "thousands" of dollars came with it. Years of frugality and thrift had left them relatively comfortable by 1956, when Ted retired from teaching. As curator at Hancock from 1961 to 1963 (in name only after 1962), he had to contend with the board's view that his modest salary should be "studied."[80] When Ted died in 1964, Faith continued to live in their small house in Pittsfield.

The Andrewses were so far from any mercenary notion of "marketing product" that the final disposition of their collection became a major problem in their lives. They were extremely reluctant to part with their beloved Shaker materials, which they considered relics of a noble culture and not "product" for sale. Around 1957, when I first visited them at their Richmond home, I was astonished to see the sizeable barn behind their house crammed from floor to rafters with every conceivable kind of Shaker artifact, almost every piece collected since 1923 (except for pieces and manuscripts in their dwelling, and in the homes of their son and daughter). By the 1950s they had to supplement the barn space with "stalls" in Pittsfield.[81] During my visit, Ted smiled at my consternation that two persons could have accumulated so much; and he was moved by my expression of delight that so much of Shaker art and culture had been saved for future generations.

In view of the Andrewses' reluctance to release any items from their collection and their spare way of life, one cannot take seriously vituperative fictions and distortions picturing the Andrewses as profit-hungry dealers pushing "product" to enrich themselves. Still, misrepresentations have skewed the historical record and should be mentioned. Much of the animus stems from the arcane "World of Shaker," a subculture of hundreds of adepts, writers, dealers, hobbyists, collectors, and religious seekers. Many in the group are serious students of Shaker history and culture, but others are a peculiar kind of Shaker cultist and have projected a field of distortion from which only a handful of professional historians have escaped. In the apt phrase of one historian, they have been feeding on the Shakers "in a parasitic fashion."[82]

Those who attribute a "commercial mission" to Ted Andrews, and by extension, to Faith, fundamentally misrepresent the character of the collectors and the history of the collection. In this regard, it is particularly interesting to examine the relation of the Andrewses to the competitive and materialistic art scene in New York City in the 1930s. It reveals much about their resolute sense of mission and their steadfast resistance to marketing. It also led to their extraordinary good fortune at the Whitney Museum of American Art and to a career-altering friendship with Juliana Force.

New York City: The Whitney Museum and the Elite Reception of "Shaker"

In the 1920s, when the Andrewses began their serious collecting, the American art world was still making an invidious distinction between "high" and "low," or popular, culture. The art and artifacts of the Shakers belonged to the low side of the cultural ledger, mere "rural" pieces not worthy of collecting or exhibiting; on the high side were European painting, sculpture, and architecture, or finely carved Philadelphia Chippendale. The young Andrews of Camp Devens days had complained in his diary of the excessive worship of all things European and the need to appreciate great new American voices such as that of Walt Whitman. The prejudice against low art was especially strong in the early twentieth century. In the words of John Cadwalader, a trustee of the Metropolitan Museum of Art, "What do you mean by American art? . . . There is nothing American worth notice."[83]

A pivotal figure in establishing the Andrewses' New York nexus was Homer Eaton Keyes, the astute and well-connected editor of *Antiques* magazine. The Andrewses had known Keyes since Ted's time at Yale Graduate School, and he became their earliest, most significant convert and loyal ally. In 1937 the newly widowed Keyes stayed at the Andrewses' Richmond farmhouse just prior to his own death. He considered the Andrews house a spiritual refuge. Late in life Faith fondly recalled him as "our first very great friend. First and last."[84]

As an art historian, Keyes was a conservative student of high art but was quick to recognize the lasting beauty of Shaker craftsmanship. Still, even for Keyes, folk art was suspect, and he remained cautious—until he read Ted Andrews's book *The Community Industries of the Shakers*.[85] The book was groundbreaking in that it deals in detail with the everyday material culture of a well-known "utopian sect." Though the tools of work and manufacture did not constitute high culture, in Ted's mind almost every object from Shaker hands possessed esthetic value.

Aware of the lingering prejudice against popular culture, Keyes began a letter in June 1930 to Ted with the comment, "Within the next few months I expect to use the few photographs of Shaker furniture which I have. This is a subject which it is not wise to feed too rapidly to the public."[86]

Keyes's "public" consisted of the high-culture tastemakers and museum leaders centered in New York City: New York gallery owners, collectors, and museum directors such as Juliana Force of the Whitney Museum; Dorothy Canning Miller of the Museum of Modern Art; Holger Cahill, director of the Federal Art Project; and Edith Gregor Halpert, the leading New York gallery owner; influential theatrical figures such as Lincoln Kirstein and Jerome Robbins, who were interested in Shaker dance; and Robert Frost and many other artists, scholars, and luminaries, all of whom became part of the Andrewses' lives.[87]

Homer Eaton Keyes, editor of The Magazine **Antiques**.

Thus, by the 1930s the Andrewses had tied into a scene and a city alive with people who were far more open to new ideas than their fellow New Englanders. As Faith remarked in an interview, "We found that in New York we had quite a different audience, more receptive, spontaneous, more civilized, more sophisticated perhaps."[88]

At the same time the intellectual tide was turning strongly in favor of the Andrewses. The long apprenticeship of American culture and art to its European master that Ted Andrews had complained about as a young man was finally coming to an end. In a diary entry of June 1919 he had lamented "all the encrusted formations which have barnacled our national art, some out of the old world, some out of the unrealities and superficialities of the new."[89]

Attitudes toward low culture had changed dramatically from 1909, when the Metropolitan Museum of Art launched what they thought was a wildly daring exhibition of early American furniture and decorative arts to "test out the question of whether American domestic art was worthy of a place in an American museum."[90] Not until 1924 did the Metropolitan open an American wing—just as the Andrewses were starting their own private "wing"

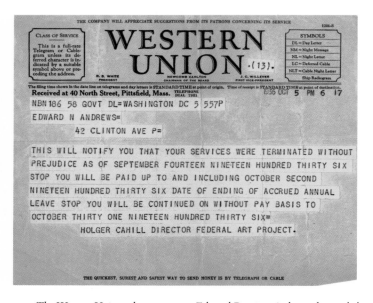

The Western Union telegram sent to Edward Deming Andrews that ended
his work with the Federal Art Project. Ironically, the sender, Holger Cahill,
and the Andrewses would become good friends later in life.
Courtesy, The Winterthur Library: The Edward Deming Andrews
Memorial Shaker Collection, contained in Box 21.

of low culture, the "rural" culture of the Shakers. And in October 1929 the Metropolitan turned down Gertrude Vanderbilt Whitney's offer of her extraordinary collection of some five hundred American paintings and sculpture, treating her emissary (Juliana Force) with insulting condescension. The Metropolitan's director, Edward Robinson, after a respectful obeisance to Gertrude Whitney's fine philanthropy, sent Force away with the comment, "What will we do with them, my dear lady? We have a cellar full of those things already."[91] The rebuff led directly to the founding of the Whitney Museum of American Art.

The Metropolitan's "test" of the acceptability of American art was no surprise to Ted Andrews. He had long been aware of the early twentieth-century art world's preferences for the art of the Old World (Europe). He believed that the ruling classes who bought art and supported museums harbored a bias against American art.

The turning point came in 1932, when Holger Cahill organized the Museum of Modern Art's exhibition titled American Folk Art: The Art of the Common Man in America, 1790–1900. Art scholars consider this event an important milestone in the acceptance of folk art. As a well-known early promoter of folk art and a leading gallerist, Edith Gregor Halpert soon made huge profits selling it, particularly to the Rockefellers. Under the influence of the artist Charles Sheeler, a close friend of the Andrewses, Halpert acquired a large Shaker collection for her country home with the Andrewses' help—just as Juliana Force had done: "Shaker" had become acceptable as folk art. The appreciation of folk art that began in the 1920s had emerged by 1932 as a new movement in the art world, and now it flowered as an aspect of New Deal populism.

The growing interest in folk art merged with the new interest in popular culture, which in turn led to the first outdoor museums, including Henry Ford's Greenfield Village (1929) in Dearborn, Michigan, Mystic Seaport (1929) in Connecticut, and Old Sturbridge Village (1938) in Massachusetts, the harbingers of an explosion of museums of popular culture after World War II.

The favorable changes in public taste and intellectual fashion and a modicum of public recognition did not, however, guarantee a comfortable living to the Andrewses, who scraped by on tiny Depression-era salaries. Ted continued teaching and Faith did secretarial work. By 1937, though they were able to buy the colonial saltbox in Richmond as a summer home, they were still enough financially hard-pressed that they shared the initial cost of the house with a cousin.

Not until August 1928 did the Andrewses get their first respectful hearing, in *Antiques* magazine, a scholarly publication serving the relatively new middle-class activity of collecting antiques. This article and another published in *Antiques* the following year describing and extolling Shaker artifacts gave the Andrewses national visibility and helped establish their scholarly reputation.[92] One specific result was that Laura Bragg, the new, reform-minded director of the Berkshire Museum in Pittsfield, became a convert. Upon learning of the Andrews Collection from the *Antiques* articles, Bragg contacted the Andrewses and helped them set up the 1932 exhibition of their collection at the Berkshire Museum.

Another even more important result of the Bragg friendship was the Andrewses' fateful entrée into the arts and museum worlds of New York City. The Andrewses instantly understood the importance of Laura Bragg's social and professional connections for the future acceptance of Shaker art and artifacts. Some forty years later, Faith wrote:

Laura Bragg had the know-how that we needed. She knew how to share her knowledge, how to share your knowledge and she brought together at a dinner meeting that evening the people she felt mattered in our collecting life. It was there we met Juliana Force, and she was a force in our life for many years to come. Laura Bragg opened up the doors for us to expand and extend our work, and Homer Keyes, along with her, particularly after we got to know Juliana Force, Carl Rollins (who published our first book). We had great gatherings, great talks, great hopes, and we accomplished far more than we ever dreamed of, I think.[93]

Even more revealing were Faith's comments on meeting Juliana Force during the Pittsfield exhibition. She remembered being thrilled that Force "was the first person to use the word 'elegant' in reference to the furniture. You can imagine what a boost that was to us."[94]

Juliana Force, swimming in funds from the Whitney fortune at the lowest point of the Depression, and spurred by competition from Laura Bragg, would redirect the Andrewses' careers almost immediately. The Berkshire Museum exhibition was hardly dismantled before Bragg, meeting with others, launched a plan to create a "Society for the Preservation of Shaker Antiquities," ostensibly to help the Andrewses but in reality to attempt to commandeer the Andrews Collection for the benefit of the Berkshire Museum. Ted and Faith appreciated Bragg's approval and help, but her enterprising move was ill conceived, badly timed, and not entirely disinterested. With a political savvy that they did not always demonstrate, the Andrewses had instead cast their lot with Juliana Force's new Whitney Museum, which promised to mount a Shaker exhibition in the cultural capital of the country. On October 26, 1932, in the earliest surviving letter between the Andrewses and Force, Ted Andrews distanced himself from Bragg's project, tactfully exposing its impracticality and its possible offensiveness to the Shakers—who would hardly welcome being shelved among the "antiquities"—but he also cleverly played up to Force's large self-interest and her even larger ambition.

Laura Bragg ca. 1930

Photographs of the Andrewses' 1932 exhibition at The Berkshire Museum. All images on this page are Courtesy of the Berkshire Museum, Pittsfield, Massachusetts

> Although we recognize the merits of such a scheme, Mrs. Andrews and I have not been active participants in this movement, first, because knowing the Shakers as we do, we foresee the advantage of an unobtrusive technique; secondly, because of certain real difficulties in finding a desirable Shaker property; and thirdly, because we do not feel that it is quite fair to you, and your plans for a Shaker room, to participate in a project which, if not duplicating at certain points what you desire to accomplish, might possibly, through undue publicity, take the edge from the surprise element or novel character of your exhibit.[95]

In her reply Force thanked Ted for his forethought in bringing these plans to her attention. Eager to stake her claim on presenting the Shakers to the public, the blatantly materialistic and talkative Force sympathized with Ted's protective attitude toward the Shakers and even lamented the loss of reticence and

religious spirit: "I am rather distressed at your letter because, of course, such an organization would materially affect my plans. I have no great sympathy for a society in connection with so reticent and religious a spirit as the Shaker tradition. It is all too scarce in the history of our country. My inspiration to preserve in this Museum that spirit is almost diametrically opposed to what I term 'propaganda.' I think you understand my attitude which I am expressing to you."

Bragg's plans for the "society" never materialized. As for the Whitney, Ted, Faith, and Juliana Force had recognized one another's real desires and aims from their earliest correspondence, and they started a mutually beneficial alliance that would last another six years. Force helped them meet people prominent in the arts, arranged to get them some financial support, and financed their first major publication. The Andrewses' New York nexus began to flourish.

Juliana Force (1876–1948), the woman whom Faith recalled as "a force in our life," was the first director of the Whitney Museum of American Art and a close friend of the founder of the museum, Gertrude Vanderbilt Whitney (1875–1942). Force had free access to Gertrude Whitney's fortune and gave many upcoming artists and scholars of the time, including the Andrewses, much needed monetary support.[96] She deeply influenced the way American art has been perceived and received. The daughter of a poor tradesman from Hoboken, whose wife had borne fourteen children in two marriages, Juliana Force escaped to New York City, where she artfully constructed the persona of an aristocrat—and got away with it, partly by dissimulation and partly by sheer brass. In the words of her biographer, "Juliana fought hard for her seigneury, overcoming poverty and an unpromising physical appearance. Impetuous generosity and extravagance were her hallmarks, but a certain arbitrariness and irrationality occasionally crept into her dealings as well."[97] Nicknamed "Mrs. Fierce," she was only five feet one inch tall, but her self-confidence, piercing intellect, and rigorous carriage made her a commanding figure.

Faith admired Force: "I thought she was a very sophisticated woman. Very. We were dealing with an entirely different personality. A very shrewd type of person and a very fine person."[98] She became a good friend of Juliana Force's perhaps because they both sought to break away from the constraints of their nineteenth-century upbringings, from the irrational control of organized religion, and from male domination of economic, social, and intellectual life.[99] But they differed in one fundamental area of life: the getting and keeping of money, and this difference would end their friendship.

Faith was thrifty and understood self-denial, while Force was extravagant and hedonistic. For Faith money was helpful, but for Force it was everything. As her biographer notes, Force's mother "instilled in her children a gripping fear of poverty and a wild desire to spend money as an act of defiance."[100] Her brother remembered that as a young girl Force would stamp her feet in a tantrum, shouting, "I won't be poor! I hate being poor! I won't be poor." She was deathly afraid of cats, and on a visit with the Andrewses to one of the empty Hancock buildings a black cat ran in front of her and she fainted away; the Andrewses thought she was dead.[101] As a relatively affluent adult she owned five houses in Europe and the United States but really could not afford them. It was her attempt to squeeze money out of the Andrewses (in the form of objects from the Andrews Collection) that broke up the friendship.

Juliana Force, Director of the Whitney Museum ca. 1940-41.
Courtesy of the Frances Mulhall Achilles Library, The Whitney Museum of American Art

But before that happened she was as generous to them as she was to the many artists she supported. Force was extremely close to her wealthy benefactor, and their work together in promoting American art from 1907 till Whitney's death in 1942 altered the face of American art. In 1907 Force helped Whitney establish the Whitney Studio in MacDougal Alley in Greenwich Village. She acted as Whitney's agent, representative, doorkeeper, and secretary and, as Whitney took on lovers, quickly became her confidante. As a team with great prescience they purchased the work not of big-name artists but of dissenting realists (equated with modernism at the time), including Robert Henri, John Sloan, George Luks, Everett Shinn, William Glackens, Thomas Eakins, and many others.

Force's keen artistic judgment and openness to new ideas enabled her to recognize the lasting worth of Shaker art and the pioneering work of the Andrewses. The Andrewses' scholarship and their collection fit in perfectly with the Whitney-Force enterprise of establishing a museum to exhibit the vernacular and the new in American art. The Whitney

Studio had become the Whitney Museum of American Art in 1931, and the following year the Andrewses represented a notable departure among the many protégés of Whitney and Force, all of whom were artists.

The surviving correspondence between Juliana Force and the Andrewses in the archives of the Whitney Museum begins in 1932 and traces a ten-year arc of friendship, business, and patronage, ending abruptly and awkwardly in 1942. The correspondence was put on hold each summer when Force sailed for Europe, while the young and worshipful Andrewses eagerly awaited missives from their magical benefactor.

The first project proposed by the Andrewses was the publication of a monograph Ted had written on his collection of Shaker gift drawings. By the spring of 1934 Ted had completed enough of the manuscript to seek a publisher, and since Force had already been awarding a stipend to the Andrewses for the gift-drawing work (and other research) since November 1932, Ted approached her about having the Whitney publish it. But Force had always focused the mission of the Whitney on artists, not publishing, and wrote a politely supportive letter of rejection on March 1, 1934, stating that "the book is not primarily a publication for the Museum to undertake. I am more sorry than I can say that this is the case, and I do hope that there will be some other way of getting this valuable contribution to American Culture published. Will you let me hear from you about this? With kindest regrets, I am Sincerely yours, DIRECTOR [Juliana Force]."[102]

Undeterred, Ted moved forward. On the advice of his stalwart friend Homer Eaton Keyes, he contacted George T. Bailey, director of the Yale University Press, and Carl Purington Rollins, a renowned printer, and sent them copies of the manuscript. When he asked Force for a letter of support, she responded willingly. Ted seemed confident about his chances at Yale, describing Rollins's great enthusiasm for the book in a letter to Force. But Yale Press turned him down, and the manuscript would remain unpublished until after Ted's death.[103]

In the same letter that reported so optimistically about the possible publication of the gift-drawing book is found the first reference to a new and fateful aspect of the Andrewses' relationship with Force: "On our next trip [Ted wrote] we will bring down the pieces of Shaker furniture which you bought last fall." These were to be added to a number of other fine Shaker pieces that would adorn her second country home, Shaker Hollow Farm, in South Salem, New York. It would be easy to assume, from Faith's account of the Andrewses' first meetings with Juliana Force in Pittsfield and at various Shaker sites, that she was one of their star converts, something of an innocent till she visited the Andrewses. Actually, Force had begun to collect Shaker furniture before 1920 and added some Shaker pieces to the Pennsylvania Dutch antiques in her second American estate, Barley Sheaf Farm, in Bucks County, Pennsylvania. Moreover, by the time she met the Andrewses, she had amassed a substantial Shaker collection at Shaker Hollow Farm. Although the Andrewses greatly deepened her understanding of the Shaker esthetic and acted as expert agents for new acquisitions, Force had long used the word "elegant" to describe Shaker work. She separated the Shaker artisans from what she called untutored "folk painters."[104] It is a myth that Force was an early convert to the Andrewses' conviction that Shaker artifacts are a form of high art—even if the museums wanted to call it folk art; she had recognized the unique value of Shaker objects before 1920.

Driven by an unquenchable acquisitive spirit, she crammed her large New York apartment with objects of every conceivable style from rococo to Victorian (for its shock value). Similarly, she filled Shaker Hollow Farm with a mishmash of outlandish leopard-print rugs and couches, modernist paintings, and colonial furniture. High-society visitors would have been the first fashionable people to see Shaker furniture displayed as a status symbol for those "in the know." In calling her place "Shaker Hollow Farm," Force reflected the newly fashionable and positive use of "Shaker," long before the massive vogue for Shaker after World War II.

Clearly Juliana Force had recognized the special worth of Shaker objects before the Andrewses ever met and married. While one must emphasize this crucial and perennially omitted fact in the Andrews story, it does not diminish the great contribution the Andrewses made in deepening Force's understanding of Shaker culture, nor their role as experts and purchasing agents; and Juliana Force became the first major New York art world figure, after Homer Eaton Keyes, to be supplied with Shaker objects. (Keyes never had much in the way of Shaker furniture, just a few small objects received from the Andrewses as tokens of esteem.)

The Andrews-Force alliance reached its peak between 1935, with the exhibition at the Whitney Museum, engineered by Force, of the Andrews Collection and other pieces, and 1937, with the publication of *Shaker Furniture*, subsidized by Force. For the Whitney's pivotal 1935 exhibition, Force

Interior photographs of Juliana Force's "Shaker Hollow Farm" ca. 1935. The "butler's desk" shown at bottom was featured in the Andrewses' January 1933 article for The Magazine **Antiques.** *The Andrewses photographed it in the snow outside their Pittsfield home before it was acquired by Juliana Force.*

made sure that the Andrewses got all the floor space they wanted and free rein to choose and arrange their Shaker objects as they liked. Faith remembered that it was "Christmas all the time. . . . It was not just the money. It was Juliana Force's influence and support. Just like that, she would get things. . . . You could feel her mind going. And she looked for ways to help us. . . . At the museum . . . we had absolutely free say and no warning about anything. We were running it all." Not until 1959, when the new American Museum of Bath, in England, invited the Andrewses to set up a permanent but much smaller exhibit, did they enjoy so great a freedom and such respectful support.[105]

A letter from Ted Andrews to Force dated April 28, 1935, outlines the scope and content of the Whitney exhibition. The Andrewses would try to show groupings of object types, as well as room settings. "Enclosed, according to your wishes, is a tentative list of Shaker furniture and accessories which we would like to show in the fall exhibit. These pieces have been visualized in galleries V and VI, both as small ensembles and with regard to the appearance of the rooms as completed units. . . . You will note that we have included, as desirable, certain pieces in your collection."[106]

The Whitney exhibition, titled Shaker Handicrafts, ran from November 12 to December 12, 1935. Andrews wrote a short essay, together with a fifteen-page checklist of the show—including, quite notably, the watercolor *East View of the Brick House*. Andrews listed the drawing in the catalogue, but it was not part of the Andrews Collection. Since it was still in the possession of the Hancock Shakers in 1935, it is apparent that the Shakers had lent it—the first time that any Shaker community lent artwork to a public exhibition. Although the museum did not document the exhibit photographically, a few snapshots appeared in a very friendly review in the *Christian Science Monitor* on December 3, 1935. The brief *New York Times* notices were politely admiring.[107]

Overall the show was a success, despite the Andrewses' dismay over the damage to six of their pieces during shipping. The exhibition reinforced the mutual admiration society established between the Andrewses and Juliana Force and the relationship would remain in full glow for another two years. Just

after the exhibit closed, Force's secretary, Anna Freeman, sent a short note to Ted: "Dear Mr. Andrews: Mrs. Force asks me to send you the enclosed check for $85 for the 'Shaker piece' you were kind enough to let her have. Mrs. Force appreciates exceedingly the modest price you put on it! Sincerely yours, Sec'y to Mrs. Force."

In return for all her patronage, however, Force wanted payback from the Andrewses in the form of items from their collection, in particular the gift drawings. In the two years following the successful Whitney exhibition, her relationship with the Andrewses began to deteriorate, mainly because of her financial problems. She had been nonchalantly living the high life at a time when most Americans were suffering economically. By 1937–38 she was in desperate need of money and had to sell her large collection. (It went secretly to Blanchette Rockefeller.)[108] After considerable negotiation and argument between Force and the Andrewses, the friendship came to a bitter end, a sad fact that the Andrewses passed over in their memoirs.[109]

The spring of 1936 witnessed two key events. Each would have a lasting impact on the friendship, one decidedly negative— the fate of the Andrewses' gift drawings; the other enduringly positive—publication of the furniture book. As artists and photographers descended on the Andrewses' Pittsfield home to document Shaker design for the Federal Art Project, Ted Andrews shrewdly decided to store the gift drawings in the vault of the Whitney Museum. His purpose was likely threefold. First, the drawings had to be in a secure environment, safe from potential theft or damage. Second, Ted did not want artists working under the auspices of the government to "scoop" him on his discovery of this unique byway of American art. Third, he quickly lost confidence in the honest administration of the program, referring in letters to the incompetence of some of the workers and the federal bureaucracy's arbitrary categorizing of Shaker art by state, e.g., New York versus Massachusetts.

Juliana Force was in full agreement with Ted's worry about security, since she was a great admirer of the gift drawings. So much so, in fact, that she felt a sense of ownership about them. Accordingly, the gift drawings were taken to New York, where they would remain for nearly two years.

In the meantime, the second key event in the Andrews-Force relationship was coming to fruition. In the early summer of 1936 Force and Carl Purington Rollins met to discuss the prospects for the publication of the Andrewses' Shaker furniture manuscript. In a show of support, Force sent a hundred dollars to Yale University Press on July 8, to "help defray expenses on Mr. Andrews book."

A poster, invitation, and handbill for the exhibition Shaker Handicrafts at The Whitney Museum of American Art in 1935.
Courtesy of the Frances Mulhall Achilles Library, Archives, Whitney Museum of American Art, New York

On October 15 of that year the Andrewses received a letter from Force's secretary informing them: "Mrs. Force has decided to sell her Shaker things and would like very much for you to advise her as to what prices to place on them. She therefore thought that perhaps you could find it convenient to come to New York some day next week and on your way stop in South Salem and look the things over. This will be of great help to her and she will be glad to pay your expenses."

Force's sudden need for money prompted her to sell part of her longstanding Shaker collection. Accordingly, in May 1937, at her request Ted and Faith Andrews catalogued her collection at Shaker Hollow Farm in South Salem and she held a private sale there on May 18 and 19. She did not sell everything but received enough cash to honor her promise to the Andrewses and to Yale to subsidize the production costs of the furniture book. On June 1, 1937, she sent a check to Yale for nine hundred dollars, thus insuring the publication of *Shaker Furniture.* The American Council of Learned Societies also contributed to the cost of publication.[110] Even though she was now approaching insolvency, Force no doubt had to send the money to Yale in part to save face, after having kept Rollins and others at Yale Press waiting an entire year for the balance of her subsidy. Soon after that payment she made arrangements to sell Cobweb, her estate in England.

In desperation, the now sixty-year-old Force turned to her twenty-year-old nephew, Carl Rieser, as a confidante, assuring him in a letter of June 9 that he was "a grown man and can face facts as well as anyone." She said that she had to change her mode of living because the government was taking more than one-third of her income, so that "I was obliged to sell all my investments at a sacrifice and my income now is only what I can earn. For all the money I give to either support or aid in supporting others, I get no exemption. . . . Do write to me and do not ever show this to anyone." She finally sold Cobweb for twenty-five hundred pounds, and her nephew sent consoling letters to England, where she had taken refuge in the Lake District.[111]

The following September the Andrewses contacted Force, asking her if there were any Shaker pieces she wished to sell. They probably wished to retrieve some precious items that they had previously sold to her. But considering the amount of money Force had already bestowed on the Andrewses and her desperate financial situation, this overture seems slightly awkward in retrospect. A reply came to them in the negative. This exchange is the first instance at which one can detect the friendship beginning to unravel.

What happened next is detailed in four brief letters between Force's secretary and the Andrewses, with a final letter coming from Force herself. It is worth presenting these texts in full, because they add yet another layer of controversy to the most iconic of all Shaker artifacts: the gift drawings. Apparently the drawings, which had been stored in the vault at the Whitney, were brought to the site to be included in the sale at Shaker Hollow. According to Faith, Force returned them to her and Ted before the sale. Nonetheless, their ownership was in dispute.

January
twelfth
1938
Dear Mrs. Andrews:

I am making an inventory of Mrs. Force's "Shaker" things and in checking up on the items I find that the "Inspirational Drawings" which Mrs. Force sent down to South Salem at the time of the Sale are not among the things that came back here after the Sale.

In order to complete this inventory it is important for me to have these drawings, as I understood from you, at the time they were sent down here, that they belonged to Mrs. Force. Will you therefore be good enough to let me know what became of them, as I feel it is my fault for not having checked up on these sooner.

With kindest regards to you and Mr. Andrews,
Sincerely yours,
Secretary to Mrs. Force

January 13, 1938

Miss Anna Freeman,

New York.

Dear Miss Freeman:

Apparently you are mistaken about the ownership of the drawings. At the time the Federal Art Project began the documentation of items in our furniture and textile collection, Mrs. Force suggested that it would be well to bring the drawings down to the museum for temporary safe-keeping. Neither we nor she wanted to have the drawings included in the federal project, and so in the spring of 1936 Mr. Andrews made a special trip to New York to deposit them at the Whitney Museum until we were through with the government work. There they stayed until Mrs. Force's sale last spring, when she brought them up to South Salem on one of her trips and returned them to us. We brought them home the same day—before the sale opened.

Please let us know if this brief outline does not clarify the situation satisfactorily. We do not want to have the slightest misunderstanding about the matter.

Sincerely,

Faith Andrews

February 8, 1938

Dear Mrs. Andrews:

I regret that an opportunity has not presented itself until now for me to respond to your letter of January thirteenth.

Your answer rather puzzled me, for I remember distinctly your calling on the telephone, when Ruth Reeves was taking the inventory at your house for the Index of American Design, at which time you said that you told her that the Inspiration Drawings belonged to Mrs. Force. At this time you also spoke to Mrs. Force and it was then that she told you to have them brought down here. I also recall very definitely that Mrs. Force sent these drawings to South Salem at the time of the Sale, particularly to be included in the Sale, and not for the purpose of returning them to you.

Recently I have had an opportunity to go over the accounting pertaining to the "Shaker Furniture Book", and I really feel, Mrs. Andrews, that Mrs. Force sincerely believes that these drawings are her only tangible result of her large investment.

Since I am almost through with the inventory pertaining to Mrs. Force's Shaker belongings, may I expect to hear from you again about these drawings before I pass it on to Mrs. Force?

Sincerely yours,

Secretary to Mrs. Force

Edward Deming Andrews photographed writing at a Shaker school desk ca. 1935.
Gift of Miriam R. and M. Stephen Miller, Collection of Hancock Shaker Village

February 13, 1938
Mrs. Juliana Force,
New York.
Dear Mrs. Force:

In view of the fact that telephone conversation seems an unsatisfactory means of our stating our position about the drawings, or you yours, we would like to suggest that you write us yourself about the matter or come to see us. If there is a doubt in your mind about ownership, it can best be straightened out by a personal conference.
Sincerely,
Edward D. Andrews

February
fourteenth
1938
Dear Mr. Andrews:

I do not see that any letter from me could make your statement in regard to the ownership of the Shaker drawings any plainer.

Miss Freeman reported to me that Mrs. Andrews said they belonged to her and not to me.

Will you be good enough to send the negatives which I asked Miss Freeman to telegraph for? I will be very grateful if you will ship these as soon as possible.
Very truly yours,
[Juliana Force]

It is difficult to say for certain what had transpired between 1936 and 1938 with regard to the ownership of the gift drawings. Certainly no surviving documentation exists of their sale or donation by the Andrewses to Force, and it seems highly unlikely that such records would have been lost or that Force possessed any written evidence of a transfer. Resort to memory of a telephone call is revealing. It is worth recalling that Juliana Force had always been somewhat devious and now was desperate.

It seems highly unlikely also that the Andrewses would have given their entire collection of gift drawings to Juliana Force, especially because Ted felt a spiritual attachment to them and he had not yet published the work about which he remained the most passionate until the end of his life, *Visions of the Heavenly Sphere*. Rather, it seems that Force may have tried to strong-arm the Andrewses into giving her the gift drawings, especially in the light of her secretary's comment, "Mrs. Force sincerely believes that these drawings are her only tangible result of her large investment." This tangential claim may refer to the thousand dollars she had sent to Yale. In his letter of February 13 in reply to the secretary's letter, Ted Andrews asked for a face-to-face meeting with Force about the matter. This request finally elicited a response from Force herself that is quite telling in its brevity, and in its limp acknowledgment of the veracity of the Andrewses' claim of ownership. Force's claim that she owned the drawings was entirely without foundation. As her biographer remarks in discussing the clash, Force had a "fix on entitlement" and "it became one of her quirks to think that if she conceived a passion for a small object owned by someone, it was fair to hint at her right of eminent domain."[112]

The falling out between the two parties marks the end of the most important patronage relationship the Andrewses would enjoy during their career. In supporting Winter and Andrews, Juliana Force became the first and most influential ally in the Andrewses' campaign to raise the level of respect for the Shakers and their arts, especially as a result of the Whitney exhibition, Shaker Handicrafts, in 1935. Moreover, without Juliana's help, the Andrewses' pioneering work *Shaker Furniture* would never have been published in the midst of the Depression.[113]

A final exchange put a farcical cap on the relationship. In May 1942, a month after the death of Gertrude Vanderbilt Whitney, Ted Andrews received a telegram from Force's secretary requesting a meeting with him. When the meeting was immediately cancelled, he wrote back expressing his dismay that "the conference you so kindly planned for Monday had to be postponed. I trust you will let me know fairly soon when one can be arranged." The next day Force's secretary telegrammed a reply.

Dear Mr. Andrews:

The telegram you received was sent by me, for Mrs. Force, confusing your name with a Director of a Museum, whom Mrs. Force wished to see, and to whom she instructed me to send a telegram making an appointment. When Mrs. Force returned, she told me you were not the "Mr. Andrews" she wanted to see.

Mrs. Force received your letter of May sixth, and asks me to write you that she cannot possibly understand why you want to see her, and that she cannot make any appointments outside of Museum affairs.

Sincerely yours,
Secretary to Mrs. Force [114]

The Tree of Light** or **Blazing Tree
painted by Sister Hannah Cohoon,
Hancock, Mass. 1845.
Andrews Collection, Hancock Shaker Village
1963.129

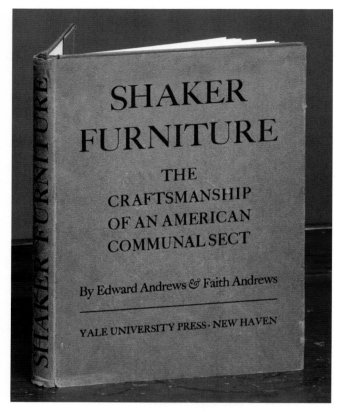

*The first edition of **Shaker Furniture** 1937.*
Collection of William and Sandra Soule

Finding a Home for the Collection

The Whitney exhibition of 1935, followed by the 1937 publication of the furniture book, established the preeminent importance of the Andrews Collection, gave the Andrewses national visibility, and started them thinking about finding a permanent home for the collection. They felt that they "were getting in very deep" and started thinking about a museum. Both Sister Sadie Neale and Sister Alice Smith felt that "there should be an institution to take over these things."[115] But the Andrewses had so deeply mingled their personal lives with their Shaker collection that they were loath to part with it. They feared transferring ownership of their "children" to institutions that would not "love" them enough.

The Andrewses' recalcitrance was expressed in the conditions they imposed on the use of the collection, principally their demand that the collection be preserved as a unit for educational purposes. Their purist conception of the Shakers and Ted's relentless emphasis on using the whole of Shaker culture for education and emulation partly explains their several failed attempts between the late 1930s and about 1964 to find a library or museum for their collection. Their lack of flexibility put off even the most receptive institutions.

The first of the Andrewses' long series of frustrated attempts to find a respectable recipient for the collection came in 1941. In January of that year Ted Andrews, aware of Eleanor Roosevelt's interest in the Shakers and her acquaintance with the Neale sisters at Mount Lebanon, wrote to her, asking, "What can we do to preserve the unique collection we have made?"[116] She responded with an expression of delight and arranged to meet with Ted at the Museum of Modern Art about three weeks later. Sincerely concerned for the continuation of his work and the preservation of the collection, she unsuccessfully tried to find a government job for him, and put him in contact with relevant officials in the capital, including Alexander Wetmore, assistant secretary of the Smithsonian Institution.

Ted tried to persuade Wetmore to accept their collection as an educational tool and to display the artifacts in period rooms. Wetmore explained that the institution, because of "our lack of space for such displays at the present time," could not accept the Andrewses' conditions. Wetmore suggested that the Library of Congress would be interested in the manuscript and print materials, saying nothing about the artifacts and furniture.[117] Wetmore was truthful. Ted was disappointed, expressing his opinion to Eleanor Roosevelt that neither the National Museum nor the National Gallery was interested in the preservation of the folk or popular arts of America. But other factors were involved.

Andrews did follow up on Wetmore's suggestion to contact the Library of Congress, and the librarian at the time, Archibald MacLeish. MacLeish responded on March 18, 1941, welcoming the books, prints, and manuscripts as a "tremendous" addition to their MacLean Collection, but noting, rightly, that "the museum material" would not be appropriate.[118]

The Wetmore-MacLeish episode reveals that already by the late 1930s the Andrewses had begun thinking about the problem of preserving their collection. They had to spend the first two decades of their career, from 1923 to 1941, trying to persuade educated Americans that the artifacts and culture of the Believers were worthy of respect and conservation. They concentrated their campaign in the arts and education worlds, succeeding in the first and failing in the second.

In the early 1950s Ted turned his attention to the completion of his most ambitious project yet: a comprehensive history of the Shakers. The resulting work, published in 1953 by Oxford University Press under the title *The People Called Shakers: A Search for the Perfect Society*, was the most thorough examination of the Shakers since the 1904 publication of *Shakerism, Its Meaning and Message* by the Shaker sisters Leila Sarah Taylor and Anna White.[119] While dated, the Andrewses' work remains a foundational text for students of Shaker history; it is not a definitive work, but it is a signal milestone in the historiography.

By 1956 the Andrewses, then in their sixties, felt more urgently than ever the need to preserve their vast collection for the future. Amherst College and Yale University were their first choices. Ted held degrees from both institutions, but once Yale laid down their welcome mat, Amherst receded from his thoughts.

Yale's allure for Ted lay mainly in its having a first-rate American Studies program that was sympathetic to the study of utopian history. In 1938 Arthur E. Bestor Jr., the founder of the historical study of American utopianism (for which he coined the term "communitarianism"), wrote a dissertation at Yale that was to become a seminal work in American social history, *Backwoods Utopias*.[120]

The Andrewses felt, with some justification, that even as late as the late 1950s most scholars did not take Shaker history seriously. One who did was the Coe Professor of American History at Yale, David M. Potter (1910–1971), a teacher venerated by his students and considered by many scholars as possibly the best American historian of his time. In June 1958, after he had left Yale for Stanford, Potter wrote a letter in support of the Andrewses to the Yale administration, noting:

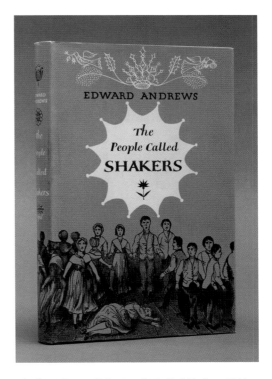

*The first edition of **The People Called Shakers** 1953.*
Collection of Hancock Shaker Village

> As the bibliography of his [Ted Andrews's] publications will show, he possesses an unrivalled knowledge of all aspects of Shakerism. He and his wife are an institute in themselves.... The exacting quality of his scholarship and also his enlarged view of the subject assures that he will develop the broad implications of the material and that he will meet rigorous standards of historical ... method.[121]

Potter treated the Andrewses with great kindness, responding with insight into their aspirations for Shaker studies, even if he felt that they had set their hopes too high. Potter wrote a very positive assessment of the significance of the Shakers in American history—which Ted was very fond of quoting.

"I am convinced," Potter wrote, "that the Shakers offer unusual opportunities for study; because of [their closely integrated culture] they do present in manageable compass—in microcosm—all the elements of a full-blown culture. This culture represented a deliberate alternative to the prevailing American culture, and therefore it offers a perspective upon American culture at large."[122]

The Andrewses thought they saw in Potter's statement some support for their conviction that the Andrews Collection could be used primarily for an educational purpose at Yale. Thus, at the beginning of his tenure as consultant for Shaker history and culture at Yale (1956–58), Ted wrote a prospectus titled "The Andrews' Teaching Collection," confidently stating, "The Shaker library and artifacts constituting the Andrews' gift to Yale University will serve as a 'Teaching Collection'—a relatively new development in education by means of the visual arts. Housed in the Yale Art Gallery, it will serve as a graphic demonstration, to students in the American Studies Program and others, of a particular, indigenous culture."[123]

In the midst of his tenure at Yale Ted was convinced that his dream of using Shaker culture as a teaching tool had come true. On June 7, 1957, in his commencement address at the Scarborough School, he proudly described the collection's role in Yale's American Studies program, as though Yale had accepted all his conditions.

Our collection of artifacts—furniture, textiles, prints, industrial products, etc.—will be housed in the Art Gallery, in a section reconstructed as an authentic Shaker interior, and so installed as to allow for rotating exhibits and convenient study. After being catalogued, the books, pamphlets and manuscripts will be deposited as a unit, in that section of the University Library devoted to Americana. The teaching course, part of the American Studies program, is open to students, on both the undergraduate and graduate levels, who are particularly interested in this aspect of our American heritage.[124]

In a letter to an old friend, T. D. Seymour Bassett, the librarian at the University of Vermont, Ted remarked that David Potter "has been a true friend, for whose constructive suggestions and sympathetic insight into our work we shall always be grateful."[125]

Unfortunately, the Andrewses soon learned that they were quite mistaken. Academic institutions are extremely jealous of their control over the curriculum and long-term commitments of space and would resist any donor's effort to have any one topic required or any one mode of exhibition stipulated, a stand that the Andrewses in their Shaker obsession simply could not fathom.[126] They unrealistically expected Yale to become a center for Shaker studies, but their dream had to compete for space and money with Yale's colossal holdings on topics of larger import in human history, such as the British Empire.

The Andrewses also argued for a separate locked section of the stacks in the Sterling Memorial Library for their rare books; they did not want them to be dispersed throughout the general collections. But Yale had no large storage area for rare books and manuscripts. (The magnificent Beinecke Library for rare books and manuscripts had not yet been built.) They also wanted a Shaker Room to be set up in the Art Gallery, but the Art Department was reluctant because of lack of space. Writing what amounted to a long letter of condolence, Potter told Ted that he felt "very badly about the way matters have developed for you and Mrs. Andrews." One of the rare persons in authority to understand the Andrewses' extreme reluctance to relinquish control of their collection, Potter noted that he was mindful "that the transit of your treasures from a personal to an institutional ownership would, at best, mean that they would not be cherished as before and that this would necessarily be saddening to you." But Potter also pointed out with his legendary tact and honesty:

I would have been glad if circumstances had developed in such a way as to lead to a continuation of your work, but I must honestly say that, although I personally feel great enthusiasm for your material and later for your way of interpreting it, I always felt that because of its rather special character, your work was unlikely to find a regular place in the curriculum and therefore that one could not expect an extension of your appointment. Since I was not in negotiation with you myself, it was not for me to state this point, but I felt it very important at the time that no misleading expectations should be implied to you, and that the appointment should be put primarily on the basis of the preparation of a full descriptive catalogue of the Collection.[127]

Thus, in early 1958 the Andrewses withdrew their gift, causing great pain and embarrassment to all involved. In 1961 they bought a house back home in their birthplace of Pittsfield.

In 1987, some thirty years later, Faith attributed the withdrawal of their gift to "personnel and policy changes that cast doubt on the future of their collection."[128] As the Yale proposal was unraveling she got to talk alone with a key new administrator, Andrew Carnduff Richie, who had not yet taken office as the director of the Yale Art Gallery. Richie had an old-school background at the Courtauld Institute in the early 1930s and showed an active disinterest in the Andrews Shaker collection. Faith recalled:

[Richie] hadn't taken over yet, but he was there and in control. And he wasn't interested in Shaker. It was very obvious. And finally I suppose it was irritating to him to be questioned by me probably, but finally he said, "What do you want me to do, give up everything I have come for and just devote myself to Shaker?" and I said I didn't think it would be a bad idea. We found that the thing was falling apart, and I think Yale regretted it, really.[129]

Ted never expressed his opinion on the reasons for the breakdown at Yale, but in a curious penciled marginal note in a document from 1962 he wrote: "That the S. project did not materialize at Yale was not the fault of the original sponsors."[130] While Ted's note shows concern that fault not be wrongly assigned, he never stated where the fault truly lay. He was not one to point fingers except when goaded. These seventeen cryptic words are all we have about his profound disappointment at losing the promised home at Yale, but they accord well with Potter's assessment, and they are typical of Ted's conscientious and nonvindictive reactions to deeply felt wrongs. His habit of kindly reaction would be sorely tested in the episode that followed.

The Hancock Story and Aftermath
Success in Bath, England, and Hopeful Beginnings in Hancock

After the failure at Yale the Andrewses suddenly found themselves the object of passionate suitors eager to take the place of Yale. By far the most attractive was the newly established American Museum at Claverton Manor in Bath, England, which was to open in 1961 and to which they made a generous at-cost sale of outstanding items from their own home.

Two American citizens, Dallas Pratt and John Judkyn, had provided the initial funding for the museum, which has since become very popular. Its Shaker room was the Andrewses' first major installation since the Whitney in 1935—and this one was permanent. Since they enjoyed total control of the installation, the Andrewses were delighted to work with Bath—"a wonderful building, a lovely countryside, an intelligent devoted staff, under inspiring leadership," Ted wrote.[131] Without much fuss they sold (at bargain prices) a small but fine selection from their collection.

Bath enthusiastically welcomed the Shaker items and respected the Andrewses' view of Shaker culture, and the Andrewses responded with exceptional warmth. Impressed with the high standards of the founders of Bath, they gave unstintingly and joyfully of their time and advice, and when by 1959 they had shipped the last precious item to England (the classic candlestand described by Homer Eaton Keyes as the "finest stand in America"), Faith wrote, "We are delighted that you, too, are pleased with the 'successful completion of our negotiations.' It has been from our first meeting a pleasure to work with you and Mr. Judkyn. For us to have had a part in making such an installation possible in England—where Ann Lee and her small band of followers 'received the divine call to establish their church in America' is indeed a privilege."[132] In their memoir of collecting, the Andrewses wrote, "The experience was a memorable one—not only because the result was so satisfying, not only because there was respect everywhere for us and our work, but also because the Shakers . . . now had a monument in their own homeland."[133] Never before had the Andrewses released prime pieces with so little regret and so much pleasure.

Many other museums and libraries were now interested. In the fall of 1958 Williams College invited the Andrewses for talks, but nothing came of that. About the same time Ted looked into the Smithsonian, which had changed greatly since 1941 and now made a place for American social history.[134] The following June Ted wrote to his friend T. D. Seymour Bassett about other possibilities:

The Andrewses' installation in The American Museum in Britain ca. 1961.

Reproduced courtesy of The American Museum in Britain (Bath, UK)

"There are at least three historical museums in this country that are interested, but we have as yet made no commitments. We still hold to the ideal (as outlined in an article in October 1957 *Antiques*) of one beautiful room, with an adjoining library, to be used as a teaching collection and study center—the sort of thing we hoped to do at Yale."[135]

As it turned out, as many as five or six other interested parties had stepped forward about the same time. Meredith B. Colket, director of the Western Reserve Historical Society in Cleveland, was especially eager to get the collection. In the late 1950s the Andrewses briefly considered housing their collection at the Pleasant Hill Shaker Community in Kentucky. In December 1960 Ted remarked to Thomas Merton, "Our collection was once slated to go there [Pleasant Hill]," but apparently it never got started. Actually, the restoration of Pleasant Hill did get started just a few months after Ted's remark. Other prospective purchasers included Wesleyan University in Middletown, Connecticut, which put forth feelers in February 1959; Williams College, in Williamstown, Massachusetts; Arthur Bestor Jr., who tried to get the collection for the University of Illinois; Sturbridge Village, Massachusetts; and the Clements Library of the University of Michigan.[136] Contrary to a frequent assumption that the Andrewses wanted money for their collection, Ted remained adamant that the collection be released only as an educational unit in a museum or university. The various sale possibilities did not interest him because the purchasers did not understand that the collection was a unit. In November 1959, just before the Hancock restoration began, Ted wrote to me:

We've initiated investigations into the market value of our library, through Goodspeeds, but were disappointed at their lack of imagination regarding the library as a whole and only got appraisals, item by item. . . . We've yet to set a price on it for two reasons: one, we don't know what it's worth, and two, we still think it should go with a "period" room in some American museum or university.[137]

Despite the plethora of choices they now enjoyed, it seems inevitable that the Andrewses would end up where they began: in the now defunct Shaker community of Hancock. As early as 1939, twenty-one years before the establishment of Hancock Shaker Village, Inc. Ted and Faith had proposed a museum to be located next to the Shaker village and had drawn up "Prospectus for a Museum of the American Shakers."[138] Had Ted finally adopted Laura Bragg's similar proposal for a society for the preservation of Shaker antiquities? World War II intervened and the project remained dormant for twenty years.

In 1959 an infinitely finer possibility emerged: a group of locals, including the Andrewses, together with a few wealthy summer residents of the Berkshires, took steps to purchase the entire Shaker village of Hancock. Ted would soon write a new prospectus for this group.

Amy Bess Miller and the Andrews Gift

Amy Bess Miller (1912–2003) and her husband, Lawrence K. "Pete" Miller (1907–1991), the editor and, later, publisher of the influential *Berkshire Eagle*, then the dominant regional newspaper, had provided (indirectly) most of the original funds

Amy Bess Miller, President and CEO of Hancock Shaker Village, Inc., ca. 1980.
Collection of Hancock Shaker Village

for the purchase of the Shaker lands and buildings and became de facto overseers of the new Shaker Village restoration. Amy Bess Miller almost immediately became the first president of Shaker Village, Inc.

Pete Miller, like Ted Andrews, was less forward in speech and action than his wife, and he had risked part of his family's publishing fortune as collateral for the loan covering the purchase price of the property. The Shaker Ministry, then headquartered at the Canterbury community, agreed to sell the property to "the Miller group" on June 28, 1960 for $125,000. (The Shakers' lawyer used the phrase "Miller group" for the purchasers, because the only members of the group who were financially exposed were the Millers.) The competing bid was higher, but it came from a party that planned to establish pari-mutuel horseracing on the property. The Ministry preferred the bid of the Miller group, a nonprofit, Shaker-friendly educational corporation, to the higher offer from persons of dubious morality.[139] The financial contribution of the Miller family made it possible to save the property and start the restoration. Additional funding would come in the form of a mortgage from the local Agricultural Bank and the promise of a loan by board member Frederick W. Beinecke—who was probably the anonymous donor who finally discharged the mortgage. But the Millers were the prime movers. Their daring commitment bestowed a prerogative, and Amy Bess Miller was determined to exercise it.[140]

Amy Bess Miller was a woman of demure demeanor but iron will. Her polished ladylike manner led some to think of her as a Southern belle, but she had left Texas at the age of eight, and considered herself a Yankee "though and through." She never attended college, but after graduating from the exclusive Miss Hall's School for girls in Pittsfield, Massachusetts, in the 1930s, she studied art history at the Sorbonne. In Paris she met Edith Wharton, who had left the Berkshires in 1911, but was still a presence. The front-page obituary for Amy Bess Miller in the *Berkshire Eagle*, the family newspaper, primly summed up her formidable personality as follows: "Petite and lady-like, she demonstrated a capacity for straight talk, for unifying divergent interests in a single purpose, and for achieving a wide variety of goals with a minimum of fuss."[141] The *New York Times* recounted her leadership role as a founder of the restoration and noted her Shaker expertise. But no subsequent notice did justice to her boundless energy and keen political sense. While the Andrewses and others were important in saving Hancock, the successful restoration is a monument to Amy Bess Miller.

Even in her office Amy Bess Miller was an elegant presence, soigné and soft-spoken. Lawrence Yerdon, the village's director from 1983 to 2005, served longer under Miller's presidency than had any previous director, and upon her death rightly noted that without her foresight and extraordinary efforts, the village would not have been saved from developers. Eventually her vision of Hancock as a tourist attraction won out: within twenty years the French editors of the first Michelin "Green Guide" to New England (1981) awarded the isolated village three stars ("Worth a journey"), equal to the two leading museums of Boston, the city of Cambridge, and all of Cape Cod.[142]

Saving and running the village was only one of Amy Bess Miller's manifold activities and accomplishments. A natural leader and an astute administrator, she held top-level positions in many areas of high culture, as well as local and national philanthropies, among them the presidency of the Berkshire Athenaeum (1944–79). She was influential in Massachusetts but was also prominent nationally.[143] Miller was clearly a person with extraordinary qualities of leadership, as well as powerful social connections. But under all the charm and politesse lurked the attitudes of a hard-nosed corporate executive. "A very determined lady," a board member from the 1970s remembered.[144]

Amy Bess Miller had been a friend of the Andrewses since the mid-1930s and accompanied them on visits to Hancock and Mount Lebanon.[145] The Andrewses believed that Hancock would be the ideal home for their collection, and Ted was happy to write a second prospectus, this time based on the reality of a new museum, Shaker Community, Inc. later renamed Hancock Shaker Village, Inc. The new museum printed his essay and sent it out as part of its first fundraising package.[146]

When, on October 13, 1960, the Andrewses drew up the text by which they gave their furniture collection to the newly established Shaker Village, Inc. they tried in one paragraph to provide for the surrender by the donee in the event that the village should fail to make proper use of the collection. Milton C. Rose, a Wall Street lawyer and a member of the Board of Trustees of Hancock, warned them that the surrender provision would prevent them from taking a tax deduction on the collection. The Andrewses' final agreement with the legal entity Shaker Community, Inc. dated December 6, 1960, shows that they refused to change the paragraph.[147] They did not share Rose's pecuniary ethic. As it later turned out, they could not enforce any complete surrender.

Shifts of Power

The Andrewses' strong assertion of their power over the collection, even before the museum opened, lay at the very heart of all subsequent discord, which was driven by issues of power and policy rather than legal guidelines.

Almost immediately disagreements arose between the president, Amy Bess Miller, and the curator, Ted Andrews, regarding the rights of the curator, the proper display of the collections, and even the date for the official opening of the village to the general public. Miller wanted to get the physical premises ready for paying tourists as soon as possible, even if the exhibits were temporary and not up to scholarly and museum standards. The Andrewses wanted to delay until they had proper displays. The Andrews also stood by their right, guaranteed by the legal agreement donating their collection, to control the "use, display, and maintenance" of the collection.

Any regard for legal niceties or fond memories of old friendship fell by the wayside as Amy Bess Miller pushed ahead with her plans for the restoration of the village, ignoring (and sometimes contesting) Ted's expert advice on dozens of curatorial decisions. Without having paint layers analyzed to determine authentic colors or consulting Ted's careful documentation, Miller ordered that most of the meeting house interior be painted a Swedish blue instead of the original flat rich red. When Ted had workers reset the Believers' grave markers in the ground, Miller ordered that they be dug up. (Although she may have been right in this instance, her way of proceeding served to deepen bad feelings.) She countered many of Ted's decisions surreptitiously, usually in his absence.[148]

While many of Miller's actions were hostile to the Andrewses on every level, it must be noted that they, in turn, showed little sympathy or understanding of the challenges of opening a huge, costly new outdoor museum dependent on the public for its revenue; the Andrewses' almost exclusive concern was the fate of their collection even before it was properly catalogued. Some years later Faith Andrews put the differences very simply: "They didn't have the same vision."[149]

However justified their grievances, the Andrewses had little chance of rectification. They confronted a formidable power: the founding Board of Trustees of the new Shaker Community, Inc. The early board consisted mostly of the post–Edith Wharton generation of the summer elite: the Wall Street lawyer Milton Rose; Carl A. Weyerhaeuser, a member of the West Coast timber baron family; and prominent locals, including Frederick G. Crane of the Crane & Co. paper mill (suppliers of currency paper to the United States Treasury). An amiable clublike atmosphere prevailed at board meetings. Amy Bess Miller invited me to join the board in the summer of 1960 on the recommendation of Ted Andrews, and for a while I felt privileged to work with local and national leaders and enjoy oysters fresh from Cape Cod.

From the very beginning Miller had started pushing the Andrewses aside, ultimately demoting Ted and forcing him to resign from the board. Her specific target was the contractual right of the Andrewses to control the "use, display, and maintenance" of the Andrews Collection. She began this process by persuading the board to appoint an outsider to displace Ted: Wilbur Hillman Glover. Glover received the title of director, ranking him higher than the curator. As Ted's superior, Glover did not feel obliged to respect the Andrewses' claimed legal rights. In her 1984 memoir of the restoration, Hancock Shaker Village/the City of Peace: An Effort to Restore a Vision, 1960–1985, Amy Bess Miller noted that Glover was a distinguished scholar, the best of fifteen carefully screened candidates, as well as an experienced administrator who had taught at the University of Wisconsin from 1931 to 1945.[150]

Wilbur Hillman Glover (1906–2002) was a graduate of the now defunct Milton College, in Wisconsin. After taking his Ph.D. at the University of Wisconsin-Madison in 1931, he did teach at three Wisconsin state colleges between 1934 and 1945 but never held a professorial position in the Department of History at the Madison campus. In 1947 the Wisconsin Historical Society appointed Glover as its first field man (1947–52). From there he won the position of director of the Buffalo and Erie County Historical Society.[151] Miller persuaded Edith Rosenwald Stern, the Sears, Roebuck heiress and a trustee, to underwrite Glover's salary for two years.

Glover had no expertise in Shaker or religious studies. As it turned out, he was in place solely to execute Amy Bess Miller's plans, which could be fully realized only if Ted Andrews were removed. He started work in mid-April 1962 and soon had his finger in every crevice of the village.[152]

The removal of Ted Andrews took the form not of a dismissal but of gradual displacement. The minutes of the Board of Trustees of December 7, 1962, make the purpose of the appointment of Glover quite clear: "Inasmuch as Mrs. Miller asked Dr. Andrews to present a Master Plan at the December 7th (1961) meeting, she has now asked Dr. Glover to present his Plan of Operation."[153] A month later, she wrote to the Andrewses, politely demanding that "those items in the collection which have not yet been received should now be brought to the village in Hancock and made available for exhibition and study as soon as possible."[154]

Glover immediately went to work on the new "Plan of Operation" to displace Ted's plans and presented the new plan to the board at its meeting of July 28, 1962.[155] One effect of the plan was to push the board to send Ted a letter stating that the Executive Committee had recommended that "the subject of your salary" be studied. Miller informed Ted that he would receive fifty-two hundred dollars a year and concluded her letter with the polite comment, "As I told you last March, it would be impossible to remunerate you for your talents and the contribution of your scholarship in this field over the years."[156] Glover's salary was much higher.

Pushed by Amy Bess Miller, who was the real director, Glover also worked hard to make daily life intolerable for Ted Andrews. On at least two occasions he intercepted important letters addressed to Andrews regarding the writing and publication of his article "Sheeler and the Shakers."[157] He put forth the simplistic and oft-repeated notion that Ted's problem was that he was "caught" between Amy Bess Miller and Faith Andrews.[158] Glover even attempted to disparage the authority of Ted's expert knowledge by finding supposed errors in museum exhibits and reporting them to Miller. He tore off some of Ted's exhibit labels and placards because he did not agree with them. He thought exhibits should have mannequins, while Andrews had long believed that "stilted dummies in costume . . . are apt to strike a contrived note."[159]

The details of one incident that illustrates the intense atmosphere surrounding the working relationship between Ted Andrews and Wilbur Glover are preserved in two memos. Ted took issue with Glover's installation of a mannequin and blanket in the meeting room of Hancock's Brick Dwelling, then being used for a costume exhibit. He drafted a memo to Glover the morning of August 15, 1962. It reads in part:

> Re: Costume room—suggestions for improvement.
> An aspect of the Shaker form of worship can be shown, as well as an early brother's costume, by placing one of the male figures in the attitude of the dance, with arms raised, palms upward. In the dance the brethren wore vests, no coats. This gives the figure historical significance. For him to be reaching into a blanket chest as though he were to take out an article of dress for whatever purpose is to miss the opportunity of making the best use of the figure. Historically, he would not be engaged in such an act in such a room.
> Until we worked on the figurines yesterday the kerchiefs were incorrectly draped on one of the female models. We should be very careful, in this field, not to improvise, but to study early portraits for the correct manner of dress.
> This can be one of our finest rooms and we should not be satisfied with anything less than the best, aesthetically as well as <u>historically</u>."

Glover's sarcastic reply, in response to Ted's professorial tone, was sure to grate on his serious commitment to authenticity and sense of expertise.

> For Mr. Andrews
> August 15, 1962
> Thank you for the memo of this morning on the Costume room. As to the Kerchief the alteration is agreed to, it having been decided previously that it should not be tied in the working-costume manner.
> As to the male figure reaching into the blanket chest, I am not aware of any prohibition against such an act and would be glad of a citation that would establish the existence of one. It is quite possible that such a rule could in any case be ignored as the rules sometimes were, although it might be better if we were to assume uniform observance of rules for our purposes. You are not of course suggesting that there is documentation establishing it as a fact that no man every [*sic*] reached into a blanket chest in such a situation.

Ted, documenting the disintegration of his position at Hancock, noted in pencil on the bottom of this memo: "Comment on above— Above a good example of pettiness, attempt to find errors in curators knowledge."[160]

Ten days later, Glover called Ted into his office and accused him of "insubordination" and "undermining his authority" and ordered him out of the room, then called him back and lost his temper over Ted's correction of an employee (identified as "R. E.") for serious mistakes in the costume room exhibit. By the end of that summer Ted, unable to endure daily harassment, had withdrawn himself from the day-to-day operations of the museum. Ever averse to contention, he commented privately, "You know as well as I do that I have always cooperated, as best I could, with the director, though he hasn't always done so with me." [161]

Glover's actions precipitated the final stage of the crisis. At a board meeting on March 30, 1963, President Amy Bess Miller stated, "Dr. Andrews serves in three capacities—donor, curator, and trustee," implying a conflict of interest, even though she herself was a donor, president, and trustee. But by the date of that board meeting, months after Ted's bitter departure from the village, she was merely seeking to rationalize her displacement of the curator. Ted was physically gone and she was in fact running the whole show.

Glover himself soon became a victim of Amy Bess Miller. By the spring of 1963 he was beginning to feel so unhappy that he turned to Ted in a private conversation. Ted recounted Glover's turnabout: "He confided to me his difficulties with the president, how his ideas were constantly being vetoed by her, and that she resented them—that his office had really been reduced to that of an 'administrative assistant.'" This little bid for sympathy did not prevent him from further denigrating Ted.[162]

What had happened, in summary, was that the Andrewses had a binding legal agreement that gave them (in practice, with Ted as curator) the right to control the use of the Andrews Collection. Miller ignored that right, and she intentionally pushed him out (or "kicked" him out, as she put it in an interview of 1993).[163]

Negotiation and Loss

The Andrewses were blindsided by Amy Bess Miller's appropriation of seemingly unlimited power, a turn of events that abruptly rendered them subordinates. Their experience in New York City with the competition for power and money and the privileged demeanor of the upper classes perhaps should have forewarned them. As executive secretary for the exclusive Women's City Club of New York, Faith had become well acquainted with the power of money and what she called "social ambition" and later described it as "Shakerism in reverse."[164] It may be that the Andrewses' willful immersion in the unworldly ideals of the Shakers and their long friendship with Miller made them less able to anticipate, and react dispassionately, to policies grounded in the self-regard of an American aristocrat and the dictates of an economic bottom line in running a museum. And they seemed unable to appreciate Miller's needs and rights as the administrator of a new museum. Dealing with the Andrews Collection was only one of her many tasks. She needed to get a museum started and opened up to paying visitors. She had to be concerned with marketing and publicity and find new capital for basic restoration. She had to develop new programs like the herb garden (her favorite project) and had to oversee the hiring and payment of staff. Above all, she had to have a budget that was adequately financed. At the beginning she was concerned with basic survival and administrative convenience, and the last thing she expected was that the Andrewses would renege on their promised gift—which they tried to do at the height of the crisis.

As the altercation came to a head, five persons played key roles: Milton C. Rose, Carl A. Weyerhaeuser, Frederick W. Beinecke, Dorothy Canning Miller, and the Andrewses' son, David Volk Andrews.

Like his parents, David Volk Andrews counted on the support of Dorothy Canning Miller, a Shaker Village trustee since 1960; but that turned out to be a wrong choice. While Dorothy Miller was an old art-world ally and friend of the Andrewses from the 1930s, she eventually sided with Amy Bess Miller.

Dorothy Canning Miller was a curious bird of passage in the history of the village and of the Andrews Collection. As one of the first curators of the Museum of Modern Art, she was something of a celebrity in the rising new museum culture of the 1930s, and Amy Bess Miller and the Andrewses eagerly courted her to join the first Board of Trustees of Shaker Village, Inc. From the 1930s to the 1960s Dorothy Canning Miller and her husband, Holger Cahill, had a long, not always harmonious, relationship with the Andrewses. They first became acquainted with the Andrewses through a shared interest in "primitive" art in the 1930s and had a common friendship with the leading gallerist and folk art dealer of the 1930s, Edith Gregor Halpert. In the 1940s and 1950s Cahill, Miller, and Halpert became avid collectors of Shaker, with the help and advice of the Andrewses.

Dorothy Miller was an early proponent of collecting "primitive folk art" for museums (a common way to view Shaker craftsmanship in the 1920s) and came to appreciate folk art through Holger Cahill. She acted as a folk art "picker" for Cahill, along with Cahill's intimate friend Edith Gregor Halpert, as they searched the Northeast from Maryland to Maine for antiques between 1931 and the early 1940s. As curator at the Newark Museum from 1920 to 1930, Cahill was the earliest proponent of folk art (also called naive, isolated, outsider, and most frequently, primitive art), and in 1930 organized the first folk art exhibition in a major museum, "American Primitives" in the Newark Museum. In 1932 Cahill became acting director of the Museum of Modern Art, where he and Dorothy Miller continued to promote folk art.

At her death, a *New York Times* art critic characterized Dorothy Miller as a "clairvoyant" who was the first to recognize and promote painters and sculptors who were to become major figures in American art, including Jackson Pollock, Mark Rothko, Frank Stella, Larry Rivers, Louise Nevelson, and Claes Oldenburg.[165]

Although Amy Bess Miller and the Andrewses had welcomed Dorothy Miller to the founding Board of Trustees, she proved a disappointment. Dorothy Miller attended very few board meetings and was too poorly informed to vote on anything that was happening.[166] For her the village was, as for other prominent summer residents, a worthwhile summer diversion; for Amy Bess Miller in her role as president, Dorothy Canning Miller was an important big-name presence.[167]

A second person whom David Andrews and his parents trusted to defend them was Milton C. Rose, senior partner of the leading New York law firm of Mudge, Rose, and one of the original trustees of the village. A friend of both the Millers and the Andrewses, Rose had a summer home in the Berkshires and an imposing apartment just off Park Avenue. He was influential enough to hire Richard M. Nixon at a moment when Nixon was languishing between elective offices. The entire Andrews family expected Rose to side with them in the dispute. But in the end, Dorothy Canning Miller and Milton C. Rose, stalwart allies in the eyes of the Andrews family, chose not to support the Andrewses, a change of sides that would have shocked them.[168]

In Amy Bess Miller's dispute with the more modestly situated Andrewses, a majority of the board members (not only Milton Rose and Dorothy Miller) sided with Amy Bess Miller. In this camp, but staying in the background, two others stood out as immensely wealthy benefactors of the village: Carl A. Weyerhaeuser and the philanthropist Frederick W. Beinecke, the heir to the Beinecke "green stamp" fortune. Rose, Weyerhaeuser, Beinecke, and Dorothy Miller constituted an especially powerful subgroup of the board and tended to follow the lead of the president.

An Attempt at Conciliation

The board finally voted to set up a conciliation committee to study the conflict and report back to the Executive Committee by early May 1963 on "a re-definition of the duties of President, Director and Curator and beyond that to make an affirmative recommendation to attempt to resolve the dispute after consultation with everyone concerned."[169] Amy Bess Miller had already "fired" Faith Andrews as a person with no official position at the village.[170]

Appointing a committee is the classic way in parliamentary procedure to avoid making a decision. But by the deadline of May 1963, this decision to form a conciliation committee was mere play-acting, because the Executive Committee of the Board of Trustees had already decided to remove Ted. The only real issue remaining was the timetable for the legal delivery of the Andrews Collection. Faced with the absurdity of being "re-defined" by the board, the thoroughly disillusioned Andrewses took legal steps, believing they could still withdraw a large part of their collection.

The Conciliation Committee set up by the board on March 30, 1963, was to include four members, one chosen by the Andrewses, one chosen by the president, the third chosen by the Executive Committee, and the fourth chosen unanimously by the other three. Frederick Crane reported: "Madam

President chose Miss Dorothy C. Miller; Dr. & Mrs. Andrews chose Professor Mario S. De Pillis; the Executive Committee appointed Professor S. Lane Faison; and these three members chose Mr. Milton C. Rose."[171] The Executive Committee's choice of Faison, the Miller family's aggressively loyal friend, reflected the Amy Bess Miller's influence on the committee. The Conciliation Committee was heavily stacked 3 to 1.

After having met twice at the home and at the law offices of Milton C. Rose in New York City on May 22, 1963, the committee decided to "redefine" Ted Andrews's position as the solution to the impasse over the direction of the Andrews Collection and the official position of Ted Andrews. At the insistence of committee member S. Lane Faison, the committee invited Glover, but not Ted Andrews, to New York for a special two-hour meeting, mostly devoted to Glover's extremely biased view of Ted. The committee decided that the parties were so far apart that it would serve no useful purpose to invite the Andrewses.[172] After discussions that lasted till 10 p.m. the committee adjourned and in the following week issued its report to the Executive Committee of the board, making the following recommendation:

> The Committee thought that Dr. Andrews should be persuaded to have his task redefined in such a manner that his scholarship, knowledge, and prestige continue to benefit the Community. The Committee agreed to ask one of its members to prepare this report and make the following suggestions, with the understanding that no final decisions be reached until it is completely discussed by the Board of Trustees:
> 1. That the existing task statements are not themselves at fault and still serve as a reasonable guide for administration.
> 2. That Dr. Edward Deming Andrews be appointed Research Consultant to the administrators of Shaker Community, Inc. to be paid a consultant's fee of $3,600.00, or an amount to be determined after mutual negotiation.[173]

The Executive Committee took action almost immediately. In a letter to the president of July 3, 1963, Frederick Crane, chair of the Executive Committee, reported that on the previous day the Executive Committee had discussed the report of the Conciliation Committee and approved it with the addition, "That Dr. Edward Deming Andrews be relieved of the position of Curator and appointed Research Consultant to the administrators of the Shaker Community, Inc. to be paid a consultant's fee of $3,600.00 or an amount to be determined after mutual negotiation."[174]

Amy Bess Miller called a special meeting of the board on August 2, 1963, with almost full attendance, including Wilbur Glover by invitation. The board voted sixteen yes votes to two no votes to accept the report of the Executive Committee with the word "reassigned" substituted for "relieved." It then voted to approve the Tasks Statement for the proposed new position of "Research Consultant" to replace the curator.[175]

The Andrewses rejected the offer, because, as Faith later reported, it was a "nebulous position of Research Consultant and a cut in pay. . . . The salary offered—$3,600.00—was less than one third the salary for the position of Director [already held by Glover]. The situation as presented left us no choice."[176] In his letter of rejection Ted Andrews stated that redefining his position did nothing to solve two problems: their loss of a legal "right of direction of the Andrews Collection" and the "complete lack of communication at the village." He said that he and his lawyer would like to meet with Amy Bess Miller "to discuss our total disassociation with Shaker Community, Inc."[177] The Andrewses were understandably concerned about the course of events and the actions of the president.

The two parties met with their respective lawyers and with David Volk Andrews on August 26, 1963, the last time Miller and the Andrewses would ever meet to discuss their differences. As Miller reported in her extensive personal memo on this meeting, Ted asked why his authority had been taken away and his salary reduced. Miller replied that he "couldn't get along with the Director." Ted's son, David, retorted, that the director could not get along with Ted. A few minutes later Ted asked again why he had been removed as curator. Miller replied that "some of his work had been inadequate and mentioned as an example the writing and placing of labels." Ted retorted that she was picking at lint, "picking here and there and there, and then making something of it." He also said that Miller had come between husband and wife, that she had ordered Faith Andrews not to come to the village, that she had said there were certain places in the village where Faith could not come. Miller pointed out the inconsistency of the statement and denied that she had ever said or meant to convey in any way such a thing. Ted accused Miller of refusing to meet with Faith and that as a result of all this humiliation her mental health was suffering.[178]

Nothing came of the meeting beyond confirming that the Andrewses would never again be associated with the village. But while the meeting settled accounts on the matters of power and personalities, a whiff of doubt hovered over the legal status of the Andrews Collection. Amy Bess Miller almost immediately wrote a vigorous and persuasive defense of the rights of the Hancock Corporation to control the Andrews Collection.[179] Finding some board members who were available on short notice, she immediately arranged to have Ted Andrews barred from the premises. When he came to pick up some belongings, she called on the local sheriff to monitor him; that was his last visit. From a purely administrative and budgeting point of view, Amy Bess Miller had a case for reassigning Ted Andrews, but strong-arming Ted and Faith only backfired.

Faith Andrews rivaled Amy Bess Miller in will and drive, but was no match in money or social connections. Despite their less elevated social status, Faith and Ted were certainly not without standing, and their work gave them a national prestige that locals did not much understand, and Miller could only envy; and they still enjoyed connections and friendships in the art and museum worlds of New York City. In the early 1960s their son, David Volk Andrews. was a vice-president of Chase Manhattan Bank, the most prestigious Wall Street bank of the time. David's attainment of equal footing with grandees of Wall Street like Louis Stanton Auchincloss allowed him to maintain a relationship of equality with Amy Bess Miller. Their letters reveal a cordial relationship even after the break between his parents and Miller. She treated him as an equal. Fearful of alienating the Andrewses' well-connected son, she wrote to him on July 18, 1962, at the moment that the Glover-Andrews disagreements had reached a crisis level and tried to involve him in a solution. She informed David that she had planned a meeting of the "greatest importance," because, she said, "Your mother and Father are anxious to have a meeting with Dr. Glover and me and have asked Milton Rose to be present also." She implored him to attend.[180] She did not tell him that Frederick Crane had already notified her of the decision of the Executive Committee to "relieve" his father from the position of curator.

As a young assistant professor from the University of Massachusetts, I did not wield much influence on the board. Far more influential and powerful was S. Lane Faison, who took a strong anti-Andrews stance, and who had made the stacking of the Conciliation Committee against the Andrewses possible. Faison, the son of a U.S. Army general, was a prominent faculty member at Williams College and was soon to become the Amos Lawrence Professor of Art. He was a college friend and later the confidante of Amy Bess Miller's husband, Pete Miller. His opinions carried great weight with both Pete and Amy Bess. But Amy Bess Miller pointedly ignored his extreme posture that the Andrewses, particularly Ted, were trying to take over the directorship of the entire restoration project.[181]

The social-political relations between the overpowering board and the Andrewses and the secret lines of demarcation among the members are amply corroborated by surviving letters, such as those exchanged by Miller and Beinecke, a sympathetic trustee who did not want his correspondence with Miller to be known to the rest of the board.[182] Their secret correspondence discusses the Andrewses as a problem. Beinecke was the only board member of sufficient stature and distance (from the issues) that Miller could consult with. She also turned to a friend with connections in the Berkshires, Louis Auchincloss; but while Auchincloss's views could influence others connected with the village, he was not a board member and had no vote. Amy Bess Miller's tight control of every aspect of the village, her social position, wealth, and personal alliances all assured her of victory over the Andrewses by 1963, when Ted left the village for good. Issues of museum policy and scholarship had given way in the end to clashes of class, personality, and sheer power.

Aside from disagreements over institutional needs and the issues of personality and power described earlier, the heart of the dispute at Hancock lay in the interpretation of the legal phrases of the original agreement giving the Andrews Collection to Hancock Shaker Village. The Andrewses, on one hand, interpreted the phrase that said the use, exhibition, display, and maintenance of the collection was "under the direction of the donors" to mean that when he became curator Ted Andrews would also supervise the use of future acquisitions and gifts, several of which he had attracted through old friendships. In Ted's words, "We should have authority over other acquisitions which affect the basic collection." He had in mind the acquisition of the closely related collections of Vincent Newton and of several other old friends, who were willing to make gifts to the village but were dissuaded upon learning of "the treatment accorded us."[183]Amy Bess Miller, on the other hand, interpreted "direction" narrowly: the curator would be curator only over the Andrews Collection and in that smaller capacity should follow the orders of the director and the president. She also repeatedly noted that she herself had made significant donations of objects to the museum.

In presenting her side of the Hancock story, Faith Andrews does make one central and incontrovertible point, that the contract of 1961 between the donors (the Andrewses) and the donees (Shaker Community, Inc. or "the Miller group") stipulated that "Said collection shall be used, exhibited, displayed, and maintained by the Donee, its successors and assigns, *under the direction of the Donors*" (emphasis added by Faith Andrews). While Faith was technically correct, the Andrewses interpreted the word "direction" too broadly.

Ted and Faith, shocked at the loss of trust and respect and horrified about what might happen to their life's work, tried to retrieve their collection, but their deed of gift was not revocable. Ted wrote the best summary of the final settlement:

> Our lawyer has been continuously on the job of settling affairs at Hancock—a tricky business, believe me. We are, as you know, totally dissociated with the project, though for the time being we are still members of the board. The lawyer is working on a so-called "termination agreement." This will allow us to retain everything, including the library, which has not already been sent to the village. Unfortunately we cannot recall what we have given. In the agreement will be a clause whereby we can compile a descriptive and interpretative catalogue of the *Andrews Shaker Collection at Hancock*, to be *finely* printed at the village's expense. This memorial of our gift is, we think, a good substitute for our earlier plan of trying to allocate all our furniture, etc. in one place at the village. A.B., Glover, etc. objected to that scheme on the score it would mean "static" installations and tie their hands. The "catalogue" will be a permanent record, and I hope a literary production. I am already working on it. Besides these agreements, we hope to receive a satisfactory monetary settlement, to be paid when the agreement is signed. Mr. Connor, of the Executive Committee, has been most helpful in the various meetings which have been held. So has David.[184]

On January 28, 1964, the Andrewses finally signed an agreement that conforms to Ted's summary. It formally revoked the original gift agreement of December 6, 1960, and conveyed all Shaker articles "which have been delivered to the premises of the Corporation in Hancock." Hancock Shaker Village (the "corporation") also agreed to print and publish a catalogue of the Andrews Collection "within a reasonable time" and also agreed to pay the Andrewses the sum of $8,666.66.[185] Most of the artifacts, including all gift drawings, remained at Hancock, while the bulk of the manuscripts, which had not been delivered to Hancock, eventually found an ideal home at the Winterthur Museum as the Edward Deming Andrews Memorial Shaker Collection.[186]

The clash between the Andrewses' ideals and Hancock's institutional needs echoed their encounters with Amherst and Yale in that the Andrewses, ever the purists, insisted on a particular interpretation of the collection, one that would not be simplified or distorted to appeal to the tourists visiting the restored village. They were also concerned about the proper storage and cataloguing of manuscripts and artifacts.

The Andrewses' contribution to the establishment of Shaker Community, Inc. extended far beyond books, manuscripts, and artifacts. While they felt humiliated by the loss of any role at Hancock, they took comfort in their unassailable national reputation. In November 1963, as the lawyers drew up the "termination agreement," Ted wrote, "Being free of commitments at Hancock, we are again independently carrying on our Shaker work, collecting and writing."[187]

The Andrewses called themselves "collector-scholars," but they were also visionaries.[188]

The Spiritual Dimension of the Shakers and the Demands of Tourism

At the heart of the dispute between the Andrewses and the corporation of Shaker Community, Inc. was a profound historical and esthetic difference about the meaning of Shaker artifacts and Shaker history. One party wished to emphasize Shaker ethics, spirituality, and esthetics; the other sought popular appeal and good tourist attendance.

For the Andrewses, the history and culture of the United Society of Believers was a sacred jewel of American civilization. Their veneration of all things Shaker led them to be extremely protective of their vast collection, to refuse to negotiate flexibly with any museum on such basic matters as displays, interpretation, and even storage of artifacts. Nor would they compromise their position that Shaker history and culture should be taught as a prominent part of American history. Their views were unreasonably rigid.

Eldress Emma B. King of Canterbury, New Hampshire, with Faith and Edward Deming Andrews at Hancock Shaker Village on July 3, 1961.
Photograph by R. Joel Librizzi for **The Berkshire Eagle.** *Collection of Hancock Shaker Village 1992.5504*

Ted believed that the culture of the Shakers was a spiritual matter and not merely art-historical. In a commencement address on June 7, 1957, he described the spiritual life of the Shakers.

The life of the Shaker was one of self-denial, self-discipline and obedience to an ideal—but he had chosen it freely, believing, as his covenant read, that as "a debtor to God" his mission lay in improving his talents in this life in that way in which he could be most useful. He was a pragmatist in his concept of mission—he wanted to utilize his talents fully. But more important, the concept was essentially a spiritual one. He felt that he was a debtor to God, and that consequently he should love all the creatures of God—should have, in Dr. Schweitzer's fine phrase, "a reverence for life."[189]

About five years later Ted wrote "Prospectus for a Museum of Shaker Cultural History," an essay that is central for understanding the history and ultimate disposition of the Andrews Collection. Writing to "educate" the board, he reflected on the need to go beyond static installations of artifacts to "the *spirit* of the Shaker culture" and asserted that such a museum must demonstrate "a sensitivity to, and sympathy for, the ideals and aspirations of this religious order." He then listed the twelve principles of "applied Christian ethics" that ought to be inculcated through the Hancock Shaker museum. He greatly admired the kind of Shaker statement that appeared in the Union Village (Ohio) covenant of 1841: "The faithful improvement of our time and talents in doing good, is a duty which God requires of mankind as rational and accountable beings." But, he reassured the board, "We do not have to believe, or live, as the Shakers did. But we have an obligation to explain why they believed, or lived, as they did."[190]

The draft "Prospectus for a Museum of Shaker Cultural History" attempted to define the course of the newly established Hancock Shaker museum and make it less touristy and more spiritual: "I would like to take this opportunity to present, in outline, what I think our philosophy, our ultimate goal should be. Unless we have such a philosophy and adhere to it with integrity, we are apt to muddle along, to improvise, to concern ourselves too much with matters of popular appeal, etc., forgetting in the process that we have a distinct, almost unique function to fulfill. We do not want the village to be just one more outdoor museum."[191] Ted's dream of perpetuating the spirit of the Believers without much regard to public tourism or the enormous expenses of restoration, struck the president of Shaker Community, Inc., Amy Bess Miller, as impractical. In any case, by 1962, when Ted wrote this particularly evangelistic statement of how the Hancock restoration should proceed, it was too late. A few months later, in what would be one of his last publications, Ted saw his work as a kind of conversion experience: "In our own case Shaker furniture and artifacts were, at first, just interesting collectibles. Appreciation of their full meaning took time and study and insight . . . and in the end [it was] a spiritual experience."[192] Ted's paean to the virtues and spirituality of the Shakers had no effect on the board of the village.

Faith Andrews agreed with Ted that "our vision" was spiritual, but her own seeking for a spiritual identity was not at all comparable with Ted's. In her 1983 manuscript history of their dispute with Shaker Community, Inc., she noted that, "as Ted often reminded the Board in the minutes," the spiritual values inherent in the Shaker culture [must be] transferred to our project. Any museum can preserve and catalogue artifacts in increasing numbers and varying quality. But to preserve the spirit, the forces out of which these artifacts came, could be accomplished only if all of us understand and profoundly believe in Shaker principles—such virtues as humility, simplicity, rectitude, neatness, order, cleanliness, communal cooperation, mutual respect and tolerance.[193]

Ted, especially, seemed to identify with the Believers' religious practice (though not their doctrine), so much so that by the early 1930s his good friend Homer Eaton Keyes could tease him about it: "Great people, the Shakers. I think you probably will become one yourself before you get through."[194]

Ted considered the Shakers' spirituality worthy of comparison with the highest spiritual practices of the Catholic monastics. That belief explains the Andrewses' warm friendship with Thomas Merton of the Trappist Abbey of Gethsemane. As Ted wrote in his reminiscences, "Of all the people we have come to know as a result of our work none is closer to us in spirit than Thomas Merton."[195] Merton went straight to Ted's spiritual heart in what was probably his earliest letter to the Andrewses. "To me," Merton wrote,

the Shakers are of very great significance, besides being something of a mystery, by their wonderful integration of the spiritual and physical in their work. There is no question in my mind that one of the finest and most genuine religious expressions of the nineteenth century is in the silent eloquence of Shaker craftsmanship. . . .

I will try to profit by their example and put into practice some of their careful and honest principles. It would be a crime to treat them superficially, and without the deepest love, reverence and understanding. There can be so much meaning to a study of this kind: meaning for twentieth century America which has lost so much in the last hundred years—lost while seeming to gain. I think the extinction of the Shakers and of their particular kind of spirit is an awful portent. I feel all the more akin to them because our own Order, the Cistercians, originally had the same kind of ideal of honesty, simplicity, good work, for a spiritual motive.[196]

The Andrewses' emphasis on "spirit" went far beyond reflecting on the otherworldliness of Shakerism. As a young soldier, Ted had read Hindu religious texts, and this interest eventually led to a spiritual friendship with the philosopher and scholar of Hinduism and Buddhism and curator of Asian art at the Boston Museum of Fine Arts Ananda Kentish Coomaraswamy, renowned in his day. Coomaraswamy, a proponent of a traditionalist Hindu religious revival and a domineering man, excluded Faith from his hours-long conversations with Ted. Faith left a vivid, and not entirely flattering, vignette of the man.[197]

Ted (and to a large extent, Faith) communed with "spirit." They attended Shaker services, when permitted, and felt the presence of the Shakers even when they were long absent from a Shaker building. In the mid-1930s Sister Alice Smith of Hancock set up a study in the old dairy building so that Ted could work on his Shaker songbook. Of this plain structure Faith remarked, "It was a lovely place, but Ted also felt the *spirit* there and Alice always had." In his last years Ted felt that the gift drawings expressed the Shaker spirit best. He called them "spiritual drawings" and the surfacing of these drawings swept him away, validating all his deepest feelings about the Shakers. His wife believed that "the shock of it never left him. It sort of tied the thing all up. It made it seem right."[198]

Ted's spiritual bent—one could almost speak of a conversion—ill prepared him for his battle in defense of Shaker purity at Hancock.

The Tragic Denouement at Hancock

The contractual claim of the village on almost every Shaker item owned by the Andrewses was incontestable. They had managed, however, to retain many precious manuscripts and books and some uncatalogued artifacts, most of which went to the Winterthur Museum.

Amy Bess Miller's memoir of the restoration, *Hancock Shaker Village*, includes a bland, ten-line description of the actions of 1961–63. "As the second season approached in 1962," she explains, "several trustees felt the need for a director and administrator. Dr. Andrews preferred to remain Village curator. . . . He was with the Village as curator until June of 1962, when he retired." A committee of the board, she explained, felt "the need for coordination" and offered the position of director to William H. Glover.

Thus did this sanitized account, published some twenty years later, pass over the Andrews crisis in the village as a nonhappening, as an amicable decision by the board and a freely chosen "retirement" by Ted Andrews. [199] Actually, Ted did not choose retirement but was forced out of his position by calculated humiliations and the sabotaging of his work.[200] Miller's date of June 1962 is inaccurate; Ted was still around as late as August.

Amy Bess Miller's relatively objective and indispensable account touches lightly on the history of the village corporation and its board but does include an indirect defense of her own role in the retention of a goodly part of the Andrews Collection, barely acknowledging the great (if reluctant) gift of the Andrewses—the very heart of the restoration. In a volume of 167 double-columned pages, she even ignores the altercation that had threatened the continuation of the restoration and that had led to an acrimonious out-of-court settlement. In her mind the omission was doubtless a matter of prudence as much as self-justification.

Eventually the issues of money, power, and class all came down to a pedestrian, legal requirement: a list of specific items, mostly furniture and other artifacts, that, by deed of gift, the Andrewses could not legally take back. As for other items, neither party could agree on what, exactly, the Andrewses had donated. Ted had done a great deal of cataloguing before he left the village, but his work was incomplete when he resigned. After Ted's removal as curator, the village and the Andrewses were fighting over a list of legally donated items. This dispute was easier to settle than the redistribution of power.

The resolution of the dispute depended on an accurate inventory of the entire village collection, and Amy Bess Miller spent almost three years working to ensure that the Andrewses could not legally take back anything they had given in their original contract of December 1961. In January 1963 she wrote to Beinecke, a sympathetic trustee (who did not want his correspondence with her to be known to the rest of the board): "I regret the fact that Andrews won't share his library with us—although we are legally the owners of it—date of delivery to be convenient to him—we cannot benefit even by having duplicates in the office.[201]

Three months later she wrote:

As you know, we were assured by Dr. Andrews in 1959 that when and if Shaker Community, Inc. became a reality his complete collection, which included his library of Shaker material, would be given to the corporation. To date he has delivered about 60% of his furniture, artifacts, and all of the inspirational drawings, —but refuses us the use of the library.

We are building up a good reference shelf of related material historical and otherwise and are gradually, thanks to you, beginning a collection of helpful documents.[202]

Events came quick and fast around Christmas 1963 and brought to an end the entire Hancock saga. On December 6 Amy Bess Miller wrote to Milton C. Rose, the most influential member of the Board of Trustees, informing him that she had received the final settlement from the Andrewses' attorney, John MacGruer, and noting, "I took it without comment and told him we would be in touch with him after our meeting Tuesday." She had already planned for this moment by scheduling a special consultation of the Executive Committee for December 10, 1963. She would pose the question: Should the board accept as valid and complete the list of items to be handed over by the Andrewses?

By Christmas Day Amy Bess Miller and her staff had completed their own inventory of those items of the Andrews gift that were the incontestable legal property of the village, and on December 26 she informed Frederick Crane:

I am glad to tell you that we have now checked the inventory and can account for all the items mentioned on their list. As you know, it was very incomplete and not definite in detail, but for our purposes I think it is satisfactory.

Many thanks for your patience in dealing with this matter which we should feel now can be concluded.[203]

The village retained the portion of the donation that Miller had described to Beinecke in her letter of March 5, 1963, with the exception that a handful of manuscripts that had already been on display would remain with the village. By the final legal settlements of December 14, 1963, and January 28, 1964, about 85 percent of the collection, according to Faith's reckoning, remained at Hancock.[204]

In 1983, nineteen years after the death of her husband, Faith presented her version of their withdrawal and resignation in an unpublished documentary history she called "The Hancock Story." On the cover sheet she states, "This treatise is not to be released during my lifetime." Using mostly photocopies of original documents, Faith honestly and forthrightly describes the struggle over the collection at Hancock and her husband's resignation. Many of the legal points she makes are not relevant here, but one or two are fundamental and a brief summary is in order.

Faith emphasizes the primacy of Ted's well-articulated dream of creating a museum "dedicated to preserving and promoting the cultural values of the Shakers." His passion was a prime mover of the Hancock museum project, and in fact the Miller group that purchased the property turned to him for an official statement of purpose. Ted offered his 1959 manuscript prospectus, which the group published as its first fundraising document: *Proposal to Save the Shaker Community at Hancock, Massachusetts: Its Importance as Part of the American Heritage.*[205] The Hancock *Proposal* was the culmination of Ted's thirty-year concern with the educational and social value of Shaker culture.

Faith framed her account with an interesting door metaphor: Part I: The Opening of the Door, and Part II: The Closing of the Door. She implies that the Andrewses did not willingly close doors.

The door opened in August 1960, with the efforts of the Millers and the Andrewses to save Hancock Shaker Village. The key word is "save." At that time, toward the end of his career, Ted was still intent on saving a culture that was about to become extinct. In a 1957 outline for one of his last classes as a Fellow at Yale, he used almost the same words he had used as a young soldier in his long-ago diary written as a young soldier.[206]

Faith Andrews saw the very first year as the beginning of a breach of faith, just as the "door" of their gift had opened. The Andrewses relied, in the beginning, on the trust and openness of an old friendship and, in their naiveté, never dreamed of demanding immediate compliance with the legal language of the deed of gift. Their daughter, Ann, remembered, "My parents felt strongly that what was happening was ethically and morally wrong." Amy Bess Miller later stated that although the village had lost its legal claim to the Andrews library, it had a "moral right" to both the library and other items.[207]

In 1990, the year of Faith Andrews's death and some half-dozen years before her own death, Amy Bess Miller came close to adopting a version of the Andrewses' spiritual interpretation of the Shakers, noting their "pursuit of perfection and their consecration to God" and affirming the intent of the village to teach and perpetuate the Shaker ideals.[208] And, ironically, in the title of her history, *Hancock Shaker Village/the City of Peace: An Effort to Restore a Vision 1960–1985* she uses the word "vision" to mean the Shakers' own vision of heaven and earth, close to the Andrewses' view of the Believers. But these were public statements stressing the positive; in a private interview of 1993 she made strongly negative statements about the Shakers.[209]

In her conduct of museum policy Miller continued to be more calculating than spiritual. Although she did not succeed in retaining all of the Andrews library and manuscripts and lost two old friends, her achievement was undeniably great: with her connections, her money, her political skill, and her drive she created a fine museum that has served an appreciative public and preserved a crucial part of Shaker culture and "vision."

The Andrewses' twenty-year struggle from 1938 to 1959 to find a safe home for their collection, without dispersing it on the open market, had not ended in Hancock in 1963. It was a chapter that had closed, with some long-term benefits to both parties. Ted Andrews died a few months after the separation agreement, and, to my surprise, he had expressed much less anger than Faith about the unraveling of their great hopes for a final, ideal home for their collection. But he was heart-broken.

After Hancock: Faith Shuts a Door at Amherst College and Winterthur Opens One

Ted's death on June 6, 1964, gave Faith a heightened sense of urgency about finding a permanent home for the rest of the collection. After the dashed hopes at Yale and Hancock, the Andrewses had turned to Ted's alma mater, Amherst College. In August 1964, a few weeks after Ted's death, Faith wrote to Thomas Merton to thank him for writing the preface to *Religion in Wood* and in particular for sending a wonderful letter of condolence. She explained the new status of the collection and the Amherst College feeler.

> You see the plan for Shaker Community Inc. where we worked so hard and with such faith—did not work out. After a year of legal hassle and great disappointment to Ted—we withdrew from the organization. However, the rare drawings and furnishings *delivered* there remain their property but the "undelivered" are in our name.
>
> This is a brief resume in order for you to see what is happening and I would greatly appreciate any thoughts you might have as to the forwarding of Ted's work. The library, as you know is a very important one—the manuscript material, printed books and pamphlets and Ted's invaluable notes which accompany it. I want very much to make this library a memorial to Ted and have thought of Amherst College, since Ted was a graduate and felt close to it. Then too they are building the Robert Frost Memorial Library—even though Frost's collection was withdrawn by his daughter Leslie.[210]

The Andrewses had first approached Amherst College back around 1958, just after the great disappointment at Yale. They had found a friend in a powerful and famous historian at the college, Henry Steel Commager. Commager encouraged Amherst to acquire the collection and was generous in giving them advice. Amherst College was welcoming enough for the Andrewses to go house hunting, but with the sudden emergence of the Hancock Shaker restoration in 1959, they had instantly switched to Hancock. After the debacle at Hancock in 1963, the Andrewses retained their outstanding library of rare books and hundreds of manuscripts, and upon the death of Ted in June 1964, Faith immediately escalated the effort to transfer the collection to a place willing to memorialize Ted. By late summer she had reinstated the connection with Amherst College—while welcoming the continuing interest of Winterthur and even making a half-hearted inquiry at Williams College.[211]

But Faith's negotiations with Amherst College and Winterthur both promised success. On October 6, 1964, less than a month after the weak feeler to Williams, Faith met with President Calvin H. Plimpton of Amherst College. Newton F. McKeon, director of the Amherst College Library, recorded the details in a memo to himself:

> In her conversation with the President she indicated that [the collection] consisted of 120+ bound volumes, 60+ manuscripts and hymnals, and 350 manuscript letters and the like. She wanted these to be kept as a unit and she began by asking whether there might not be a room for them. She proposed adding a Shaker table and framed prints but President Plimpton discouraged her from this and told her we could not provide for them. She was told by both that there would be a place for these materials in Special Collections, and they could be kept together as a single collection. She left expressing the desire that she hear from me about our interest.[212]

The college responded warmly. "It is my hope," wrote McKeon, "that you will look with favor on Amherst as a permanent home for your collection. For us this would be an occasion for rejoicing." Following Faith's meeting with President Plimpton and others, Plimpton reported that "Professor Commager . . . took fire at the thought" that he could use the documents for teaching purposes.[213] McKeon even sent her architectural drawings that showed exactly where the collection would be housed in the library, which was still under construction at the time.[214] Faith wanted a special room with a Shaker table, but McKeon emphasized that the collection must be open for research and not be "locked up." On December 31, 1964, McKeon wrote to her that she should now "formally communicate" her intentions to President Plimpton.[215]

In the meantime President Plimpton, apparently alerted by museum gossip, worried about the legal availability of the collection. Writing to Amy Bess Miller on January 20, 1965, he reported on Faith's offer and stated, "I also gather that some of these books and manuscripts have already been given to the Hancock Shaker restoration, and I am told that you have a letter or a deed of gift of these very books. Hence, before we proceed any further with Mrs. Andrews, I would be grateful if you could straighten me out on this matter, I have not corresponded with Mrs. Andrews about these questions."[216]

Amy Bess Miller responded immediately and assured Plimpton that he was free to proceed:

In January 1964 we entered into a settlement agreement with Mr. and Mrs. Andrews as a result of which the earlier agreement [the gift agreement of December 1960] was revoked. The Andrewses agreed at the time that all items in their collection of Shaker articles which had been delivered to Hancock Shaker Village were indeed the property of the Corporation. Therefore we have no legal claim to anything now in Mrs. Andrews' possession.[217]

On the same day that Miller was writing to Plimpton, Faith was writing to McKeon. She agreed on the suitability of the location of the collection and assured him that she would "cooperate fully and that my whole aim is to make the library a useful and creative one."[218] That she fully intended to carry out her oral commitment was very clear. Indeed, two weeks before President Plimpton and Amy Bess Miller had exchanged letters, Faith wrote to me about her latest meeting with Plimpton and exclaimed, "All that is needed now is a letter from me to Plimpton!"[219]

She never sent that letter.

Almost three months went by before Faith contacted Amherst College again, this time implying clearly that she would not formalize the oral agreement:

I have been giving a great deal of thought to the destination of the Shaker library. While I have every reason to favor Amherst, I have not been able to come to a definite decision. You all have been most kind and understanding regarding my situation, and I trust will bear with me until such time as I can clarify my own thinking.[220]

Faith was struggling with the awkward fact that she was negotiating with Winterthur, which had always been quite friendly to the Andrewses, now re-emerged as the best possible home for the collection. Since Amherst College had met her installation requirements and since she had made an oral commitment to give the collection to the college, she was undoubtedly feeling guilty about not signing a formal agreement. This embarrassing denouement explains why, in all subsequent interviews, as well as in the *Fruits of the Shaker Tree of Life*, she omitted any mention of this unfulfilled gift.

There is no record of her contacting Amherst College again.

Years later, in 1976, she did write to Professor Commager again, asking him whether "Amherst would consider giving an award to Ted's contributions in this field," but the college never responded.[221]

The end of the Amherst College negotiations in 1965 threw the door to Winterthur wide open. Winterthur had long been friendly to the Andrewses. In 1957, recognizing the Andrewses' preeminence in the field, Charles Montgomery, director of the Winterthur Museum, invited them to consult on the installation of a Shaker room at the museum. At that time they formed a warm relationship with the founder, Henry Francis du Pont, as well as with John Sweeney, the associate curator.[222]

On April 10, 1962, Ted had delivered a lecture at the Winterthur Museum on Shaker life and culture before a large and select audience that included the Winterthur Museum staff, graduate students in the Winterthur Program, and Winterthur guides. Entitled "The Shaker Arts in Culture: Forces behind the Forms," the lecture was a stunning success, inspiring the Senior Research Fellow Charles F. Montgomery to write a letter to Amy Bess Miller that can only have left her with a bitter aftertaste. "Yesterday," he began,

I had the great pleasure of listening to one of the most splendid lectures on American arts and culture that I have ever heard; and I thought, perhaps, that you would be interested in knowing how beautifully Dr. Andrews related the culture, the arts and crafts, and the life of the Shakers. Never have I heard a more sensitive or scholarly survey of a people and its culture.

His bubbling postscript unwittingly added to his recipient's discomfort:

> P.S. Perhaps I ought to tell you that I strongly urged Dr. Andrews to have a recording made of his introductory lecture here; which, combined with slides, would, I think, make a wonderful introduction for your visitors before they start a tour of your building at Hancock.[223]

Ted's triumph came at the very moment the troubles at Hancock were intensifying. After the warm reception at Winterthur, Ted's expertise was once again validated. It was a gratifying upturn in the last twenty-four months of his life.

It was also an auspicious moment for the fate of the collection, because by the spring of 1962 the Andrewses had already decided to withdraw their gift from Hancock. Impressed with Winterthur's dedication to the highest standards of museum scholarship and practice, and delighted by Henry Francis du Pont's generous hospitality and respect for their work, the Andrewses had nurtured the relationship, and, while still at Hancock, had even transferred some personal pieces (not on the inventory of the gift to Hancock) to Winterthur. This transaction came to the attention of Amy Bess Miller, who promptly brought it to the attention of the Board of Trustees as a possible breach of contract.

Having made a final legal settlement with Hancock Shaker Village in January 1964, the Andrewses felt free to locate a suitable place for their library of books and manuscripts. Not until April 1965, when Faith finally got out of her entanglement at Amherst College, was she free to plan for a transfer to Winterthur.[224] In March 1967 Faith was able to deliver the bulk of the collection to Winterthur. As noted elsewhere, most of the furniture and other artifacts, including the rich collection of gift drawings, remained at Hancock, while the books and manuscripts went to Winterthur. The beautifully housed and administered Edward Deming Andrews Memorial Collection at Winterthur has become a standard research center for any scholar researching Shaker history.

Completing "the Work" and Preaching the Spirit

Because Faith had been so deeply conflicted about the final choice for the library collection, settling it at Winterthur was a major achievement. Though devastated by Ted's death, she was able, within three months, to resume work on various projects. She focused her energies on completing a catalogue of the collection. Before Ted's death, the couple had written what she called "the outline" of the catalogue, and, together, they were about to check it against the record that Ted had worked on at the village.

Faced with five unpublished manuscripts after Ted's death, Faith sought and received a lengthy interview with Professor Henry Steele Commager at Amherst College. She thought that was an appropriate way to start, because Amherst was Ted's college and because he had known Commager. Always direct, she asked him, "What do I do about these manuscripts?" and "What do I do with my life now?" Commager told her she could have an agent or do it herself. She chose the latter course and remembered "that was quite a day in my life."[225]

After conferring with Commager, Faith asked me to help her with the task of finishing Ted's books. She confidently reported to Thomas Merton, "A young friend of ours in American history—a student of the Mormons—is willing to undertake with me the completion of these [final three] chapters."[226] But for professional reasons I had to refuse; she was extremely disappointed and gradually, as she aged and I got on with my professional life, we lost touch but never broke the bond of friendship.

The final settlement between the Andrewses and the village required that the village publish a definitive catalogue of the portion of the collection that went to Hancock. Shortly after Ted's death, Faith wrote to Thomas Merton that "in our 'legal' withdrawal from the Village, they agreed to publish a 'Catalog of the Andrews Collection' now at Hancock. Ted's thought was that in the future—when the present personnel had left—it would be a record—one which would stand out from the many inferior additions [i.e., inaccurate descriptions of particular items in the collection]. Ted had written the foreword—a beautiful essay—and completed the listing."

Faith thought that the village would begin work on the definitive catalogue almost immediately. Herewith in the book before you, the village has finally fulfilled its obligation, delayed over forty-five years until the former "personnel" were gone.

Determined to finish "the work" after Ted's death, Faith took on the daunting task of preparing Ted's last works for publication, and first on her list was the much discussed catalogue, a legal requirement and a moral touchstone. Because of the checkered history of the bequest and the discontinuities between 1955 and 1964, she confronted intractable problems, such as Yale's reluctance to release Ted's voluminous notes on the provenance of various items in the collection. An even greater problem was lack of access to her husband's unfinished notes on the catalogue; she was forced to start a new "record" or catalogue wholly independent of the cataloguing previously done at the village. For this new beginning she needed to visit the village in person to examine original objects, lists, and records.

So in September 1964 Faith sent a formal note to Amy Bess Miller, stating that she wanted to have her catalogue ready "to present to the Publications Committee [of the Board of Trustees of the village] before winter." "There are some difficulties involved," she explained, "which I think you can clear up for me and I would like to discuss this with you so that the project can be completed and I can go on to the next one."[227] Among the "next ones" she would eventually finish her joint work with Ted on the history of their careers as collectors, *Fruits of the Shaker Tree of Life*, together with one of the two earliest works Ted wrote—and one that meant most to him—*Visions of the Heavenly Sphere*. Amy Bess Miller had to allow Faith to enter the village, but her secret response was to make it difficult for Faith to gain direct access to the Hancock collection. She instructed her staff to enforce museum rules as strictly as possible, commenting, "This would apply to Faith."[228]

Faith continued the work of managing their collection, even after most of it had found a home. The challenge of preserving Ted's and her conception of the purity of Shaker culture kept her busy during the last twenty-six years of her life, and though handicapped toward the end by blindness and a wheelchair, she promoted the work with undiminished devotion, until her death in 1990 at the age of ninety-four. The Andrewses considered the preservation of manuscripts, books, and artifacts only one part of their mission, which was animated, in Faith's words, by a sense of participation in Shaker life:

Even though we came in [at] . . . the very end of the culture, we didn't feel badly about it, about its being so near the end. We felt so happy to have seen what they did and to have seen first hand and to have known the people, I don't think it could have been done any other way.[229]

Faith's regular use of the phrase "the work" in referring to their mission echoes the religious language of the Shakers, the Mormons, and other groups who spoke of "the work" of proselytizing and building up the kingdom.

The religious element in the Andrewses' vision led them (especially Ted) to do a good deal of sermonizing on the ethics of the Shakers as a system of values to be emulated. In letters, proposals, and other documents, Edward Deming Andrews repeatedly wrote of his dream or vision for the use of his collection. He did not dare be so specific about what Yale or Amherst should teach, but in his later prospectus for Hancock he listed the following:

1. The doctrine of perfectionism, particularly in all kinds of workmanship.

2. The virtues of simplicity and humility.

3. The practice of scrupulous neatness and order.

4. Charity and hospitality. The "right uses of property."

5. Racial and religious tolerance.

6. The concept of equality of rights and responsibilities as between the sexes and all stations of life.

7. The concept of consecrated labor, and respect for manual labor. Variety of labor as a source of happiness.

8. Education for character. The power of good example. Recognition of ability and talent.

9. The importance of temperance, physical health, hygiene.

10. Love of the land.

11. Kindness to dumb animals.

12. Active concern for world peace.

These twelve points could easily pass for a standard list of liberal secular virtues, even now, half a century later. Psychologically these virtues were a projection of Ted's own standards of kindness, gentleness, and liberality. But none of them could be considered directly religious. So, why did he feel compelled to define them as Shaker?

Doubtless in his own soul Ted had journeyed far beyond secular humanism, seeking to share the Believers' thirst for God. If it was moral, it was Shaker. In Shaker perfectionism, simplicity, work, and peace he could see equivalents in Merton's contemplative order. Surely his yearning for the spiritual dimension must explain his closeness to the guru Ananda Kentish Coomaraswamy. Ted's old goal of somehow inculcating Shaker teachings ended only with his formal resignation from Hancock in 1963 and his death a year later.

Had he lived, Ted would have joined Faith in rejoicing at the opening of doors at Winterthur, and in fact he had already begun to enjoy Winterthur's friendly welcome and appreciation of his initial gift of books and pamphlets.[230]

As the Andrewses made their happy transition back to the work, the pain of Hancock was already receding into history, and they felt that they had to explain that history to distant friends like Thomas Merton and Barry Bingham Sr., both in Kentucky. Bingham was a publisher of national repute and a leading supporter of the restoration of Pleasant Hill, which the Andrewses thought was better run than Hancock.

In November 1963 Ted wrote to Merton, describing the breakup at Hancock with calm forbearance. Ted had just attended the funeral of Robert Frost and was distressed at the "turbulent times." Reporting also on why he had not written recently, he summarized the events as follows:

> For us they have been troublous [times] too, for we found that we could not condone the policies and behavior of those administering Hancock community, who have power and money but questionable ethics and little real understanding of the Shaker heritage. For two years or so we have tried to maintain our standards, but matters got worse, and finally there was no alternative to our total dissociation with the project. But we are back to our own independent work again, writing articles, and preparing a supplement to the furniture book and an economic history of the Shakers. Though the culture was in a sense a monk's one, a sub-culture, it is strange how rich it is, and we never seem to exhaust the possibilities of research and interpretation.[231]

Ted died six months later.

I was never enamored of Ted's fixation on the necessity of using the Shaker experience as an instrument of education. Indeed, I found it exasperating; but because of his regard for me as well as my respect for him as a much older scholar, I was reluctant to challenge his educational notions.[232] Having lived through the Andrewses' major disappointments, I came to understand, some fifty years later, that he belonged to the

Photograph of Thomas Merton by Sibylle Akers.
Used with permission of the Merton Legacy Trust and the
Thomas Merton Center, Bellarmine University.

generation of John Dewey and shared the widespread American veneration of education as the instrument of social and cultural progress; for Ted, educational progress could be promoted by studying the Shakers and their "principles." I greatly respected him as a very gentle man with a too-strong historical obsession. Even the Andrewses came to admit, later in life, that their painful experiences in finding a home for their collection arose from their insistence on the educational use of the collection.

The intense bond between Faith and Ted led her to be ultrasensitive to any criticism of him, and there is little doubt that her strict religious upbringing gave her a passionate moral focus and a strong will in stark contrast to the personality of her gentle, soft-spoken husband. But they worked harmoniously together, creating a new world of Shaker scholarship.

The Andrewses never realized Ted's vision of preserving Shaker culture as a single, undivided unit encompassing hundreds of artifacts, as well as manuscripts and books, to be used to inculcate the spirit of the Shakers. On some deep level they believed they were saving a culture. That, of course, cannot be done. But in a very meaningful sense they did succeed in their life's work: a highly significant and invaluable achievement of historic preservation, a pivotal benefaction to American culture.

In a letter to Faith Andrews in 1970, the Hancock Shaker sister Olive H. Austin got it right: "[Your] work of love on this most worthwhile subject will go down in history and [your] names will always be spoke of and remembered as the greatest authority on Shaker lore."[233]

Bibliographical Note

There are very few secondary works of serious scholarship on Shaker history. Most recent works, especially the less scholarly books and essays, inevitably do take a stance, implicit or explicit, on the work of the Andrewses and their collection. The most common view of the Andrewses' work (particularly of Ted's 1953 history) is that it was pioneering but is now dated.

Among the best works of serious scholarship on the Shakers are Patricia J. Brewer, *Shaker Communities, Shaker Lives* (Hanover, N.H.: University Press of New England, 1986); Lawrence Foster, *Religion and Sexuality: Three American Communal Experiments of the Nineteenth Century* (New York: Oxford University Press, 1981); Clarke Garrett, *Origins of the Shakers: From the Old World to the New World* (Baltimore: Johns Hopkins University Press, 1987); and Stephen A. Marini, *Radical Sects of Revolutionary New England* (Cambridge: Harvard University Press, 1982).

The primal account is Edward Deming Andrews's *The People Called Shakers: A Search for the Perfect Society* (New York: Oxford University Press, 1953; new enlarged edition, New York: Dover, 1963). Although a professional historian could argue with Andrews's narrative method, and although the work is now somewhat dated, it has acquired the status of a primary source. For a detailed and excellent account of the Shakers after 1876, see parts 4 and 5 of Stephen J. Stein, *The Shaker Experience in America: A History of the United Society of Believers* (New Haven: Yale University Press, 1992). As noted in the text, Stein criticizes Andrews, among other things, for focusing on the period before 1865.

Numerous writings of the hobbyists, enthusiasts, and amateur historians in the "World of Shaker," especially regarding the Andrewses, have some value. But the independent Shaker scholar Stephen J. Paterwic aptly describes these works as showing "very little research, and even less thought" (in his very positive review of Glendyne Wergland's, *One Shaker Life: Isaac Newton Youngs, 1793–1865* [Amherst: University of Massachusetts Press, 2006], in *Communal Societies* 26.2 [2006]: 188–90).

In the light of the condescension of some later writers, it must be remembered that not only did Ted and Faith Andrews save much of a culture in the form of artifacts and manuscripts, but Ted, through his groundbreaking monographs on Shaker music and Shaker gift drawings, opened up these and other aspects of Shaker life to the world of scholarship.

Manuscript Collections

Primary sources for the history of the Andrews Collection are surprisingly extensive, though most are in manuscript form.

The manuscript sources for my account may be found in two main archives: the Edward Deming Andrews Memorial Shaker Collection at the Winterthur Museum, Garden, and Library in Winterthur, Delaware (EDAMSC), and the Uncatalogued Institutional Archives, Amy Bess and Lawrence K. Miller Library, Hancock Shaker Village, Hancock, Massachusetts (HSV archives). These two archives are the richest in original materials, many of which were submitted in the form of carbon copies of typescripts. Since the 1970s there has been so much photocopying of Andrews materials in some collections (though none from Winterthur and few from Hancock) that it is often difficult to determine, in the various collections, whether a document is the "original" photocopy or the copy of a copy. This distinction can be significant because penciled marginalia in some photocopies are illegible. In short, the most authentic "originals" of many documents are the old typewritten carbon copies.

The great collection of Andrews materials at Winterthur (EDAMSC) forms the core of any research on the Andrewses. Ann E. Andrews Kane, the daughter of Edward Deming and Faith Andrews, kindly gave me free access to all the restricted boxes. The EDAMSC manuscripts include correspondence, drafts of speeches, articles, notes, brochures, and clippings. E. Richard McKinstry, the Andrew W. Mellon Senior Librarian at Winterthur, has described and annotated the printed and manuscript items of the Andrews Collection in his invaluable guide, *The Edward Deming Andrews Memorial Shaker Collection* (Published for the Henry Francis DuPont Winterthur Museum; New York: Garland, 1987). Faith Andrews regarded the publication of this guide as the culmination of a lifetime of collecting and of preserving materials; she believed that her bequest would preserve the life and spirit of the Shakers—and the memory of her husband.

The Hancock Shaker Village archives also include a large number of nonpaper primary sources, mainly recordings on compact disks and audiotapes.

Other significant manuscript collections consulted include the Ann E. Andrews Kane personal collection, Palo Alto, California; the Emma B. King Library, Shaker Museum and Library, Old Chatham, New York; and the Mario S. De Pillis Sr. private collection.

I am indebted to Ann E. Andrews and her husband, Tom Kane, for permitting me to examine the Andrews manuscripts in their possession, most notably the Camp Devens (now called Fort Devens) journal. This journal is indispensable for understanding the mind of Ted Andrews, his ideals and ambitions, and particularly his very early interest in the culture of the Shakers

The Emma B. King Library has a rich collection of materials relating to the Andrews, which includes the Hugh Howard papers and the Helen Upton papers.

My private collection of manuscripts includes mostly correspondence relating to the Andrews family and the relationship of Edward Deming and Faith Andrews to the Hancock Shaker Community, Inc., known since the 1960s as Hancock Shaker Village, Inc.

As an old friend of the Andrewses and as a fellow board member at Hancock Shaker Village, Inc., I accepted the invitation to write this essay as a moral duty: to cut through the gossip and amateurism of the so-called World of Shaker and provide a sympathetic but objective account of the Andrewses and their collection. Unfortunately, in distancing myself from unsavory incidents from the early 1960s, I had discarded a large part of my collection of correspondence from the 1950s and 1960s, never dreaming that I would be asked to revisit that period as an aged historian; but one large folder did survive my attempt to mollify memory, and I have drawn on those surviving manuscripts. My modest collection will go to the Winterthur Library.

The Hancock years of my friendship with the Andrewses were costly to me academically. We first met in 1956, and at the height of the Hancock struggle (1961–63) I stood alone as their one remaining ally. My involvement with Hancock demanded a huge investment of time and energy in the very first years of my career, when publications were the only road to promotion and tenure. The deans made it clear that historical restoration did not bring "national visibility" to the university. The politics of museum-building were enervating and destructive. But I do not regret my stand.

Primary Sources

The following is a short, select list of some of the most important primary sources I consulted. A. Donald Emerich's "Publications of Edward Deming Andrews and Faith Andrews" (listed in full under "Printed Works") is currently the most complete bibliography of the works of Edward Deming Andrews and Faith Andrews.

Andrews, Edward Deming. "Camp Devens Journal, June 4, 1919–April 20, 1920." Collection of Ann E. Andrews Kane, Palo Alto, Calif.
    This is a key document for understanding Edward Deming Andrews. Unfortunately, two leaves covering July 31 to October 2, 1920, in the crucial period of Andrews's intellectual debates (with himself as well as others), have been torn out. Also in the Kane collection are five earlier journals running from March 20, 1906, to March 18, 1914; dating from the age of twelve to his sophomore year at Amherst College, these contain early hints of his introspective idealism.

——. "The Shaker Arts in Culture: Forces behind the Forms." CD recording of lecture delivered at Winterthur, Delaware, April 10, 1962, HSV archives. This lecture had a great impact on the faculty and staff and provided the seed for Winterthur's eventual acquisition of the Andrews manuscript collection.

Andrews, Edward Deming, and Faith Andrews. *Fruits of the Shaker Tree of Life: Memoirs of Fifty Years of Collecting and Research.* Stockbridge, Mass.: Berkshire Traveller Press, 1975.

——. "Prospectus for a Museum of the American Shakers." 1939. Copy of typescript. Manuscript Collection, HSV archives.

——. *Religion in Wood: A Book of Shaker Furniture.* Bloomington: Indiana University Press, 1966.

——. Photographs by William F. Winter. *Shaker Furniture: The Craftsmanship of an American Communal Sect.* New Haven: Yale University Press, 1937; reprinted, New York: Dover, 1950.

Andrews, Faith Y. "The Hancock Story." Typescript. 1983. EDAMSC.

——. Interviews by Robert F. Brown. Pittsfield, Mass., January 14, 1982–April 23, 1982, EDAMSC. Transcript of audiotapes in the Smithsonian Institution, Archives of American Art.

Emerich, A. Donald. "A Conversation with Faith Andrews," December 2, 1972. Transcript of audiotapes, EDAMSC.

Miller, Amy Bess. Interview by Andrew Vadnais, June 4, 1993, mp3 digital recording on two CDs, HSV archives.

[Young, Ann]. "The Hugh Howard Papers Regarding Edward Deming Andrews and Faith Andrews and Their Life of Research and Writing about the 'Shakers' (the United Society of Believers in Christ's Second Appearing)." [2004.] Emma B. King Library, Shaker Museum and Library, Old Chatham, N.Y.

Printed Works

Berman, Avis. *Rebels on Eighth Street: Juliana Force and the Whitney Museum of American Art.* New York: Atheneum, 1990.

Emerich, A. Donald. "Publications of Edward Deming Andrews and Faith Andrews: A Select Chronological List." In A. Donald Emerich, comp., *Shaker Furniture and Objects from the Faith and Edward Deming Andrews Collections Commemorating the Bicentenary of the American Shakers.* Washington, D.C.: Published for the Renwick Gallery of the National Collection of Fine Arts by the Smithsonian Institution Press, 1973.

Miller, Amy Bess. *Hancock Shaker Village/the City of Peace: An Effort to Restore a Vision, 1960–1985.* Hancock, Mass.: Hancock Shaker Village, 1984.

Miller, M. Stephen. *From Shaker Lands and Shaker Hands.* Hanover, N.H.: University Press of New England, 2007.

Ott, John Harlow. *Hancock Shaker Village: A Guidebook and History.* 4th ed. Hancock, Mass.: Hancock Shaker Village, 1976.

Pollock, Lindsay. *The Girl with the Gallery: Edith Gregor Halpert and the Making of the Modern Art Market.* New York: Public Affairs Press, 2006.

Richmond, Mary L. *Shaker Literature: A Bibliography.* 2 volumes. Hancock, Mass.: Shaker Community, Inc.; distributed by University Press of New England, 1977.

Notes

[1] The book that established them nationally was Edward Deming Andrews and Faith Andrews, photographs by William F. Winter, *Shaker Furniture: The Craftsmanship of an American Communal Sect* (New Haven: Yale University Press, 1937; reprinted, New York: Dover, 1950). This book is not to be confused with their *Religion in Wood: A Book of Shaker Furniture* (Bloomington: Indiana University Press, 1966), a different, later, work with different plates, not all of which show furniture.

[2] See Malcolm's psycho-historical essay, "Strangers in Paradise: How Gertrude Stein and Alice B. Toklas Got to Heaven," *New Yorker*, November 13, 2006, 54–61, which describes the politics of ownership of great Impressionist art, its sudden increase in value, the role of Ernest Hemingway, Stein's bequest, and the querulousness of human testimony.

[3] See also Malcolm's *Two Lives: Gertrude and Alice* (New Haven: Yale University Press, 2006), which contains most of her *New Yorker* article. She also wrote a well-informed appreciation of the work of the Andrewses in "The Modern Spirit in Shaker Design," in A. Donald Emerich, comp., *Shaker Furniture and Objects from the Faith and Edward Deming Andrews Collections Commemorating the Bicentenary of the American Shakers* (Washington, D.C.: Published for the Renwick Gallery of the National Collection of Fine Arts by the Smithsonian Institution Press, 1973).

[4] Edward Deming Andrews (EDA), "Camp Devens Journal, June 4, 1919–April 20, 1920," Ann E. Andrews Kane personal collection, Palo Alto, Calif. Ellipses in the original.

[5] Retold in a slightly different form in EDA and Faith Andrews, *Fruits of the Shaker Tree of Life: Memoirs of Fifty Years of Collecting and Research* (Stockbridge, Mass.: Berkshire Traveller Press, 1975), 21–22. See Faith Andrews, interview by Robert F. Brown, Pittsfield, Mass., January 14, 1982; Uncatalogued Institutional Archives, Edward Deming Andrews Memorial Shaker Collection, Winterthur Museum, Garden, and Library, Winterthur, Delaware (hereafter EDAMSC). See also, later in this volume, Christian Goodwillie, "The Andrewses and the Shakers."

The obituary for EDA in the *Berkshire Eagle* (June 8, 1964), then owned by the Miller family, old friends of the Andrewses but by then alienated from them, erroneously dated the bread-purchase incident in 1925 and implied vaguely that EDA's real interest arose from antique collecting and not from the bread-purchase incident: "It was in the 1920s that antique-collecting first began to interest Dr. Andrews in connection with a small antique business operated at the Clinton Avenue House where the family lived." As EDA's journal entry of June 1919 (quoted earlier in the text) shows, he was quite fascinated by the whole of Shaker culture several years earlier. Faith herself in a late interview also used the erroneous 1925 date; e.g., Peter Andrews, "A Conversation with Faith Andrews," November 25, 1982, audio recording on CD, Amy Bess and Lawrence K. Miller Library, Hancock Shaker Village [HSV], Hancock, Mass. (hereafter HSV archives).

Ironically, the Andrewses themselves came to accept the folkloric bread-purchase version of the birth of their interest in collecting. The *Berkshire Eagle* obituary quotes EDA as commenting three decades later: "It was a tremendous revelation to us. It was a whole way of life that we hadn't really been aware of, even though we had lived only a few miles away from it most of our lives."

[6] Ann E. Andrews Kane, conversation with the author, October 2, 2006.

[7] The Andrewses told of their loaf of bread experience very early in their careers. See *Berkshire Eagle*, October 22, 1932.

[8] Stephen Bowe and Peter Richmond, *Selling Shaker: The Commodification of Shaker Design in the Twentieth Century* (Liverpool: Liverpool University Press, 2007); Stephen J. Stein, *The Shaker Experience in America: A History of the United Society of Believers* (New Haven: Yale University Press, 1992). Using such words as "romanticizing" and "sentimentalizing" to describe EDA's treatment of the Shakers, Stein suggests that EDA misperceived the historical reality of Shaker life. Such terms, however, are not very useful in historical analysis.

[9] For examples, see Bowe and Richmond, *Selling Shaker*, 268; and Stein, *Shaker Experience*, 374.

[10] Shirley Lawton Houde, "Water for Soldiers," unpublished, unpaginated manuscript history, ca. 1939, Shirley Historical Society.

[11] Seth Chandler, *History of the Town of Shirley, Massachusetts, from Its Early Settlement to A.D. 1882* (Shirley: Published by the Author, 1883), 497–501.

[12] Houde, "Water for Soldiers," section 15 (concluding section; not all sections are numbered).

[13] Robert Adam to Christian Goodwillie, e-mail message, March 9, 2006, De Pillis private collection. Frank Lawton remained in touch till old age. See Frank Lawton to Ted and Faith Andrews, May 25, 1933, and January 7, 1934, EDAMSC.

[14] Five extant early diaries that begin in 1906 are in the Kane collection.

[15] EDA, Journal, July 17, 1919.

[16] Hugh C. Davis (b. 1922), of Leverett, Mass., son of Edward Morris Davis, interview by the author, October 2006; *Encyclopedia Britannica*, 2007 edition, s.v. "Davis, William Morris"; Robert Adam (b. 1949) of Shirley Center, Massachusetts, telephone interview by the author, October 27, 2006; Chandler, "Lawton," in *History of the Town of Shirley*, 497–501. See also Houde's description of her parents' program for helping the morale of young soldiers in "Water for Soldiers."

Robert Adam, head of the department of preservation carpentry at the North Bennet Street School (Boston) and a leader of the Shirley Historical Society, came to know the history of the Lawton family very well through his friendship with Shirley Lawton Houde. Also, Adam lives in the Benton MacKaye house, historically known as the Betsey Kelsey House (1835), and in 2003 he purchased the rundown Shaker infirmary for a dollar and had it moved from near Route 2 to a site opposite the MacKaye house in Shirley Center, where he restored it with the help of his students. Telephone interview with Robert Adam of Shirley Center, Massachusetts, by the author, October 27, 2006; Walecia Konrad, "HAVENS: That's No Museum, That's My Home," *New York Times*, July 18, 2003.

[17] Houde, "Water for Soldiers," section for April 1919, n.p.

[18] EDA to his mother, postmarked March 8, 1918, holograph, Kane collection.

[19] From EDA's poem "Bit of the Old," October 1918.

[20] Thomas Kane, e-mail message to the author, March 5, 2006, De Pillis collection. Kane, a long-time professor at Stanford University, married Ann Andrews in 1951. In a letter of March 8, 1918, to his mother, EDA expressed dismay at vile crimes against the Jews in Austria and the Ukraine, Kane collection. His Camp Devens journals contain references to Catholic and Jewish friends, such as George Flanagan, Tarcisio Tarquinio, and Herman Silverstein.

[21] EDA to his mother, March 8, 1918.

[22] Andrews, interview by Brown, 32.

[23] A. Donald Emerich, "A Conversation with Faith Andrews," December 2, 1972, transcript of audio tape recordings, EDAMSC.

[24] Faith Andrews, interview by Laura Beach, August 1987, *Antiques and the Arts Weekly* [the Bee Publishing Company, Newtown, Connecticut], September 4, 1987, 59.

[25] Obituary of Seldon Deming Andrews, *Berkshire Eagle*, September 18, 1950.

[26] Certification of active army service August 25, 1917, to April 4, 1919, War Department, Adjutant General's Office, Washington, D.C., July 3, 1942, Andrews Archives, box 1, EDAMSC.

[27] Emerich, "Conversation with Faith Andrews."

[28] Andrews, interview by Brown, 9.

[29] Ibid.

[30] EDA, "The Shakers in a New World," *Antiques*, October 1957, 340.

[31] See "Biographical Note," Charles C. Adams Papers, 1915–68, New York State Library, Albany.

[32] Andrews and Andrews, *Fruits*, 139, 190.

[33] For a detailed discussion of the history of Shaker boundary maintenance, see Stephen C. Taysom, "Divine Resistance and Accommodation: Nineteenth-Century Shaker and Mormon Boundary Maintenance Strategies" (Ph.D. diss., Indiana University, 2006).

[34] Andrews and Andrews, *Fruits*, 88.

[35] See Goodwillie, "The Andrewses and the Shakers."

[36] Stein, *Shaker Experience*, 374. By selectively quoting some sentences taken out of context, Stephen Stein has insinuated that a few key Shakers, such as Sadie Neale, did not like the Andrewses.

[37] See Sister Sadie Neale Diary, HSV archives; Sadie A. Neale to Faith Andrews, April 1, 1932, EDAMSC.

[38] Andrews and Andrews, *Fruits*, 91.

39 Ibid., 104–5.

40 Emerich, "Conversation with Faith Andrews," 28.

41 *Berkshire Eagle*, October 22, 1932.

42 Andrews and Andrews, *Fruits*, 190.

43 Hancock membership records, HSV archives.

44 Faith Andrews, interview by James Thomas, president of Shakertown at Pleasant Hill, Kentucky, at a reception given in honor of Faith Andrews at the Shaker Museum and Library, Old Chatham, N.Y., reported in the *Berkshire Eagle*, October 25, 1982, and cited in Donna B. Mattoon, "Scholar Honored in Old Chatham for Her Studies of Shaker Sect," *Berkshire Eagle*, November 25, 1980.

45 Emerich, "Conversation with Faith Andrews," 4.

46 Ibid., 8.

47 John Patterson Maclean, *A Bibliography of Shaker Literature, with an Introductory Study of the Writings and Publications Pertaining to Ohio Believers* (Columbus, Ohio: Fred J. Heer, 1905). MacLean, "Unappreciated Donations" (broadside), [Franklin, Ohio, 1904], Library of the Western Reserve Historical Society, Cleveland, Ohio, tells the story of MacLean's withdrawing his gift of over nineteen boxes of books and "relics" from the unreceptive Ohio State Historical and Archaeological Society. Mary Richmond justly remarked that "Shaker scholarship owes a debt to his efforts to place [Shaker] materials in libraries where they have been preserved and made available for Shaker Studies." Mary L. Richmond, "About the Shakers," in *Shaker Literature: A Bibliography*, 2 vols. (Hancock, Mass.: Shaker Community, Inc.; distributed by University Press of New England, 1977), 2:76.

48 Megan M. Kennedy, "'This place is not meant for recreation. It is meant for inspiration.': The Legacies of Clara Endicott Sears" (master's thesis, University of Massachusetts at Amherst, 2005), 21, 66.

49 Clara Endicott Sears to EDA, December 8, 1926, EDAMSC, is the earliest extant letter I have found between Sears and the Andrewses. See also Emerich, "Conversation with Faith Andrews," 44.

50 Stein, *Shaker Experience*, 374. Stein attributes the phrase "Antique Pilgrims" to the Shakers, implying that, as a group, they felt a strong hostility toward the Andrewses. That implication is a myth. Neale soon became a fast friend, as documented elsewhere in this essay. For an account of the rise of collectors of Shaker materials in the early twentieth century, see Brian L. Bixby, "Seeking Shakers: Two Centuries of Visitors to Shaker Villages" (Ph.D. diss., University of Massachusetts at Amherst, 2008), chap. 4, "Death and Collectors, 1875–1950."

51 Sadie A. Neale to the Andrewses, October 13, 1942, Winterthur folder SA 1697.20 (no. 978), EDAMSC.

52 Emerich, "Conversation with Faith Andrews," 8.

53 Andrews, interview by Brown, 87, 89, and elsewhere. In their crusade to save and find a home for the materials of a disappearing culture, the Andrewses resembled another young idealist of a later generation named Aaron Lansky, who, at the age of twenty-three, decided to save the world's Yiddish books and indeed single-handedly rescued thousands of Yiddish books from dumpsters, attics, cellars, and living rooms in Canada and the United States. Aaron Lansky, *Outwitting History: The Amazing Adventures of a Man Who Rescued a Million Yiddish Books* (Chapel Hill, N.C.: Algonquin Books of Chapel Hill, 2004), ix.

54 Daniel Fraser, *The Divine Afflatus: A Force in History* (Boston: Published for the United Society of Shirley by Press of Rand, Avery, & Co., 1875). Writers of Ted's generation, like H. L. Mencken, also used the word.

55 Andrews, interview by Brown, 56.

56 EDA, "Prospectus for a Museum of the American Shakers," 1939, HSV archives.

57 Andrews and Andrews, *Fruits*, 186; Edward Deming Andrews II, e-mail messages to the author, December 19, 2006, and September 20, 2007, De Pillis collection. Edward Deming Andrews II is EDA's grandson.

58 Andrews and Andrews, *Fruits*, 172.

59 The publishers of Merton's extensive correspondence have dwelt on only a small fraction of narrowly edited selections of Merton's vast correspondence. Paul M. Pearson, director and archivist of the Thomas Merton Center at Bellarmine University, Louisville, Kentucky, has prepared a collection of the Merton-Andrews correspondence for publication in 2008.

60 Merton's letter to the Andrewses is quoted in Andrews and Andrews, *Fruits*, 174. The hymn was first "sung by the Saviour and Mother Ann" on February 21, 1845 (ibid.).

61 Thomas Merton, introduction to Andrews and Andrews, *Religion in Wood*, xiii. While the comment may have some metaphorical truth, Merton, in the embarrassingly inaccurate sentence that followed it, wrote: "Indeed the Shakers believed their furniture was designed by angels—and Blake believed his ideas for poems and engraving came from heavenly spirits." The Shakers believed no such thing.

62 Mark Van Doren, typescript statement (1964?), box 1, Andrews folder, EDAMSC. Probably written at the time of EDA's death.

63 Homer Eaton Keyes, preface to Andrews and Andrews, *Shaker Furniture*, vii.

64 For an excellent analysis of gender conflicts, see Glendyne Wergland, "Gendered Conflict and Consensus in Shaker Society" (paper delivered at the annual conference of the Communal Studies Association, September 29, 2007, Kirtland, Ohio). For a good general summary of commercialization and internal disputes, see Stein, *Shaker Experience*, 337–432.

65 The earliest and still one of the best examples of the more analytical approach to the Shakers is Lawrence Foster, *Religion and Sexuality: The Shakers, the Mormons, and the Oneida Community* (New York: Oxford University Press, 1981).

66 The "concretion" phrase is found in Louis Miles, "Shaker Men and Women Together and Apart: Regulated Behavior Described in Five Documents," *The Shaker Messenger* 13, no. 1 (January 1991):6. Stein used the "frozen view" in *Shaker Experience*, 376. The Andrewses' neglect of the later period and their idealization of Shaker purity and religion has come under frequent attack, most forcefully by Stein. Stein, for example, terms EDA "a preacher and proselytizer" because he so admired Shaker self-discipline and self-denial and because he believed (in EDA's words) that their "experiment in primitive Christianity has been replete with lessons of value to all mankind" (376). But as I have tried to show, the proselytizing was necessary and positive in the 1920s and 1930s. Ironically, Stein himself argues that "classic Shakerism was a product of this [1787–1826] Formative Period"—a statement that contradicts his own general thesis that emphasizes the later period (xvi).

67 See Stein, *Shaker Experience*, especially 373–78, a compendium of common anti-Andrews criticisms.

68 Andrews and Andrews, *Shaker Furniture*, 65.

69 Susan Sontag, *On Photography* (London: Penguin, 1977), has been the most influential and persuasive work on the question of what a photograph means.

70 Stein, *Shaker Experience*, xiii.

71 The Ken Burns documentary is *The Shakers: Hands to Work, Hearts to God* (PBS, 1984).

72 Stein, *Shaker Experience*, 381.

73 Bowe and Richmond, *Selling Shaker*, 268 and n. 243, quoting from *The Observer* (London). The journalist in *The Observer* is apparently following Stein's picture of the Andrewses as sly, profit-seeking operators; Stein asserted that the Andrewses "and others pressured the aging Shakers to surrender their possessions. These 'friends' of the Believers, in turn, made substantial profits and built impressive private collections." Stein, *Shaker Experience*, 397.

74 Hugh Howard and Jerry V. Grant, "Reinventing the Shakers," *Eastfield Record*, no. 11 (Winter 2002–3). Ann Andrews Kane told me in September 2006 that Howard had promised to write a biography of EDA, and she had unwisely given him complete access to all the manuscripts in her possession in Palo Alto from about August 1991 to May 1992 for a biography he never wrote. Grant, now librarian at the Shaker Museum and Library, Old Chatham, New York, served briefly as director/curator at the Hancock restoration. Old Chatham's hostility to EDA as a competing collector goes back to the wealthy founder of the museum, John S. Williams, who told one bookseller not to offer any rare titles to EDA because he was "difficult." Mario S. De Pillis to EDA, December 21, 1959, carbon copy, De Pillis collection. Another longstanding source of anti-Andrews statements in the "world of Shaker" is a small group of later converts at the Sabbathday Lake community led by Brother Ted Johnson, the de facto leader of Sabbathday Lake from 1960 to his death in 1986. Johnson did not know the Andrewses. He did live with some half dozen Shaker sisters from the defunct Alfred community, and two of these spoke negatively of the Andrewses.

75 In an interview given late in life Faith spoke of selling antiques from the Clinton Avenue house to help finance Ted's studies at Yale, but her dates are vague. Digital recording of "Interview with Faith Andrews 1.m4a" held at the Shaker Seminar at Mount Lebanon 1982, HSV archives. Because of a teaching job at New Haven High School, Ted did not begin his graduate work in earnest till 1925.

76 EDA to Dallas Pratt, January 19, 1958, printed in Flo Morse, "Creating a Shaker Room," *America*

in Britain (publication of the American Museum in Bath) 36 (1998): 8. When a mistake was made in delivering one of the finest pieces in the Andrews Collection, EDA declined to accept a compensatory check sent by Pratt. The Andrewses had inadvertently sent the wrong furniture piece, one of lesser quality.

77 Keyes to Faith Andrews, New York, September 3, 1937, box 5, SA 1381 (#743), Correspondence, EDAMSC.

78 Andrews, interview by Brown, 138–40. The interview corroborates my own memory.

79 Ibid., 87.

80 Amy Bess Miller to EDA, July, 30, 1962, HSV archives.

81 Andrews, interview by Brown. "Stalls" were rented spaces in garages and other buildings for long-term storage.

82 Stein alludes to this "parasitic" subculture several times in *Shaker Experience*; see xvii, 409–10, 441, 442.

83 Quoted in Avis Berman, *Rebels on Eighth Street: Juliana Force and the Whitney Museum of American Art* (New York: Atheneum, 1990), 5. The dominance of high art has not entirely faded. In the fall of 2007 a single Philadelphia Chippendale tea table sold for $6.8 million, twenty to thirty times the price of any comparable Shaker piece. See Wendy Moonan, "Antiques: Tea Tables Times Two," *New York Times*, January 11, 2008.

84 Andrews, interview by Brown, 15.

85 EDA, *The Community Industries of the Shakers* (Albany: University of the State of New York, 1933).

86 Homer Eaton Keyes to EDA, June 5, 1930, EDAMSC.

87 For a good picture of that close-knit and intensely competitive world, see the many Andrews references in Berman, *Rebels on Eighth Street*.

88 Emerich, "Conversation with Faith Andrews," 23.

89 EDA, Camp Devens Journal, June 28, 1919. EDA was summarizing with approval the talk by Percy MacKaye, a leading member of the Lawton's salon in Shirley Center, Massachusetts.

90 Quoted in Darryl Thompson, "Eleanor Roosevelt and the Shakers: The Andrews Contacts," *Shaker Messenger* 14.2 (July 1992): 8.

91 Quoted in Berman, *Rebels on Eighth Street*, 263.

92 Edward Deming Andrews and Faith Andrews, "Craftsmanship of an American Religious Sect; Notes on Shaker Furniture," *Antiques* 14.2 (August 1928): 132–36, and "The Furniture of an American Religious Sect," *Antiques* 15.4 (April 1929): 292–96.

93 Emerich, "Conversation with Faith Andrews," 11. Rollins is wrongly transcribed as "Rounds" in the typescript. Moreover, Faith misspoke in saying that Rollins "published" their book (Andrews and Andrews, *Shaker Furniture*); he merely designed it. Rollins was a leading typographer and book designer in his day.

94 Andrews, interview by Brown, 49.

95 EDA to Juliana Force, October 26, 1932, Archives of the Whitney Museum of American Art, New York.

96 Emerich, "Conversation with Faith Andrews," 14.

97 Berman, *Rebels on Eighth Street*, 10. See also 9, 14, and 19.

98 Andrews. interview by Brown, 50.

99 Berman, *Rebels on Eighth Street*, 33.

100 Ibid., 20, 24.

101 Faith Andrews, Oral History, July 20, 1987, HSV archives.

102 Juliana Force to EDA, New York, March 1, 1934, Whitney Museum archives.

103 EDA, *Visions of the Heavenly Sphere: A Study in Shaker Religious Art* (Charlottesville: University of Virginia Press, 1969). A fine sequel and expansion is Daniel W. Patterson, *Shaker Gift Drawing and Gift Song: A Study of Two Forms of Shaker Inspiration* (Sabbathday Lake, Me.: United Society of Shakers, 1983).

104 Berman, *Rebels on Eighth Street*, 146–47.

105 Andrews, interview by Brown. 32, 95; Faith's statement also quoted in Berman, *Rebels on Eighth Street*, 384, with further details about Force's actions and loss of financial flexibility when the Whitney was incorporated as a nonprofit institution ten days after the Shaker opening. On Bath, see Andrews and Andrews, *Fruits*, 168–69.

106 Whitney Museum archives.

107 "Shaker Art," *New York Times*, November 17, 1935 (unsigned); Walter Rendell Storey, "Folk Art Inspires the Designer: In Current Exhibits He Can Study Old Types of Simple Furniture," *New York Times Magazine*, November 24, 1835. Storey (b. 1881), a conservative expert on Chippendale, viewed the Shaker works as "folk art" of superior artistry.

108 Lindsay Pollock, *The Girl with the Gallery: Edith Gregor Halpert and the Making of the Modern Art Market* (New York: Public Affairs Press, 2006), 142–43, 186, 212–13. Force had approached Halpert seven years earlier for money to support her lavish lifestyle; Halpert sold thirty German and Shaker antiques to Abby Aldrich Rockefeller. Berman, *Rebels on Eighth Street*, 309.

109 Andrews and Andrews, *Fruits*, 147.

110 Andrews, interview by Brown, 44.

111 Berman, *Rebels on Eighth Street*, 399–400.

112 Ibid., 403. My account of the fight over the drawings agrees in every respect with Berman's (403–4).

113 Ibid., 317.

114 All primary source materials used in this section are housed in folder 3, Juliana Force, Director, 1930–48, and folder 7, Museum Records 1930–39, Shaker Furniture Publications, Whitney Museum archives.

115 Emerich, "Conversation with Faith Andrews," 38.

116 Thompson, "Eleanor Roosevelt and the Shakers," 6. See also Darryl Thompson, "Eleanor Roosevelt: The Shakers and the Meaning of Craftsmanship," *Shaker Messenger* 13, no. 3 (September 1991): 13–15.

117 Alexander Wetmore to EDA, February 28, 1941, in ibid., 7; EDA to Mrs. Eleanor Roosevelt, March 5, 1941, in ibid.

118 Archibald MacLeish to EDA, March 18, 1941, folder SA 1377 (#739), EDAMSC.

119 *Shakerism, Its Meaning and Message: Embracing an Historical Account, Statement of Belief and Spiritual Experience of the Church from its Rise to the Present Day* (Columbus, Ohio: Press of Fred J. Heer, 1904).

120 Arthur E. Bestor Jr., *Backwoods Utopias: The Sectarian Origins and the Owenite Phase of Communitarian Socialism in America: 1663–1829* (1950; 2nd, enlarged edition, Philadelphia: University of Pennsylvania Press, 1970).

121 David M. Potter, extract of a letter, June 18, 1958, recipient not identified, but very likely an official at Yale University. Andrews Archive, box 1, EDAMSC.

122 Quoted in EDA, *A Proposal to Save the Shaker Community at Hancock, Massachusetts: Its Importance as Part of the American Heritage* ([New Haven]: Connecticut Printers, August 1960), 3.

123 EDA, "The Andrews Teaching Collection," undated, box 1, Restricted Collection, EDAMSC.

124 EDA, "Scarborough Address," June 7, 1957, 2, box 1, Restricted, EDAMSC.

125 EDA to T. D. Seymour Bassett, June 1, 1959, EDAMSC. Bassett had heard a very sympathetic (to EDA) account of the Yale fiasco and reported it to EDA in a letter of May 20, 1959, photocopy, Shaker Museum and Library, Old Chatham, N.Y.

126 I was finishing my doctoral work at Yale in 1950s and heard of some of the negotiations.

127 David M. Potter to EDA, Palo Alto, Calif., November 8, 1957, box 1, Restricted Collection, EDAMSC; photocopy in the Shaker Museum and Library, Old Chatham, N.Y.

128 Liz Stell, "Preserving the Shaker Tradition," *Berkshire Week*, supplement to the *Berkshire Eagle*, September 4, 1987, 11. Faith was the guest of honor marking the twentieth anniversary of her bequest of the Edward Deming Andrews Memorial Shaker Collection and the publication in 1987 of E. Richard McKinstry's guide to the collection. See also Andrews, interview by Brown, 118–20.

129 Andrews, interview by Brown, 121–22.

130 Marginal note in EDA, "Prospectus for a Museum of Shaker Cultural History," 3, draft of an essay, handwritten on yellow lined legal pad paper, EDAMSC.

131 EDA to Mario S. De Pillis, aboard the "Rotterdam," holograph, De Pillis collection. Pratt, an American, was related to Beatrice Cartwright, of an old family of English gentry; he was a psychologist. Judkyn, an antiques dealer, was an Englishman with American citizenship. Both men enjoyed sizeable inheritances, and they maintained a town house in New York, as well as a residence in England. Judkyn ran a small antiques business in New York. See Gaynor Kavanagh, "Exhibition Review," American Museum in Britain, Claverton Manor, Bath, *Journal of American*

History 82.1 (June 1995): 135–38; John Sweeney, a friend of Pratt and Judkyn's and a former curator at the Winterthur Museum, telephone interview by the author, November 17, 2006. In 1971 the museum secretary told Edward Deming Andrews II that his grandparents had sold (not donated) the Shaker pieces to the American Museum. Edward Deming Andrews II to Mario S. De Pillis, e-mail message, December 1, 2006, De Pillis collection.

132 Faith Andrews to Dallas Pratt, March 30, 1959, in Morse, "Creating a Shaker Room," 8.

133 Andrews and Andrews, *Fruits*, 169.

134 Faith Andrews to Mario S. De Pillis, holograph, October 21, 1958, De Pillis collection. The Andrewses' extensive correspondence with the Smithsonian may be found in the Smithsonian archives, Record Unit 192, United States National Museum, 1877–1975, box 538.

135 EDA to T. D. Seymour Bassett, June 1, 1959.

136 EDA to Thomas Merton, December 19, 1960, carbon copy, EDAMSC. On Colket, see Mario S. De Pillis to Meredith B. Colket Jr., New Haven, Conn., June 11, 1958, and Colket to De Pillis, June 20, 1958, both in De Pillis collection. Interestingly, the chairman of the Art Department at Wesleyan, Samuel M. Green, argued against his own institution, urging the Andrewses to consider Hancock first. Samuel M. Green to Faith Andrews, February 26, 1959, box 1, Restricted, EDAMSC. In October 1958 James Phinney Baxter, president of Williams College, along with some department heads, met with the Andrewses; two trustees were very enthusiastic and visited the Andrewses, but nothing came of it. Faith Andrews to Mario S. De Pillis, October 21, 1958, De Pillis collection; EDA to Mario S. De Pillis, December 3, 1958.

137 EDA to Mario S. De Pillis, [December 1959], De Pillis collection.

138 EDA, "Prospectus for a Museum of the American Shakers," 1939, HSV archives. An article in the *Berkshire Eagle,* December 8, 1938, reported that the Andrewses made the first public announcement that they intend to establish a Shaker museum for the preservation of Shaker culture.

139 With her usual candor, Faith Andrews covers these and other issues at Hancock in her interview by Robert F. Brown (140, 151); see also Amy Bess Miller, *Hancock Shaker Village/the City of Peace: An Effort to Restore a Vision, 1860–1985* (Hancock, Mass.: Hancock Shaker Village, 1984), 18–25. Amy Bess and Pete Miller were the only significant legal persons in the purchase, but the Shaker lawyers used the term "Miller group" in recognition of other persons advocating the purchase. A good sense of the difficulties involved in purchasing the property and getting a museum started may be found in the minutes of the Steering Committee of the Hancock Community Project, June 26, 1960, at the home of Mr. and Mrs. Lawrence K. Miller, edited typescript, EDAMSC. The exact nature of the Millers' collateral is not clear. But the risk to Pete Miller's family assets was real. I remember vividly a meeting of the Board of Trustees of HSV at which Miller upbraided his wife for her cavalier attitude toward the safety of his financial commitment.

140 For a sense of the prominence of the Miller family in the region and Pete Miller's personality see Rinker Buck, *First Job: A Memoir of Growing Up at Work* (New York: Public Affairs, 2002).

141 Mary-Jane Tichenor and D. R. Bahlman, "Civic Leader Amy Bess Miller Dies at 90," *Berkshire Eagle*, February 23, 2003. See also obituary by Eric Pace in the *New York Times*, February 26, 2003. Amy Bess Miller was born in El Paso, Texas, the daughter of Elizabeth Avery Taft Williams and Frederick R. Williams, a company doctor for a copper firm. When Amy Bess was eight, her family moved to Worcester, Massachusetts, where her uncle Frank Channing Smith was a trustee and president of the Worcester Museum and a prominent citizen of the city. Although her father was not wealthy (she deeply resented being called an "heiress" by the locals of Pittsfield), Miller did enjoy myriad connections to the economic and social elite of her day. She was at ease discussing the Wharton novels with the well-known literary critic, novelist, and Wharton scholar Louis Stanton Auchincloss. Auchincloss, a cousin of Jacqueline Bouvier's (later the wife of President John F. Kennedy), was an estate lawyer in the Wall Street firm of Hawkins, Delafield, and Wood, from which he retired in 1986. On Auchincloss, see James W. Tuttleton, "Louis Auchincloss at 80," *New Criterion* 16.2 (October 1997), which spells out the importance of upper-class connections before World War II. I am grateful to Margo Miller, the eldest of Amy Bess Miller's four children, for providing some genealogical details in an interview of February 5, 2008.

142 *Michelin Tourist Guide: New England*, 1st edition (Clermont-Ferrand, France: Michelin et Cie, 1981).

143 Amy Bess Miller was a trustee of Miss Hall's School (1941–2003), a member of the Board of Trustees of the Massachusetts Audubon Society, a member of the Kennedy Memorial Commission (1967), a member of the Board of Trustees of the American Antiquarian Society, a member of the Board of Overseers of the Berkshire Medical Center, and a member of the Board

of Incorporators of Edith Wharton Restoration, Inc. She also held leadership positions in several other high-level organizations. Among her many accolades were four honorary degrees received between 1970 and 1987. John Harlow Ott, director of the village from 1970 to 1983 and later executive director of the National Heritage Museum in Lexington, Massachusetts, characterized Amy Bess Miller as "a powerhouse," running the village, supervising on-site events, such as craft fairs, forwarding the publication of books, and all the while doing fundraising.

144 Frederick Rudolph, interview by the author, December 9, 2007.

145 Miller, *Hancock Shaker Village*, 18.

146 Oddly, EDA wrote a third version in 1963 just as he was leaving Hancock. Never printed or published, this prospectus repeated his old educationist view that Shaker culture represented a "microcosmic civilization" that could be used as a way of approaching the study of America cultural history. EDA, "Prospectus for a Museum of Shaker Cultural History," 3, photocopy of holograph, about 1963, Shaker Museum and Library, Old Chatham, N.Y. Ann Andrews Kane states that this was written on the threshold of the third season at Hancock (i.e., spring 1963), by which time her father had already left. See "Notes by Ann on Tapes," holograph, undated, photocopy, Shaker Museum and Library, Old Chatham. While EDA expressed similar ideas in 1959, the 1963 statement is the best of his many expressions of the mission to teach Shaker culture, which he reduces to twelve specific themes emphasizing "the humanistic and the spiritual" (quoted in the last section of this essay).

147 Milton C. Rose of Mudge, Stern, Baldwin, & Todd to Mrs. Edward Deming Andrews, November 7, 1960, HSV archives. See appendices for text of the agreement.

148 On the unhistorical choice of paint colors, see EDA to Mario S. De Pillis, April 25, 1963; for the grave markers, see EDA to Mario S. De Pillis, May 4, 1963, both in the De Pillis collection. The meeting house was finally dedicated on May 30, 1963.

149 Andrews, interview by Brown, 151.

150 Miller, *Hancock Shaker Village*, 146.

151 I am indebted to Paul S. Boyer, Merle Curti Professor of History Emeritus, University of Wisconsin–Madison, for making inquiries at the University Archives and the Department of History. Glover's appointment as field worker is also mentioned in Clifford L. Lord and Carl Ubbelohde, *Clio's Servant* (Madison: State Historical Society of Wisconsin, 1967), 404. See also the obituary for Wilbur H. Glover in the *Buffalo News*, October 27, 2002. He retired in 1975.

152 EDA to the author, April 11, 1962, De Pillis collection.

153 Minutes of the meeting of the Board of Trustees of HSV, December 7, 1962, HSV archives.

154 Amy Bess Miller to the Andrewses, January 25, 1963, HSV archives. Quoted in the Andrewses' reply reproduced in minutes of the meeting of the Board of Trustees of HSV, March 30, 1963, HSV archives.

155 Wilbur H. Glover, "Plan of Operation," mimeograph, attached to the agenda of the meeting of the Board of Trustees of HSV for July 28, 1962, typescript, HSV archives.

156 Amy Bess Miller to EDA, undated [late 1962?], carbon copy in HSV archives.

157 EDA, "Sheeler and the Shakers," *Art in America* 53 (February 1965): 90–95.

158 EDA to Mario S. De Pillis, June 18, 1963, De Pillis collection.

159 EDA to Dallas Pratt, January 19, 1958, printed in Flo Morse, "Creating a Shaker Room," *America in Britain* (publication of the American Museum in Bath) 36 (1998), 5.

160 Glover to Andrews, typewritten note, August 15, 1962, EDAMSC; EDA to Mario S. De Pillis, May 5, 1963.

161 For interceptions, see EDA to Edith Gregor Halpert, director of the Downtown Gallery, Pittsfield, Mass., September 27, 1963, Sheeler Letters, EDAMSC. See also EDA to Halpert, January 17, 1963, ibid. "R.E." was probably Ross Edmund, who had studied art history at the University of Illinois at Chicago.

162 EDA to Mario S. De Pillis, May 5, 1963, De Pillis collection. For Glover's defense of himself, see "Minutes of the Shaker Community Conciliation Committee's Meeting with Dr. W. H. Glover in the office of Mr. Milton C. Rose," compiled by Mario S. De Pillis, EDAMSC. For EDA's instructions to me as his representative on the committee, see EDA to Mario De Pillis, April 15, 1963, EDAMSC. In his instructions, EDA was very specific in citing his distrust of the operation of the committee. As for Glover, EDA believed Miller had "built up purposely a wall between the director and us—one that she bases on our [supposed] jealousy." He also accused her of making false statements against Faith. EDA, memo "For Your Portfolio," April 9, 1963, De Pillis collection.

163 Amy Bess Miller, interview by Andrew Vadnais, June 4, 1993, mp3 digital recording on two CDs, HSV archives.

164 Andrews, interview by Brown, 91.

165 Michael Kimmelman, "Dorothy Miller Is Dead at 99; Discovered American Artists," Obituary, *New York Times*, July 12, 2003. Juliana Force and Gertrude Whitney, contemporaries of Miller, surely equaled her in clairvoyance, if only for their daring support of the Ashcan School of painters.

166 EDA to Mario S. De Pillis, April 15, 1963, De Pillis collection.

167 Dorothy Canning Miller (1904–2003) was born in Hopedale, Massachusetts. Adin Ballou, the abolitionist preacher and reformer, founded Hopedale in 1842 as a Universalist commune of "Practical Christians," but it did not last long: it was disbanded between 1856 and 1868. By the time Miller was born, the utopia had become the ideal company town owned and operated by the Draper Corporation. Her affluent family left when she was quite young and she grew up in Montclair, New Jersey. Upon graduating from Smith College in 1925, Miller completed an apprenticeship in 1926 at the Newark, New Jersey, art museum and promptly accepted a job offer in the same institution, where she met Cahill. From there she went on to a distinguished career of museum work, mostly as a curator at the Museum of Modern Art (1932–69), where she first encountered the Andrewses. Cahill, Halpert, and Miller were members of the New York art world elite but not lasting friends. Cahill adopted the name Edgar Holger Cahill. He was born in Iceland as Sveinn Kristyan Bjarnson. See Wendy Jeffers, "Holger Cahill and American Folk Art," *Antiques*, September 1, 1995. Most of my account of Cahill is based on Jeffers's research. See also Vivien Raynor, "Establishing Folk Art's Pedigree," *New York Times*, February 12, 1995.

168 For over sixty years Milton C. Rose (1904–2002) practiced trust and estate law at Mudge Rose Guthrie Alexander & Ferdon. Before bringing in Nixon, Rose had already brought John N. Mitchell, Nixon's future attorney general, into the firm in 1967. Rose was very proud of the business Nixon brought into the firm. By 1967 the firm had changed its name to put Nixon first: Nixon Mudge Rose Guthrie & Alexander. In 1969 President Nixon appointed Mitchell (who had managed his campaign) U.S. Attorney General. See the obituary of Milton Rose, *New York Times*, March 21, 2002.

169 Minutes of the meeting of the Board of Trustees of HSV, March 30, 1963, HSV archives.

170 Amy Bess Miller's summary "firing" of Faith Andrews is documented in, among other places, Faith Andrews, "The Hancock Story," typescript, Pittsfield, Mass., 1983, 9759 A565, HSV archives. Since various copies of "Hancock Story" have been repaginated by hand and since several copies have pages missing, I have not supplied page references for this short document. Faith's typescript includes photocopied documents. Some copies of "The Hancock Story" have marginal comments made by Faith after she had prepared the original typescript. Scores of original documents (including my own letters) have been photocopied for other collections with no calendar specifying the location of the originals, let alone variants. Unless otherwise noted, I have used the version in the HSV archives.

171 Memorandum "Report and Recommendation," from the Conciliation Committee to Frederic G. Crane, chairman of the Executive Committee of the Board of Trustees, undated but within a week of the meeting of May 22, 1963, HSV archives. The memorandum is an attachment to the minutes of the Special Meeting of the Board of Trustees, held on August 2, 1963, "to hear the report and recommendation of the Conciliation Committee, to hear the recommendations of the Executive Committee, and to take action."

172 Glover's farrago of falsehoods did not all appear in the minutes of that meeting and I reported them in detail to EDA, who refuted Glover's statements in a private memo to me. EDA to Mario S. De Pillis, June 18, 1963, De Pillis collection. For Glover's statements, see the "Minutes of the Shaker Community Conciliation Committee's Meeting with Dr. W. H. Glover," May 22, 1963, HSV archives and De Pillis collection.

173 Memorandum from the Conciliation Committee to Frederick G. Crane, Chairman, Executive Committee of the Board of Trustees," May 1963 with Appended Statement, HSV archives.

174 Frederick G. Crane, chairman of the Executive Committee, to Mrs. Lawrence K. Miller, July 3, 1963, HSV archives.

175 Minutes of the special meeting of the board of trustees, August 2, 1963, HSV archives. Amy Bess Miller amended the typescript of the minutes to remove Lawrence R. Connor's intemperate anti-Andrews comments ("Mr. Connor said that . . . we shouldn't be 'scared' of the Andrewses [and] . . . that we shouldn't play around with prima donnas"). The two no votes were David Volk Andrews and Catherine White. My abstention was not recorded.

176 Andrews, "Hancock Story." Although already physically gone from the village by the summer of 1963, EDA rejected the humiliating offer of figurehead "consultant." See his letter in ibid.

177 EDA to Mrs. Lawrence K. Miller, August 9, 1963, HSV Archives.

178 Amy Bess Miller, handwritten memo (to herself) of the meeting of August 23, 1963, dictated on August 26, 1963 to a typist, 2, HSV archives. The typescript version omits some words and phrases and adds others.

179 Amy Bess Miller, memo, Re: Andrews Collection, September 11, 1963, ibid.

180 Amy Bess Miller to David Volk Andrews, July 18, 1962, HSV archives.

181 Faith Andrews, in "Hancock Story," describes Faison's blunt assertion of the power of the "directors of the Shaker Community, Inc." over mere employees like the Andrewses. My report to the Andrewses on the December 14, 1963, board meeting, in a letter to them dated January 14, 1964, includes notes on Faison's hostilities; a carbon copy is in the De Pillis collection. Faith quotes one of my defenses (included in the minutes only after I had vigorously demanded its inclusion) in "Hancock Story." Faison's interventions against the Andrewses are well documented in EDA's correspondence in the De Pillis collection. For EDA's instructions to me, as his representative, regarding Faison, see EDA to Mario S. De Pillis, April 15, 1963, De Pillis collection. For Faison, see the obituary by Douglas Martin, "S. Lane Faison Jr., 98, Dies; Art Historian and Professor," *New York Times*, November 14, 2006. Having taken time off from college, Pete Miller graduated (class of 1931) two years after his friend Faison.

182 Amy Bess Miller did not make arrangements for the preservation of her papers and not all of them have remained at the HSV archives.

183 EDA to Mario S. De Pillis, April 15, 1963, De Pillis collection.

184 EDA to Mario S. De Pillis, November 2, 1963, De Pillis collection.

185 Agreement between Edward Deming Andrews and Faith Y. Andrews and Shaker Community, Inc. (the Corporation), January 28, 1964, HSV archives.

186 As the sole sympathetic member of the Board of Trustees I felt helpless to defend actions taken against EDA, none of which came before the board.

187 EDA to Mario S. De Pillis, November 2, 1963, De Pillis collection.

188 EDA and Faith Andrews, "Prospectus for a Museum of the American Shakers." HSV archives. Amy Bess Miller thought that the Andrewses may already have planned for a way to preserve Shaker materials as early as July 1932, when they organized an exhibition of Shaker furniture and artifacts at the Berkshire Museum in Pittsfield, Massachusetts. Miller, *Hancock Shaker Village*, 20. But she very probably confused EDA's later proposals with Laura Bragg's 1932 plan for the Society for the Preservation of Shaker Antiquities, discussed earlier in the text.

189 "Scarborough Address," June 7, 1957, 5, EDAMSC. The reference to Albert Schweitzer strikes a false note. In the 1950s citing the name of Albert Schweitzer was a way of invoking the value of religion as a humanitarian activity. Spiritually the Shakers were far removed from Schweitzer's beliefs.

190 EDA, "Prospectus for a Museum of Shaker Cultural History," draft of an essay, handwritten on yellow legal-pad paper, 3–5, EDAMC. The list appears in other places and includes: "1. The doctrine of perfectionism, particularly in all kinds of workmanship. 2. The virtues of simplicity and humility. 3. The practice of scrupulous neatness and order. 4. Charity and hospitality. The 'right use of property.' 5. Racial and religious tolerance." His wording in this manuscript differs from a final version of his list of Shaker virtues quoted extensively in the final section of this essay. This draft prospectus is not to be confused with EDA's final version of April 4, 1958, entitled "A Project in Shaker Conservation," typescript, box 1, Restricted, EDAMSC, which was the seed for the eventual restoration of HSV. EDA proposed the village as a home for the collection.

191 EDA, "Prospectus," 1.

192 EDA and Faith Andrews, "Sheeler and the Shakers," 95. Though Faith signed jointly as the author, Ted wrote the text.

193 Andrews, "Hancock Story." Faith is quoting from EDA's "Report of the Curator," p. 8 of the minutes of July 28, 1962.

194 Homer Eaton Keyes to EDA, February 2, 1934, EDAMSC.

195 Andrews and Andrews, *Fruits*, 170. This statement occurs in an entire chapter devoted to Merton. As E. Richard McKinstry notes, the common interest was the Shakers "as part of a larger spiritual community." McKinstry, comp., *The Edward Deming Andrews Memorial Shaker Collection* (Published for the Henry Francis DuPont Winterthur Museum; New York: Garland, 1987), 311. Stephen Stein expressed his disdain for both Merton and EDA in the first sentence

of his book, *Shaker Experience in America*, unaware of their revealing friendship—rooted in their common admiration for Shaker religion and culture.

196 Thomas Merton to EDA, December 12, 1960, EDAMSC.

197 Andrews, interview by Brown, 54–55. Coomaraswamy brought along his fifth wife and left it to Faith to take care of the wife and their sick dog and do the cooking.

198 Ibid., 110; emphasis in the original. EDA used the term "spiritual drawing," but Daniel W. Patterson proposed the term "gift drawings" in his *Gift Drawing and Gift Song: A Study of Two Forms of Shaker Inspiration* (Sabbathday Lake, Me.: United Society of Shakers, 1983), basing his interpretation of the meaning of the words "spirit drawings" and "inspirational drawings" and the Shakers' use of the word "gift" (xi). Most writers on Shaker topics now accept Patterson's term.

199 Miller, *Hancock Shaker Village*, 146.

200 I have documented various instances of attempts to undermine EDA's work in other parts of this essay, but a convenient summary of the situation at the very end of the Andrewses' tenure may be found in the minutes of the meeting of the Board of Trustees of HSV, March 30, 1963, HSV archives. It does contain false statements by Glover and Amy Bess Miller, as well the preposterous statement by Faison that the Andrewses' donor agreement did not give the Andrewses the right to take over the "direction" of the entire Shaker Community, Inc. Amy Bess Miller heavily edited the minutes of March 30, 1963, to remove extremely prejudiced statements against the Andrewses. See her handwritten alterations in the draft typescript, HSV archives. The Andrewses' attorney, John MacGruer, was especially concerned about the alteration of these and subsequent minutes. EDA to Mario S. De Pillis, April 18 and April 22, 1963.

201 Amy Bess Miller to Frederick W. Beinecke, January 7, 1963, HSV archives.

202 Ibid., March 5, 1963.

203 Mrs. Lawrence K. Miller, president, to Frederick G. Crane, December 26, 1963, HSV archives.

204 See the documents in Miller, "Hancock Story."

205 New Haven, Conn., August 1960. Amy Bess Miller later asserted that EDA wrote the brochure "with" Carl Purington Rollins and his wife, Margaret. Miller, *Hancock Shaker Village*, 26. Actually EDA wrote it alone. Preliminary drafts in EDA's handwriting are in EDAMSC. Rollins, Printer to Yale University and a prominent typographer, designed the brochure and saw to its printing but did none of the writing. Amy Bess Miller described this eight-page brochure as a powerful part of the initial fundraising effort: a letter that went out to twelve hundred potential supporters. The letter proudly stated that arrangements had been made to acquire the important collection of Dr. and Mrs. Andrews. She did not mention that much of EDA's pamphlet was devoted to using the village and its collections as an educational tool (a prudent omission)—or that EDA had been the original proponent of the restoration. Miller, *Hancock Shaker Village*, 26.

206 In the class outline, EDA emphasized that the purpose of collecting artifacts was to understand the importance of a given culture, and to do so, as in the case of the Shakers "before it becomes extinct." EDA, "Notes for first seminar at Yale (Library 2/27) [1957?]," index cards, handwritten, card 1, EDAMSC.

207 Ann Andrews Kane, e-mail message to the author, March 13, 2006, De Pillis collection; Margaret Rollins to Newton F. McKeon, January 29, 1965, Amherst College archives. Taking the side of Amy Bess Miller, Rollins wrote: "In the final settlement with Ted, we retained all that had been turned in to us freely plus 5 cartons of day books, records books, etc, which the Andrews attempted to claim as 'personal property.' Actually the deed of gift states that they give everything they possess pertaining to the Shakers." Rollins added: "Now the shaker museum has no legal claim on anything not in its possession—according to Amy Bess Miller, 'no claim except a moral claim.'!"

208 Amy Bess Miller, introduction to John Harlow Ott, *Hancock Shaker Village: A Guidebook and History* (Hancock, Mass.: Hancock Shaker Village, 1976), 9.

209 Miller, interview by Vadnais, digital recording on CD, HSV archives.

210 Faith Andrews to Thomas Merton, August 18, 1964, EDAMSC, photocopy of original at the Abbey of Gethsemane. Emphasis in the original.

211 Margaret Rollins, still a board member in 1964, mentioned a supposed offer to Williams College in a letter to Newton F. McKeon, January 29, 1965, Amherst College Archives. Rollins wrote that in September 1964 Faith had "offered the 'Andrews library' to Williams College—with the stipulations as to its set-up and use. Fred Rudolph called Amy Bess about this." Frederick Rudolph (b. 1920) was a prominent professor of history at Williams and became a trustee of Hancock in the 1970s. In an interview with the author on December 9, 2007, Rudolph did not recall any

subsequent negotiations—let alone the phone call of forty-three years before. There is no further mention of it after the phone call, and Amy Bess may have discouraged the offer.

212 McKeon's memorandum to himself on Faith's talk with President Calvin Plimpton and later with Associate Library Director Charles T. Laugher, on her "considering giving the collection to Amherst," in the "Mrs. Edward D. Andrews folder," Newton F. McKeon file, Amherst College Archives. The quoted text is the entire memo.

213 Newton F. McKeon to Faith Andrews, October 9, 1964, ibid.

214 Faith Andrews to Calvin H. Plimpton, October 28, 1964; Newton F. McKeon to Faith Andrews, December 7, 1964, ibid.

215 Newton F. McKeon to Faith Andrews, October 9, 1964, and December 31, 1964, ibid.

216 Calvin H. Plimpton to Amy Bess Miller, January 20, 1965, ibid.

217 Amy Bess Miller to Calvin Plimpton, January 27, 1965, ibid.

218 Faith Andrews to Newton F. McKeon, January 27, 1965, ibid

219 Faith Andrews to Mario S. De Pillis, January 11, 1965, De Pillis collection.

220 Faith Andrews to Newton F. McKeon April 11, 1966; McKeon responded immediately on April 13 with an understanding and sympathetic letter, Amherst College Archives.

221 Faith Andrews to Henry Steele Commager, November 18, 1976, Commager Papers, ibid.

222 In the Andrews interview by Brown, 167, Faith asserted that the person inviting them in 1957 was Joseph Downs, but Downs had died in 1954. Thus, the person inviting them must have been Ted's great admirer, Charles Montgomery, who succeeded Downs as director of the Winterthur Museum. Montgomery served from 1954 to 1961. See also John Sweeney to EDA, November 5, 1957, EDAMSC. Nevertheless, the Andrewses did know Downs, who had acquired Shaker objects for Winterthur and had received advice from the Andrewses.

223 Charles F. Montgomery to Mrs. Lawrence K. Miller, April 11, 1962, box 1, Restricted, EDAMSC. Oddly, Montgomery addressed the letter to Amy Bess Miller's home address. The lecture is available on a CD (misdated May 11) in the HSV archives.

224 A minor dispute in March 1964 briefly muddied relations. A few weeks before his death EDA wrote to John Sweeney, curator at Winterthur: "Now that the legal ends of our 'community' experiment have been tied up, we would like very much to clear the record on the matter of Joe Butler's report to Madam President. . . . We are soon to send our letter of resignation as members of the board and would like to include a clarifying statement from Mr. Butler. It is an unpleasant subject and we regret to have to involve you in any way—however, it rankles in our minds and I am afraid will until it is righted." EDA to John Sweeney, March 20, 1964, EDAMSC.

Sweeney died in May 2007, so that I could not ask him to explain the issue of Joe Butler's misrepresentations. About a year before Sweeney's death, Christian Goodwillie conducted an interview with Sweeney that throws light on the relationship of the Andrewses to Winterthur. See John Sweeney, interview by Christian Goodwillie, tape and CD, HSV archives.

225 Andrews, interview by Brown, 161.

226 Faith Andrews to Thomas Merton, December 7, 1964, EDAMSC; photocopy of original at the Abbey of Gethsemane.

227 Mrs. Edward Deming Andrews to Mrs. Lawrence K. Miller, September 12, 1964, HSV archives.

228 Copy of an untitled museum rule with Amy Bess Miller's handwritten annotation ordering her staff to require Faith's strict compliance, typescript dated September 8, 1964, HSV archives.

229 Andrews, interview by Brown, 78.

230 EDA to Mario S. De Pillis, April 13, 1963, De Pillis collection.

231 EDA to Thomas Merton, November 19, 1963, photocopy from original in the Abbey of Gethsemane. See also Faith Andrews to Barry Bingham, January 11, 1964, EDAMSC.

232 Nevertheless, I did once write a blunt criticism of their insistence (mainly Ted's) on using the collection as an educational tool. See Mario S. De Pillis to EDA, December 31, 1958, De Pillis collection.

233 Olive H. Austin to Faith Andrews, March 15, 1970, EDAMSC.

Staircase, First Loft,
Brick Dwelling,
Hancock,
Massachusetts, 1830,
photographed by
William F. Winter
ca. 1930.

Courtesy, The Winterthur
Library: The Edward
Deming Andrews Memorial
Shaker Collection,
No. SA 469

The Andrewses and The Shakers

By Christian Goodwillie

Edward Deming Andrews ca. 1922.
Collection of the Family of David V. and Phyllis C. Andrews

Buried deep within the voluminous archives of the Edward Deming Andrews Memorial Shaker Collection at Winterthur lies an unpublished manuscript in Faith Andrews's hand. Written sometime after 1981, this unfinished reminiscence of the Andrewses' life and work contains a telling line—crossed out immediately after it was written. Describing the Andrewses' 1923 entrance into the Brick Dwelling at Hancock, Massachusetts, she wrote: "Pandora's box was empty compared with our first glimpse beyond the kitchen door."[1] Perhaps the realization that this was the moment at which their life's work began, coupled with memories of the broad range of emotions unleashed, caused her to rethink the statement. According to the Greek myth, the contents of Pandora's Box included greed, vanity, slander, lies, envy, pining and—remaining at the bottom after the others had been unleashed—hope. In truth, the comparison of Pandora's Box to the beginnings of the Andrewses' relationship with the Shakers could not have been more appropriate. While this idea may seem hyperbolic in relation to some of the earliest scholars of Shakerism and collectors of Shaker objects, the complexity of the Andrewses' career, and the personal relationships involved, brought up all of these emotions. However, this aspect of the Andrewses' story has been overemphasized in recent years by revisionist scholars who tend to downplay the essential facts pertinent to the Andrewses, as well as the enormity of their accomplishments.

Edward Deming and Faith Andrews revered Shaker religion, life, culture, and material culture. Together the couple made the pursuit of all things Shaker the central, consuming passion of their lives. They befriended the Shakers. They purchased objects, they sold objects, and they gave away objects. They wrote more on topics related to the Shakers than anyone has since, or likely ever will again. It is to them, that we who study the Shakers owe the existence of major collections at five institutions and in numerous private holdings. Had the Andrewses not pursued these objects many would likely not exist today. Despite this simple fact, the politics of the "Shaker world" preclude easy extensions of gratitude. Some cannot consider the Andrewses without negative notions, although detractors may not understand the origin of such perceptions. Many of these perceptions stem from the Andrewses' dealings with the Shakers themselves. This essay attempts to document and contextualize the complex relationship between the Andrewses and the Shakers. Perhaps an honest reassessment of the Andrewses' relations with the Shakers will provide a firmer foundation from which to assess their achievements.

As a child growing up in Pittsfield, Massachusetts, Faith Andrews was aware of the Shakers. In an interview in 1982 she recalled her mother's warning: when walking on Pittsfield's main thoroughfare, North Street, "if I met the Shakers I must be polite but not stop them and not want to talk and not stare. I never forgot that. Little did I know what they would mean to me later."[2] Faith's mother had attended Shaker meetings at Hancock before worship services were closed to the public.[3] Mario S. De Pillis has demonstrated that Ted Andrews wrote of his interest in the Shakers as early as 1919. Clearly, despite the dwindling number of Believers at Hancock, Massachusetts, and Mount Lebanon, New York, the Shakers remained in the consciousness of people in the Berkshires.

Edward Deming Andrews met Faith Young at a dance in Pittsfield in 1919. Faith decided to go to the dance alone in the hope of meeting someone, a bold move for a young woman at that time. Ted had just completed his service in the army and was looking for a teaching job. The couple married in 1921 and moved to Concord, Massachusetts, where Ted found employment. In the summer they returned to the Berkshires, living in the Andrews family home, a large Victorian house in Pittsfield. Their passion for antique collecting grew as they toured New England in a Model T Ford looking for early American furniture. As Faith described it: "We had quite a good start with early, very fine early American things. There was no end to our collecting. We found very fine Queen Anne pieces. We found highboys, and we were able to document everything. We found paintings, early American paintings, it was a whole new world opening up." She recalled a particularly fine highboy acquired in Stephentown, New York. Upon meeting the woman who had sold it Faith was told: "Yes, your husband was here. He went through this house like a dose of salt." During those summers the Andrewses earned extra cash running an antique business out of their house in Pittsfield. They kept notes on where and from whom they acquired each piece, forming a habit for the careful documentation they practiced while building their Shaker collection.[4]

The story of the Andrewses' first encounter with the Shakers at Hancock in September 1923 has been retold many times. Contrary to popular belief, they did not enter the Brick Dwelling on their first visit to buy a loaf of bread but rather were asked inside on the second visit.[5] The Pandora's Box opened on that day contained not only Shaker objects but living Shakers, whose personalities and internecine "family" squabbles would bear heavily on the Andrewses' increasing efforts to acquire all things Shaker. It is notable that the first Shaker with whom they became personally acquainted, Sister Alice Smith, would be among the most controversial.

By the time of the Andrewses' first contact with the community at Hancock in 1923, the Shakers had been in a steady decline since the 1850s, and there were only six remaining Shaker villages: Mount Lebanon and Watervliet, New York; Hancock, Massachusetts; Canterbury, New Hampshire (the last members of the Enfield, New Hampshire, community relocated to Canterbury that year) and Alfred and Sabbathday Lake, Maine.[6] The dissolution of some of the eastern, and all the western, Shaker societies, as well as the cooperation of leading Shakers from Mount Lebanon, had made a large amount of manuscript and printed material available to collectors and dealers. Wallace Cathcart, John Patterson MacLean, H. H. Ballard, Edward B. Wight, Walter F. Prince, and Clara Endicott Sears blazed a trail early in the twentieth century by gathering Shaker materials for institutions and private collections. Although the Andrewses began collecting later, they were able to gather materials of equal (and often greater) importance than these earlier collectors. Their success is due in part to the length of their interaction with the Shakers and in part to the fact that the communities at

The original south door of the 1830 Brick Dwelling at Hancock, Massachusetts. This is the door through which the Andrewses entered when they first met the Shakers in 1923. Collection of Hancock Shaker Village

Mount Lebanon, Hancock, and Alfred closed during this interaction. Some people, a few Shakers among them, have perceived the Andrewses as "culture-vultures" who circled the decaying villages, befriended aging members, and waited for the chance to pick the carcass clean. This view has been grossly inflated and reinforced in recent scholarship through selective quotations of original source materials by those seeking to build their own reputations as scholars of Shakerism by undermining the Andrewses' character and, by extension, their work. However, there does appear to be some justification for these more negative views of the Andrewses in Shaker sources, as well as in the Andrewses' own writings.

Collecting is, by its nature, competitive and can sometimes be a dirty business where perceptions of greed and favoritism sow the seeds of distrust and enmity. Shaker families were not immune to these influences. Their members, though termed "brother" and "sister" by faith, were not above seeking their own interests first, often at the expense of others in their own family. The ties of blood shaped the "sisterhood" of Sadie and Emma Neale of Mount Lebanon's Church Family in a different and even more complex dynamic than what one finds among those Shakers unrelated by biological kinship. In their relationships with these Shaker families and their members, the Andrewses entered a minefield studded with explosive issues of hierarchy—and by extension the legitimate authority for the disposal of community property, as well as personal relationships colored by generational differences. Along the way the Andrewses were confronted numerous times with opportunities requiring decisions—based on an interpersonal cost-benefit analysis. The cost-benefit equation usually comprised the cost to their personal relations or friendship with a particular Shaker (or their reputation in the Shaker family as a whole) and the possible benefit to their ambitions as collectors and scholars. This was the reality of doing business under the magnified scrutiny of Shaker families with relatively few members that were edging toward extinction.

A key difference between the Andrewses and other early collectors are the conditions under which they operated. Unlike Sears, Cathcart, Prince, or Ballard, they were not collecting under the auspices of an institution (in Sears's case, the institution was of her own founding). This fact has bothered some critics of the Andrewses, particularly since the Andrewses actively participated in buying, selling, and trading Shaker materials. These critics must then place men such as John Patterson MacLean and Edward B. Wight in that same arena, because they too were involved in dealing Shaker materials during their own activities as collectors and scholars. The Andrewses' tangled relationships with a multitude of public institutions is exhaustively documented in Mario S. De Pillis's essay in this volume. The Andrewses' efforts to collect and study the Shaker materials were in large part limited only by their own creativity in devising ways in which to acquire, document, and disperse Shaker objects. This freedom from an overarching framework of institutional boundaries and employment obligations was probably a major factor in their prodigious achievements as authors, collectors, and independent authorities on the Shakers and their culture.

According to Faith Andrews's later account, Sister Alice Smith was the Andrewses' first friend among the Shakers. Smith had been brought to the Hancock Shakers in 1893 as a girl of nine. Born in Norwich, Connecticut, in 1884, she signed the Church Family covenant in 1905 and grew to become one of the important "burden bearers" in a Shaker family comprised mostly of young girls and elderly women. It seems to have been Sister Alice who answered the door on both the first and the fateful second visit by the Andrewses to Hancock. It is worth recounting in full Faith's later recollection of the crucial moment that they entered the 1830 Brick Dwelling on their second visit: "The second time we went back for more bread, we were asked to go into the kitchen and sit down while they prepared the packaging. And what we saw was a great shock to us. It was like stepping back into a medieval home. The kitchen had a stone floor and the built-in arches. It was like nothing we had ever seen. That was the beginning."[7]

Ethel (left) and Alice Smith (right) photographed ca. 1895. Ethel would eventually leave the Hancock Shakers, but Alice remained at the community until her death in 1935.

Courtesy, The Winterthur Library: The Edward Deming Andrews Memorial Shaker Collection, No. SA 59

Although Alice was certainly a dedicated sister, authoring a manuscript about Hancock entitled "History of Our Home,"[8] she welcomed the attentions of a young, attractive couple from outside her sequestered family. As the couple put it in their memoir *Fruits of the Shaker Tree of Life*: "There was nobody left in the family with whom she could share her thoughts. She was waiting, it seemed for someone else who cared."[9] Through her the Andrewses were able to gain access to many buildings at the relatively dormant village of Hancock.

The first Shaker object the Andrewses acquired at Hancock was a turned wooden bowl (page 102).[10] As Faith recalled: "Gradually we got through Sister Alice to meet the rest of them, only five or six then and they were elderly with the exception of Alice and another sister and we got to know them very well. They were a poor family. There was money, but not available to that particular family and so the few things that they—well they had many things to sell, they weren't using because they were getting fewer in number every day and there were locked rooms [we] were eventually taken into and almost anything had its price that we wanted to ask about."[11] It is unclear who had the authority to determine the price and availability of items the Andrewses were interested in acquiring. One of the central tenets of Shaker belief is that property is owned in common. This belief is expressed in *The Testimony of Christ's Second Appearing* as follows: "All the Believers, who came together in the full order and covenant of a Church relation, possessed all things jointly; neither said any of them that ought of the things which he possessed was his own; but every thing was possessed in a perfect law of justice and equity, by all the members."[12] The authority for disposal of property held in common is made explicit in the following section of the Shaker *Compendium*: "All the consecrated property of the Society is held in trust by trustees belonging to each community."[13] However, as with most issues in regard to Shakerism, different practices seem to have prevailed at different times in different communities.

The issue of authority is further complicated by the changing nature of the Central Ministry and Trustees' Order in the late nineteenth and early twentieth centuries. Following the closing of the period of the "first parents" of the Shaker gospel, considered to have ended with the death of Father James Whittaker in 1787, there was a clear need for a structured hierarchy of leadership within the Shaker movement. Initially organized by Father Joseph Meacham at New Lebanon, New York, in 1787, the Ministry (subsequently referred to as Central, or Parent) typically consisted of two Elders and two Eldresses. This Central Ministry had spiritual oversight of all the Shaker communities established during the eighteenth and nineteenth centuries. The Shaker communities were then organized into Bishoprics—clusters of two or three communities usually in geographic proximity to one another. Each of these Bishoprics had its own Ministry, answerable to the Central Ministry at New Lebanon. The Bishopric Ministry would regularly travel among the communities under their jurisdiction, making appointments of Elders, Eldresses, and Trustees in the families within those communities.

As the nineteenth century wore on, and Shaker villages began to close, many of the properties were sold, and leadership duties were consolidated. The Hancock Bishopric Ministry was formally dissolved in 1893. The day book kept by an unidentified Shaker at Hancock recorded the change: "June 18, 1893: The Hancock Ministry is abolished. The Ministry of Mt Lebanon take henceforth Mt Lebanon, Watervliet, Hancock and Enfield under their charge."[14]

Eldress Frances Hall seated outside the Trustees' Office at Hanock, Massachusetts, ca. 1930.
Collection of Hancock Shaker Village 1987.2265

The result of this consolidation was the creation of a combined Central (or Parent) Ministry that had authority over all the remaining Shaker communities, as well as local authority for the four communities remaining of the old First and Second Bishoprics: Mount Lebanon and Watervliet, New York; Enfield, Connecticut (closed in 1916); and Hancock, Massachusetts. Elder Joseph Holden had moved from Mount Lebanon to Hancock in 1892 to represent the combined Ministry at that community. After the Hancock Trustee Ira Lawson died in 1905, Elder Holden assumed a dual role as Central Ministry Elder and, specifically, Trustee for the Hancock community. He filled this dual role until his death on April 24, 1919. On May 8, 1919, Sister Mary Frances Hall of Hancock was appointed Trustee for that Society. In 1923, the year of the Andrewses' first visit to Hancock, none of the members of the Central Ministry was in residence there. And none did reside there until 1939 when Hall was appointed a member of the Central Ministry.[15]

Final authority for the disposition of materials owned by the Hancock Shakers should have been in her hands. However, this does not seem to have been the case. In the absence of written documentation from the early twentieth century at Hancock, much about this period can only be gleaned from the reminiscences of eyewitnesses to those days. From sources both inside and outside the Shaker community at Hancock it is clear that relations were not good between members living in the Brick Dwelling of the Church Family and Trustee Frances Hall.

Eldress Fannie Estabrook standing outside the Brick Dwelling at Hancock, Massachusetts, July 10, 1931.
Collection of Hancock Shaker Village 1987.2285

Caroline Helfrich was the Eldress at the Church Family at Hancock until her death in 1929. Fannie Estabrook was appointed Eldress in 1929 and served in that capacity until her death in September 1960 (the community closed on October 14, 1960). Because of the lack of cooperation between the Church Family Eldresses and Trustee Frances Hall, the Andrewses by default should have been dealing mainly with Eldresses Caroline and Fannie as the officially appointed leaders of the Church Family. The Eldresses in turn should have sought the approval of Trustee Frances Hall for the sale of any items from the community. From the surviving evidence this protocol was rarely, if ever, observed.

One witness to these times was Clara Sperle (later Clair Zeitlin), a young girl from Yonkers, New York, who was brought to live with the Hancock Shakers by her father after her mother's death from tuberculosis. Clair arrived at Hancock on Halloween night of 1925.[16] When interviewed in 2005 she had not been in contact with the Shakers, or the "world of Shaker," since her last visits to Hancock in the late 1940s. Clair's reminiscences proved to be remarkable in terms of her unprompted recall of names, places, and personalities at Hancock and within the wider Shaker world of the 1920s and 1930s, including Elders Walter Shepherd and Arthur Bruce, and Eldress Prudence Stickney—none of whom was in residence at Hancock.

Each girl in the care of the Hancock community was overseen by a specific Sister. Clair was overseen by Eldress Fannie Estabrook and had the opportunity to be in her company during most days. Clair had much to say about the presence of the Andrewses at the "brick house" (as she referred to the 1830 Brick Dwelling).

Clair Zeitlin: I know you know all about Mr. Andrews. Edward and Faith Andrews. I always wanted to look like his wife. She was tall and willowy. She was just beautiful. Little girls always have ideal women that they'd like to be. I said, "Oh, she is so pretty." Well, Mr. Andrews bought up a lot of Shaker furniture, and some of it was unbeknown to who was supposed to be in charge of that kind of work, of selling them. If there was anything to be sold it was to go through, like, if they went to Eldress Fannie and said, "I want to buy this little table," see, but there was a lot of little things that were under the table, if you know what I'm trying to say. And Alice was in with them, she was very friendly with them. So, she was going along with some of that and she shouldn't have, and Eldress Fannie found it out and she said, "You don't sell this furniture under-handed like that, it doesn't get sold." But they were kind of under the table, you know, she was selling them low, Alice was. And Mr. Andrews had a home out in Pittsfield. And we used to go out when we were shopping or something, Eldress Fannie and I, we'd stop off, you know, to rest a little bit and so forth, so—every piece of Shaker furniture they had was in there.

Christian Goodwillie: So Eldress Fannie could see.

Clair Zeitlin: Sure she could see. That's why we stopped off there occasionally, 'cause she'd say "What's going on?" See there's no need to steal from them. You don't need to steal from anybody, just ask, you know, and if it's reasonable, and they can work things out—

Christian Goodwillie: So did Alice get in trouble then with Fannie?

Clair Zeitlin: I imagine she got told. But there was never any fighting or yelling or none of the quarreling, none of that was ever there [in the Brick Dwelling], that was taken care of I guess down at the office.

Clair entered the community at the age of eight and left at the age of nineteen. However, despite her young age, she seems to have been unusually perceptive with regard to the internal politics of the Hancock community, particularly the relationship between Alice Smith and Frances Hall. She stated the following about Frances Hall:

> Well, she wasn't a Shaker, she wasn't really a dyed-in-the-wool Shaker, she was but she wasn't, you know what I mean, I don't know maybe when she was a girl she was more devout or something, but anyways, she was in the Trustees— Elder Arthur and Elder Shepherd, Walter Shepherd, See I'm just a kid only 10, 12 years old so I don't know the details, all I know is that Eldress Fannie would come down and say so you go out and play on the swings till I get through— There was some cahootsie stuff going on between her [Alice] and Frances. I don't know how to put it, they weren't going through the right channels. Alice would take it upon herself to sell some furniture which she had no business to do.[17]

Eldress Fannie Estabrook with Clara Sperle (later Clair Zeitlin) in 1928.
Collection of Hancock Shaker Village 1990.4386

It is indisputable that Alice Smith was the conduit through which a huge amount of furniture and other materials was sold out of the Hancock Shaker community. Whether she had the authority to dispose of such materials is open to debate. A comparison of the way in which she dealt with Charles C. Adams, director of the New York State Museum, and how she dealt with the Andrewses provides helpful insights into the complexities of selling communal property. Her dealings with the Andrewses in the 1920s are barely documented. However, by the early 1930s she was working quite openly with Charles Adams in assembling and building an outstanding collection of Shaker materials. An excerpt from one of the earliest instances of their correspondence seems to indicate that Smith was aboveboard in her dealings.

Nov. 1 1931.
Dear Doctor Adams:
    I have talked with Eldress Fannie—about the different things you wish to have, and she is willing to let you have anything we can spare— but she thinks as I do—that the best thing to do is for us to come to Albany, look the things over—also get a better idea of what you need.
    It really is a "<u>huge</u>" job to find out about it all—the more I study it, the more I marvel at the work the older & early Shakers accomplished.

Be assured I will do all I can to help you—and wish I was able to do more—but feel that we can do quite well—even at this late day.

Wishing you success—I am

Very cordially yours—

Alice M. Smith

Additionally, a tripod stand with a single drawer bearing a gift inscription from Eldress Fannie Estabrook to the Andrewses dated Christmas 1930 also belies Clair Zeitlin's perception that Eldress Fannie was opposed to helping the Andrewses build their collection (page 179). However, as much as the Andrewses were welcomed to the Hancock community and brought into the secluded confines of the Brick Dwelling, their position as outsiders was subtly reinforced. Faith Andrews remembered ruefully: "When we ate at Hancock, it was in the Ministry dining room, which we were rather inclined not to like, because it isolated us from the rest of the family. But we realized it was an honor."[18] Faith Andrews let time soften the blow of this gesture, recasting it as a privilege to have eaten where the Ministry had once taken their meals. In reality, it was an honor to be asked to stay and dine "with" the Shakers, but the separation of the Andrewses from the family was plain. Clair Zeitlin later recalled the glee with which, as a child, she had noted the Andrewses' disappointment at supping apart from the Shakers.

Sister Lillian Barlow and Brother William Perkins at Mount Lebanon's Second Family ca. 1930.

Collection of Hancock Shaker Village 1989.3947 (Barlow), 1992.5672 (Perkins)

The first evidence of any interaction between the Andrewses and any of the Mount Lebanon families is in a pair of letters written to Ted and Faith by Sister Lillian Barlow and her co-worker William Perkins at Mount Lebanon's Second Family in 1929. These letters shed light on the relationship, and specifically the Second Family's reaction to the Andrewses' first published article in the August 1928 issue of The Magazine *Antiques*.

Jan 5th /29

Mr & Mrs Andrews,

Dear friends,

You have had our best wishes for the season all the time, and moreover I have attempted several times to tell you in writing, and failed. Christmas founds us all very worn and tired largely because the spirit of Christmas does not prevail in the Shaker Village, and past Christmases have been frought with much sorrow.

Yours was one of the very few greetings which had any meaning of the real spirit of Christmas, and free from balderdash.

For yourselves we have great respect to use no larger term, and your comings are very welcome, and it is fine to see your close affection for each other. My best wish for you is—that you may write something of your selves into the common page of life that others may profit thereby. Human relationships at their best have always something divine in them, and you are able to bear witness to this. I trust this is not too personal a letter, and that you will understand I mean every word of it, nay more, that it merely points to what I would have you understand of ourselves. So we wish that for you every day may find a new birth of the Christ spirit, and every day a new opportunity for doing good.

Yours sincerely,

Sister Lillian & Bro. William

"Every day is a fresh beginning,

Every day is the world made new.

Susan Coolidge."

March 19th/29

Mr. E.D. Andrews

Dear Friend,

I want to tell you now why I like your essay on "Shaker Arts and Crafts."

It is distinctly different from anything I have ever read on the subject.

It shows the patient delving into a subject you have considered worth while; and a honest expression of what you <u>really know</u> with characteristic gentleness. It is kind. It is free from subtle flattery so many people find necessary to boost semi-truthful statements. Usually we find in other writings about the Shakers cheap opinions by superficial observers in which truth has little part, mostly intended to bring the writer financial gain, or a mere publicity, the true subject matter being almost entirely neglected.

But you have come to know us intimately. You are familiar with our daily life. You have seen the sunshine as well as the shaddow, as well as the struggles of our difficult life. You have caught some of the blessedness we feel in our brother and sister associations; the joy of unselfish companionship, and the share and share alike of everything that is good.

As a literary achievement it is fine; but not a whit better than what we hope for and have a right to expect from your combination.

You see—while you were learning to know us, we were exercising our privileged opportunity to know you as close patient and persistent observers well able to arrange facts in an interesting and orderly manner.

Our good Sister Lillian joins me in this appreciation and all good wishes for future successes.

Yours sincerely,

Sister Lillian and W.A. Perkins

Will return the writing in the near future. WAP.

[overleaf] Sister Lillian has found the key to desk[19]

Sisters Emma (seated) and Sadie Neale at Mount Lebanon, New York, ca. 1930.

Courtesy, The Winterthur Library: The Edward Deming Andrews Memorial Shaker Collection, No. SA 4

Faith Andrews credited Alice Smith with laying the groundwork for the Andrewses' first visit to the Church Family at Mount Lebanon. There they met the Neale sisters, Sadie and Emma. Faith described them thus:

They were a great pair. They were blood sisters, so it happened toward the end of their Shaker life they were living together in the one family for the first time and like many blood sisters, they didn't get along too well together, but as Shaker sisters they managed. And when we got to know them better we asked Sister Sadie about Emma and the differences, because we detected them and Sadie was very frank with us and she said well, she said, "You see, Emma is commercial and I am agricultural." Now by agricultural Sadie meant she was a postmistress, garden deaconess, school teacher, she had a hand in almost everything from the beginning of her life there.[20]

The Andrewses would make a lifetime friend in Sadie but found dealing with Emma Neale to be problematic at best. The Andrewses' persistence in exploring the buildings at Mount Lebanon would yield some of their greatest treasures but also test the bounds of their relations with both Neale sisters.

According to an interview conducted with Faith in 1972, Ted Andrews was the first to make contact with the Neale sisters.[21] The exact date of the first visit is not known, but Faith stated it was in the "very late 1920s."[22] The first time she met Sadie Neale, Faith recalled, she was at the Ann Lee Cottage (an old dwelling house of the Center Family), "sitting on that so-called throne, a platform that had been built to elevate the sisters' chairs and needlework table, so they could look out the windows over the main road, the Shaker Road, and get the light. Sometimes we would find Sadie looking out the window at the hills, especially if there was a storm coming. She loved the view. It gave her strength."[23] This "throne" would eventually find its way into the Andrews Collection (page 186).

A letter in the Andrews Archives at Winterthur from Emma Neale to Faith Andrews helps to date the beginning of their interaction.

February 4, 1929:

Mrs. Faith Andrews

Friend

A reply to your letter has been delayed by sickness & death of one of our very Elderly sisters & many other cares incident to the home.

In regards to any of the past[?] incidents of our handiwork or old time furniture there is little left to show as it has mostly been sold. If the sale at present contemplated goes through & we know of anything worthy of holding to the view of coming generations will let you know. We will not be able during the cold weather to visit the closed up buildings.

With all good wishes to you & yours I am,

Yours Respectfully

Emma J. Neale[24]

The Andrewses begin to appear in the personal diary of Sadie Neale in 1929. A string of entries from that year illustrate that while the Andrewses may have been quite excited about their new Shaker friend, she perhaps did not always share their enthusiasm:

March 26: Mr and Mrs Andrews come to look over old furniture in afternoon. I use some time going around with them.

March 28: Mr and Mrs Andrews come in the afternoon to look at old furniture. Use up considerable of my time.

May 2: Wait on Andrews couple in afternoon who come to pick up old furniture.

May 9: The Andrews couple come in afternoon and pick up more old ware.

June 13: Mr and Mrs Andrews calls in afternoon.

August 27: Andrews couple come in afternoon. Select two or three old pieces and use considerable of my time.

October 21: The Andrews couple call in afternoon, and many other non essentials.

November 13: Andrews come over in afternoon and I go to South family with them and other places. They pay me 25.00 on account.[25]

It would be premature to allow these first impressions of Sadie Neale to color one's perception of her regard for the Andrewses over the next nineteen years of their acquaintance. Subsequent correspondence and actions show that Sister Sadie became quite fond of Ted and Faith, even if she seemed initially bothered by their visits. Sadie was apparently much easier to do business with than her sister Emma. Faith recalled her understanding of the underlying meaning of Sadie's referring to Emma as "commercial":

All she cared about was people who had money, making her friends the money people where Sadie was content to get money for the family through her gardens. Money meant everything to [Emma]. When she would offer to sell us something, it was only because she would double the price and think we wouldn't be able to buy. But it was always a piece we could not resist. And so we did, we bought from both of them, but mostly from Sadie.[26]

It is impossible to document the truth in these allegations, but there is no doubt that whenever possible the Andrewses preferred to deal with Sadie Neale.

By 1929 the Andrewses began to cast the net wider than Berkshire County, Massachusetts, and Columbia County, New York. A letter written by Eldress Prudence Stickney of the Sabbathday Lake community, apparently subsequent to a visit by the Andrewses, documents the first offerings of Shaker material from Maine.

August 31, 1929

My Dear Friend:—I am sorry to keep you waiting so long for an answer to your questions about the old fashioned things made by the Shakers, but have been so lame, it was hard for me to get around.

Table in basement at Office— $6.00

Table in sewing room— $5.00

Table in canning room— $10.00

Bureau at Office— $25.00

Yellow Sink— $10.00

Work bench in meeting house— $15.00

3 Children's spool beds, $5.00 each— $15.00

Eldress Prudence Stickney of Sabbathday Lake, Maine.
Collection of Hancock Shaker Village
1992.5645

I have one spool bed six feet by 1 foot 3 inches if you want it @ $8.00 and 2 chairs in perfect condition, made by the Shakers here if you should want them at $7.00 I will put new listing seats into them, and they will be like new. I mention these as the sister who went around with you thought you might like them. I hope the items I am sending you, will help you in your writings.

Thanking you for your kindly interest in us, I am

Your Sincere Friend

Prudence A. Stickney[27]

Scholars who imply that the Andrewses took advantage of Shakers impoverished by the Great Depression to buy furniture should note the date of this ample and generous offering.[28]

The last family at Mount Lebanon to which the Andrewses gained introduction was the North Family, by 1930 the home of those Central Ministry members in residence at Mount Lebanon. Faith Andrews credited Sadie Neale with providing a "proper introduction" to the members at the North.[29] In all likelihood the fact that the Neale sisters were Trustees of the Society, as was Sister Annie Rosetta Stephens, provided the appropriate connection for the Andrewses. They would come to regard Sister Annie Rosetta as their closest friend at the North, where they did much early collecting; but I have found very little in the way of documentary evidence of the Andrewses' relationship with the North Family.

The Andrewses were already in contact with the Canterbury, New Hampshire, Shaker community by 1930. The following letter from Sister Josephine Wilson (a Trustee for the Church Family who would be appointed to the Central Ministry in 1939) answers an earlier letter written by the Andrewses. Reading it one gets a sense of the humble tone the Andrewses' letter must have taken. Eldress Josephine's humorous reply goes far to reassure the Andrewses of their welcome at Canterbury (the words in red are reproduced below as they originally appeared in the typewritten letter):

April 28, 1930

Dear Friends,

We are glad to have you come around to our opinion, that the trip here and home again on the same day is too much, and we shall be happy to have you stay with us over night. You have not stayed long enough at one time to call it a visit, nor to get acquainted. We have your things you left behind you in safe storage, and perhaps we shall be fortunate to be able to show you some things that have come to light during Housecleaning time,—sometimes they do. I think your suggestion is a good one, to come the latter part of May, and then we may have more leisure to be with you,— we hope so at least. You say, "It is kind of us to bother with you." Now look the word bother up in Webster's Dictionary, and see if the definition applies to friends. POTHER means to make a stir, —better use this next time, for I will grant you do this, but are not guilty of being a BOTHER.[30]

Eldress Josephine Wilson of Canterbury, New Hampshire.
Collection of Hancock Shaker Village 1988.3348

Nineteen-thirty also saw the beginning of the Andrewses' interaction with Charles Adams of the New York State Museum. Adams had already begun building a Shaker collection for the State Museum based on materials from the Watervliet, New York, community, as well as items acquired from Sister Jennie Wells at Mount Lebanon's North Family. Adams and the Schenectady photographer William Winter had been working together since at least 1928 on an exhibition of Winter's photographs of Shaker buildings and artifacts. Winter wrote Adams on January 4, 1930, expressing his frustration with documenting this unfamiliar subject.

Dear Dr. Adams,

At last I have all of my Shaker work in proof. Using these prints as the basis I have arrainged a tentative photographic exhibit. The results however are not at all what I would prefer. My feeling with regard to the whole affair is something like this.

Since I last saw you I have been working on a literary research; collecting all the data I can. Already I have made some progress at understanding the spirit of Shakerism, and I want to go ahead and do more work along that line. What I have now compared with what I can have after several more weeks in the field makes me desire to postpone the show.

As you know I have had no plan. In 1928 I went ahead motivated by interest and by the feeling that what I had before me was valuable but how and why I was not sure. The experience of last year; the careful study of the 1928 prints and the literary research have now led me to set up a plan. If I could carry it through, the result would be a collection of photographs of great story telling and historic value, and many of them beautiful photographs.

The main trouble with the 1928 series is that many of the important features of Shakerism are not represented,— the story is not complete. Most of the pictures are beautiful records and with them as the basis I would go on, re-photographing some but to a greater extent adding new prints to the series so that it will be complete. This time I would work from my plan or "continuity."

Cordially yours,

Winter[31]

Charles C. Adams, Director of the New York State Museum ca. 1930.
Courtesy of the New York State Museum, Albany, N.Y.

A letter from Adams to Winter dated February 27, 1930, describes Adams's first meeting with the Andrewses, and the ideal solution to Winter's lack of knowledge and a "complete story" in presenting his Shaker photographs.

Dear Mr. Winter:—

A few days ago Mr. and Mrs. Edward D. Andrews, of 42 Clinton Avenue, Pittsfield, Mass., who had been to Mount Lebanon and had seen Sister Jennie Wells, came in to the Museum to see our Shaker Collection. . . . Sister Wells had told them of you and our plans for the exhibit. Andrews is a graduate student of education in Yale University and is planning a book on the Shakers. They have already made valuable collections of objects and literature. I showed them all I could, considering the crowded conditions of storage, and they were keenly and enthusiastically interested. They appear to be very fine people indeed, and I believe that you will like them, and it looks as if we can get excellent cooperation from them.

I enclose a copy of a letter just received from them. What do you think of the whole situation? Could we not arrange a meeting here some week and talk matters over? They expressed their eagerness to meet you. I will wait until I hear from you before replying to the letter.

We are just ordering a lot of costumes from Jennie Wells, and she writes me that she has secured additional things for our collection. She has been quite ill and is resting up at Mount Lebanon.

Very sincerely,

Chas. C. Adams[32]

An excerpt from Winter's reply marks the beginning of a landmark collaboration between the Andrewses and Winter.

March 2, 1930
Dear Dr. Adams.

I shall be happy to meet you and your Pittsfield friends anytime you desire. I think it would be splendid to have their aid.

Their offer to prepare a "circular to give a general informational background" is gracious, and if possible I think it should be printed. It would be a perfect compliment to the exhibit. I have no idea, however of what it would cost.
Cordially yours,
Winter[33]

An entry in Charles Adams's notebook documents the first meeting of the Andrewses, Winter, and Adams: "04/19/1930 <u>Winter</u> and I went to Pittsfield to see the <u>Edw. D. Andrews</u> . . . collection. I talk over our plans with Mr. and Mrs. Andrews. . . They have a great amount of Shaker furniture and <u>clothing</u>, etc."[34]

Ted Andrews would find a kindred spirit in William Winter. Winter captured the sacred austerity and drama latent in Shaker objects and architecture. With his camera he realized in visual terms Ted's own idealized inner vision of what the Shakers represented. Andrews and Winter first spoke at length about their prospective work in May 1930. Andrews wrote in glowing terms to Adams about these meetings:

Photographer William F. Winter ca. 1930.
Courtesy, The Winterthur Library: The Edward Deming Andrews Memorial Shaker Collection,
No. SA 1391.2

May 22, 1930
Dear Dr. Adams—

Mr. Winter has been here twice this week and we have had some enthusiastic conversations which we all regretted your not having been in on. Hope we can all get together soon—
Yours
Edward D Andrews[35]

In the meantime the Andrewses began to work with Adams on an exhibition, as well as the writing of the book that would become *The Community Industries of the Shakers*. Additionally, the Andrewses began to sell Shaker objects to Adams for the collection of the New York State Museum. A letter dated February 25, 1930, illustrates these processes.

Dear Dr. Adams:

Our conversations of the other day were a genuine pleasure and stimulus to our interest in the Shakers. We have been looking over our acquisitions from a broader point of view, and have found several items pertaining to the economic history of the sect which we think you would find gratification in owning.

The April exhibit should be of great interest. We would consider it a privilege to help you in any way possible; and if you would like us to prepare a circular to give a general informational background to the exhibition, please be free to enlist our services. Old records are constantly coming to light, and it will not be long we feel, before a valuable survey of the industrial life of the Shakers, in New York as well as in other states, can be written.

Cordially yours,

Faith and Edward D. Andrews[36]

From Charles Adams's notebooks, on deposit at the New York State Museum, we have a rare parallel perspective to the Andrewses' experiences as collectors navigating the political shoals of the Shaker families at Mount Lebanon and Hancock. Despite Adams's earlier contacts with the Watervliet Shakers and Mount Lebanon's North Family, he seems to have gained access to the Church Family only through the Andrewses. The following excerpts from his journal suggest that Ted Andrews, omnipresent at Adams's earliest visits with the Neale sisters, was carefully shepherding their interactions. It is possible that the Neales were relying on Ted Andrews for his help in business dealings with Adams. However, it seems equally plausible that Andrews was looking out for his own collecting interests. This help appears to have been welcomed by Adams at first, but over the next few years the goodwill between the two parties seems to have diminished.

[Mount Lebanon, N.Y.]

Oct 11. 1930. They [the Andrewses] think that it is necessary <u>not</u> to let one Shaker family know about our relations to others!—the Andrews

Also think <u>Jennie Wells</u> can not help much here. Are inclined to think that she charged us <u>high</u> and tells others we can pay for objects! Thinks we must work largely and independently of her out here.

He Andrews wishes to prepare a book on <u>Shaker furniture</u>. I told him that if he did not wish to make it a money venture, we might be able to publish such a <u>report</u>. Asked him to send me a letter[37]

After that first visit, Andrews wrote to Adams on behalf of Sister Sadie Neale, discussing terms for the sale of certain objects and advising quick action in retrieving them because of the sale of the Church Family property to the Lebanon School (later renamed the Darrow School).

Oct 28, 1930

Dear Dr. Adams—

Sister Sadie Neale is willing that you should have the corn sheller for $10—The entire broom-making outfit, consisting of the several items you saw, with accessories, she would be willing to dispose of at a minimum of $30.00. The latter machinery is Shaker made, as you know, while the three or four corn shellers which I have seen are not; in fact two of them have in stencil outside patents of a comparatively late date. It might be good strategy to take the broom machinery at least, as such a sale would doubtless lead to further cooperation in your enterprises on the part of the Neales. There is an interesting Shaker-made machine for packaging herbs, and no end of other industrial equipment. Sister Sadie is anxious to have the broom paraphernalia removed as soon as possible, in case you decide to take it. The school people are assigning a caretaker to the property at an early date, and as the property with certain exceptions already belongs to them, certain embarrassments may be eliminated by such early action.

Hoping to see you soon,

Edward D Andrews[38]

A string of further entries in Adams's notebooks show how closely Ted Andrews worked with Adams through 1930 and 1931 in selecting and acquiring mainly industrial artifacts from the Neale sisters at Mount Lebanon's Church Family.

Nov. 15, 1930
Saw Sister Sadie Neale
Sister Emma Neale
E.D. Andrews of Pittsfield came also.
    We could not get the broom machine out of the bldg. Andrews showed me a number of desirable things which we should get, including mitering machine, hemp machine, corn cutting (3 or 4) machine for canning corn.

Nov. 20, 1930
Church Family, Mt. Lebanon
Sister Sarah (Sadie) Neale and Dr. Andrews. Gave Andrews proof of Circular No. 2 by him. Andrews and I went about and selected a number of objects that we thought desirable. There is a great quantity of desirable industrial materials, particularly metal and wood working tools.

Dec. 10, 1930 Church Family Shakers
Dr. Andrews was there waiting with Sister Sadie Neale at the <u>Post Office</u>.

Dec 30, 1930 Mt. Lebanon Shakers
    The Andrews of Pittsfield also came. We got a large number of tools for metal and wood working and many more things of interest. Lassiter and the Andrews also received a number of things. The Andrews helped much in picking out things and in getting Sister Sadie's release of them.[39]

Sister R. Mildred Barker and Eldress Gertrude Soule with Edward Deming Andrews at Hancock Shaker Village on August 4, 1961.
Collection of Hancock Shaker Village
1996.5929 (top) and 1996.5930

   Concurrent with the Andrewses' deepening relationship with the Neale sisters, and the related dealings with Charles Adams, were their efforts to extend their reach into the Shaker communities in Maine. Eldress Prudence Stickney at Sabbathday Lake continued to be their contact in the north. The community at Sabbathday Lake, colloquially referred to as the "least of Mother's children in the east," was poor in finances but rich in membership.[40] By 1931 Eldress Prudence and the Central Ministry were carefully weighing the decision to close the struggling Alfred community and consolidate its members at Sabbathday Lake. This action had been considered since 1926, but was now essential due to financial pressures. Sister R. Mildred Barker, originally from Alfred, later wrote a history of that community. She recounted the decision to close in the following terms, beginning in 1927:

Still the financial status of the family did not progress. For a number of years the sisters served chicken dinners and light lunches to summer tourists. This helped, but was not enough. There had been talk of consolidating with the New Gloucester Society [an alternate name for Sabbathday Lake] for a number of years. Eldress Prudence Stickney of the New Gloucester Society as well as the Maine Ministry was most considerate and understanding, and while she was desirous for this consolidation, she did not press for its acceptance. The New Gloucester family needed the added members that such a move would bring, and Alfred needed the financial security. Together they would forseeably become one prosperous family. Therefore, after careful consideration and reflection, it was decided in February, 1931, that the move should be made. It was started at once with both families working together to finish the move as soon as possible. On May 28, 1931, a little over three months after the decision was made the two families were one.

Brother Delmer Wilson of New Gloucester was appointed one of the Trustees of Alfred in order that he might assist in the disposition and sale of the property.[41]

The years surrounding the closing of Alfred were incredibly painful for those Shakers who were compelled to leave their lifelong home. The Andrewses were a constant presence during this transitional time. For Eldress Prudence and Brother Delmer, the Sabbathday Lake Shakers overseeing the sale of furnishings and other objects from the buildings at Alfred, the willingness of the Andrewses to buy almost anything that was made available must have seemed a financial blessing. However, for the Alfred Shakers, witnessing the dispersal of their physical heritage inspired negative opinions of the Andrewses that have been passed down in oral history among the Sabbathday Lake Shakers even to the time of this writing. An interwoven examination of the written and oral sources for the period can at least present evidence of, if not pass judgment on, the Andrewses' actions.

The Andrewses made their first visit to examine objects from Alfred in May 1931. The visit is documented in the diaries of the Sabbathday Lake Shakers Eugenia (Gennie) M. Coolbroth and Delmer Wilson:

May 14 – Mr. and Mrs. Andrews come to see about some antiques.

May 15 – Mr. and Mrs. Andrews come up and see Eldress Prudence; they buy over $200.00 worth of antiques.[42]

May 15 – Mr. & Mrs. Andrews of Pittsfield Mass bought quite a bit of furniture.[43]

Eldress Prudence followed up on the Andrewses' visit with a few letters offering more items that had been gathered as the Alfred buildings were being cleaned out by Brother Earl Campbell of Sabbathday Lake.

May 16: My Lovely Friends:— Would it be too much of you to itemize some of the things, the old cord bedstead, warming pan, tall jar, as those belonged to Br. Earl [Campbell], and give the price of those. I do not think there are any other things of his, so you need not bother with the others. I hope you found something at Alfred that helped you with your collection.[44]

This photo of Brother Stephen Gowan appeared in an article entitled "Alfred Sad As Shakers Pack Up to Leave Old Home Forever" in the Boston Evening Transcript.
Courtesy, The Winterthur Library: The Edward Deming Andrews Memorial Shaker Collection, Box 16.

May 25th: My Dear Friends: . . . Earl found another cross leg table at Alfred, and brought it over here, and he wants to know if you would care for this one. We want you to have the first offer. I found a picture of the village that you hoped to get, so I will send it with his drawings when he goes. I was so glad to get it for you.[45]

Wednesday [May 27]: My Very Dear Friends: . . . The Alfred Shakers will come tomorrow so we have much to do to be prepared to meet them. Earl will take care of the things you got at Alfred, and after a little rest, and a lull in the work, will take your things to you. He is a jewel of priceless worth, and I could not get along with all the burden I carry, if I did not have him. He is "one of my boys," and he sticks by. Now my dears, I presume you were referring to the old cheese press in the meeting house? We ought to get $50.00 for it, but that may be more than you feel like paying. I think the old cheese presses are very scarse. I do not know of any others, do you?

Don't forget us after you are done with buying, for you will always be as welcome as the flowers in June. We did enjoy your short stay with us so much.[46]

The Andrewses returned to Maine quickly to follow up on these offerings. By the time of their next visit, the Alfred Shakers had been relocated to Sabbathday Lake. Oral history within the community at Sabbathday Lake has preserved stories of the Andrewses' visit to Alfred earlier in May, while the Shakers were still in residence. Brother Arnold Hadd, who joined the Sabbathday Lake community in 1978, recalls some of the stories he heard from former Alfred Shakers:

There are only a few stories about the Andrewses that have been told here. Sister Elsie McCool repeated the first story.

When the announcement was made that the Alfred Community would close and consolidate with Sabbathday Lake (1931) it became apparent that we had a shortage of workrooms for all the new Sisters. As the Ministry's Shop was no longer being used Eldress Prudence decided to clean it out for them. Sr. Elsie was one of those assigned to help with the task. Eldress Prudence gave the young Sisters items in the rooms as she said the Andrewses would hound her to give these pieces to them. Rather than see them dispersed without a reason Eldress Prudence decided to keep the objects in the family.

Sister Mildred Barker and Sister Ruth Nutter told the other story. They were both Alfred Shakers and they stated that the Andrewses would go through any building they wanted to without permission looking at items they wanted to buy. When the truck from Sabbathday Lake would arrive to take a load of goods [back to Sabbathday Lake] the Andrewses would watch what was being loaded. If there were anything that they wanted then they would follow the truck home and before a piece was off loaded they would ask to purchase it.

Of course the Community was devastated at losing their home and they were all busy trying to sort and salvage and keep things going until the move. Most of the time someone would be crying and the Andrewses would barge on through without any thought of what the people were going through the only thing they cared about was getting first crack at the antiques.

When the Andrewses came to pick up their antiques they stayed overnight at the Office. They were given a tour of the Village by Earl Campbell the following morning and it was he who gave them the Elder Joshua Bussell drawings as they were being stored in the upper part of the Ox Barn along with other items from Alfred. He neither had permission nor authority to do so, but he did it anyway.[47]

The Andrewses selected more antiques in late May, and these were shipped down to Pittsfield by a moving company. These events are again recorded in the diaries of Coolbroth and Wilson.

May 30 – Mr. Andrews comes to get another load of old-fashioned things.[48]

June 5 – A big moving van arrived last night to move antiques to Pittsfield Mass got loaded and started and rear end gave out in axle.

Telephoned to Springfield for repairs & stop here tonight.

June 6 – Moving van repaired and left for Pittsfield about 4 P.M.[49]

June 6 – The men leave in the truck after they are stranded with Mr. Andrews load of antiques.

According to an interview with Faith Andrews, one truckload of antiques purchased from Alfred was destroyed in a fire on its way to Pittsfield. It seems likely that this was the load on the truck that was delayed in its departure from Maine and may account for the relatively small amount of Maine Shaker furniture that is known to have been collected by the Andrewses in comparison with the numerous items listed for sale in the correspondence of Eldress Prudence. The Andrewses made at least one more visit to Maine in October 1931, capping a busy year of collecting for the couple, awkwardly juxtaposed against the human drama unfolding among the Shakers there.

October 5 – Mr. and Mrs. Andrews come to take the rest of their things.

October 6 – Mr. and Mrs. Andrews take their things to-day.[50]

Perhaps the most important objects collected by the Andrewses were the "gift drawings." The Andrewses initially referred to these striking works on paper as "inspirationals" or "inspirational drawings"; they and others have also called them "spirit drawings." The Shaker scholar Daniel Patterson convincingly argues for the current name of "gift drawings," based on the fact that these images were a visual parallel to the songs and testimonies that came to the Shakers as gifts from the spirit world so profusely in the 1840s and 1850s.[51]

According to the account published in the introduction to the Andrewses' monograph on the gift drawings entitled *Visions of the Heavenly Sphere*, Sister Alice Smith at Hancock first revealed the existence of the drawings to the Andrewses in the late 1920s. The exact date is uncertain, but circumstantial evidence suggests it was no later than 1931. Ted Andrews's account is worth quoting in full, if only for comparison with later accounts of the momentous occasion given by Faith.

In the retiring-room of the family dwelling of a New England Shaker community we were talking one evening in the 1930s with a sister of that religious order. When the conversation turned to the various modes by which a reticent sect expresses its inner spirit, she grew thoughtful and then said: "I have something to show you which I have kept secret since I was a child of eight I want your opinion about it." She then opened a chest in a corner of the room and took out an illuminated scroll entitled "An Emblem of the Heavenly Sphere." As we looked at it, she was silent and watchful. Our reaction was one of delight and wonder; we did not know, after ten years' acquaintance with this secluded folk, that they ever attempted to depict the signs and objects of the spiritual world. Seeking an explanation for the document's nature and source, we learned that Sister Alice had rescued it from wastepaper consigned to an oven, had hidden it away, and as she grew older, had treasured it increasingly as a precious, if somewhat mysterious, expression of the Shaker soul. "My showing it to you was a test," she afterward declared. "If you had shown any evidence of levity in your response, I was prepared to keep it as mine alone. I would have known that 'the world' could not understand."[52]

Sister Alice Smith sent this photo of her room to her blood sister Ethel, who had left the Shakers many years earlier. She wrote on the back: "I took this of my room, so as to get the Arbutus back of your photo, but was not near enough—have another one when I get the time to print it, this is just a little peek."
Courtesy, The Winterthur Library: The Edward Deming Andrews Memorial Shaker Collection, No. SA 493

This account has come under much scrutiny and criticism from those who are suspicious of its romanticism. Ted Andrews's original manuscript for *Visions of the Heavenly Sphere* is in the Andrews Archives at Winterthur. It remained unpublished at his death in 1964, despite the fact that the Andrewses had been working toward its publication since the early 1930s. The typescript for the book is in the Andrews Archives at Winterthur, with emendations in Ted Andrews's hand. The date of the typescript is unclear, as is how much time may have passed between the momentous evening when Sister Alice unveiled the drawings and the Andrewses' written recollections.

Faith Andrews gave accounts of the encounter with Alice Smith on at least two subsequent occasions. The first was in an interview with A. D. Emerich in preparation for the exhibition entitled *Shaker* at the Renwick Gallery in 1973–74. In this account, rather than rescuing the drawings from the fire, Sister Alice considers burning them herself if the Andrewses had not recognized their value.

> One evening in [Alice Smith's] room, she said she would like to show us a roll of paintings she had and to see what we thought of them. She went to a large cupboard and produced this quite considerable roll, maybe half-a-dozen sheets, carefully unrolled them, and spread them out on the floor. We were shaken by the experience. I think the first we saw was the Tree of Life. It seems to be everyone's favorite today. On occasion she had shown them to others, who thought them funny and had laughed at the strange angels flying about, and the airships. That hurt Alice, because to her they were sacred sheets, and she had made up her mind to burn them if even we thought them ludicrous. She gave them to us with love. . . . Alice found others, and Sadie Neale, and Elder Arthur Bruce at Canterbury.[53]

The final recounting of this story came during Faith's interview by Robert Brown in 1982.

> We saw quite a bit of Alice and we came to know her so well that we were allowed to come and visit evenings with Alice in her room, which was a beautiful room. And this one night, she had been talking to us quite a bit about herself and her Shaker life, feeling a little bit discouraged by the way things were then, having been overworked, being the youngest one there, and she told us that she decided that she again would open this chest in the closet and take out the roll of drawings which she had done, maybe three or four times before, to show to people, and found that people laughed and ridiculed them, and she had made up her mind that if the Andrews felt that way she would destroy them as they had planned originally. And when she unrolled the drawings, there were perhaps six there, and we were speechless, fortunately. We didn't know what we were looking at, but we knew it was very precious and there was only the sound of our breathing. We couldn't talk about it. And Alice had said would you like to take them and study them? And we did. Then the Shakers from other communities heard about these drawings and other drawings became available.[54]

The closet door of Sister Alice Smith's retiring room in the 1830 Brick Dwelling, Hancock, Massachusetts. In some of the accounts of the Andrewses first look at the gift drawings they are said to have been stored in this closet.
Collection of Hancock Shaker Village

Daniel Patterson was informed in 1980 by Olive Hayden Austin, a former Hancock sister and close friend of the Andrewses', of further circumstances surrounding the drawings that predated the Andrewses' involvement with the Hancock Shakers. Sister Olive's account squarely contradicts that which Sister Alice supposedly related to the Andrewses.

Mrs. Olive Hayden Austin, who was raised from childhood at Hancock, says that she never heard any of the older Shakers speak about the paintings and that she has a different recollection of their rediscovery: "It wasn't until about the year 1925 when we young folks were doing our spring cleaning in the attic that Sr. Alice found a couple of them in the very top most cupboard where no one had bothered to clean for ages. We all dropped our dust cloths and mops just to study them, they were so beautiful. Sr. Alice took them to her room and we never saw them again." Mrs. Austin recalls the discovery of a second set in the early 1930s, when Sister Alice was showing the Andrews around the village. "The meeting house," she says, "had been closed for years but opened up to show them the interior of the building. Up stairs in the Ministry Sisters retiring room, again in one of the top most cupboards is where the bulk of these paintings were found."[55]

Because of the obvious conflict among these accounts, the actual events surrounding the offering and transmission of the Hancock gift drawings to the Andrewses will probably never be known. Perhaps Alice Smith romanticized the story. Perhaps the Andrewses did so when they wrote their account well after the death of Sister Alice in 1935. Some scholars of Shakerism point to the murkiness surrounding the unearthing of the gift drawings as evidence of the Andrewses' romanticization of the Shakers or of their own special relationship with individual Shakers. The important fact is that the drawings have been preserved for the public in the Andrews Collection at Hancock Shaker Village.

Sister Alice Smith in the 1830 Brick Dwelling, Hancock, Massachusetts.
Courtesy, The Winterthur Library: The Edward Deming Andrews Memorial Shaker Collection, No. SA 63

The revelation of this first cache of drawings whetted the Andrewses' appetite for more examples. The Andrewses wrote to Eldress Prudence late in 1930, or early in 1931, to inquire about the availability of drawings they had seen at Sabbathday Lake. These were likely not gift drawings, but perhaps other village views executed by Brother Joshua Bussell. According to Brother Arnold Hadd the two gift drawings in the collection at Sabbathday Lake could not have been known to the Andrewses at this time. One had not yet been rediscovered where it was stored in the Ministry Shop, and the other was given to Brother Delmer Wilson by Sister Alice Smith of Hancock in the early 1930s.[56] We do not have the Andrewses' original letter, only Eldress Prudence's reply:

January 13: My Dear Friends: . . . About the pictures. I do not feel I can spare them from our Museum which we have in our old Church, and we have gathered all we could of Shaker things, which is the apple of my eye. How I would have loved to have gone to New York and seen your display. It must have been wonderful, and I hope you did well.[57]

Sisters Emma and Sadie Neale and Rosetta Stephens at Mount Lebanon each showed examples to the Andrewses. Tantalizing references to the drawings are also found in Charles Adams's notebooks. His desire to obtain some for the New York State Museum, as well as his envy of the Andrewses' possession of at least one example, are apparent.

May 25, 1931
Church Family Mt. Lebanon
     From the North Family, Winter and I went over to see <u>Sister Sadie and Emma Neale</u> in their <u>new quarters</u>. . . . Sister Emma showed us some <u>beautiful drawings</u> made by Sister <u>Polly Reed</u> who drew the world map, of spiritual visions. These were described by the persons who had the visions and Sister Polly Reed drew them. <u>The Andrews have one of these drawings framed</u>. Sister Sadie has also <u>some</u> of these <u>drawings</u>. These were said to be <u>pen work</u> and were in some cases <u>beautifully colored</u>.
     We went to Pittsfield to see the Andrews. They have been getting new valuable materials but he as not made progress on the Handbook because of sickness in the family.[58]

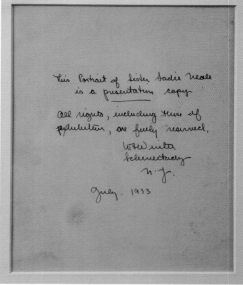

Sister Sadie Neale, as photographed by William F. Winter. "This Portrait of Sister Sadie Neale is a <u>presentation</u> copy/All rights, including those of exhibition, are fully reserved/W F Winter/Schenectady/N.Y./July 1933."
Collection of Miriam R. and M. Stephen Miller

Adams was a frequent visitor at Hancock late in 1931. He was working with Sister Alice Smith to assemble a large collection of Shaker materials from the community. This collection, the largest single collection of documented Hancock materials with iron-clad provenance, still resides at the New York State Museum. Adams's notebooks record visits to Hancock in October, November, and December of 1931. In his notebook entry for December 10 he recorded seeing the gift drawings with excitement.

I took the 8:30 AM bus for Pittsfield, Mass, to visit the Hancock Shakers and look over the objects collected for sale by <u>Sister Alice Smith</u>. Arrived about 9:35 AM and spent the time to near 12 noon looking over the materials collected by her. I went over the list which she had prepared and she added many items. She had done wonderfully well and her prices are very reasonable.

Sister Alice showed me <u>several</u> of the <u>colored drawings</u> of the visions made about 1840–1850. She gave <u>one</u> to Dr. Andrews.[59]

The one drawing already in the Andrewses' possession by this time was likely the Polly Collins work *An Emblem of the Heavenly Sphere*. Ted Andrews describes the work as the initial drawing shown them by Sister Alice in his introduction to *Visions of the Heavenly Sphere*. Additionally, *An Emblem.* was documented by William Winter during his work with the Andrewses.

Charles Adams's dealings with Alice Smith seem to have been quite out in the open. A body of correspondence between Adams and Smith also exists for the years 1931 through 1934. It seems doubtful that she could have sold so many items from the community, and asked older members about the use and history of many, without the full cooperation and knowledge of Eldress Fannie Estabrook. In a letter dated November 29, 1931, Smith told Adams: "I have made the price of each piece as reasonable as I could—you know in such matters I cannot do just as I would like to but have to consult with Eldress Fannie—just speaking for myself—I would like to see every thing go into the Museum free of charge."[60] The answers to further questions of the extent of Trustee Frances Hall's approval or involvement are unknown.

A group of Shakers from Sabbathday Lake traveled to Pittsfield in late May and early June 1932 to visit their co-religionists at Hancock and Mount Lebanon, as well as the Andrewses. Sister Alice Smith also took the group, consisting of Eldress Prudence Stickney, Sisters Jennie Mathers, Iona Sedgley, and Brother Earl Campbell, to the New York State Museum on May 31 to see their Shaker collection. In a letter of thanks to Charles Adams, Sister Alice wrote, "Doctor Andrews has helped so much in making our people see and feel the worthwhileness of preserving all we can."[61]

In a letter written directly to the Andrewses Eldress Prudence overflows with gratitude and warmth toward the couple:

June 7th [1932]: My Lovely Friends: We arrived home Sunday noon, warm and tired, and home looked good to me, but I had the time of my life, visiting old scenes and seeing old friends. It will be a rich golden memory to me as long as I live. One of my happiest memories are of you two dear ones. How I did enjoy the time spent with you. To know and to feel the deep reverence you have for the old Shaker things, did my heart good. Every touch was full of love and devotion, for those who have given their lives in full consecration to God's work, and I am thankful for everything you have that belonged to us. You seem more like Shakers, than many who have worn the garb, and made outward profession. There was pure elevating influence in your home that we all realized. We all loved you from the first, but love you more now, since we have been in your dear home. . . . It was a great privilege to me to see my loyal Pittsfield Shakers once more, and spend every extra moment with them, for I always called it my "other home," so close they have always been to my heart.[62]

The Andrewses' October 1932 exhibition at the Berkshire Museum was one of their greatest early triumphs, and as Mario S. De Pillis notes in his essay, it would connect them to Juliana Force and opportunities at the Whitney Museum in New York. The involvement and presence of the Shakers at so many events associated with the exhibition validated the Andrewses' expertise in the eyes of the public. The *Berkshire Eagle* followed the exhibition closely. An article covering the opening noted: "One of the pleasantest features of the exhibition was the approval set upon it by the presence of several of the Shakers. Eldress Sarah Collins, Brother Benjamin De Rue [*sic*], Sisters Alice Smith, Olive Hayden, Elizabeth Belden, Rosetta Stevens [*sic*], and Sadie Neal [*sic*], of the Church, North and Hancock Families, and Sister Adelaide of the South Family, received the guests with Miss Laura M. Bragg, director of the museum, Dr. and Mrs. Andrews, and Mr. Winter."[63] An article in the next issue reported that Emma Neale and Elder Walter Shepherd had given gallery talks and that Ted Andrews had introduced Elder Walter, who, in turn: "thanked Dr. Andrews for what he is doing to honor the Shakers."[64] For one final gallery talk Sister Sadie Neale introduced Faith Andrews, and the *Eagle* commented: "The presence of several sisters and brethren from Mount Lebanon and Hancock yesterday, as has been the case on the other days when gallery talks have been given, put the finishing touch of perfection upon the program of a rare and pleasurable afternoon."[65]

Elder Arthur Bruce of Canterbury,
New Hampshire.
Collection of Hancock Shaker Village 1988.3308

The Andrewses contacted Elder Arthur Bruce of Canterbury, New Hampshire, in 1933 regarding the gift drawings in that community's possession. A draft of the letter written to Elder Arthur shows the diplomacy with which Ted Andrews inquired about those drawings.

> Dear Elder Arthur—
>
> I ~~Have just written to Mr. Cathcart to go to Cleveland soon.~~ We are planning a trip to Canterbury in the near future ~~probably~~ sometime in May, Before we go, I wanted information, ~~on~~ if possible, on one matter.
>
> Would it be permissable for us to obtain photographic records of the drawings, or inspirational sketches, which are in the possession of the Canterbury society, ~~it~~ and similar to the ones which ~~you~~ we showed to you in my study. We are interested, <u>not in obtaining them</u>, but merely in documenting them. I would make camera studies ~~of the~~ right there, and ~~be~~ it would not be necessary to remove them from your office. We already have permission to record similarly the drawings from the Hancock society, & one owned by Sister Rosetta. Sister Emma also has allowed us to see two or three of hers. We are anxious to make our study as complete as possible, & every additional item will clarify the whole (we will be under the greatest obligation to you is you will allow us this privilege.) I think there was an early map of New Lebanon ~~also~~ which I would also like to copy.
>
> Most sincerely—[66]

Andrews shortly received a favorable reply from Elder Arthur, who also provided the Andrewses with a letter of introduction to Wallace Cathcart and Wilfred Boulanger, the Father Superior of the La Salette Seminary at the former Shaker site in Enfield, New Hampshire. If one reads between the lines of his reply it is evident that Elder Arthur wants to make it clear that the Andrewses were still welcome at Canterbury. It is unknown why this sort of diplomacy (as also evidenced in the previously cited letter from Eldress Josephine Wilson) was necessary. Perhaps the initial contacts between the Andrewses and the Canterbury Shakers were not congenial. However, Elder Arthur's trust in the Andrewses and their work speaks for itself:

May 2, 1933

Dear Mr. Andrews:-

Irving and I are planning to be your way next week and we are wondering if it would be of moment to you if we brought along the drawings for you to photograph.

Do not infer from this that we want to interfere in any way with your trip to this place. We merely make this suggestion for you to consider.

I may go down to Maine tomorrow for a day or two. I leave home on a short trip and may take in Sabbathday Lake.

With best wishes, as always, believe me

Sincerely yours,

Arthur Bruce.[67]

The single surviving letter from Alice Smith to the Andrewses in the Andrews Collection at Winterthur is a bizarre piece, full of allusions (seemingly in reference to a possible theatrical production about the Shakers) and not entirely comprehensible. However, compared with the formal tone of her correspondence with Charles Adams, the style of this letter provides an excellent insight into the intimate relationship that Sister Alice had with the Andrewses, who apparently had frequent evening visits with her.[68] The letter also provides a window into the conservatism of the sisters at Mount Lebanon, especially on the matter of religious confession; Sister Alice reacted strongly against these attitudes.

March 3, 1933: "Dear Friends: I am sending you the itemized list of "goods"—that you have bought during the past few years—just as I noted each purchase—Please do not feel that I am sending this, as a bill is usually sent, but I wanted you to see where you <u>stood</u> on the matter, & hope you find it correct & that it corresponds with your own account, but if I have made any errors, let me know. You will see that it is not a large sum—but there is no hurry—just because of this list being mailed. I could have given it to you last evening if I had thought, but my mind was <u>elsewhere</u>. I was so glad to have you here again, and while I do not feel so <u>very</u> keen on <u>our</u> last evenings subject, still it brought you out here, & that was no bad <u>luck for me</u>, & I hope it means none for you. There seems to be a strange feeling at work . . . & I know it all will mean something definite in the end—and no doubt add greatly to your experience and education absent especially the last flare? I feel as I think it over, that you should look the matter up—so that you will have the facts from both sides—this knowledge will possibly be of use in the future; especially if this play does come out. Perhaps we can think of the best way to obtain the needed information. . . . I am very certain that you will both be able to handle the matter well—I was worried at first—for you—but on thinking it over. & talking with you—I feel different, and our own people "spill over" in such queer ways, & when you least expect it, so now I am glad this has come up- -, <u>now</u> if the movies move [?] into Lebanon next summer—we will know why—, really there are as strange things as this that have happened—& you know, these kind of people, send a trunk well ahead of them, and while I am sorry to admit it, such [?] always seem to make deep impressions on some of our people. No doubt but Emma Neale, would see "supernatural powers" even in Betty Compson—& Lillian Gish etc etc, if she also saw the bank roll - - I suppose I "am queer"—as usual—but that's how I feel, so I am glad this matter came into our hands—now I am going to be a regular "watch dog"—and hope nothing escapes me—& I can often <u>guess</u> as well as "reckon"—so heres good luck to you—and thank you for all your good work—and sincere interest—"I am with you in the furnace heat, as the old song says—Excuse this card letter but I never measure a letter before hand—Much love—Alice

P.S.—Do you suppose that Rosetta would be alright to talk this over with—if she could be away from the North Family—I think she should be on the lookout—for there may be others sent there—for more "confessional news," & they would be silly enough to think that the whole world was "going Shaker," all of a sudden—& they had done it, I believe in letting our light shine but on the right people—Of course I might have been caught too, but do not think so, if she had really mentioned as personal matters as the Confession subject & this matter in Florida, but she was very careful what she said to me—I know she has her mind made up—about the way Shakers confessed—& they have got to do it—that way—so there is no use in any one trying to explain it. I know I never get down on my knees—& never was required to, no doubt that's my whole trouble, well that's that, to change the subject—tell me if you like the new marmalade better than the old.

Of the earth earthy

Sincerely Alice[69]

During 1934 Sister Alice set up a room for Ted Andrews to use for his writing in the Dairy building (today referred to as the Sisters' Shop and Dairy) at Hancock. Ted was beginning work on the book that would ultimately be published as *Shaker Furniture: The Craftsmanship of an American Communal Sect*. Homer Eaton Keyes, editor of *Antiques* magazine and an early advocate of the Andrewses' work, had a chance to visit the Andrewses during this time. Faith recalled his reaction on entering the Dairy: "Alice had fixed a study for Ted in the dairy and it was very austere because she just had a table and a chair and a small chest of drawers for his work and he worked there. He did a lot of writing there. And when Homer Keyes stepped into that room, I'll never forget what he said, he said 'There is peace here.' He was practically speechless about the feeling."[70]

William Winter visited Hancock often to photograph furniture in the Brick Dwelling, Sisters' Shop and Dairy, Meetinghouse (demolished 1938), and larger Sisters' Shop and Store (demolished in 1958) at the community. Clair Zeitlin had colorful remembrances of this time:

> *Clair Zeitlin:* I loved the dairy, I used to get it ready for Mr. Winters [*sic*] he took the photographs. Eldress Fannie would say, "Clair, Mr. Winters called, he's gonna come out for pictures," so I'd go up and clean up the dairy upstairs. They had a big loom upstairs, great big. I'd dash down there after school and get everything clean and tidy and ready.

> *Christian Goodwillie:* So you would set up a lot of the pictures for him.

> *Clair Zeitlin:* Yeah. I loved to. He'd tell me what he wanted. I would work with him when he'd come. See, he'd suggest this and that and I'd say I'll get you this and I'll get you that. I spent some time with him to see what he wanted.[71]

The west entrance of the Dairy, or Sisters' Shop, at Hancock, where Edward Deming Andrews wrote much of the book Shaker Furniture. (top) Eldress Fannie Estabrook with Clara Sperle (later Clair Zeitlin) and unidentified visitors at Hancock, Massachusetts, ca.1930.
Collection of Hancock Shaker Village, Noel Vincentini 1935, 1987.2283 (bottom)

Interior photographs of the meeting room of the 1786 Meetinghouse at Hancock, Massachusetts, taken before its demolition in 1938.

Courtesy, The Winterthur Library: The Edward Deming Andrews Memorial Shaker Collection, No. SA 477 (top), SA 478 (bottom)

The Andrewses' close relationship with Sister Alice Smith, their Shaker friend of longest standing, came to a tragic end with her death from stomach cancer on February 20, 1935, at the age of fifty. Clair Zeitlin was with Alice on the night she died in extreme pain in her retiring room in the Brick Dwelling. She recalls the scene:

> Alice got stomach cancer. She suffered terrible one night and I stayed right with her till she died. Alice Smith, she died in my arms one night. She did. She had cancer, she was so sick, she suffered so bad. And I stayed in her room, yes, I remember Alice. She used to sit there at that loom. She was a nice woman. She used to make me the nicest things, she used to make me beautiful dresses.[72]

Sister Alice was buried in the Shaker cemetery at Hancock. Ted Andrews was one of the pallbearers. At some point before her death, exactly when is not known, she gave (or possibly sold) the rest of the gift drawings from the Hancock community to the Andrewses.

The Andrewses' first opportunity to consider preserving Shaker material culture on a large scale came in 1938. The social situation at Hancock's Church Family had deteriorated to the point that Trustee Frances Hall was almost completely estranged from the rest of the family living in the Brick Dwelling. Faith Andrews recalled that Frances Hall "was not on speaking terms with the people in the big house." "I remember," she said,

that the trustee had notified the people in the red brick dwelling that in order to save money, or repair, she was going to take down the meetinghouse . . . one of the most beautiful buildings. And she started to get the workmen lined up and we felt very very badly about that . . . so in our rush and eagerness to do something, we went over to Sadie Neale and told her what was going on and we said we would be satisfied just to get the meeting room if we couldn't get the whole building. We couldn't afford to get the building and move it.[73]

Relying on their deep friendship with Sadie Neale, the Andrewses approached her with the news from Hancock. "More than anything else," they felt, "she wanted the Shaker work to go on: as example, as inspiration, as part of the historic process."[74] The fullest version of the subsequent exchange comes from an interview with Faith, who reported:

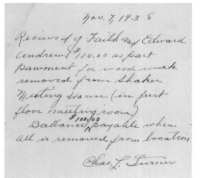

[Sadie said,] "Do you know what it would cost you to get the meeting room?" That is where the dances were. And we said, "No, but we'll find out and we'll come back and tell you." So we found out. We went over and saw the people who were going to take the building down and they gave us a price for saving the meeting room, eight or ten more windows, all in perfect condition and painted that pale heavenly blue, two stoves to heat that room, just a magnificent place, and built-in pieces, and we went back that afternoon and told Sadie and Sadie said "Yea, you wait a few minutes." And she went into her bedroom . . . and took the covers off her bed and reached under the mattress and pulled out a little satchel and sat on the bed and counted out the money and gave it to us. And that was the most amazing thing. She said "Yea, if you want it, it's yours."[75]

Photographs of the 1786 Meetinghouse at Hancock, Massachusetts, taken during its dismantling in 1938. The Andrews' receipt from contractor Charles Turner of Pittsfield for salvage of the interior woodwork.
Courtesy, The Winterthur Library: The Edward Deming Andrews Memorial Shaker Collection, No. SA 376, SA 377 (Meetinghouse), SA 1702.1 (receipt)

It is ironic that a Shaker sister would have to lend money to outsiders in order to save the interior of a Shaker meetinghouse situated four miles from her home. However, Shaker families had a tradition of economic independence, and the Shakers were not terribly sentimental about buildings within their communities, an attitude that extended even to the meetinghouse. By lending the Andrewses money to save the interior of the Hancock Meetinghouse Sadie Neale was quietly demonstrating her personal regard for the Shaker past, as well as her respect for the intentions of the Andrewses in saving it.

Before the 1786 meetinghouse was dismantled in November 1938, the architect Henry Seaver documented the interior, probably at the behest of the Andrewses. Elevation drawings of the one of the pairs of south doors, nine pages of written notes, and a striking watercolor of the meeting room survive in the Andrews Collection at Winterthur. Once Frances Hall had received payment from the Andrewses, the woodwork was taken to the Andrewses' barn at their Richmond farmhouse. A portion of it was sold to the American Museum in Britain, where it is still installed in the Shaker Room. The remaining woodwork was eventually given to Hancock Shaker Village. In truth there is little to distinguish the raised-panel jambs and moldings from other New England country Georgian woodwork of the 1780s. This similarity in itself is instructive in demonstrating that the distinctive Shaker style evolved slowly, and in conjunction with the principles of the faith.

The stewardship of Hancock Shaker Village in caring for this interior architecture is open to debate. Ted Andrews was appalled that much of the original peg rail was cut up to fit the 1793 Shirley, Massachusetts, Shaker Meetinghouse after it was relocated to Hancock in 1962. He complained about it in a memorandum to the museum president Amy Bess Miller:

> The director and president used, without authorization, pegboard on the first floor which was not the property of Shaker Community, Inc., but still that of Mr. and Mrs. Andrews. This was done despite my request to the superintendent that no use should be made of this material, as it was part of the complete meeting room of the old Hancock church which we bought at the time of the dismantling and hoped some day to restore. This original material was painted over with the false color and cut to fit space![76]

Curator, and eventual Museum Director, John Ott's salvage of the two east doors of the meetinghouse from a Ministry Shop coal bin in 1968 plainly shows, however, that the practical Hancock Shakers had little regard for their outmoded meetinghouse. Nonetheless, there is no doubt about the extraordinary prescience of the Andrewses and Sister Sadie in saving the woodwork. Currently, a substantial amount of the remaining interior is catalogued and stored at Hancock, forming a remarkable assemblage of eighteenth-century interior architecture by Shaker hands.

The Andrewses' continuing closeness with Sister Sadie Neale seemed to only further sour their relations with Sadie's natural sister, Emma. Charles Adams's notebooks record the tension and paranoia afflicting the Neale sisters and their hired assistants as competition for the remaining artifacts of the Church Family increased. Because no correspondence between the Andrewses and the Neales exists for the late 1930s into the early 1940s we must rely on Adams's notebooks and Sadie Neale's diary for a window into the period.[77] In a notebook entry dated December 8, 1939, Adams states:

> Cornell had told [New York State Museum curator William] Lassiter and Chamberlain that Emma and Sadie were at loggerheads. Cornell works for Emma, and another man for Sadie. Sadie has tried to have Emma get rid of Cornell as Andrews does not like him, he claims that the Andrews stole from Sadie! The situation is very bad. The wagon seat figured by Andrews in his book belongs to the wagon at Mt. Lebanon.

Sister Emma Neale in front of the 1824 Meetinghouse at Mount Lebanon, N.Y.

Collection of Hancock Shaker Village

Emma gave me a long story of the wills made by persons and that they had no authority to do so. Lassiter had heard the story and that the Court ruled that as they no longer had religious services they no longer had a legal religion! The wills have caused a lot of trouble.

In Sadie's <u>presence</u> Emma said she would give me some textiles! This showed her favorable attitude. I had suggested to Emma that she will the pictures to the St. Mus. She thinks that these should not have been allowed out of official possession. Letterhead came from the Western Res. His. Soc. about some that they had. <u>Kath</u>. Allen, a Jewess, had let them go.

She said some had made a business out of the Shakers matter. I said we did not. She asked me about Andrews, I said they had made it a business. I asked what she thought and she said she would not tell. I said you asked me! Told her not to repeat what I said and I trusted her.[78]

The issue of individual legal wills among the Shakers cited by Charles Adams demonstrates just how far Shaker customs and order had declined at the Church Family. How could an individual Shaker have any other will than to leave all of his or her possessions to the united interest reflected in the Shaker covenant? Emma Neale's derision of the deceased Eldress Catherine Allen for her Jewish ancestry (Allen's mother was Jewish) is quite shocking, given Allen's noted dedication to the faith. At the time of her death in 1922 she was the First Eldress in the Central Ministry. Finally, the frequent hostile remarks made against the Andrewses (and unproven regarding the allegations of theft) indicate that Emma's animus toward them had reached a fevered pitch. Despite her advanced years she was still sly enough to trick Adams into a frank confession of his thoughts about the Andrewses while coyly withholding her own.

Given Emma's attitude toward the Andrewses in December 1939, it is all the more curious to find the following entry in Sadie's diary for January 17, 1940: "Andrews calls to see Emma about some drawings."[79] Is it possible that Ted Andrews could have secured the gift drawings held by Emma Neale despite her strong personal feelings against him? It seems so.

Emma Neale had written to Wallace Cathcart, librarian of the Western Reserve Historical Society in Cleveland, on June 26, 1939, regarding his request to help identify some of the gift drawings sold to the society by Eldress Catherine Allen.

Esteemed Friend

In reply to your esteemed favor I would be very glad to verify any writings or drawings you have which might stand in the name of Polly Reed who in my estimation was the greatest penman, and most artistic person in our community.

If Eldress Catherine gave them to you from Lebanon they must be hers. There was some made in other places, Watervliet Canterbury &c but I would not consider them equal to her's.

I have some which I have kept hidden from sight as they were the expression of a deep religious inspiration and so was very precious to the one possessing them. I still have them and would not wish to make it public as they have been sought so many times.

Your's Sincerely Emma J. Neale

A detail from [heart shaped cutout for] Rufus Bishop by Sister Polly Jane Reed, Mount Lebanon, N.Y. 1844.
Andrews Collection, Hancock Shaker Village 1963.121

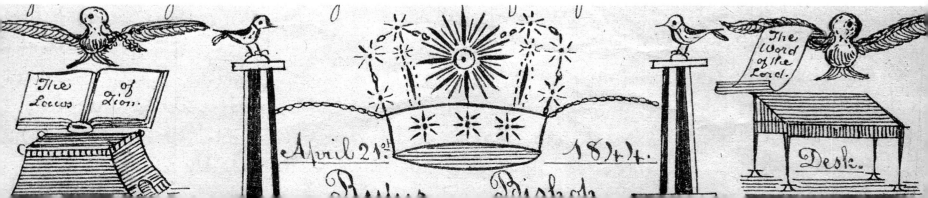

A further letter to Cathcart written July 27, 1939, offers confirmation of the gift drawings in Emma Neale's possession at that time, a view of the general condition of the Shaker societies, and also a veiled insinuation likely referencing the Andrewses.

Esteemed Friend

In a previous letter I think I told you retiring Polly Reed was the greatest or one of the greatest women the Shakers ever raised. Her Spiritual drawings as gifts from former Leaders were beautiful but to me sacred. All her Maps & Charts &c drawn with pen & brush never had her name. One of the two Hemispheres before Maps were common was a wonderful piece and now hangs in the Museum in Albany N.Y. but no name attached. This was made in 1856. I grew up under her training so you will see why I appreciate your respect for the Shakers and would not have you think I object to having the many things that Shakers have done with unnoticed skill some of it represented in the Museums as Shaker products but the Shakers strove to have it in the name of the Community rather than the individual which might cause some rivalry. It would not need to if we were all of one pattern. In our closing days much has bought for a very small price and sold by antique dealers for a very great price. Some have not passed as antique dealers but that was what they really were. You speak of Elder Irving passing away. It is indeed a great loss and [leaves] Canterbury without a male. There are about 34 sisters mostly middle age & younger but no children as they as others have ceased to take them as there is no future in our present condition. We will go out in our present form but I really believe will rise again if under another name. (<u>Principles never die</u>) Forms may change as conditions demand.

To sum up our present condition is quite unsettled altho' they have arranged an order who they designate as Ministry and Trustees combined I am still a Trustee only one position at my age is enough. At Lebanon Eldress Ella Winship is Minister at the head Agent of the Trustees & head of the North Family at Mount Lebanon. Eldress Rosetta Stephens lives with her as associate Eldress & one of the Trustees. Sadie Neale & myself are both Trustees we are all that is left of the Church Family. We live in one of the Church Family buildings which was reserved when that property was sold until we no longer needed it. There are four members in what was once the 2nd Family, There are 12 members at The North Family, Frances Hall at Hancock is Minister & Trustee that completes the four that are Ministry & Trustees all four sisters not a brother. How it will work out we cannot tell. We are in a very unsettled condition and I may not have made very clear but may later.

Sincerely Your's Emma J. Neale[80]

Charles Adams's notebook records the frenetic and almost humorous details of his next visit to Mount Lebanon: trying to get decent photographs of the sisters in their proper dress, negotiating for goods, and listening to jealous carping about favoritism and the influence of the Andrewses.

02/06/1940

Chamberlain with his auto took Lassiter, Baldwin & myself to Mt. Lebanon to make plans to deliver by truck the purchases from the North & Church families.

Baldwin made another trial to get a good photo of <u>Eldress Sarah Collins</u>.

I spoke to Eldress <u>Lillian Barlow</u> about 2 sets of the knock down parts of all the kinds of <u>chairs</u> she makes, and a photo of the lathes. She wishes to clean up before any photos of the lathe.

Then went to see Cornell about the Emma sale. Then Lassiter and I walked to see the Neales.

They were friendly. I told Emma about the Western Res. His. Soc. collection. She again spoke of the Sister Allen who should not have disposed of the MSS., but was always after money, a Jewess.

Sister Sarah Collins of Mount Lebanon, New York.
Courtesy, The Winterthur Library: The Edward Deming Andrews Memorial Shaker Collection, No. SA 28

Emma brought out a pair of yellow deerskin gloves with silk needlework, which she priced highly.

Called at Heynigers office to get Shakers No. of Peg Board & copies of School booklets.

Then went to the North Family and took new photo of Rosetta—she changed to Shaker dress—he also took photo of Sister Martha Wetherell, more of the corn drying pans.

Jennie [Wells] called me aside and said Rosetta did not wish to sell to me the medicine bottles I had once selected from the bldg. back of their house. Told her I cared more for Shaker friendship than the bottles etc! She added a note about the Andrews that was not favorable and suggested Rosetta was favorable to the Andrews! I don't see the meaning of this![81]

Shortly thereafter the headmaster of the Lebanon School paid a visit to Adams, where the main topic of conversation again seemed to be the Andrewses. Heyniger was not in favor of the Andrewses' collecting efforts, and his wildly exaggerated fears indicate that he must have heard news of Ted Andrews's recent acquisition of Emma Neale's gift drawings.

02/27/1940

Visit by C. Lambert Heyniger Darrow School, New Lebanon, N.Y.

He had met the Andrews and was shown some of their materials but seemed aloof and wondered how they made a living! He also told Lassiter that they had told Heyniger that they had about 50 of the spiritual drawings!![82]

Sister Emma Neale had always favored Charles Adams over the Andrewses in her dealings. The last glimpse we have of Emma Neale and Charles Adams competing against the Andrewses comes in an Adams notebook entry for June 6, 1941:

Sister Emma Neale photographed ca. 1937 by L.J. Peterson.
Collection of Hancock Shaker Village 1989.3975

Shaker Visit / Church Family / Emma

5. Andrews report that all their Ch. Fam. belongings go to Andrews. Emma refuses to grant this and will prevent this by writing.[83]

It seems impossible that the Andrewses could have actually talked Sadie Neale into willing all of the possessions of the Church Family to them. While Emma Neale was clearly under that impression, in the absence of documentary evidence we can never know the truth.

A plaintive letter written to the Andrewses by Sadie Neale on October 13, 1942, shows just how much Sadie had come to rely on the Andrewses' visits and friendship:

Where? Oh where are our Antique Pilgrims? And where is the Scarborough School and the Dean and Instructor thereof? I would like some more reliable information than the newspaper gives. . . . But what I want to know most at the present time is where are our Antique Pilgrims? With much love yours ignorantly Sadie A. Neale.[84]

"Antique Pilgrims" the Andrewses may have been, but they were also dear friends and confidantes to many Shakers during their lives.

Sister Emma J. Neale died at Mount Lebanon on November 28, 1943. Her sister Sadie moved to Hancock shortly thereafter, finally passing away on February 17, 1948. With Sadie Neale's death also came the end of the Church Family of the Mount Lebanon Shakers, the first Shaker family gathered into order in 1787. Sister Sadie had worked with the Andrewses to preserve some of the most valuable Shaker artifacts, among them the first written form of the covenant dating to 1795, and the 1786 interior of the meetinghouse at Hancock.

Sister Sadie Neale photographed ca. 1937 by L.J. Peterson.
Collection of Hancock Shaker Village 1989.3975
A detail from [heart shaped cutout for] Sarah Ann Standish by Sister
Polly Jane Reed, Mount Lebanon, N.Y. 1844.
Andrews Collection, Hancock Shaker Village 1963.123

Ted Andrews's major work *The People Called Shakers: A Search for the Perfect Society* was published in 1953. Heralded upon its publication as the most comprehensive study of the Shakers yet published, it was not above criticism from the very people it celebrated. The most noted example of this criticism came from Brother Ricardo Belden of Hancock.

Brother Ricardo wrote a letter to the book's publisher, Oxford University Press, and also gave an interview to an Albany newspaper disparaging the book. The Andrewses preserved both in their papers given to Winterthur. This act of preservation alone speaks volumes of the Andrewses' commitment to documenting the complete story of their interactions with the Shakers, good or bad. Faith Andrews was careful enough to place a prefatory note of her own with Brother Ricardo's letter:

Brother Ricardo Belden photographed in front of
the Tannery, Hancock, Massachusetts, ca. 1958.
Collection of Edgar and Beverly Crete

> This letter <u>to</u> the <u>Editor</u> of Oxford Press expressing his dislike of our history is typical of Bro Ricardo—A member originally of Enfield Con Society, he was left on the steps of the Village Shaker church when he was a very young baby. His clothes indicated that he came from a "well-to-do-family." At that time a boy named Charlie Ross was missing (probably kidnapped) & the Shaker story has not been verified. Newspapers of the day would doubtless carry a full story. However, Ricardo's reputation as a Shaker leaves much to be desired.[85]

Brother Ricardo's letter, dated October 1953, expresses very specific concerns with *The People Called Shakers.*

> Dear sirs.
>
> I have read the book The People Called Shakers. I do not like some parts of it, as they are sayings of people of the outside world and are no part of the Shaker works or teachings. Such as are printed on page 46 and other pages in the book.
>
> On page 139 the picture of the square order shuffle is in disorder and not in proper form.
>
> On page 232 the picture of Frederick Evens [*sic*] is no likeness of him, I met F. Evens several times in my life and remember him well.
>
> On page 154 the picture is not a good representation of Believers worship.
>
> On the front of the jacket the picture does not represent any form of ower worship in my time, it is disorderly and misleading.
>
> On the back of jacket the picture of the singing meeting is disorderly. Brethren should not sit with knees crossed in a meting when Sisters are present.
>
> Yours cincerely,
>
> Ricardo Belden.
>
> I was placed with the Shakers at Enfield Conn. when I was 4 years old and I united in the marches and dances from childhood up to the time they stopped useing them in their worship, I still know how to perform them.
>
> I see on the back of the jacket a statement that E.D. Andrews is the highest authority on the Shakers, he is not an authority high or low on the Shakers, Thare is no authority on the Shakers <u>other than the Shakers themselves</u>.
>
> Ricardo Belden
>
> [separate enclosure]
>
> Dear sirs.
>
> I have not made <u>two copies</u> of my writing, for it is not easy for me to write, and I have other things to do.
>
> You may make as many copies as you wish.
>
> Yours Ricardo Belden
>
> This is not to be published.[86]

Brother Ricardo Belden in his shop at the Brothers' Shop, Hancock, Massachusetts, 1935.

Library of Congress, Prints & Photographs Division, photograph by Samuel Kravitt, LC-DIG-ppmsca-07479

Brother Ricardo's objections were further aired in an article published on November 15, 1953, in the *Pictorial Review.* The article, entitled "New Books Records History of Area Shakers," gives a brief overview of the sect and then allows the Shakers to comment on Andrewses' work. Brother Ricardo is quoted in a passage that appears under the tongue-in-cheek subheading "Shakers Aroused":

Over at Hancock, Mass., a white-bearded patriarch, Brother Ricardo Belden, who will be 85 on Dec. 22, and is senior of only two remaining male Shakers, is outspoken in his righteous wrath. He consented to be quoted on this much: "I consider it a very unfair writing about the Shakers. Some of it will be misleading to the Outside World, and some absolutely false statements are made about the Shaker order. Andrews, or any other person in the Outside World, cannot be an authority on the Shakers except the Shakers themselves."

Without a copy of the book at hand, Brother Ricardo would not cite specific examples of what he means. "Read it and you will see," he says.

One of the sisters at Hancock backs up the criticism of "The People Called Shakers," albeit a bit more mildly. She thinks the author included some unfavorable items needlessly. "Whatever they say, they can't harm us," is her placid view. "We have proved ourselves above it."[87]

Although surviving letters written by the Andrewses in the 1920s and 1930s do not contain references to Sister Olive Hayden of Hancock, she would become a close friend of the couple's in later years. Sister Olive was brought to Hancock on Halloween night of 1903 at the age of seven (Clara Sperle would arrive exactly twenty-two years later on that same date). As Olive matured she became the music teacher to the girls in the community, while fulfilling many other roles as caretaker to the aging sisters. She left the community at the age of thirty-nine on August 15, 1935 and eventually married Morris Austin and settled in Connecticut.

When the Andrewses began their collaboration with Amy Bess Miller to restore the Shaker village at Hancock, Olive Austin was one of the first people interviewed extensively in connection with the project. She had known the Andrewses from their visits to Hancock in the 1920s and 1930s and quickly rekindled a warm friendship with Faith Andrews—a friendship that would grow deeper in the shared grief of losing their husbands.

The first of seventeen letters from Olive in the Andrews Archives at Winterthur is dated August 2, 1961. The last one is dated January 23, 1977. Through reading these lengthy letters (along with numerous brief Christmas and birthday greetings), one gains a sense of the depth of the friendship that existed between Olive and Faith. The correspondence covers the period when both women lost their husbands, providing an especially interesting insight into what this experience was like for Olive, who was raised a Shaker. Sister Olive also offers up valuable memories of her time at Hancock. The excerpts that follow address issues relevant to the Shaker world in general and demonstrate that the Andrewses' relations with the Shakers were not solely based on the eventual acquisition of Shaker objects.

Aug 2, 1961

Dear Friends:

Your lovely note received and I was certainly thrilled to be called Sister Olive.

I think I still am a Shaker at heart for my thoughts constantly turn to my dear home and all the precious souls I was privileged to live with.

When I think of the weeks, months and years of untiring work Dr. Andrews has done I feel grateful to him and to you also. I am sure the remaining Believers also owe him a great debt of gratitude for what he has done for the future generations.

The next letter was written after a visit to Hancock Shaker Village in its new incarnation as a museum.

Nov 4, 1962

I was so pleased when I saw what has been done to the old poultry house. It was in such a terrible state the last time I was there. Then too the old meeting house from Shirley; how beautiful it looks a perfectly darling building. It seems so wonderful to see my dear old home being restored. I dream so much of the dear saintly people I lived with. Only those who have been brought up among the Shakers can know what beautiful lives they lived.

Olive Hayden Austin in 1943.
Collection of Hancock Shaker Village 2002.7274

The next letter suggests that Faith had taken Olive into her confidence regarding the troubles at Hancock Shaker Village, Inc.

June 10, 1963

Dear Faith:

How can I ever thank you enough for the beautiful little Shaker doll? I do love it so much, it is exquisite; every little detail of her clothing is so perfect.

I shall always prize it and think of you and your love and interest in everything pertaining to the dear "Believers."

I did enjoy visiting you in your dear little home and seeing your fine Shaker furniture, Morris and I thought it was most lovely.

Dear Faith; I was so sorry to hear of your trouble and worry.

I shall pray that every thing will come out right and that harmony will prevail for naturally I love Hancock Community Inc. the place of all my childhoods fond and pleasant memories.

No other spot on earth will ever be so dear to me for I was certainly priviledged to know some of the early members and they truly "practiced and lived what they preached." I loved them dearly and prized my <u>Gospel relation</u>.

The little chest you had upstairs brought back loving thoughts of my dear caretaker, Sister Emoretta Belden, I told you it was hers. She was so good and sweet, no mother could ever be more gentle than she was to me; she was second Eldress in the Church family.

Olive's poignant memories of childhood Christmases spent at Hancock, as well as her thoughts on a recent visit to Sabbathday Lake, Maine, color the next letter.

Dec 12, 1965

The middle of October we took a little vacation and went up to Maine as we love it up there so much. Called at the Shakers and they were so pleased to see us, the village is kept up so nice, every building all freshly painted and the Ministry's shop all restored and furnished as it used to be.

This time of year always makes me feel sad, for our Christmas plays which we put on for the older ones were always so lovely, we were weeks preparing and rehearsing. What a happy time it was for everyone, Alice was our coach. Our meeting room and dining room was trimmed with princess pine and how fragrant it was.

We sang carols in the halls and those who were working in the kitchen decorated the dining room tables most beautiful.

If I could live my life over again I would choose to go to the Shakers, that is if they too were in existence, I had such a happy childhood there, wish the young people of today could have what I had.

You and your husband did so much to interest people in the Shaker way of life, I have read and reread his books, many, many times and think they are wonderful, I am sure everyone owes you both so much gratitude for your fine contributions along these lines, Shaker history.

The next letter contains a heartfelt tribute to Ted Andrews from Sister Olive in response to the gift of a copy of the Andrewses' recently published book *Religion in Wood*. Ted Andrews had been dead for two and a half years by this time, so Olive's unsolicited tribute must have touched Faith deeply.

Jan 1, 1967

Dear Faith:

How shall I ever express enough thank yous for the perfectly beautiful gift which you sent me?

It is such a lovely, lovely book in every way, how I treasure it for it brings back such wonderful memories of days gone by when I gaze on the pages and see the dear rooms and furniture from my old Hancock home.

It is so wonderfully compiled and I know it took many hours of work and study to finally place it before the public.

I realize more and more that as time glides on posterity is going to owe so much to Dr. Andrews and you for your devoted study to the Shaker way of life and to their artifacts.

No other historians have given so much to the world as you have in the way of Shaker lore.

Dr. Andrews works are Masterpieces and his name will be spoken of with great appreciation by countless numbers of people long after the last Shaker member has vanished from the earth.

We all owe him a great debt of gratitude. I thank you again dear for this priceless book, I <u>love it</u>.

I hope you had a lovely Christmas; the season has never seemed the same to me since I left home, every year we younger people used to put on plays and invite the Lebanon people over, it was a delightful time for us.

As a child we all had to look back on our years, take an inventory of our lives and see and acknowledge our little faults and how we could improve.

We had to visit our Eldress and have a confidential talk with her.

Also at this time each child had to sacrifice something special in the way of toys to give to the poor children as we always had as much again at Christmas. It was a lovely custom I think for it taught us to be unselfish.

I had a wonderful caretaker, I doubt if my own mother would have done more for me, I was left an orphan and what a fortunate child I was that my father recognized the true worth of the Shakers, it was his wish that I be placed among them at his passing. Could any father be wiser than he was?

Here, in a letter surely unique in the annals of Shaker-related correspondence, Olive shares the news of the death of her husband, Morris.

Nov 26, 1967

My Dear Faith:

Here it is almost the end of the year and I sit alone writing you this unhappy letter.

Faith, I lost my dear husband six months ago on the 10th day of May. I just could not write to anyone for I was in such a state of shock, it has been a most terrible experience to go through.

I know you went through it also so I am not informing you of anything you have not suffered yourself. I know you loved your dear husband as I loved mine.

The letter goes on in a very personal tone about Olive's sense of loss and subsequent loneliness.

In the next letter Olive thanks Faith for a copy of *Visions of the Heavenly Sphere*. She also shares lengthy and detailed reminiscences of her childhood at Hancock, as well as her thoughts on the ongoing restoration of Hancock Shaker Village.

March 15, 1970

Dear Faith:

How can I possibly express my gratitude to you for compiling such a wonderful work of art as 'Visions of the Heavenly Sphere.'?

How many, many hours of research and study you and your dear husband must have put into this work.

It is the most beautiful book I think I have ever seen and I don't know how I can ever thank you enough for sending it to me.

I do so love your "Shaker Order of Christmas," I have read and reread it many times.

Do you know a great deal of what you have written was still in existence in my childhood days?

I remember Eldress Caroline and Sister Emoretta gathering clothes together to put into the box for the poor, some of my own little dresses and underwear went into this box and every one of we children had to part with two of our toys for under priviledged children. I remember how hard it was to part with these treasures but we were made happy again when we found ever lovlier toys under our tree Christmas morning.

Oh, it truly was a beautiful life, I was a happy little girl at the Shakers, my caretakers was so wonderful to me, the only mother I ever had.

You wrote about the Sisters going to the Eldress to open their minds, even the little children did this. Once every month we went to our Eldress and told her how we were progressing and even our little misdemeanors which so often occur among children. She was always so loving and kind and ready to show us the right way.

I dearly loved our Eldress, I wonder if you ever knew her, she was a wonderful mother to all her young people, truly a born leader and we all looked up to her with much devotion and respect.

It does not seem possible that this wonderful way of life has passed.

The beauty, the serenity of the Shaker life to think I was priviledged to enjoy it and know so many of the saints who lived among them.

My heart aches today for the purity, the unselfishness and gracious ways of these dear people.

I am happy my Hancock home is now a monument to these dear consecrated people.

Was glad to hear that the wonderful old stone barn has been made safe and strong again.

Hancock was truly a lovely Society a "City of Peace" nestled in the arms of the beautiful Berkshires.

We young people knew all the wonderful trails in those hills and hours were spent in walking, picking berries, gathering nuts and having picnics up the mountain side.

You and Ted's laborious work of love on this most worth while subject will go down in history and your names will always be spoken of and remembered as the greatest authority on Shaker lore. This is as it should be for you have both devoted your entire life to this cause that future generations may study and know that such a wonderful people as the Shakers did live upon this earth of ours.

The final few exchanges in the correspondence touch on the Shakers at Sabbathday Lake and offer bittersweet reflection on life within and outside a Shaker community. Olive's remarks on the 200th anniversary of Mother Ann's arrival in America are surprising and suggest that Shakerism, ever changing, had evolved past what she had known as a young woman.

July 26, 1971

I did enjoy visiting with the Maine Shakers for it had been eight years since I last saw them. I missed seeing Sister Ethel Peacock so much for she was such a live wire, full of fun, also Sister Della Haskell whom I always liked very much, they were both from Alfred. Eldress Harriet Coolbroth certainly had a nice family of young people but they are fast going now.

Oct 17, 1971

It was wonderful to see you again, and Eldress Gertrude I know was delighted to be with you and have a chance to talk, she is a dear little person. I truly feel for her for her burdens are very heavy.

We enjoyed a wonderful dinner it was so delicious, and I thought of Alice through it all and of the wonderful evening we spent at your home on Clinton Street way back in the year 1930. It seems like such a long time ago and indeed it is.

So much has happened since then, we have both known much joy and sorrow during the forty and one years.

Aug 6, 1974

Today is the two hundreth anniversary of Mother Ann's landing in America. How this country has changed since her day, some things for the better, others sad to day is not so good. I suppose they are having a big celebration at S. D. Lake but just as happy I'm not there, wonder what Mother Ann would say if she should return, she wouldn't be able to recognize the Truths she taught I'm sure.

Right around the time of this last letter from Sister Olive to Faith Andrews there occurred one more incident of the Shakers' involvement with the Andrewses and their work. Faith had prepared for Syracuse University Press an updated edition of the 1933 publication *The Community Industries of the Shakers*. The new book, entitled *Work and Worship of the Shakers*, was to be published in 1973 by Syracuse University Press. Apparently, the editor of the press sought out the opinion of Brother Theodore Johnson, a member of the Sabbathday Lake community, regarding the merits of the work. Brother Ted (as he was known) had become friendly with the community in the late 1950s. He eventually joined (a topic of great controversy and well beyond the scope of this essay) and helped bring in new, younger members to the family. It is unclear what his objection to the Andrewses' work were. Brother Arnold Hadd has been unable to locate a copy of Johnson's letter in the library at Sabbathday Lake. Likewise, a call to Syracuse University Press yielded no results. The only documentation of what happened is in Robert Brown's 1982 interview of Faith Andrews, which quotes Faith as follows:

The editor [of Syracuse University Press] must have asked Mr. Johnson about the Andrewses because he wrote back that it would be a great mistake for them to publish this book. That we were not scholars. If we were, we were a form of armchair scholars and he was quite shocked at the prospect of it. And he was very convincing. And the editor evidently convinced the director that they had best not after getting this word from the head librarian.[88]

Faith Andrews's reference to Brother Ted as "the head librarian" (although he was head of the library at the community) is intentionally dismissive of his membership in the community. This attitude was tantamount to a political stance within the Shaker world surrounding the admission of Theodore Johnson as a member. Leaving this issue aside, Brother Ted, a Fulbright scholar and graduate of Harvard Divinity School, was certainly qualified to give a professional opinion on the Andrewses' work. Johnson's letter to the editor only temporarily delayed the publication of *Work and Worship*, which was issued in 1974 by the New York Graphic Society. Curiously, Brother Arnold Hadd recalled that *Work and Worship* was sold by the Sabbathday Lake community: "When I was a young man and visiting here the museum shop carried that book. Br. Ted did all of the buying for that shop so whatever he might have felt was by the mid 1970s altered."[89]

The Andrewses' life-long study Shakerism and collecting of Shaker objects were built on a firm foundation of relations with the Shakers. But human relationships are seldom simple and inevitably involve joy and pain. The Andrewses' interactions with the Shakers as a whole were never as simple as the Andrewses themselves sometimes portrayed them. Additionally, the Shakers' internal relations, within families, communities, and the entire United Society, were even more complex and have yet to be fully understood by historians. In the light of these facts it is impossible to pass judgment on fifty years of friendship and business among such a large and diverse group of people. In assembling this corpus of documents relating to the Andrewses' interactions with the Shakers I have endeavored to present original source material in an impartial manner. Some recent scholars have been particularly harsh toward the Andrewses. It is my hope that this book, and the beautiful collection it presents, will spark a reevaluation of the early twentieth century Shaker world and the Andrewses' place therein.

Notes

1 Uncatalogued archival document located in restricted archives, Edward Deming Andrews Memorial Shaker Collection, Winterthur Museum, Garden, and Library, Winterthur, Delaware (hereafter EDAMSC). The estimate that this five-page narrative was written after 1981 is based on internal evidence.

2 Faith Andrews, interview by Robert F. Brown, Pittsfield, Mass., January 14, 1982, 4, uncataloged archival document, EDAMSC.

3 A. Donald Emerich, comp., *Shaker Furniture and Objects from the Faith and Edward Deming Andrews Collections Commemorating the Bicentenary of the American Shakers* (Washington D.C.: Published for the Renwick Gallery of the National Collection of Fine Arts by the Smithsonian Institution Press, 1973), 25.

4 Andrews, interview by Brown, 9–12.

5 Ibid., 16.

6 See Priscilla Brewer, *Shaker Communities, Shaker Lives* (Hanover, N.H.: University Press of New England, 1986), 143; and Stephen Paterwic, "Who Were the Shakers?" in M. Stephen Miller, *From Shaker Lands and Shaker Hands* (Hanover, N.H.: University Press of New England, 2007), 13.

7 Andrews, interview by Brown, 16.

8 Alice May Smith, "History of Our Home," ms. no.13,377, Emma B. King Library, Shaker Museum and Library, Old Chatham, N.Y.

9 Edward Deming Andrews and Faith Andrews, *Fruits of the Shaker Tree of Life: Memoirs of Fifty Years of Collecting and Research* (Stockbridge, Mass.: Berkshire Traveller Press, 1975), 93.

10 Emerich, *Shaker Furniture*, 24.

11 Andrews, interview by Brown, 16.

12 Benjamin Seth Youngs, *The Testimony of Christ's Second Appearing* (Albany: Printed by E. and E. Hosford State-Street, 1810), 509.

13 Frederick W. Evans, *Shakers. Compendium of the Origin, History, Principles, Rules and Regulations, Government and Doctrines . . .* (New Lebanon, N.Y.: [Charles Van Benthuysen & Sons, Printer], 1867), 44.

14 Day Book, 9784.H2 H235 acc. #370, Hancock Shaker Village, Pittsfield, Mass. (hereafter HSV).

15 In 1938 Frances Hall had been named Trustee of the Watervliet, New York, community, and in 1943 she would be appointed the sole Trustee of the remaining North Family of New Lebanon. Much of the careful unraveling of the who, what, when, and where of the post-1892 Shaker Central Ministry was accomplished by Stephen Paterwic and Brother Arnold Hadd in their excellent article "Gospel Ministry," *Shaker Quarterly* 24 (Winter 1996): 3-30. See particularly p. 6 for a discussion of how the roles of Ministry and Trustee tended to merge from the late nineteenth century on.

16 Elizabeth Belden, "List of arrivals, departures and deaths at Hancock," 1893–1943, ca. 200 pp. # 9757 B425, ID #5217, blue dot, HSV.

17 Clair Zeitlin, interview by Christian Goodwillie and Gary Leveille, February 26, 2005, Delray Beach, Fla. Original recordings on deposit at HSV.

18 Emerich, *Shaker Furniture*, 29.

19 Andrews Archives, folder in box 5 (no acc. no.) Lillian Barlow and William Perkins, EDAMSC.

20 Andrews, interview by Brown, 17.

21 Emerich, *Shaker Furniture*, 26.

22 Andrews, interview by Brown, 20.

23 Emerich, *Shaker Furniture*, 27.

24 Andrews Archives, folder SA 1697.1 (#974) Emma J. Neale, EDAMSC.

25 Sadie Neale, diary, 1929, ms #1112, call number 9758, HSV.

26 Andrews, interview by Brown, 18.

27 Andrews Archives, box 9, folder SA 1697.2 (#975) Prudence Stickney, EDAMSC.

28 Hugh Howard and Jerry V. Grant, "Reinventing the Shakers," *Eastfield Record*, no. 11 (Winter 2002–3), 13.

29 Emerich, *Shaker Furniture*, 29.

30 Andrews Archives, box 9, folder: SA 1697.16 (# 976) Josephine Wilson, EDAMSC.

31 Winter Collection, Curatorial Files, New York State Museum, Albany.

32 Ibid.

33 Ibid.

34 Charles Adams notebooks, ibid.

35 Andrews File, ibid.

36 Ibid.

37 Charles Adams notebooks, ibid.

38 Andrews File, ibid.

39 Charles Adams notebooks, ibid.

40 According to Brother Arnold Hadd of the Sabbathday Lake, Maine, Shaker community: "The least of Mother's children in the east was coined by Elder Otis and it seems to have been repeated by other communities in referencing the multitude of problems here." E-mail to the author, December 13, 2007.

41 R. Mildred Barker, *Holy Land: A History of the Alfred Shakers* (Sabbathday Lake, Me.: Shaker Press, 1986), [unpaginated, second page from the last].

42 14-DJ-140 1931 [Coolbroth, Eugenia M.] Diary, Shaker Library, Sabbathday Lake, Me.

43 14-DJ-100 1931 [Wilson, Delmer C.] Diary, ibid.

44 Andrews Archives, box 9, folder SA 1697.9 (#975) Prudence Stickney, EDAMSC.

45 Ibid., folder SA 1697.10.

46 Ibid., folder SA 1697.11. Dating this letter was achieved through the use of the perpetual calendar at http://www.accuracyproject.org/2009calendar.html, which provided evidence that the Wednesday at the beginning of the letter would have been May 27, the day before the Alfred Shakers arrived at Sabbathday Lake as documented by Sister R. Mildred Barker (see *Holy Land*).

47 E-mail to the author, September 2, 2007.

48 14-DJ-140 1931 [Coolbroth, Eugenia M.] Diary.

49 14-DJ-100 1931 [Wilson, Delmer C.] Diary.

50 14-DJ-140 1931 [Coolbroth, Eugenia M.] Diary.

51 Daniel W. Patterson, *Shaker Gift Drawing and Gift Song: A Study of Two Forms of Shaker Inspiration* (Sabbathday Lake, Me.: United Society of Shakers, 1983), p. xi.

52 Edward Deming Andrews, *Visions of the Heavenly Sphere: A Study in Shaker Religious Art* (Winterthur, Dela.: Henry Francis DuPont Winterthur Museum, Inc., 1969), 3.

53 Emerich, *Shaker*, 39.

54 Andrews, interview by Brown, 29–30.

55 Patterson, *Shaker Gift Drawing*, 7.

56 E-mail to the author, January 3, 2008.

57 Andrews Archives, box 9, folder SA 1697.8 (#975) Prudence Stickney, EDAMSC.

58 Charles Adams notebooks, Curatorial Files, New York State Museum.

59 Ibid.

60 Alice Smith Collection, ibid.

61 Ibid.

62 Andrews Archives, box 9, folder SA 1697.12 (#975) Prudence Stickney, EDAMSC.

63 "Shaker Exhibition at Museum Opens with Large Reception," *Berkshire Eagle*, October 11, 1932.

64 "Mount Lebanon Shakers Speak Here in Appropriate Setting," *Berkshire Eagle*, October 15, 1932.

65 "Describes Work of Shaker Sisters," *Berkshire Eagle*, October 22, 1932.

66 Andrews Archives, box 3, folder: Shaker Inspirational Drawings (1) SA 1384 (#746), EDAMSC. The finished letter, presumably sent to Elder Arthur, is unlocated.

67 Andrews Archives, box 3, folder SA 1369 (#731), EDAMSC.

68 The Andrewses wrote of their "intimate talks in her retiring room," in *Fruits*, 94. The presence of outsiders (one of whom was male) in the retiring room of a Shaker Sister would not have been possible in earlier times. It is likely that very little correspondence survives between the Andrewses and Alice Smith because of their close proximity and frequent personal visits.

69 Andrews Archives, box 9, folder SA 1697.26 (# 979) Alice Smith, EDAMSC.

70 Andrews, interview by Brown, 28.

71 Zeitlin, interview by Goodwillie and Leveille.

[72] Ibid.

[73] Andrews, interview by Brown, 36.

[74] Andrews, *Fruits*, 90.

[75] Andrews, interview by Brown, 37.

[76] Andrews Archives, uncatalogued document, "Report on the Color in the Meeting House at Hancock Shaker Village," by Edward Deming Andrews, Curator, Shaker Community, Inc., April 29, 1963, EDAMSC..

[77] Sadie Neale's diaries for 1929, 1935, 1938, 1939, 1940, and 1943 are held at HSV. The diary for 1938 records the following visits by the Andrewses:

February 25 The Andrews call in afternoon.
April 22 Mr Andrews calls for a short time.
April 26 Andrews calls in afternoon.
May 11 The Andrews call today.
May 12 The Andrews call again today.
July 7 Andrews calls.

In the back of the journal under "Accounts":

"August 10 Andrews takes desk from P.O. brings check for 20 dollars." Sadie Neale's Diary for 1939 records the following visits by the Andrewses:
March 1 The Andrews call for a short time this AM.
June 14 In afternoon go to the Andrew's home in Richmond.
August 22 The Andrews call for a short time.

[78] Charles Adams notebooks, Curatorial Files, New York State Museum.

[79] Sadie Neale, diary for 1940.

[80] Correspondence, Mount Lebanon, NY, WRHS IV A-50, Shaker Collection, Western Reserve Historical Society, Cleveland, Ohio.

[81] Charles Adams notebooks, Curatorial Files, New York State Museum

[82] Ibid.

[83] Ibid.

[84] Andrews Archives, box 9, folder SA 1697.20 (# 978) Sadie A. Neale, EDAMSC. Stephen J. Stein took this letter badly out of context in his book The Shaker Experience in America: A History of the United Society of Believers (New Haven: Yale University Press, 1992).

[85] Restricted archives, EDAMSC.

[86] Ibid.

[87] C. R. Roseberry, "New Book Records History of Area Shakers," Pictorial Review, November 15, 1953.

[88] Andrews, interview by Brown, 176.

[89] E-mail to author December 21, 2007.

Shaker furniture photographed outside of the Andrewses' Pittsfield, Massachusetts home.
ca. 1930

Courtesy, The Winterthur Library: The Edward Deming Andrews Memorial Shaker Collection, No. SA 601, SA 600, SA 643

South Family Dwelling
Mount Lebanon, N.Y.
ca. 1930

*Courtesy, The Winterthur
Library: The Edward Deming
Andrews Memorial Shaker
Collection, No. SA 460*

Introduction to the Catalog

The selection of objects illustrated on the following pages were all at one time in the possession of Edward Deming and Faith Andrews. Today these objects are held in collections at Hancock Shaker Village, The Metropolitan Museum of Art, The Winterthur Museum, The American Museum in Britain, and in numerous private collections. Although this book was published to coincide with the exhibition *Gather Up The Fragments: The Andrews Shaker Collection*, the catalog that follows is not strictly a catalog of that exhibition. Rather, I have made an effort to track down objects that held particular significance for the Andrewses—objects of exceptional craftsmanship, previously unpublished objects, and finally, mundane objects that help to display the sheer breadth of the Andrewses' collecting activities.

Unraveling the true extent of the Andrews Collection at Hancock Shaker Village has been a tremendous undertaking for me and for Hancock Shaker Village Registrar Michael Vogt, (and Jessica Kuhnen before him). It may be impossible to ever complete the record of objects at Hancock given by the Andrewses. Most of the collections records written by Edward Deming Andrews were removed from the site after he resigned as curator of the fledgling museum in 1962. While I was able, with the help of E. Richard McKinstry and Jeanne Solensky at Winterthur, to locate some of these records, others have thus far eluded me. Quite a bit of new information about specific objects is published for the first time in the captions that follow, but much still remains to be learned. Where the community of origin is listed as "Unknown Community," the object was more than likely acquired at either Mount Lebanon, New York, or Hancock, Massachusetts—where the Andrewses did the majority of their collecting. While the Andrewses were very careful to document the furniture that they acquired, they were much less particular in documenting the large collections of tools, housewares, textiles, and other object types that they amassed.

Jane F. Crosthwaite of Mount Holyoke College has been generous enough to share her expertise in interpreting the intriguing Shaker gift drawings. Dr. Crosthwaite, who has long studied the drawings, offers here some new insights into their content and meaning. Scholar and collector M. Stephen Miller also has thoughtfully provided the lion's share of information concerning objects collected by the Andrewses, he and his wife Miriam. Collectors Thomas R. and Ann Andrews Kane, Phyllis Andrews, Edward Deming Andrews II, J.J. Gerald and Miriam McCue, Thomas and Jan Pavlovic, Bob and Aileen Hamilton, Andrew Epstein, John Ribic and Carla Kingsley, J. Richard and E. Barbara Pierce, William and Sandra Soule, David and Virginia Newell, and Gene and Karen Faul all helpfully provided information on dimensions, materials, and provenance for pieces in their respective private collections.

Dimensions have been provided wherever possible. These should be read as follows: height, by width, and by depth. For objects where there is a circular dimension read: height, by diameter. Fixed-handled objects have been measured to include the handle in their overall height. Accession numbers given for objects in the Andrews Collection at Hancock Shaker Village have three fields. The first is the year in which the object was accessioned, the second is the collection number for a group of objects, and the third is the number of that specific object within that collection. Where a third field is not given it means that there is only one object in that collection. The name Mount Lebanon has been used throughout when referring to objects from the New Lebanon/Mount Lebanon community. In order to differentiate itself from the nearby town of New Lebanon, the Shaker community officially changed their name in late 1861 to Mount Lebanon, when a post office was opened there.

Christian Goodwillie, May 2008

Bowl, Hancock, Mass. 19th century
6 ¾" x 19 ½"

This humble kitchen bowl was the first Shaker object acquired by the Andrewses from Sister Alice Smith at Hancock, Mass., circa 1923. It was turned from a single piece of hardwood and finished with red paint. The shape of the bowl has changed over time from round to oval as it has dried and shrunk. The bowl remained in the collection of the Andrews family until 1993. **Shaker Furniture** *plate 11.*

Collection of J. Richard and E. Barbara Pierce.

Bowl, probably Mount Lebanon, N.Y. 19th century
7 ¾" x 25 ¾"

Used in one of the many gardens at the Mount Lebanon community, this bowl is turned from a single piece of pine and painted red with a black stencil reading "GARDEN" on the bottom. "6 ¼ lbs" is hand painted on the bottom. A through-crack has been carefully repaired by stitching the two sides together with wire.

Andrews Collection, Hancock Shaker Village 1962.413.0002

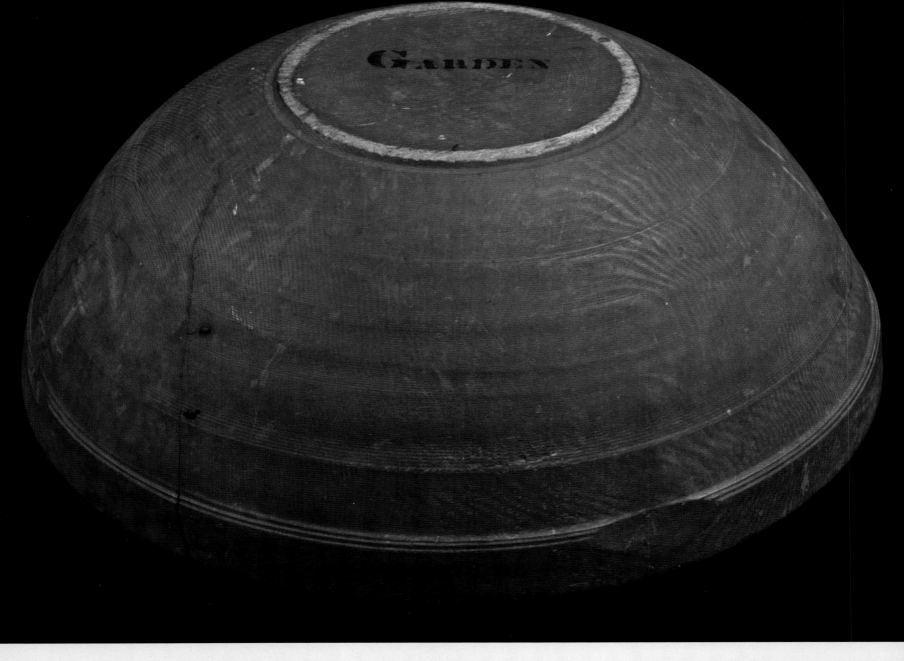

Bowl, probably Mount Lebanon, N.Y. 19th century
8 ½" x 23"

This bowl is turned from a single piece of hardwood. It is painted red with a black painted stencil reading "GARDEN" on the bottom. A crack in this bowl has been repaired with iron screws.

Andrews Collection, Hancock Shaker Village 1962.413.0001

Storage Boxes, probably Mount Lebanon, N.Y. 19th century
2 ³/₈" x 3 ³/₄", 2 ¹/₈" x 3 ³/₄"

The sides and lid rim of these diminutive boxes are made from thin strips of steam-bent wood glued with a lap joint. They are lined with paper on the inside and outside. The example on the left is painted a bright orange and flecked with miniscule black "dashes" in paint or ink. The box on the right was originally painted a similar bright orange (probably using red lead), and overprinted with a yellow/ brown paint, and then heavily varnished. The flat top and bottom of the box on the left uses thin wood discs while the domed top and the bottom of the other are constructed of pasteboard. These boxes have long been colloquially referred to as "orange peel boxes."

Collection of Miriam R. and M. Stephen Miller (left)
Andrews Collection, Hancock Shaker Village 1962.319 (right)

Paper Box, Mount Lebanon, N.Y. 19th century
2 ¹/₄" x 3 ¹/₈" x 4 ³/₄"

The Shakers often reused surplus printed ephemera to line boxes, or simply printed newer labels on the blank reverse side of surplus large broadsheets. Some of the most intriguing and practical Shaker-made objects are pasted together storage boxes constructed from unused printed materials. This diminutive box is made of an unused seed bag intended to package ¹/₄ lb. of the North Family's White Field Carrot seeds. The box was used to store chalk.

**Andrews Collection, Hancock Shaker Village
1962.036**

SHAKERS'
WHITE FIELD CARROT.
1-4 lb.—25 cts.
Apply rotten manure, plough deep and fine, sow (from
the 1st to the 20th of May) in drills 14 inches apart,
cover the seed half-an-inch deep, and thin to 4 inch.

N. F. New Lebanon, N. Y.

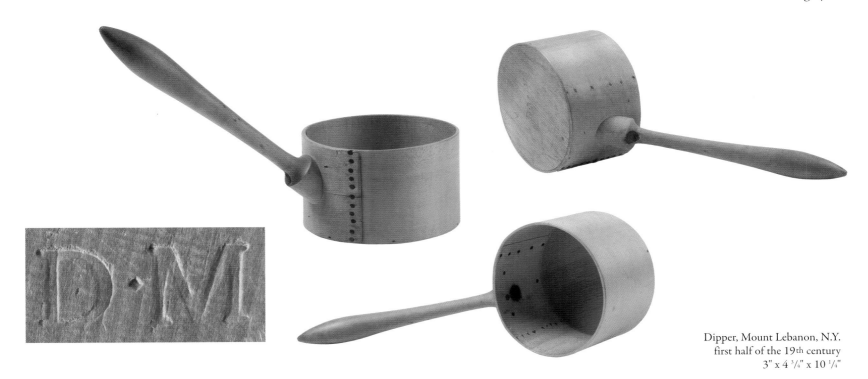

Dipper, Mount Lebanon, N.Y.
first half of the 19th century
3" x 4 3/4" x 10 1/4"

One of the many products to bear the maker's mark of Church Family Trustee David Meacham Sr. (1743-1826) are wooden dippers. The handle is turned from a hardwood and riveted into the side with an iron bolt. The side is made of steam-bent maple lap-joined with copper tacks. The bottom is a single disc of clear pine. The handle is attached at an angle and was shaped to conform perfectly to the curve of the side. The iron bolt that joins the handle and side is fixed by a nut on the underside of the handle. The nut was carefully filed to maintain the smoothly turned collar at the base of the handle. Dippers were sold in "nests" of different sizes, similar to oval boxes. Brother Isaac Newton Youngs wrote a brief history of the manufacture of dippers at New Lebanon in his 1856 manuscript A Concise View of the Church of God. "Dipper making was introduced as early as 1800. and in some years there was considerable done,— both for the Chh's use, and for sale. About the year 1842 there was much improvement, by erecting machinery to go by water, for planing the bottoms and rims, and cutting out the bottoms, making the handles, &c. Of late years but little has been done at the business."[1]

Courtesy, Winterthur Museum 1962.0038

Measure, probably Mount Lebanon, N.Y. or Hancock, Mass., 19th century
3" x 4"

Measures for dry goods were an essential part of rural life in the farmyard, shops, and kitchens. Shakers at the Second Family, Mount Lebanon; Church Family, Hancock; and Church Family, Tyringham; manufactured measures for their own use and for sale to the outside world during the first half of the nineteenth century. This example is made of steam-bent maple, lap-joined with copper tacks. A pine disc forms the bottom. The printed label bearing the number "5" may denote the size of this example, as measures, like dippers and oval boxes, were sold in nests of various sizes.

Collection of Dr. John R. Ribic and Dr. Carla Kingsley

Round or Spit Boxes, Mount Lebanon, N.Y., 19th century
Dimensions by row, left to right.
Front: 2 ¹/₄" x 7 ³/₈"; second: 3" x 7 ⁵/₈, 2 ¹/₂" x 7 ³/₄";
Third: 4 ³/₈" x 9 ⁷/₈, 4 ³/₈" x 9 ¹/₂", 3 ⁵/₈" x 10 ¹/₄";
Fourth: 4 ⁷/₈" x 11 ¹/₂, 5 ¹/₄" x 12", 5 ³/₄" x 10 ⁵/₈", 4 ³/₈" x 10 ¹/₈".

Many visitors to Mount Lebanon during the nineteenth century recorded the presence of spit
boxes, or spittoons, in Shaker buildings. Margaret Hall, who visited June 10, 1827, wrote of
the beauty of the floors in the 1824 meetinghouse, noting that "in the corners are spitting boxes that
the boards may be preserved from such contamination."² Authoress Harriet Martineau writing between
1834 and 1836 approved of the quality of every aspect of the Shaker village, right down to "their spitting-boxes,—
for even these neat people have spitting-boxes—show a nicety which is rare in America."³ An anonymous visitor who published their account
under the pseudonym "H" on August 10, 1836 wrote "even in the kitchens and dairy, spittoons are to be seen, filled with a fine and delicate kind
of shavings."⁴ The ten round boxes grouped in this photo may not have all been spit boxes, but some certainly were. Those with stenciled markings
were possibly used in the meetinghouse or by the Ministry (M), or in the meeting room (M.R.) of a Shaker dwelling house. Almost invariably these
boxes are made of steam bent maple for the side and pine for the bottom. The rim is applied and butts against the top edge of the side wall from which the
fingers have been cut. Looking at a spit box from above one marvels at how the maker joined the fingers and rim to the sides with copper tacks, carefully
merging the components for a smooth meeting point of uniform thickness. These boxes were manufactured in a process similar to oval boxes. Brother Isaac
Newton Youngs of Mount Lebanon described the technological evolution of the process at his home community: "Formerly the rims were sawed out in a
common sawmill, which did the work slowly and imperfectly. The heading & rims were planed by hand. But about the year 1830 the sawing was done by
a buz saw, and the heading planed by water. And shortly after a planing machine was erected, (say in 1832) to plane the rims, which performed the work
admirably."⁵ Among the boxes pictured are examples with both hand, and machine-planed, bottoms; some display circular saw marks on the sides, while
others have no visible tool marks. All, except row 2, box 1, (which is orange) are stained with a yellow pigment, probably chrome yellow.

Spit Box, Mount Lebanon, N.Y. 19th century
3 ⁵/₈" x 10 ¹/₄"

The black stenciled "M" on this spit box may indicate that it was used by the Ministry, or perhaps in a meeting room of a Shaker dwelling, or in the meetinghouse itself. This detail photo reveals the wood grain, visible under a thin wash of yellow paint (probably chrome yellow). The box was constructed so that the grain runs perfectly horizontal to the bottom. This method is ideal in that the wood has been steam bent for the greatest strength and flexibility. The side wall can expand and contract evenly in different climates with less of a chance for splitting around the tacked fingers or top and bottoms, or along the circular side walls. The spit box has the same notched and flattened finger, or "swallowtail," joints used on oval boxes and carriers.

Brother Isaac Newton Youngs recorded in the Church Family Journal a frightening instance when the "Great House," or Church Family Dwelling, was almost destroyed by a fire— kindled in a spit box! "November 1837, Sab. 5. Fire was found in the southwest garret of our great house, in a spitbox! how it came there is difficult to tell. It had burnt thro' the bottom of the box & some on the chest it stood on. Lucy Clark first discovered it, & it was well it was found in season."⁶ Sadly, this magnificent building— built in 1788— did eventually succumb to fire on February 6, 1875.

Andrews Collection, Hancock Shaker Village 1962.641

Round Box or Dry Measure, Unknown Community, ca. 1820
7 ⁷/₈" x 19 ¹/₂"

An unusually large example of a lap-joined oak (sides) and pine (bottom) dry measure or round box. It is joined with iron tacks and the lighter color of the wood at the top edge of the side indicates that is was probably lidded originally.

Andrews Collection, Hancock Shaker Village 1962.700.0009

Measure, Hancock, Mass. ca. 1820
7" x 12"

This measure bears the initials "D.G." referring to Trustee Daniel Goodrich Jr. of Hancock. The Hancock Shakers made and sold nests of measures to the outside world. This example has oak sides and a pine bottom. It is fastened with iron tacks.

Andrews Collection, Hancock Shaker Village 1962.457.0004.1

Round Boxes or Dry Measures, Unknown Community, ca. 1830
3 ¹/₂" x 13 ⁵/₈", 3 ⁵/₈" x 12 ⁵/₈"

The example on the left is maple (sides) and pine (bottom). The circular saw marks on the side and machine-planed bottom suggest a date of post-1830. It is finished in the yellow wash so commonly found on Shaker woodenware. On the right is a box similar in size and materials, finished in an opaque salmon colored paint. The chief difference between the two is the applied rim on the example at right. A detailed view of where the rim and box sides are carefully interleaved and joined shows the complexity of design in this seemingly simple object.

Andrews Collection, Hancock Shaker Village 1962.457.0013, 1962.457.0014

Firkins, Mount Lebanon, N.Y. 19th century
11 ¾" x 13 ⅝", 8 ⅞" x 9 ¾"

Firkins were made for a variety of uses within Shaker communities. These examples both have the typical bent hardwood handle— with rounded underside— and cotter pin construction typical of Mount Lebanon cooperage. The staves and bottoms are either pine or basswood staves. The firkin on the left is butt jointed with iron hoops binding the staves. A butt joint is found most commonly on Mount Lebanon cooperage. The iron hoops have been clipped at the corners where they are bolted together. It is finished in a red wash. The firkin on the right is anomalous, though has strong provenance of having been collected by the Andrewses at Mount Lebanon. The staves in this example are joined with a "U" shaped notch, not typically associated with Mount Lebanon, and the hoops are steam-bent ash fastened with copper tacks. The tips of these hoops where they are joined are beveled in a triangular shape similar to the "fingers" found on oval boxes. It is finished in blue and black paint with "NUTMEGS" carefully painted on the rim of the lid. The staves on both firkins are chamfered on the bottom inside edge to prevent splitting, and the bottoms of both are set into a channel cut into the staves.

Andrews Collection, Hancock Shaker Village 1962.463.0001ab, 1962.468.0001ab

Brother Isaac Newton Youngs of Mount Lebanon, New York, noted the following activities, illustrative of the process of gathering materials for cooperage, in the Church Family Domestic Journal for 1836:

March 1836

w. 2 Edward Fowler went up north about cutting up a large pine tree that our folks have bot lately.

fr. 18 The big pine tree . . . was brot home. The tree must have been about 200 feet high. It was 300 years old.

May 1836

th. 5 Henry Markham & Artemas Markham, coopers, are putting up a quantity of cooper stuff, to season. It is out of the big tree, mentioned March 18th.[7]

Pail, Mount Lebanon, N.Y.,19th century
11" (to top of extended stave) x 12 ⅝"

This pail exhibits another form of swing-handle construction from Mount Lebanon, this time joined to the inside of the vessel. The staves on this example are butt jointed. Two have been left long where the cotter pin attaches to a hardwood bail. A close look at the handle reveals that the underside is rounded to conform to the hand. The width of the handle also flares out at the ends where it is attached. Note the beveled edge on the handle end, a simple preventative measure to avoid splitting. The steam-bent ash hoops are joined by tucking the opposing ends into a notched hook. The pail is finished with a bright yellow paint on the exterior, and a white paint inside. "Harriet G. Augusta" is written on the bottom in pencil.

**Andrews Collection, Hancock Shaker Village
1962.460**

Pail, Canterbury, N.H., ca. 1850
7 ⁷⁄₈" x 10 ³⁄₈"

Canterbury, New Hampshire, along with Enfield, Connecticut and Enfield, N.H., produced large amounts of cooperage during the 19ᵗʰ century. This lidded pail from Canterbury exhibits many of the hallmarks of cooperage from that community. The staves are joined with a "V" shaped notch typical of that community, and chamfered at the bottom (like Mount Lebanon examples). The wire bail is set into a diamond-shaped bail plate (really strap iron cut on the diagonal) that has been relieved at the top to accommodate the iron rim. The turned hardwood handle has a double central scribe line and chamfered ends to prevent splitting. The bottom is turned, and beveled at the outer edge to fit into the staves. The numeral "1" is stamped into the bottom, and a "5" is stamped into the underside of the lid. The rim and hoops are iron. The exterior is finished in a yellow paint and the inside has a clear varnish.

Collection of the Family of David V. and Phyllis C. Andrews.

Kindling Carrier, probably Mount Lebanon, N.Y.
mid-19th century
14 ³/₄" x 19 ⁷/₈" x 10 ³/₈"

This dovetailed carrier was used to bring kindling to the small cast iron stoves that provided heat in Shaker shops and dwellings. The pine walls and bottom bear the marks of a machine planer. A steam-bent ash handle is affixed to the inside walls with copper tacks. The underside of the handle is rounded to conform to the hand. The finish is a yellow wash (probably chrome yellow). This example could be similar to the "box with bail to put wood and shavings in" made by Brother Isaac Newton Youngs in 1839.[8]

Andrews Collection, Hancock Shaker Village 1962.018

Tray, Mount Lebanon, N.Y. mid-19th century
5 ⁷/₈" x 18" x 11"

Constructed of carefully dovetailed pine with a chrome yellow wash, this small tray was probably used in a dining room or kitchen. Note the carefully rounded edges of the ends and handholds.

**Collection of Bob and Aileen Hamilton
Photograph Courtesy of Willis Henry Auctions, Inc.**

Round Carrier, Mount Lebanon, N.Y. mid-19th century *(top left)*
10" x 14 ⅝"

This round box, with maple sides and a pine bottom, (similar to examples on page 111) has been fitted with a fixed handle of the same form used on firkins and pails illustrated in this book. It is finished with a dark red stain, joined with iron tacks. The initials "JB" are carved into the top center of the handle.

Andrews Collection, Hancock Shaker Village 1962.459

Pail, Mount Lebanon, N.Y. mid-19th century *(top right)*
5" x 8 ¾"

The handle is the only characteristic of this pail typical to most other Mount Lebanon examples. Early museum records indicate that this was used as a "milk or calf" pail. The bottom is pine, and steam bent hardwood forms the side and hoops. The hoops in this example are joined with an unusual number of tacks in a novel pattern. The pail was originally lidded.

Andrews Collection, Hancock Shaker Village 1962.461

Round Box, Unknown Community, mid-19th century *(at left)*
7" x 12 ⅝"

A few surviving journals kept by Hancock Bishopric Elder Grove Wright are in the Andrews Collections at Winterthur. Elder Grove records impressive production statistics of cooperage at Hancock, Mass., and Enfield, Conn. Scholars have yet to identify the characteristics of cooperage from those communities due to a relative dearth of documented examples. However, clues in Elder Grove's journal referencing wire bails and the use of oak for side walls make it possible that this lidded box (or pail?) was a product of the Hancock Bishopric. The "headers," or top and bottom, are machine planed pine. The hardwood sides bear circular saw marks; the lid rim is oak. The hardwood hoops are straight-lapped and tacked. The crudely carved wooden ears tacked to the side indicate that the handle was a retrofit. The wire and hardwood handle are stylistically distinct from Mount Lebanon and Canterbury examples. A split on the side wall is repaired with four tin plates tacked to the inside. These plates were affixed prior to the application of the orange wash used as a finish on both the inside and outside.

Andrews Collection, Hancock Shaker Village 1962.464.0002

Oval Carriers, Mount Lebanon, N.Y. mid-19th century
7 ½" x 10 ½" (top), 11" x 15" (bottom)

Oval carriers, both lidded and unlidded, were a natural outgrowth of the oval box industry at the Church Family, Mount Lebanon. Typically pine "headers" (tops and bottoms) were joined to steam-bent maple sides by finely cut, iron-tacked finger joints. The example at top appears to be a primitive early attempt at retrofitting a bent hardwood handle to an oval box. The two components must have been joined at the same time since both bear a red paint finish. The use of thick wooden shims to provide clearance for the attachment of the handle to the sides indicates this carrier was likely constructed prior to the refinement of the process. Additionally, the handle ends continue to the bottom of the side wall and are cut square. The example at bottom, finished in a clear varnish and joined with copper tacks, displays the more delicate handle typical of Shaker carriers produced at many of the New England and New York communities into the early twentieth century. Note the carefully rounded handle-ends and underside. These two carriers are illustrated on page 85 of the catalog that accompanied the 1973 exhibition **Shaker***.*

Collection of Miriam R. and M. Stephen Miller (top)
Collection of Dr. John R. Ribic and Dr. Carla Kingsley (bottom)

Round Carrier, Mount Lebanon, N.Y. 19th century
4 ⁷/₈" x 14 ³/₄"

This round carrier, likely used in a Wash House, is constructed of ash sides and rim, a pine bottom, and typical Mount Lebanon hardwood handle. The sides bear circular saw marks and are lap-joined with iron tacks. The inside end of the side wall has been carefully beveled to prevent splitting. The carrier is finished all over with an orange wash (probably red lead). "Fine shirts" is written across the front in ink, and "2# 4 oz" is written in faint pencil on the rear outside wall.

Andrews Collection, Hancock Shaker Village 1962.391

Round Carrier, Mount Lebanon, N.Y. 19th century
7 ¹/₄" x 10 ³/₄"

An even more utilitarian round carrier is this swing-handled, chrome yellow example. The hardwood side is lap-joined with iron tacks. The exterior edge of the side wall at the join is beveled as in the previous example. The bottom is a single disc of pine incised with the letter "H."

Andrews Collection, Hancock Shaker Village 1962.460.0003

Round Carriers, Mount Lebanon, N.Y. 19th century
7 ⅛" x 11 ⅜", 5 ⅝" x 12 ⅝", 5 ½" x 9 ¼"

The first two examples here have the Mount Lebanon handle form so commonly used, while the third is a slight variant (lacking the shaped handle ends). The bottoms are all pine, joined to the hardwood sides by iron tacks (first two) and wooden points (third). The second carrier is finished in a red wash inside and out and is marked in pencil "1# 15oz." This is similar to the "Fine Shirts" carrier illustrated opposite.

Andrews Collection, Hancock Shaker Village 1962.462, 1962.460.0002, 1962.760

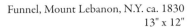
Funnel, Mount Lebanon, N.Y. ca. 1830
13" x 12"

This unusual piece of cooperage has the butt-joined pine (or basswood) staves typical of Mount Lebanon wares. It is bound with iron hoops clipped at the corners. The bottom is formed of two equal pieces of machine-planed pine into which the hardwood spout has been set. The exterior is finished with a yellow paint, the interior is unfinished.

Andrews Collection, Hancock Shaker Village 1962.390

Potty Pail, Mount Lebanon, N.Y. ca. 1830 *(opposite)*
13 ³⁄₄" x 12 ¹⁄₂"

This potty pail bears the trademark of Church Family Trustee David Meacham Sr. (1743-1826) found on so many products made for sale to the outside world. Examples of this type also survive without the trademark, indicating they were made for use both inside and outside of the community. The pail is constructed of butt-joined pine (or basswood) staves, bound together with iron hoops clipped at the corners. The top and bottom ends of the staves are chamfered on the inside edge to prevent splitting. The steam-bent ash handle is of typical Mount Lebanon construction. A separate hardwood rim with a flange nailed to the underside can be removed for emptying the chamber pot within. A single disc of pine with a turned hardwood handle threaded into it forms the top. The outside is painted yellow, and the inside a brownish-red for easy cleaning. The three legs on which this pail stands are actually staves of extended length.

Andrews Collection, Hancock Shaker Village 1962.076

Brother Isaac Newton Youngs wrote this summary of the cooperage industry at the Church Family at Mount Lebanon in his year end summary for 1838:

Of the Coopering business.

There has been consider-able of this done every year for many years.— but the particular amounts of the quantity yearly made is lost. Henry Markham is the principal one in that branch & has been since the year 1807— always doing a good deal every year & some years working at it nearly all the time: others have occasionally worked with him.— He says the work done yearly would average as much as 100 tubs, & 300 pails, in one year— There was 300 tubs made on year & 700 pails another year.[9]

By 1856, when Brother Isaac wrote his "Concise View" the cooperage industry had largely ceased. The death of Brother Stephen Henry Markham in 1846, as well as the availability of mass-produced cooperage from outside sources, were the chief causes.

Coopering.

The branch of Coopering has been supported from the first. There was some done at first at making barrels, but this did not continue long. The principal part of the business was making tubs and pails, both for the use of Believers & for sale.

There was some machinery, & a set of tool furnished in the course of a few years, after which there was but little improvement for many years: but much good and substantial work was done, which found ready market.

Of late factories for coopering have been erected abroad in the world which have reduced the price below what we could afford, and the business has become pretty much dormant, except a little for home use, repairing and mending old work, &c. The scarcity of timber was also one cause of the failure of the business among us.[10]

Wall Clock, Mount Lebanon, N.Y. ca. 1830
10 ¹/₈" x 10" x 4 ¹/₂"

Brother Isaac Newton Youngs was one of the most skilled craftsmen at the New Lebanon Shaker community. Artifacts of many different varieties scattered throughout this book are testament to his prodigious talents. As the Andrewses noted, this clock seems to fit the description of Numbers 12, 13, 14 and 15 in the journal where Youngs recorded his clock making activities. "February 1830. 13. Finished two timepieces, Nˢ 12 & 13. No. 12 I put in the washhouse, & No. 13 in the machine shop. These were a plain style with tin front plates, pivot-holes boxed with brass or silver. Wheels of cherry— the pillars screwed into the back board which forms the back plates. Made to hang on a pin, with no case but a boxing round the wheels." "November 1832. 29ᵗʰ. Finished two timepieces. No's 14 & 15. Chiefly made along with the two last mentioned, in the same style. One I put in the Deaconesses shop & the other, [15] in the physician sisters' shop."[11] **Shaker Furniture** *plate 4.*

Andrews Collection, Hancock Shaker Village 1975.245

Wall Clock, Mount Lebanon, N.Y. 1840
34 ½" x 11" x 4 ⅛"

This wall clock is one of a series of six begun by Brother Isaac Newton Youngs in 1840. This example is Number 21 in the carefully recorded chronology Brother Isaac kept of his clock making. It was the fourth in the series of this type. Of five surviving examples (number 20 is unlocated) this is the only one made of butternut rather than pine. Additionally, this example has a full glass front, as opposed to a pine panel on the lower door. The half-round projection of the back of the case has been drilled to allow the clock to be hung from a peg (or "pin" as the Shakers called them). The inside of the case is finished with a thin chrome yellow wash. The mechanism is a weight driven 24 hour movement. The escape wheel, bushings and suspension springs are brass; the pivots are steel; and the hands and the minute and hour wheels are thin hammered iron. The other wheels and pinions are wood. Brother Isaac inscribed the backs of the faces of many of the clocks he made. This one bears the following inscription: "21./Made by Isaac N. Youngs./May 12th. 1840./O Time!, how swift that solemn day rolls on/When from these mortal scenes we shall be gone!!!" [12] **Shaker Furniture** *plate 42.*

Andrews Collection, Hancock Shaker Village 1962.590

School Desk, Mount Lebanon, N.Y.
early 19th century
27 ¾" x 69 ¾" x 26"

School Bench, Mount Lebanon, N.Y.
early 19th century
25 ⅞" x 68 ¾" x 14"

Teaching Clock, Watervliet, N.Y. 1870,
9 ¾" x 9 ¾" x 1"

Side Chair, Watervliet, N.Y., ca. 1840,
38 ½" x 18 ⅝" x 13 ¾"

Hanging Shelf, Mount Lebanon, N.Y.
ca. 1850
28" x 59" x 8"

This image recreates the William Winter photograph used as plate 35 in *Shaker Furniture*. The school desk was acquired from the Church Family at New Lebanon in 1928.[13] The Andrewses made many exciting discoveries in the Church Family school house, recalling unabashedly in ***Fruits of the Shaker Tree of Life*** that "Many a time we had peered through the basement windows . . . Little, we suspected, had been moved out since the house was raised in 1839. So, when we were finally given the key and permission to explore, all the pleasure of anticipation was ours."[14] The Andrewses' forays into the building netted books, pamphlets, charts and maps, many copies of Isaac Newton Youngs's ***A Short Abridgement of the Rules of Music***, and two desks of this type. Made of cherry, it has six work places, each with a lidded compartment presumably used to hold books, papers, and writing materials. When the lids are opened they hinge down to create a writing surface supported from below by a bracket that swivels out of the skirt. Small brass spring catches secure the lids when closed. The bench was found with the desk. The teacher's clock hanging in the corner was acquired from the Watervliet Shakers. It is dated 1870. The book shelf screwed into to the peg rail was formerly used in a schoolroom at the North Family at New Lebanon. The chair, books, and candlestick in this image are not the ones that were used in the original image. The chair was collected by the Andrewses and is from the Watervliet, N.Y. community as indicated by its steeply beveled and arched slats (which graduate in height from top to bottom), as well as the turning on the pommels (or finials). The woven ash-splint seat, which is original, is joined with the same type of hook and eye cutting as the Pierce's Freegift Wells chair. This chair is stamped "10" on the front right post.

Andrews Collection, Hancock Shaker Village School Desk 1962.046, School Bench 1962.047, Teaching Clock 1962.048, Side Chair 1962.493, Hanging Shelf 1962.193 1962.048

This photograph was made for a stereoview of the inside of the Church Family's school sometime around 1870. School desks of the type illustrated on this page are plainly visible.

Collection of Hancock Shaker Village 1991-5296

School Desk, Mount Lebanon, N.Y., ca. 1840
28" x 96" x 20"

The Andrewses acquired a number of this type of school desk from the Church Family school house, to which they were granted access by the Neale sisters. Constructed of ash, pine, and cherry, these desks were used throughout the 19th century at the school house and are documented in numerous historic photos and illustrations. The desk is divided into four work spaces with a lidded compartment/writing surface and two holes for ink wells. The turned legs stand in contrast to the plainer desk illustrated opposite. The square tops form the corners of the case where the skirt boards are mortised in. Each writing surface has double breadboard ends to reduce warping and splitting. Jerry Grant and Douglas R. Allen have documented that the desks were likely built, or at least planned, by Brother Isaac Newton Youngs, who described and illustrated very similar desks in a letter of 1839 to his brother Elder Benjamin Seth Youngs at South Union, Kentucky.[15] Brother Isaac was involved at the time in the construction of the school house.

Collection of Ann Andrews Kane and Thomas R. Kane

Case of Drawers, Enfield, Conn. 1849
27 ½" x 24" x 18 ¾"

This is one of the more important pieces collected by the Andrewses. It is signed twice, once on the inside back of the case, and once on the back of a drawer, by Brother Abner Allen of Enfield, Connecticut. The main inscription reads "Enfield, Conn. May 16, 1849. Abner Alley. A.E. age 66." The construction details have enabled scholars such as Jerry Grant and Tim Rieman to attribute a number of other pieces to Brother Abner. The drawer sides, which taper in thickness from bottom to top, are a key hallmark of his joinery. This case is made of butternut with pine secondary wood and hardwood pulls. Two small brass casters with maple wheels are attached at the rear underside of the case. It has been owned by the Andrewses, the McCues, and is now in the Pavlovic collection. **Shaker Furniture** *plate 20.*

Collection of Dr. Thomas and Jan Pavlovic

Sewing Desk, Enfield, N.H. ca. 1830
35 ½" x 38 ¾" x 26 ¾"

This early desk is a design forerunner of sewing desks produced by the Shakers in Maine, New Hampshire and Enfield, Connecticut in the 1860's and 1870's. It is constructed of birch and pine with hardwood knobs and finished with a deep red wash. A flat work surface can be pulled out from under the counter. The Shaker Village at Enfield, New Hampshire, closed in 1923, and the remaining Enfield Shakers moved to Canterbury, bringing much of their furniture with them. This was well before the Andrewses began to collect beyond the Shaker communities of New York and Massachusetts. Consequently, few Enfield pieces were collected by the Andrewses. In 1933, Elder Arthur Bruce of Canterbury, New Hampshire, supplied the Andrewses with a letter of introduction to the Father Superior of the La Salette Seminary which had taken over the old Enfield site. It is unknown if the Andrewses visited the Enfield, New Hampshire village as a result. Therefore, we cannot be certain if this piece was acquired from the Seminary, the Shakers or a private source. Curiously, a number of small copper tacks, similar to those used in oval box construction, have been nailed on the underside of one of the gallery drawers. **Shaker Furniture** *plate 32.*

Collection of Andrew D. Epstein

Sewing Desk, Hancock, Mass. ca. 1840
29 ⅛" x 31 ¼" x 22 ⅝"

A number of examples of this type of sewing desk exist with varying drawer configurations, leg styles, and the presence or absence of a drop leaf. The case is made of cherry and maple, with butternut drawer fronts and pine secondary wood. The lipped drawers and delicately turned hardwood pulls are similar to other Hancock examples. The most unusual aspect of this piece is a steel and brass locking mechanism located behind the central drawer. When engaged an internal mechanism locks all the drawers in place. **Shaker Furniture** *plate 33.*

Collection of Dr. Thomas and Jan Pavlovic

Sewing Desk, Hancock, Mass. ca. 1830
27" x 37" x 24"

Acquired at Hancock in 1929, this desk has a rear drop leaf that is supported on a swivel-bracket built into the back of the case.[16] Two rods can also be pulled out from under the top to support a cutting board. The side panel of the case and rear legs are splayed for additional stability, a design feature documented in other known examples of this type. The cherry case and butternut drawers are finished with a dark pigmented varnish. Pine and poplar are the secondary woods. The fruitwood pulls and hepplewhite legs that taper on the insides from the case bottom down are similar to those found on other Hancock pieces. **Shaker Furniture** *plate 33.*

Reproduced courtesy of The American Museum in Britain (Bath, UK), 1959.67

Sewing Desk, Mount Lebanon, N.Y. 1843
28" x 32 ½" x 23 ½"

One of the most striking pieces acquired by the Andrewses is this sewing desk made by James X. Smith in 1843. The front edge of the maple rim has a 32" rule screwed to it for measuring cloth. The middle drawer front is stamped "Jas. X. Smith New Lebanon N.Y" on one side and "1843" on the other. Cabinetmaker John Kassay identified that the case, top, and drawer fronts are cherry, the side panels are butternut, and pine, basswood, and sycamore are secondary woods. The beaded molding around the drawer openings, and the beaded edge on the tapered legs, are unusual feature of this piece. Faith Andrews used this piece by her bedside for many years.

The Metropolitan Museum of Art, Friends of the American Wing Fund, 1966 (66.10.18)
Photographs ©The Metropolitan Museum of Art

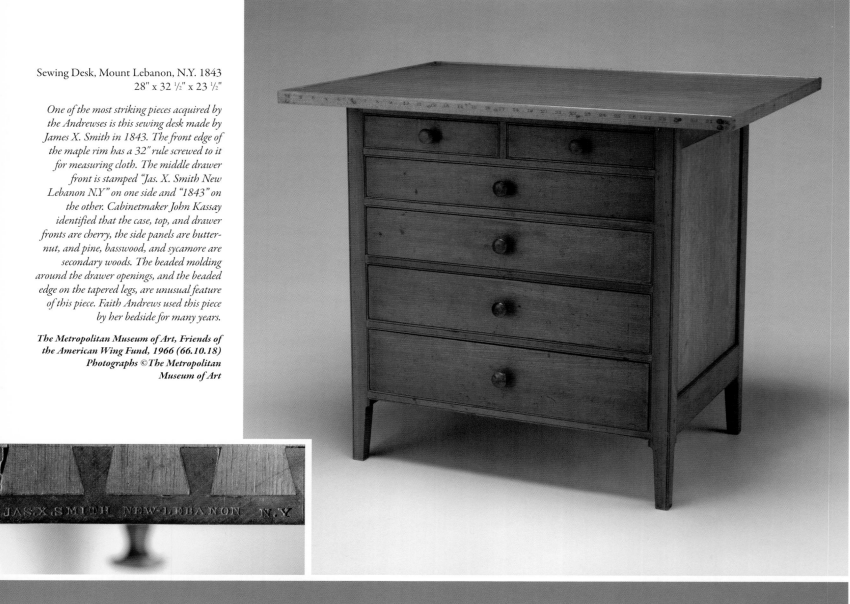

Counter, Hancock, Mass. ca. 1830
32" x 45" x 30"

Unpublished manuscript notes written by Ted Andrews in 1937 describe this piece as follows: "From the Watervliet Shakers. Curly maple, slightly stained with Shaker red wash. The drop leaf provided additional space. Found in 1927."[17] *In* **Fruits of the Shaker Tree of Life** *the Andrewses provided further information on its acquisition: "In whatever room it is placed, our curly maple tailoress counter still stands— in our memory— in the sunlit shop at the South family at Watervliet, whither we were guided, in the last years of that community, by Sister Jennie Wells."*[18] *It is illustrated in the Andrewses' first article for The Magazine* **Antiques** *which was published in August 1928. Subsequent research has suggested that this counter must have been made by a craftsman of the Hancock Bishopric, possibly Elder Grove Wright. It has the tapered drawer sides typical of Elder Grove's work. A number of similar counters survive with varying drawer configurations, some of which also have curly maple drawer fronts and pine secondary wood. It is strange that a piece with such strong Hancock Bishopric characteristics was acquired from the Watervliet, New York Shakers, but not impossible.* **Shaker Furniture** *plate 30.*[19]

Reproduced courtesy of The American Museum in Britain (Bath, UK), 1959.64

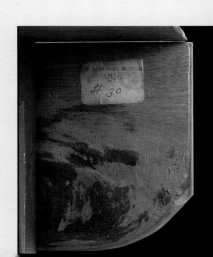

Drop Leaf Table, probably Mount Lebanon, N.Y. ca. 1820
28" x 30" (leaves extended) x 40 ⅛"

*In **Shaker Furniture** Ted Andrews attributed this piece to the Second Family of Mount Lebanon. However, in an unpublished inventory of the couple's furniture written circa 1937 (the same year **Shaker Furniture** was published) Andrews wrote: "Found in the neighborhood of Mt. Lebanon in 1929. Probably a unique, certainly an unusual piece. When found the feet and stretchers were missing. The feet were restored with the feet of table 11 [pictured bottom right] as a model. The leaves are held up by "butterfly" shaped supports. The drawer extends the length of the frame."[20] The stretcher base table whose legs were used as a basis for the restoration of this table was published in The Magazine **Antiques** in January 1933 (see photo lower right). It was found in the basement of a Second Family dwelling at Mount Lebanon where it had been used as an ironing table. This table has some elements in common with other, presumably later, Mount Lebanon drop leaf tables. The skirt and legs splay from 9 ¾" to 12 ¼". The wing shaped brackets, held in at the top by iron staples, and resting on a wooden support that is through-mortised into the case, are a crude predecessor of those found on presumably later examples (see page 134). Finally, the use of cherry wood and the ovolo molding at the bottom edges of the skirt are similar to other Mount Lebanon drop leaf tables. Despite the confusion between the Andrewses' published and manuscript notes on the piece the physical evidence supports a Mount Lebanon attribution.*
***Shaker Furniture** plate 7.*

Andrews Collection, Hancock Shaker Village 1966.200

The image at left was made by Noel Vincentini in 1935 for the Index of American Design. The drop leaf table is shown with a Hancock swift clamped to the top.

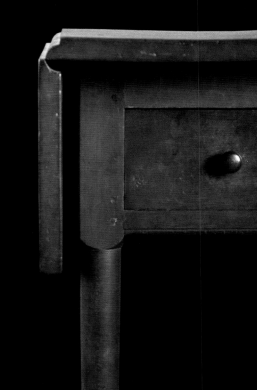

Drop Leaf Table, probably Mount Lebanon, N.Y. ca. 1820
25 ¾" x 26 ⅝" (leaves extended) x 26 ⅞"

*The Andrewses acquired this table from Sister Sadie Neale. Its diminutive size, and
written provenance transmitted through the Andrews family, indicate that it may
have been made for the use of children in the care of the Mount Lebanon Church
Family. Cherry is the primary wood with pine secondary. The drop leaves are supported
by square wooden rods that extend from the skirt. The skirt and legs of this table are
vertical, as opposed to the splayed form of other Mount Lebanon drop leaf tables. To
illustrate this difference we have photographed this table in front of a splay-legged
example not collected by the Andrewses. The drawer of this example closes flush with
the skirt, a notable difference from the presumably earlier table depicted opposite.
Someone, probably a Shaker, has written "Not for Sale" on the drawer bottom
in chalk. The table was on display at the 1932 Berkshire Museum exhibition,
as well as the 1935 Whitney exhibition.* **Shaker Furniture** *plate 20.*

Collection Bob and Aileen Hamilton

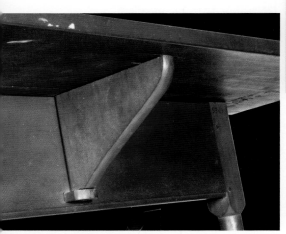

Drop Leaf Table, Mount Lebanon, N.Y. ca. 1840
26 ¹/₈" x 27 ³/₈" (leaves extended) x 36 ¹/₄"

A number of examples of splay leg tables from Mount Lebanon survive. It is possible that this table was one of the group referred to in a January 1837 journal entry by Brother Isaac Newton Youngs: "David Rowley has undertaken to make a quantity of cherry tables, to furnish the great house, in the various rooms— has begun 20 tables."[21]
The Andrewses collected this example at the Church Family prior to 1932 when it was exhibited at the Berkshire Museum in Pittsfield, Massachusetts. The table is made of cherry and finished with a lightly pigmented red wash. The drop leaves are supported by a more refined version of the butterfly brackets than those on the table pictured opposite. **Shaker Furniture** *plate 41.*

Reproduced courtesy of The American Museum in Britain (Bath, UK), 1959.69

Drop Leaf Table, Hancock, Mass. ca. 1840
28 ⅛" x 33 ⅛" (leaves extended) x 35 ½"

Written provenance from the Andrews family states that this table was acquired from Eldress Fannie Estabrook at Hancock prior to 1934. It may have been used in the Ministry's dining room, a smaller antechamber to the large family dining room in the 1830 Brick Dwelling. The table is cherry with pine secondary and exhibits the swelled turning to the legs, and diminutive fruitwood and brass pulls commonly found on Hancock furniture. The grain visible on the end of the central top board shows the careful selection of materials made by Shaker crafts-men to insure that a table would not cup or check over time. The top surface on this remarkable example lays perfectly flat.

Collection of Bob and Aileen Hamilton

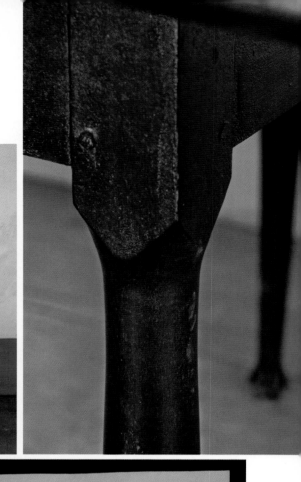

Drop Leaf Table, Alfred, Me. ca. 1830
27 ³/₄" x 35 ¹/₂" (leaves extended) x 43 ¹/₂"

This is one of a pair of black painted tables acquired by the Andrewses from the Maine Shakers around 1931 when Alfred was closed and many of the furnishings there were sold. The frame is cherry, the top is maple with poplar secondary wood. There are two lipped and dovetailed drawers of unequal length–one 14 ⁴/₈" long, the other 16 ³/₄" long, each with a large brass pull. Two pivoting supports hold the leaves in their upright position. The square posts of the case, which transition into legs with a swelled turning and button foot, are found on other examples of Maine Shaker furniture. Except for restored paint on the top surface of the top boards, the piece retains its original, black paint. This table, with its leaves in the extended position, was used as a writing desk by Faith Andrews in her home on Whittier Avenue in Pittsfield. While working at it she compiled and edited the last major work by the Andrewses, their memoir of collecting entitled **Fruits of The Shaker Tree of Life***.*

Collection of Miriam R. and M. Stephen Miller

Faith Andrews
11 Whittier Avenue
Pittsfield, MA 01201

Shaker Collection of Edward D. & Faith Andrews

ALFRED DROP LEAF TABLE WITH PAIR OF DRAWERS

One (the larger and finer) of a pair of matched but
disimilar drop leaf tables from the Alfred, Maine
community - fine drawers with old pulls at each end -
cherry, (h) 28" x (w) 43½" x (d) 16" [with leafs folded
down] - turned legs with ball foot - old black paint
with finish worn/removed on top of table surface.

DOCUMENTED - shop drawings and photograph in Handberg's Shop
Drawings of Shaker Furniture - family notes certify its Alfred
origins (as does a family label on underside of table) - it was
built by the same maker of the smaller companion table.

PROVENANCE & HISTORY - Purchased by the Andrews directly from the
Alfred, Maine Shakers ca. 1931 or 1932.

In the interview of Faith Andrews in the Renwick Gallery
Catalog of the exhibition of Shaker furniture from the
Andrews' collection, she commented:

"...Alfred was about to close...the sisters
had already left Alfred, but there was still
furniture, and we bought heavily...".

The turning of the legs is masterful, with a beautiful
graduation from the square form at the top, to the half-
ball configuration at the floor line.

The drawers are nicely and finely constructed with a lipped
overhang on three sides.

ANDREWS FAMILY NOTES - This, with its companion, was a favorite
Shaker piece of Faith Andrews. It was a "piece they chose to live
with", and graced both family residences, first at Clinton Avenue,
and later Whittier Avenue, in Pittsfield.

For many years, it was in the Andrews' study, and used as a study
desk by Mrs. Andrews.

Ann Andrews Kane   *July 20, 1990*
Ann Andrews Kane

Drop Leaf Table, Alfred, Me. ca. 1830
26 ¹/₂" x 25" (leaves extended) x 31"

*This slightly smaller version of the table shown opposite was photographed at the Andrewses "Shaker Farm" in Richmond, Massachusetts, for the **The Golden Treasury of Early American Houses** by Richard Pratt.*

Collection of Dr. Thomas and Jan Pavlovic

Table, Sabbathday Lake, Me. ca. 1830
23 ¼" x 38" x 22 ½"

*In various sources the Andrewses list three different locations where they found this table in the community at Sabbathday Lake. In **Shaker Furniture** (1937) they state it was "used in the washhouse;"[22] in unpublished manuscript notes about their own collection written circa 1937 they state it was "From the canning room of a shop;"[23] and finally, in notes prepared in the early 1960s they wrote it was from "the kitchen or buttry."[24] A description recounted in **Fruits of the Shaker Tree of Life** seems to also identify this table: "One of our most prized pieces, a low splay-legged table, will always mean Eldress Prudence Stickney; it was standing in a dark passage in a basement buttery or bake-room."[25] Despite its confused history, its solid splay-legged form with maple legs and skirt would have provided needed stability for use in any of these workshops. Additionally, the breadboard ends on the pine top would have prevented warping and checking. The photo below was made around 1935 by photographer Noel Vincentini working on the Index of American Design for the Federal Art Project. The Sabbathday Lake table is visible along the wall of the dining room in the Andrewses' Pittsfield home, opposite a Hancock trestle table now in the collection of The Metropolitan Museum of Art (see page 166). **Shaker Furniture** plate 9.*

Andrews Collection, Hancock Shaker Village 1962.045

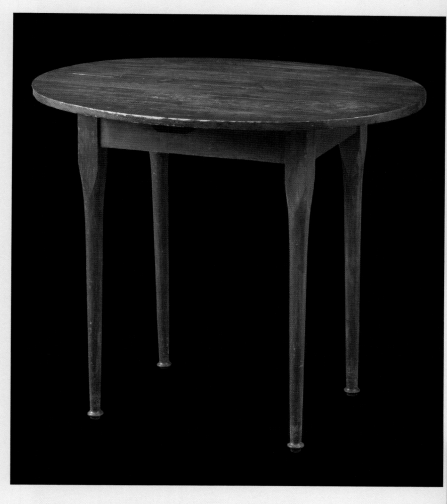

Table, Alfred, Me. ca. 1830
26 ⅛" x 30" x 22 ⅝"

The Andrewses acquired this table as Alfred was closing in 1931. It was used in a Sisters' Shop. The top is pine, the skirt and legs are birch. Note the turning of the foot, it is quite similar to the Alfred drop leaf tables illustrated on the previous pages. **Shaker Furniture** *plate 9.*

Collection of the Family of David V. and Phyllis C. Andrews

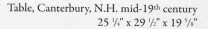

Table, Canterbury, N.H. mid-19th century
25 ¼" x 29 ½" x 19 ⅝"

This table has a pine top with breadboard ends and maple skirt and legs. Its overall form, particularly the square to round transition in the slender legs, divided by a small ring turning, are similar to other tables with provenance from Canterbury. This example shows traces of a red wash finish which has mostly worn away. **Shaker Furniture** *plate 38.*

Collection of the Family of David V. and Phyllis C. Andrews

Table, Mount Lebanon, N.Y. mid-19th century
23" x 24 ½" x 14 ½"

This unusual table is one of the few Shaker pieces known with decorative inlay. The case is cherry with pine secondary. On the top are two small diamond shaped inlays made of bird's eye maple. The legs taper gradually on the insides and are chamfered at the bottom. Written provenance from the Andrews family states that this table was acquired from Sister Sadie Neale of the Church Family at Mount Lebanon. The piece was one of Faith Andrews's favorites and was passed on to her daughter. An Andrews family note remarks: "Sadie told me [Faith] that a Shaker must have had fun with that table." [26]

Collection of J. Richard and E. Barbara Pierce

Table, Mount Lebanon, N.Y. ca. 1760/1825
26 ¼" x 32 ¼" x 22 ⅝"

*This table is unique in the corpus of identified Shaker furniture. The date "1825" is written on the drawer bottom. However, as Shaker furniture scholar and maker Tim Rieman has noted, this Queen Anne style table likely predates the Shakers.[27] The drawer was retrofitted to the piece presumably around 1825. At the same time the original ogee bracket aprons on either end (visible from underneath) were covered over with plain skirt-boards notched into the legs. The table was illustrated in the Andrewses' second article for The Magazine **Antiques** in April, 1929. This piece was eventually sold by the Andrewses and subsequently acquired by Shaker collectors Dr. Gerald and Miriam McCue in 1952.*

Collection of J. J. Gerald and Miriam McCue
Photographs Courtesy of Willis Henry Auctions, Inc.

Benches, Mount Lebanon, N.Y. ca. 1820
16" x 47 ³/₄" x 9 ⁵/₈", 16 ¹/₄" x 73 ⁵/₈" x 11 ⁵/₈"

These pine benches show the pointed arch cutouts found on early meetinghouse and dining benches from Mount Lebanon. The example at top has a molded edge on the seat and is finished in a dark stain. The example at bottom, which is considerably longer, is finished in an orange paint. **Shaker Furniture** *plate 1 (top), plate 5 (bottom).*

Collection of the Family of David V. and Phyllis C. Andrews

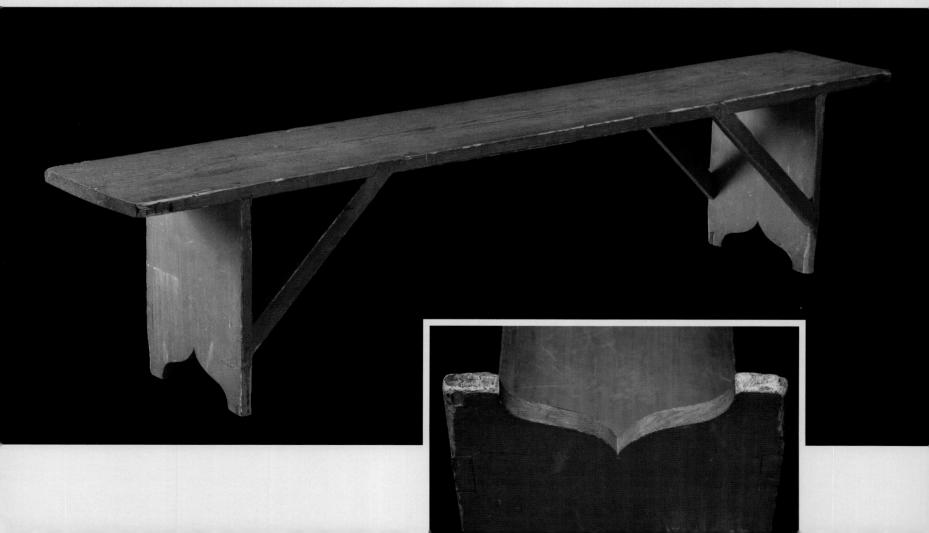

Meetinghouse Bench, Enfield or Canterbury, N.H. ca. 1830
32 ³/₈" x 120" x 14 ¹/₂"

The seat and back of this bench are each made from one piece of wood. The thirty-nine tapering spindles are dowelled into the seat and back. It is finished in a dark stain. The seat is shaped to accommodate the sitters. The legs and stretchers have a swelled turning and are dowelled. The seat is pine and the spindles are birch.

Andrews Collection, Hancock Shaker Village 1962.138

Settee, Mount Lebanon, N.Y. second-half of the 19th century
32" x 71" x 30 ½"

"A unique piece from the North Family, New Lebanon, which was the novitiate or gathering family of that community. It was here that visitors from the world were received, and it was probably for the convenience of such inquirers, or travelers, that the settee was made." [28] This piece is made primarily of cherry wood. The frame is heavily dovetailed and the back posts curve backwards to accommodate the sitter. The slats are notched at the ends where they mortise into the posts. The square legs are chamfered at the corners and then turned. The arm-posts are tapered, and the front posts have a small ring turning at the base. Note the curved ends of the arms and the turned knobs that served as attachment points for the seat. This piece is illustrated in the April 1929 issue of The Magazine **Antiques. Religion in Wood** *page 85.*

Andrews Collection, Hancock Shaker Village 1962.119

Canning Table, Mount Lebanon, N.Y. ca. 1830
25" x 55" x 20"

"A room at the north end of the main dwelling, North Family, New Lebanon, was used by the kitchen sisters for canning, preserving, pickling, candy making and so on. In it stood this long, low table— really two four legged stands with a single bread-board top— painted a dark red, as were so many pieces designed for kitchen or bake-room use. Apparently only one drawer was needed; another would have been 'superfluous.' We call it our 'male and female' table."[29] *This table was illustrated in the January 1939 issue of The Magazine* **Antiques. Religion in Wood** *page 35.*

Collection of Dr. John R. Ribic and Dr. Carla Kingsley

Washstand, Mount Lebanon, N.Y. ca. 1860
27 ¾" x 24 ½" x 14"

This pine washstand is finished in an orange wash. The bottom shelf rests loosely on supports attached to the tapered, square legs. The corners of the backsplash are rounded off where it joins the sides, which have an ogee profile. The top surface has a circular cutout used to hold a wash basin. The top of this washstand is similar to other examples attributed to Brother James Calver. **Shaker Furniture** *plate 40.*

Collection of Dr. John R. Ribic and Dr. Carla Kingsley

Washstand, Mount Lebanon, N.Y. ca. 1820
36" x 56 ³/₈" x 17 ³/₈"

*The Andrewses acquired this piece from the North Family at Mount Lebanon. The size of this washstand indicates it was likely made for use in an area
other than a typical Shaker retiring room. Scholar and cabinetmaker John Kassay suggests a possible use in an infirmary or nurse shop.[30] It is made almost
entirely of pine, save the pulls, which are maple. The top overhangs the case asymmetrically by 3 ¹/₄" on the right side. However, small hardwood pegs on
both sides of the case suggest the piece was not designed to be set into a corner. The large knots on the splashboard are unusual for Shaker work, perhaps
further indication of the rough use intended for this piece. Traces of a yellow ochre wash are found on the exterior.* **Religion in Wood** *page 33.*

Collection of the Family of David V. and Phyllis C. Andrews

Washstand, Mount Lebanon, N.Y. ca. 1840
30" x 46" x 22 ½"

*This interesting combination of a washstand and case of drawers was acquired from Sister Sarah Collins of the South Family at Mount Lebanon. Painted a deep red-brown, it is a much more refined example than the one pictured opposite and appears to have originally been a built-in. The unfinished strip at the bottom, probably from where a floor molding had been applied, as well as the splashboard specifically constructed for use in a corner, point to a built-in use. The washstand was illustrated in the article "Antiques in Domestic Settings" in the January 1939 issue of The Magazine **Antiques. Shaker Furniture** plate 21.*

Collection of Dr. John R. Ribic and Dr. Carla Kingsley

Cupboards, Mount Lebanon, N.Y. ca. 1860
65 ³/₈" x 46 ³/₈" x 19 ¹/₄", 66" x 47 ¹/₂" x 19 ¹/₂"

*Edward Deming Andrews's reminiscence of finding these pieces is highly evocative of what it must have been like to explore the buildings at Mount Lebanon: "The 'nurse shop' at the North family, New Lebanon, was located on the second floor of the second family dwelling. In one long narrow room, brightly lighted by south windows there were two identical cupboards to hold the medicinal herbs grown in the physic gardens and widely used in the Shaker infirmaries. Herb labels are pasted on the outside of the four deep drawers. The wood is butternut."[31] In another document Andrews wrote: "Through the kindness of Sister Rosetta Stephens we obtained both pieces."[32] Shaker furniture scholar and cabinetmaker Tim Rieman dates these pieces to circa 1860 based on the use of butternut, which is rarely seen in earlier Mount Lebanon pieces. Both cupboards have full plank sides, and the back of the case is constructed of horizontal boards that run all the way to the floor. The drawers are divided for the storage of medicinal herbs. The intact labels pasted to the front of the example in the Andrews Family Collection read: Lemon Balm, Catfoot, Tanzy, Peppermint, Wormwood, Mother Wort, and Cohosh. The labels pasted to the front of the example in the collection of Hancock Shaker Village read: Slippery Elm, Mug Wort, Hyssop, Yarrow, Elder Flowers, Lobelia, Horehound, Sweet Fern, Liver Wort, Summer Savory, Ma[?], and Arsmart. In the catalog for the 1973 exhibition **Shaker** Faith Andrews remembered the example at left: "was filled with herbs when we bought it."[33]*

**Collection of the Family of David V.
and Phyllis C. Andrews (left)
Andrews Collection, Hancock Shaker Village
1962.411 (right)**

Double Desk, Mount Lebanon, N.Y.
ca. 1840
84 ¼" x 48" x 16 ⅝"

"When we first saw this desk it had stood for many years in the corner of a room in an abandoned herb shop at the Center Family or Second Order of the New Lebanon Church. The aged sister who sold it to us recalled that it was originally used by the trustees or deacons of that order." [3A] *This impressively large secretary, or desk, was made for the use of two individuals. Constructed of pine with fruitwood drawer pulls, it is finished all over with a bright orange wash (probably red lead). The writing surfaces fold down from the front and are hinged to the case. A series of divided pigeonholes are provided for each user. Some of these still bear faded, illegible labels. One of the most interesting construction features of the piece are the two small drawers on either side of the center stile. They have been relieved on the sides, back, and bottom to allow the necessary clearance for them to be pulled out. Was this by design of the cabinetmaker who built the desk, or an afterthought once he realized that the drawers would be blocked when the case front was affixed? This piece was displayed at the 1932 Berkshire Museum exhibition.* **Shaker Furniture** *plate 36.*

**Andrews Collection,
Hancock Shaker Village 1962.007**

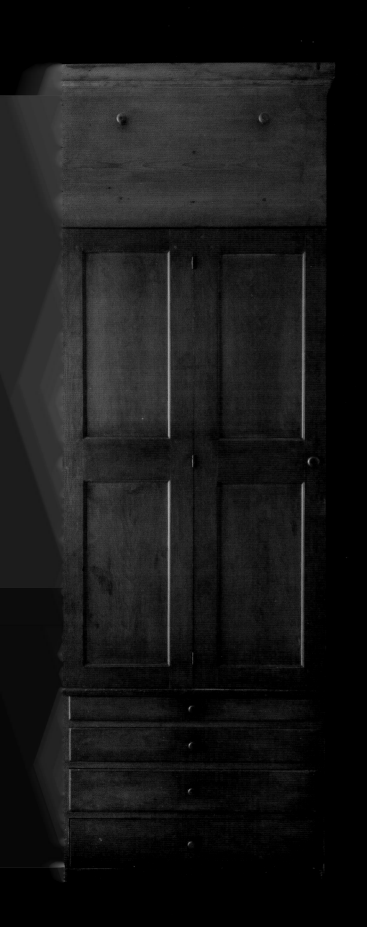

Cupboard and Case of Drawers, Mount Lebanon, N.Y. ca. 1840
95" x 31 ¹/₂" x 15 ³/₄"

This tall cupboard over drawers was probably built for the Mount Lebanon school house that was constructed in 1839 on the site of the old hatter's shop. The door is hinged in the middle and thus can be opened partially or fully. A series of shelves, dividers, and graduated doors facilitated the storage of school books and supplies. Maps and educational charts were hung from the pegs on the upper case-front. The exterior is pine, with an unknown hardwood secondary. It is finished in an orange-brown pigmented wash. Many of the design details of this piece are similar to those of the double desk illustrated on the previous page. Sister Sadie Neale sold this piece to the Andrewses.

**Collection of the Family of David V.
and Phyllis C. Andrews**

This photograph of the interior of the school room was made around 1870 for a stereoview. The large cupboard at left is clearly visible in the background with a framed picture hung from the upper pegs. **Photograph courtesy of Richard Brooker.**

Case of Drawers with Cupboard, Mount Lebanon, N.Y. ca. 1820
77 ¼" x 29" x 11 ⅝"

The Andrewses acquired this very plain (even by Shaker standards) piece from a shop at the North Family of Mount Lebanon. The correct orientation of the piece, i.e., does the cupboard belong on top or bottom, has been debated over time. However, the presence of drawer stops on the rails would indicate the present orientation, as William Winter photographed it for Shaker Furniture. The entire piece is pine and covered in a chrome yellow wash (with a modern overvarnish). The cupboard door is reinforced on the top and bottom with horizontal end boards, similar to breadboard ends, to prevent warping. This piece is unusually shallow and bears the scratch marks of a large dog all along the right side. It is one of a handful sold by the Andrewses to Dorothy Canning Miller Cahill, an early curator at The Museum of Modern Art in New York City, and the wife of Federal Art Project Director Holger Cahill. **Shaker Furniture** *plate 23.*

Gift of Dorothy Canning Miller Cahill,
Collection of Hancock Shaker Village 2004.003.0002

Cupboard with Case of Drawers, Mount Lebanon, N.Y.
ca. 1820
72" x 28" x 14 ³⁄₄"

Ted Andrews's unpublished notes on this piece are quite informative: "The best piece of furniture which we obtained directly from the Shakers themselves is a lovely cupboard case with its original warm yellow finish. Interior a chrome yellow. Wood; pine. It was one of Sister Sadie Neale's favorite pieces, and for a long time stood in a room adjacent to her sewing room, first at the Church and then at the Center family, New Lebanon, in what was known as Ann Lee's cottage. She had promised it to us, and redeemed this promise after the New Lebanon Church was sold and she was moved to Hancock. Illustrated in The Magazine **Antiques**, *October, 1957."* [35] *The raised panel on the cupboard door is indicative of a slightly earlier construction date for this piece.*

Collection of Bob and Aileen Hamilton

Cupboard, Mount Lebanon, N.Y. ca. 1830
87" x 34" x 15"

Collectors Gerald and Miriam McCue began acquiring Shaker objects in 1946. The McCue's soon crossed paths with the Andrewses and purchased a number of pieces from them. Among the first was this double cupboard finished in a red wash. Dr. McCue carefully recorded all of his Shaker purchases in notebooks he kept over the years. From his notebook we know that Ted Andrews asserted this piece was used for linens and glassware in the Nurses' Shop, Church Family, Mount Lebanon. The cut feet and flat door panels are typical of Mount Lebanon furniture. The doors are each 41" high, forming an evenly divided facade.

Collection of J. J. Gerald and Miriam McCue
Photograph Courtesy of Willis Henry Auctions, Inc.

1. <u>Infirmary Cupboard.</u>

Purchased from E.D. Andrews, who says "it came from the Nurse Shop, Church Family, New Lebanon. Made c. 1825-30. Used for linens, and for glass jars and bottles."

(opposite)
Cupboards, Hancock, Mass. or Mount Lebanon, N.Y. ca. 1800
85 ¼" x 35 ½" x 13 ¼"
80" x 37 ⅝" x 17 ¾"

Ted Andrews's unpublished notes on the Andrews Collection contain the following reference: "Large, high cupboard with two paneled doors, painted red. Hancock Church weave shop. (Now at Shaker Farm.)" [36] *Frustratingly, this could apply to either one of these cupboards. The example at far left was in the collection of Ann Andrews Kane and Thomas R. Kane until 2005, and the example at left is in still in the collection of the Family of David V. and Phyllis C. Andrews. Both have raised panels and show evidence of hand-planing, indicating an early construction date; and both are painted red. However, the presence of small brass pulls, commonly found on Hancock pieces, on the example at far left, makes it more likely that it is the one Andrews described above. Additionally, John Kassay attributed the piece to Hancock in* **The Book of Shaker Furniture.**

Collection of David D. and Virginia Newell
Collection of the Family of David V. and Phyllis C. Andrews

(right) Cupboard, Hancock, Mass. or Mount Lebanon, N.Y.
ca. 1790
81" x 36 ½" x 14 ½"

The raised panels, "H" hinges, and pointed arch feet all suggest this cupboard was built towards the end of the eighteenth century. It is finished in red paint. The door appears to have been reused from a building. The current owners were friends with Faith Andrews towards the end of her life. They recalled: "When we would sit with Faith by her desk at her home on Whittier [Avenue in Pittsfield, Massachusetts], this cupboard was at our side. Several times, Faith pointed to it with pride as the cupboard that held all their references when Ted and she wrote **Shaker Furniture.**"

Collection of Dr. Thomas and Jan Pavlovic

Case of Drawers, Mount Lebanon or
Watervliet, N.Y. ca. 1830
70 ³⁄₈" x 37 ¹⁄₂" x 18 ¹⁄₂"

*The case of this piece is fully dovetailed,
with straight-cut feet extending from the
sides. The cornice molding and dovetailed
base are applied. The base is similar to
other case pieces attributed to both
Mount Lebanon and Watervliet,
New York. The simple cornice is more
commonly seen on Mount Lebanon
examples. However, the subtle graduation
of the drawers is found on pieces from
Watervliet—making a definitive
attribution difficult. Traces of red paint
remain on the piece which appears to be
constructed entirely of pine.*

**Collection of the Family of David V. and
Phyllis C. Andrews**

Cupboard and Case of Drawers,
Mount Lebanon, N.Y. ca. 1830
74 ¹⁄₄" x 32 ⁷⁄₈" x 16 ⁷⁄₈"

*This unusual piece consists of a fully finished
case of drawers with single plank sides extending
upwards to a cupboard framed on top. Like the
example opposite, this piece has an applied
dovetailed base. Traces of yellow ochre paint
remain, although the piece appears to have
been refinished. This cupboard over drawers
seems to have barely escaped a fire. A large
burn-mark is visible on the right side. A lamp
or candle may have tipped over and briefly
been in contact with the case side.*

**Collection of the Family of David V.
and Phyllis C. Andrews**

Cupboard, Mount Lebanon, N.Y. ca. 1830
62 ¼" x 44" x 5 ½"

This cupboard, formerly built in to a wall, was constructed for the unique purpose of storing the numerous labels used in the medicinal herb industry at Mount Lebanon. Originally, it was at least one bay larger (the left cupboard was cut down the central stile), and may have been even longer than that. Many labels are still attached to the divided pigeonholes on the interior. The whole case is finished in a red wash.

Andrews Collection, Hancock Shaker Village 1962.473

Cupboards, Mount Lebanon, N.Y. ca. 1830
16 ¼" x 11 ½" x 5 ¼"
30" x 12 ¼" x 2 ¾"

These utilitarian wall cupboards were both acquired at Mount Lebanon. The example above, built entirely of cherry, it was likely hung from a nail (the hole is too small to admit a typical Shaker peg). It was found at the North Family and published in the January 1933 and October 1936 issues of The Magazine **Antiques.** *The other cupboard, made of pine, was used for storing spools and was screwed (or nailed) to the wall through the back. The interior of the spool cupboard is finished in a bright chrome yellow. The exterior is finished in a thin red wash. The pull, hinges, and latch (to keep it closed) are brass.*

Andrews Collection, Hancock Shaker Village 1962.154
Courtesy, Winterthur Museum 1970.0199

Chest, Mount Lebanon, N.Y. ca. 1840
36" x 43 ½" x 18 ¾"

This pine chest, possibly used for the storage of textiles, has the cut feet typical of similar pieces from Mount Lebanon. The pulls are turned from fruitwood and the escutcheon is stamped brass. It is finished in a yellow-orange, or "pumpkin," wash. The Andrewses acquired this example from the South Family. **Shaker Furniture** *plate 19.*

Collection of Bob and Aileen Hamilton

Chest, Mount Lebanon, N.Y. ca. 1840
29 ⅛" x 41 ¾" x 18 ⅝"

This one-drawer example, stained red, is similar in most respects to the one pictured above. The lids of both chests pictured on this page have breadboard ends. The cut feet are solid blocks of wood that are part of the sides of the chest and dovetailed into the bottom rail. The interior of the chest is fitted with a dovetailed till with a hinged top. Although scholars of Shaker furniture have attributed the piece to Mount Lebanon based on construction and style, unpublished notes written by Ted Andrews suggest it may have been acquired at Hancock: "A one drawer chest, with bracket feet, painted the typical "Shaker red"— once in the Collection— is now owned by Dr. and Mrs. Thomas R. Kane of Havertown, Pa. Origin was Hancock." [37]

Collection of Bob and Aileen Hamilton

Chest, Mount Lebanon, N.Y. 1837
27 ½" x 41" x 18"

This chest was featured in the Andrewses's first article on
Shaker furniture in the August 1928 issue of The Magazine
Antiques. It is built of pine and finished with red paint
and bone escutcheons. The lid has breadboard ends typical
of Shaker chests. The case is dovetailed and outfitted
with iron hinges and screws and steel and brass locks. The
original keys remain with the piece. It has been attributed
to Brother Gilbert Avery who moved between various
families at Mount Lebanon, but was buried at Canaan. In
Shaker Furniture the Andrewses state: "Tradition ascribes
the chest to Gilbert Avery." [38] If Avery did construct this
chest he was sixty-four years old at the time. The following
is written on the back of the case: "Made April. 1837.
Canaan." An illustration of the piece, made by an artist
working at the Andrewses' home, was published in **The
Index of American Design. Shaker Furniture** plate 19.

Collection of the Family of David V. and Phyllis C. Andrews

Chest, Mount Lebanon, N.Y. ca. 1840
37" x 44" x 19 ½"

*This chest was photographed by William Winter in the
1930s. That photograph was eventually published in
Religion in Wood (p. 29), where the chest is described as
being from Hancock, ca. 1830. However, similar chests
known to have been constructed at Mount Lebanon
suggest that this piece was also made there. It was
acquired from Sister Rosetta Stephens at the North
Family in 1939 by Dorothy Miller Canning Cahill. She
was a curator at The Museum of Modern Art and
married to Federal Art Project Director Holger Cahill.
Mrs. Cahill purchased pieces from the Andrewses in the
1930s, and it is probable that the Andrewses were
involved in her acquisition of this chest. She eventually
joined the Board of Trustees at Hancock Shaker
Village, Inc., and donated this and other pieces
upon her death in 2003.*

**Gift of Dorothy Canning Miller Cahill,
Hancock Shaker Village 2004.003.0001**

Cupboard, Mount Lebanon, N.Y. or Hancock, Mass.
ca. 1830
25 ½" x 23 ⅛" x 14 ¾"

This small cupboard is something of a mystery. The construction of the base and shape of the feet are seen on pieces from Hancock, Mount Lebanon, and Canterbury and Enfield, New Hampshire. These facts, combined with a lack of notes pertaining to its provenance, make a firm attribution difficult. The piece appears to be constructed of pine and varnished. A similar small cupboard— referred to as a "pan cupboard"— is illustrated in the January 1933 issue of The Magazine Antiques.

Collection of the Family of David V. and Phyllis C. Andrews

Trestle Table, Hancock, Mass. ca. 1830
28 ½" x 96 ½" x 31 ¼"

"Found in 1926 in the basement of a dwelling-house in West-Pittsfield formerly owned and used by the Shakers. Probably used as a family dining-table by the East family, Hancock Shakers. One end has been sawed off about two inches. Only restoration consists of end-strips on top. The table passed from our possession in 1926, and was repurchased in 1929 at forty times its original cost." [39] *The table is made of maple, pine and basswood. The posts are square with chamfered edges. The feet are very slightly arched and the top edges have been rounded off. This table was illustrated in the October 1936 issue of The Magazine* **Antiques. Shaker Furniture** *plate 3.*

The Metropolitan Museum of Art, Friends of the American Wing Fund, 1966 (66.10.1) Photographs ©The Metropolitan Museum of Art

Trestle Table, Mount Lebanon, N.Y. ca. 1830
27 ½" x 240" x 34"

This massive trestle table was found by the Andrewes in the upper loft of a Shaker mill building located to the west of Mount Lebanon. They recounted the story in **Fruits of the Shaker Tree of Life.**

At the West family in New Lebanon, New York, nestled in the woods, there was an old stone grist mill built, according to the end-irons under the north gable, in 1824. The overshot wheel was in ruins, but the mill itself, with one remaining family dwelling, was structurally sound. The property had passed from Shaker hands into the possession of a New Yorker who manufactured drugs. He had remodeled the house, and was engaged in some pharmaceutical venture on the third floor of the mill.

It was an unlikely repository of artifacts, but it was about the only building in the New Lebanon settlement we had not explored. So one autumn day we drove down the narrow lane which was its outlet to the world. No one was at home, but the door of the mill was open, an invitation which could not be resisted. On the ground floor, a dimly lit cavern, there was some long disused machinery. There was nothing on the second floor. But after climbing the wide open stairway to the top story, we saw, standing along the north wall under the windows, a magnificent Shaker trestle dining table, twenty feet long! Its top was coated with grease and grime and littered with dirty bottles. Someone, to raise its height, had put bed-rollers on its three arched supports or legs. But it had its original dark red finish and was as sound as the day it was made. Correspondence with the owner followed. He had no use for the piece, and we were glad to accept his price, plus carting, which was no easy matter.[40]

Dining tables of this size appear to have been in use at the Church Family of Mount Lebanon before the series of dietary reforms instituted in the Society beginning in the 1830s. Brother Isaac Newton Youngs wrote the following in May 1836:

"m. 20 A change is made in the position of the dining tables. The brethren's table formerly consisted of one long table, standing north & south— now there are three short ones, standing east & west, & those who choose meat sit at one table, there are but 8 of those."[41]

The four-board top of this example is pine and the trestles are birch. This table was a centerpiece in the 1932 exhibition at The Berkshire Museum. **Shaker Furniture** *plate 2.*

Andrews Collection, Hancock Shaker Village 1977.003

Bake Table, Mount Lebanon, N.Y.
ca. 1840
28 ¼" x 66" x 22 ⅜"

The Andrewses acquired this table from "the bake-room of the 'North House' at New Lebanon." [42] *The entire piece is made of pine and finished in a deep red paint. The lower shelf lies loose on two runners and can be removed. The purpose of the curious cutouts on the back of the sideboards is unknown, but perhaps they were added later to allow clearance for a steam pipe in the North Family Dwelling. The bake table was documented and published in The Index of American Design.* **Shaker Furniture** *plate 11.*

Collection of William and Sandra Soule

Shaker Sister slicing bread, **Frank Leslie's Popular Monthly,** *September 1873,* **Collection of Hancock Shaker Village 1963.190**

Bread Cutting Table,
Mount Lebanon, N.Y. ca. 1830
28" x 35 ½" x 25 ½"

If nineteenth century illustrations and photographs didn't verify the use of this type of table it would be hard to believe it was used to cut something as soft as bread. The heavy iron blade is double-hinged to the back of the table top so that it can be both raised and lowered and swiveled from side to side. The top is surrounded on the three sides by a dovetailed rim. This example was acquired from the South Family at Mount Lebanon. **Shaker Furniture** *plate 10.*

Andrews Collection, Hancock Shaker Village 1963.190

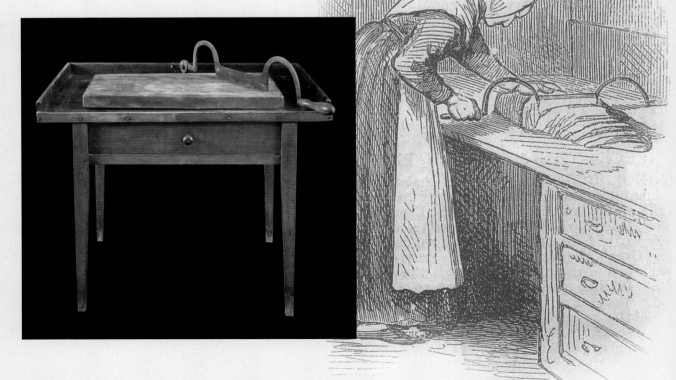

Stand, Mount Lebanon, N.Y. ca. 1820

The Andrewses speculated that this stand may have been used as a "preacher's stand" at Mount Lebanon. There was preaching at Shaker meetings open to the public, but it is undocumented that such stands were used as most Shaker preachers spoke extemporaneously. Whatever its use, this strikingly primitive and tall piece is unique among identified Shaker stands. Its stick leg form points to an earlier date of construction. Ted Andrews recounted the humorous story surrounding its acquisition in **Fruits of the Shaker Tree of Life.**

At one vendue held at a country estate near the New Lebanon community, we learned that among "the articles too numerous to mention" was an unusual stick-leg extension reading stand which sounded Shaker, and when we came to the preview, found to be Shaker. It was an early piece, stained a soft pink, in original condition. We could visualize a tall Shaker elder or the "public preacher"—perhaps Frederick W. Evans himself—standing before it as he read from the scriptures or *The Testimony of Christ's Second Appearing.* How we wanted it! And how determined we were to get it!

The day came. There were crowds there. Waiting for the cherished piece to be put up we mingled with the people, impatient and anxious. And when it was time, we found ourselves in different parts of the yard.

Someone started bidding, at five and then ten dollars. Others joined in. The bids went up to twenty, twenty-five, thirty dollars. I was getting panicky. Faith usually took the initiative on such occasions, but I couldn't see her, or hear her—naturally, as her method was to signal to the auctioneer with a nod, or with a shake of the head. When the bidding had gone to fifty, most of the bidders dropped out. But one does not lose a prize for a few dollars, so I joined in with sixty dollars. A solitary competitor bid sixty-five. I raised it to seventy. The other person went up another five, and then what happened? Each bidder now being curious to know his or her opponent, there was recognition at last. My competitor was my wife![43]

Andrews Collection, Hancock Shaker Village
1962.810

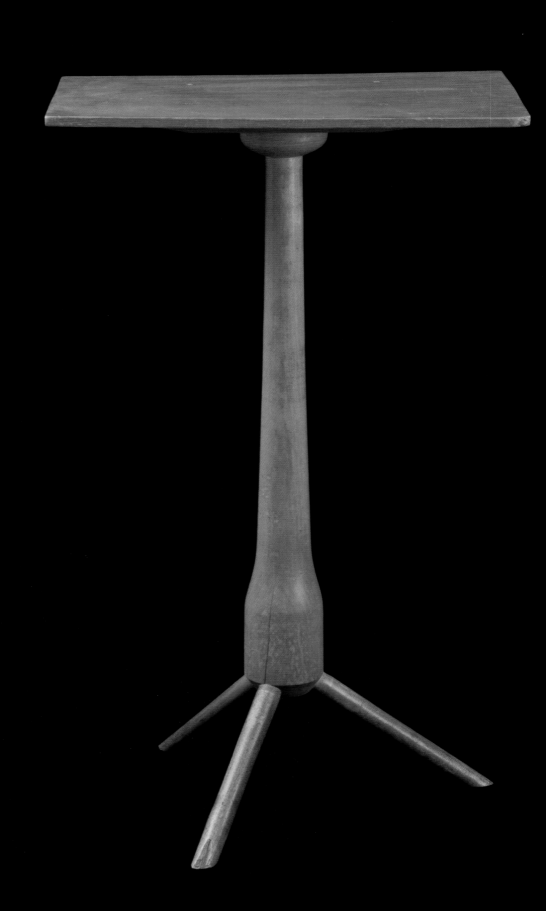

Stand, Mount Lebanon, N.Y. ca. 1820
25 ³/₈" x 24" x 16"

The stand at right exhibits a wider range of turning than other early Mount Lebanon examples. The bottom is of sufficient diameter to admit the mortised-in peg-legs, but then the diameter of the pedestal is quickly diminished, until it again expands to support a turned round base to which the drawer frame is screwed. The drawer is housed in a dovetailed frame and the top has breadboard ends to prevent warping. This stand was acquired from the Church Family.

**Andrews Collection, Hancock Shaker Village
1962.009**

Stand, Mount Lebanon, N.Y. ca. 1820
24 ¹/₈" x 18 ¹/₄" x 12 ⁵/₈"

The stand at left is one of a number of primitive stands acquired by the Andrewses at the Church Family. The top on this example can be raised and held in place by a set-screw. The finish is a dark paint. The unusual round wooden block that forms the base is 2 ¹/₄" thick and has a diameter of 10".

Collection of the Family of David V. and Phyllis C. Andrews

Stand, Mount Lebanon, N.Y. ca. 1820
25 ³/₈" x 24 ¹/₂" x 15 ⁷/₈"

With the exception of the rimmed edge on the top this example is nearly identical to the stand illustrated on page 171. Stands with rimmed edges have been traditionally associated with the garden seed industry and were possibly used for seed sorting. The legs are maple, the pedestal is cherry, and the drawer and top are pine. The piece is finished with both yellow and salmon washes. It was found: "one hot July day, in an upper room of the earliest meetinghouse, long ago converted into a three-story garden-seed house after the second meetinghouse, a much larger barrel-roofed structure was built in the early 1820s [1824]." [44]

Collection of Dr. Thomas and Jan Pavlovic

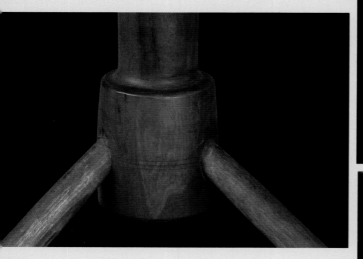

Brother Charles Ferdinand Ganebin photographed outside of the Church Family Dwelling at Mount Lebanon ca. 1935. His business card is illustrated below.
Collection of Hancock Shaker Village 6171 (business card)

C. F. Ganebin,

MT. LEBANON.

N. Y.

Stand, Mount Lebanon, N.Y. ca. 1820
26" x 18 ¾" x 12 ⅝"

The Andrewses recounted their efforts to acquire this stand in **Fruits of the Shaker Tree of Life.**

Brother Ferdinand was one of the last male members of the Church family at New Lebanon. His retiring room was in the basement of a large brick dwelling, a well-lighted room looking out over an orchard and hills to the south. When we knew him he was well along in years, infirm and long past productive labor. Most of his time was spent in this room, though we sometimes came across him taking a short walk, moving slowly along with the aid of a Shaker cane.

One day we paid him a visit. What we talked about is now forgotten, but the memory of our first sight of the stand beside his bed is still distinct. It was the only piece of Shaker-made furniture in the room. There was nothing on the stand, no book, no pipe, no glass of water. It seemed to have no use.

However, after inquiring further if it could be purchased, we were informed that it was "Ferdinand's stand," that it was his favorite piece and that it did have a use— he placed his watch on it at night! And to make sure it remained at his bedside one foot was screwed to the floor.

That was that. It did no good to suggest that another stand, a new one perhaps, be substituted for the one we coveted. Ferdinand would sorely miss the one he had used for over fifty years. We would have to wait.

After some seven or eight years Brother Ferdinand no longer had need to put his watch on the stand at night. And when he was no longer in time, the sisters kept their promise to let us have what time had withheld so long.[45]

This story, more than most, presents the unabashed acquisitiveness that certainly helped the Andrewses build their collection, but left a sour taste in the mouths of some. The rectangular rimmed top and drawer of this stand are similar to the previous example, but the gradually tapering pedestal and Queen Anne legs represent a step forward chronologically in design for Shaker stands. The top, drawer, and drawer case are pine, the pedestal is birch, and the legs are cherry. A close up view of the front leg shows the screw hole (now filled in) made by Brother Ferdinand as he tried to save his beloved watch stand.

The Metropolitan Museum of Art, Friends of the American Wing Fund, 1966 (66.10.20)
Photographs ©The Metropolitan Museum of Art

Stand, Mount Lebanon, N.Y. ca. 1830
25 ¹/₄" x 15 ³/₄"

*This elegant stand has one of the most interesting
histories of any piece the Andrewses collected. It, and
an identical twin, were acquired from the Second
Family. In **Fruits of the Shaker Tree of Life** the
story was recounted thus:*

> We did obtain, or more properly speaking,
> successfully beg several pieces from this
> loyal Shakeress [Sister Lillian Barlow]—
> pieces which we were proud to own, as the
> Second family numbered among its mem-
> bers the best craftsmen in the society.
> [Perhaps Andrews is referring to the state
> of craftsmanship at Mount Lebanon in the
> 1920s, when Sister Lillian and Brother
> William Perkins were the only remaining
> craftspeople. His statement cannot
> blanketly apply to the corpus of furniture
> made at Mount Lebanon during the
> nineteenth century.] Two of the finest
> items in our own collection came from this
> source: a pair of cherry lightstands— light
> in weight as in function— which we have
> always felt are perfect examples of Shaker
> design. The tops are round and thin, the
> slim posts subtly taper, the umbrella feet
> are simple arcs. Delicately proportioned
> and refined in line, they are studies in pure
> geometric form, symbols of the highest
> ideals of the Shaker faith.[46]

*This stand was published in the Andrewses' first
article in the April 1928 issue of The Magazine
Antiques. The magazine's editor Homer Eaton
Keyes subsequently referred to it as "the finest stand
in America."[47] The stand was one of the Andrewses'
most prized possessions for over thirty years.*

*Collectors Dallas Pratt and John Judkyn
approached the Andrewses in 1958 while in the
process of establishing the American Museum in
Bath, England. Pratt recounted meeting the
Andrewses, and acquiring some of the finest pieces in
their collection, in a memoir, writing:*

We had early on decided to have a Shaker collection in the museum, and studied the book on furniture by Edward and Faith Andrews. We saw an exhibition of items from the Andrews Collection in the Yale University Art Gallery. Based on this, and on choices made from photographs in their book, we called on the Andrews, in the house they were renting in New Haven from our friends the Vietors, and presented them with a list of our desiderata. The Andrews studied it in silence. 'Well' said Faith, 'you have very good taste!' Although somewhat reluctant to let us have the cream of their collection, they were finally persuaded by the thought that it would be the first appearance of Shaker artefacts in England, whence the first Shakers, led by Mother Ann Lee, had emigrated in 1774.

A piece which they kept in their house, because they were so fond of it, and which we fell in love with at first sight, was a small round-top table with crescent shaped feet. This we purchased with the rest, and all were shipped by the Andrews to Claverton. However, we were dismayed to find no table with crescent feet in the shipment— in its place was another table of less distinction. When we politely informed the Andrews that we had purchased the former, we received a <u>mea culpa</u> letter, saying the slip had been made probably because they could hardly imagine selling their favorite. An exchange was duly made. Since then I've always insisted that the table is one of the two items in the whole museum collection too precious to be loaned out.[48]

Ted Andrews explained the shipping error in a letter to Pratt dated May 3, 1959:

We can't understand how the mistake was made in regard to the round stand. Mrs. Andrews' theory is an interesting one— the round stand was purchased by us some twenty-five years ago and was called by Homer Eaton Keyes 'the finest stand in America.' It has held a special place in our collection and enjoyed a sort of immunity from the world so-to-speak. In other words— we had the perfect 'block.' She may be right! However, our chief concern now is to correct the error.[49]

An excellent article by Flo Morse recounts the entire story of this strange affair.[50] *The American Museum's policy of not loaning this stand is still in effect today, and one can hardly blame them— it being a prize so hard won!* **Shaker Furniture** *plate 13.*

Reproduced courtesy of The American Museum in Britain (Bath, UK), 1959.75

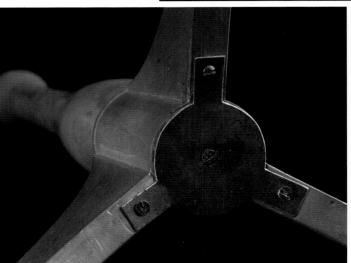

Stands, Mount Lebanon, N.Y. ca. 1840
25 ¹/₄" x 17 ¹/₄", 25 ¹/₄" x 17 ¹/₄"

*This form of stand represents the height of refinement among those produced at Mount Lebanon. A continuous curve can be traced from the end of the leg to the underside of the top. The legs, which taper in both width and height, are dovetailed into the pedestal. An iron plate provides an additional join between these elements. A cleat, with beveled edges, is screwed to the underside of the top. This assembly then screws onto the threaded top of the pedestal. The example at right has the ghost of a pair of scissors, or perhaps a wick trimmer, burned into the finish. The example at left was exhibited in the 1932 exhibition at The Berkshire Museum. One of these stands is illustrated in **Shaker Furniture**, plate 16.*

A photograph made by Noel Vincentini in 1935 for the Index of American Design shows a cherry stand of this type in the attic of an unidentified building at Mount Lebanon.

Andrews Collection, Hancock Shaker Village 1962.194, 1962.008

Stand, Hancock, Mass. ca. 1830
26" x 17 ⁵⁄₈" x 21"

The drawer on this stand can be opened in both directions. Both it, and the yoke that holds it, are beautifully dovetailed. Scholar and cabinetmaker Tim Rieman noted the unusual number and combination of woods used to construct the piece, finding cherry, pine, poplar, maple, birch, and fruitwood (knobs), all present.[51]
Ted Andrews wrote the following notes about the piece in unpublished notes on the collection: "The exposure of the dove-tailed drawer— which may be pulled out from either side for the convenience of two workers, aptly illustrates one of Ruskin's dicta, that 'the essential and necessary structure of an object should never be lost sight of nor concealed by secondary forms or ornament."[52] **Shaker Furniture** *plate 15.*

Andrews Collection, Hancock Shaker Village 1962.15

Stand, Hancock, Mass. ca. 1830
25 ⁹/₁₆" x 19 ⁵/₈" x 16 ¹³/₁₆"

This classic sewing stand is a slight variant of the example on page 178 but with a swelled pedestal and mortised spider-legs found on other Hancock sewing and candle stands. The finely-made dovetailed yoke of cherrywood which holds the drawer is threaded onto the pedestal. The top is made of figured basswood and the dovetailed drawer is made of pine and has brass pulls. This stand provides a touching window into the personal relationship that the Andrewses had with Eldress Fannie Estabrook of Hancock. The underside of the drawer is inscribed in pencil: "Presented to our dear friends/Faith and Edward Andrews./ Christmas 1930/From your Shaker friends/Hancock Mass./Fannie Estabrook." Ted Andrews could have been referring to either this stand or the example on page 178 when he wrote in previously unpublished notes: "Found at the Hancock dwelling-house 1930. The drawer is exposed and runs two ways through a narrow dovetailed frame. An unusual specimen. Only two similar examples are known."⁵³ Stands of this form are unique to the Hancock Shaker community.

Collection of Andrew D. Epstein

Stand, Hancock, Mass. or Enfield, Conn. ca. 1840
23" x 19" x 16 ¾"

*The small brass pulls and exposed dovetails are details similar to other one and two drawer stands made in the Bishopric. Many of these Hancock Bishopric stands display the same beveled edges on the undersides of the legs, as well as a neatly cut foot. The pedestal of this example has a simple swelled turning, as opposed to the ring turnings on the stand shown on page 181 (top). This stand was published in the Andrewes' article for the April 1929 issue of The Magazine **Antiques** and was also on display at the 1932 Berkshire Museum exhibition (note the label affixed to the drawer bottom).* **Shaker Furniture** *plate 15.*

Collection of the Family of David V. and Phyllis C. Andrews

Stand, Hancock, Mass. or Enfield, Conn. ca. 1840
25 ¾" x 20 ¼" x 17 ¾"

The pedestal of this example has one the most curvaceous turnings seen on eastern Shaker stands of the mid-nineteenth century. Western Shaker stands generally have thicker pedestals and are more heavily turned. The exposed dovetails and brass pulls of this stand are hallmarks of its Hancock Bishopric origins.

Collection of Dr. John R. Ribic and Dr. Carla Kingsley

Stand, Hancock, Mass. or Enfield, Conn. ca. 1850
25 ⅜" x 22" x 19"

The square top, spider legs, and more simply turned pedestal are the chief differences between this stand and its near cousin shown on the pages 182-183. This stand was exhibited at the 1932 Berkshire Museum exhibition.

Collection of the Family of David V. and Phyllis C. Andrews

Stand, Hancock, Mass. or Enfield, Conn.
ca. 1860
23 ¼" x 20 ½" x 18 ⅛"

A number of two-drawer stands survive that were made in the Hancock Bishopric. Upon being released from his position as Senior Elder in the Bishopric Elder Grove Wright settled at the Enfield, Connecticut community. His personal journal for 1860 records the process of making two-drawer work stands:

Thursday, May 3: I began to make two work stands for Elder Sister Clarissa

Friday, May 4: I work making stand legs &c.

Monday, May 7: I work at making stands

Wednesday, May 9: I am at work on the stands

Saturday, May 12: I made the 4 drawers for the two stands[54]

Elder Grove's prominence in Bishopric leadership, and the constant rotation among Hancock, Tyringham, and Enfield, as well as his demonstrated collaboration with other cabinetmakers such as Elder Thomas Damon, make community attributions of two-drawer workstands very difficult, and arguably irrelevant. The tiger maple legs and drawer fronts, turnings on the pedestal, and the red wash make this stand a very fine example. The builder has achieved a beautiful effect by "book matching" the tiger maple legs so that the wood grain radiates in opposite directions. The horizontal grain of the pedestal forms a stunning visual bridge between the legs. The edges of the top have ovolo cutouts, a decorative feature found on some Bishopric stands.

Collection of Bob and Aileen Hamilton

WEDNESDAY, MAY 9, 1860.

Cloudy all day, with a
little sprinkling of rain.
The sisters cleaned out shop
I am, at work on the stands

SATURDAY, MAY 12, 1860.

Pleasant weather, but dry.
I made the 4 drawers, for the
two stands.

Details from Grove Wright's journal for 1860.

Courtesy, The Winterthur Library: The Edward Deming Andrews
Memorial Shaker Collection, No. SA 822.

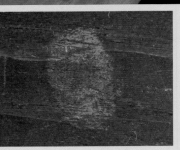

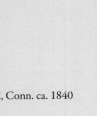

Desk, Hancock, Mass. or Enfield, Conn. ca. 1840
28" x 24 ⅝" x 18"

Ted Andrews described the circumstances surrounding the acquisition of this piece in **Shaker Furniture***: "This desk, similar to ones found at Enfield and possibly made at the Connecticut society, was used for a long time in the retiring room of a Church family deaconess at Hancock. Most of the Enfield pieces (used in the schoolrooms) lack the molding at the base of the desk box."* [55] *This piece was originally finished with a bright orange wash (probably red lead). A finger or thumb print of the Shaker who painted it has been preserved on the desk top. Bright remnants of color are also visible on the underside of the legs and in the turnings of the pedestal. The pedestal is threaded into a cleat which is attached to the desk bottom. The snake-legs end in a delicately cut foot that provides stability to the top-heavy form. The desk top was originally covered with a tacked-on writing surface which has long since disappeared. This piece was published in the Andrewses' article in the April 1929 issue of The Magazine* **Antiques***.* **Shaker Furniture** *plate 37.*

Andrews Collection, Hancock Shaker Village 1962.191

Rack, Mount Lebanon, N.Y. ca. 1830
27 ⅛" x 57 ¾" x 12"

This rack was acquired by the Andrewses from the South Family at Mount Lebanon. It was photographed by Noel Vincentini for The Index of American Design just inside a door of the South Family Dwelling in 1935. Barely visible in the image is a cupboard door on the upper left of the piece. The door has since disappeared. The rack is utilitarian in the extreme, and displays the clean lines and essential functionality so prized in Shaker craftsmanship.

Collection of the Family of David V. and Phyllis C. Andrews

Throne, Mount Lebanon, N.Y. ca. 1830
9 ³/₈" x 57 ¹/₄" x 30 ¹/₄"

*This simple pine "throne," finished in a red wash, was used by the Andrewses' friend Sister Sadie Neale. In their memoir **Fruits of the Shaker Tree of Life** the couple recorded a beautiful reminiscence of Sister Sadie and her useful throne.*

"On inclement days, and as she grew less active physically, Sadie was usually found in her retiring room, seated under a window on a sort of dais (a platform called a "throne," large enough for a chair and a sewing desk) which provided better light for sewing and reading, and a western side view of the Lebanon Valley she loved. After a few remarks on weather, health and the news of the day, the conversation invariably turned Shaker. Once, we recall, as we were discussing the dance-songs which were an integral part of the worship of the sect, she descended from her "throne," her cheeks aglow and her eyes alight, to demonstrate for us the shuffling steps, the bowings and turnings of the old song, "The Gift to Be Simple."[56]

Andrews Collection, Hancock Shaker Village 1962.491

Layers of Evidence: Poetry, Hymnody, and Industry in a Box

By M. Stephen Miller

Within the large and storied legacy of the Andrewses' scholarship and collecting were some humble, "quiet" objects; one of these was a storage box measuring approximately twenty inches long, thirteen inches deep, and fifteen inches high. Unfortunately, the uncovering and preserving of its precious contents necessitated the incremental destruction of the box itself, and no photographs are known to exist that show it in its original state.

It is not known when and where the Andrewses found this piece but most likely it was at Mount Lebanon, New York, in the 1930s. The box sat in the basement of Faith Andrews's home in Pittsfield until her friend Ed Sawyer of West Stockbridge, Massachusetts, acquired it—most likely in the early to mid-1980s. Ed then sold it to Dave and Nancy Dawson, dealers from South Glastonbury, Connecticut, from whom I bought it in September 1985. The box appeared to be made of heavy papers or cardboard with the outside covered in old green paint. There was a decided sturdiness and heft to it; it weighed about three pounds. The rectangular body of the box was fitted with an unattached lid, the top of which was initially dome-shaped. By the time I acquired the box the dome had collapsed and was slightly concave. The appeal of the box for me was its interior lining—a collage of broadsides advertising Shakers Pure Lemon Syrup and printed on yellow papers. Since the interior had never been exposed to light, the yellow color was strong and vibrant. But the moist environment of the basement it had been in for so long had left the surface of the paper spotted with a moldlike growth.

My first step in dealing with the contaminated surface of the inner lining was to seek the advice of a professional paper conservator. After several weeks of study and analysis, he concluded that the only way to save the broadsides from continuing deterioration was to remove them from the box; and he cautioned that this action could result in the destruction of the box itself. Nonetheless, since no other complete examples of this particular broadside were then known—and none has appeared in the more than twenty years since—we agreed to try. The results were both gratifying and surprising.

Tom Edmondson, then of Torrington, Connecticut, was the paper conservator. His first task was to slowly and patiently remove the broadsides from the box using steam and a spatula. He then removed the mold growth from the surface with baths of mild chemicals. His next task was to de-acidify the papers

Shaker Lemon Syrup Broadside and Bottle
Collection of Hancock Shaker Village, ID #6495 and 1967.030

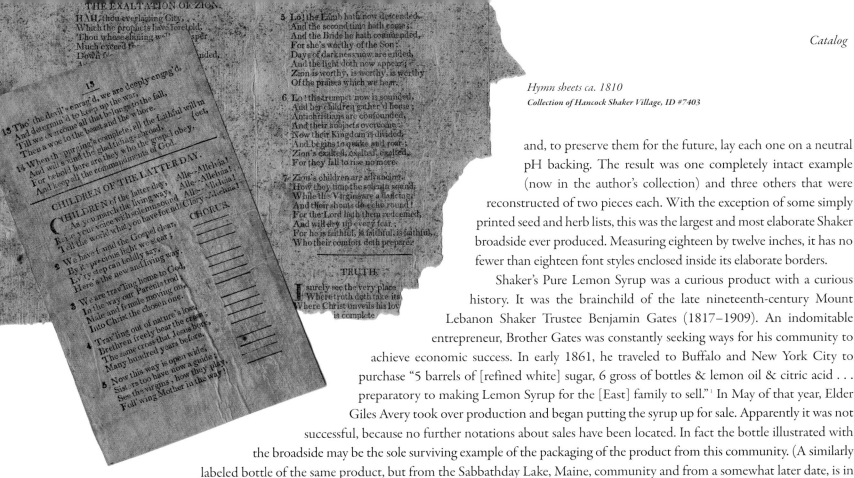

Hymn sheets ca. 1810
Collection of Hancock Shaker Village, ID #7403

and, to preserve them for the future, lay each one on a neutral pH backing. The result was one completely intact example (now in the author's collection) and three others that were reconstructed of two pieces each. With the exception of some simply printed seed and herb lists, this was the largest and most elaborate Shaker broadside ever produced. Measuring eighteen by twelve inches, it has no fewer than eighteen font styles enclosed inside its elaborate borders.

Shaker's Pure Lemon Syrup was a curious product with a curious history. It was the brainchild of the late nineteenth-century Mount Lebanon Shaker Trustee Benjamin Gates (1817–1909). An indomitable entrepreneur, Brother Gates was constantly seeking ways for his community to achieve economic success. In early 1861, he traveled to Buffalo and New York City to purchase "5 barrels of [refined white] sugar, 6 gross of bottles & lemon oil & citric acid . . . preparatory to making Lemon Syrup for the [East] family to sell."[1] In May of that year, Elder Giles Avery took over production and began putting the syrup up for sale. Apparently it was not successful, because no further notations about sales have been located. In fact the bottle illustrated with the broadside may be the sole surviving example of the packaging of the product from this community. (A similarly labeled bottle of the same product, but from the Sabbathday Lake, Maine, community and from a somewhat later date, is in the author's collection.)

The Shakers marketed Pure Lemon Syrup for two seemingly disparate purposes: as a food product (for making a refreshing beverage at home) and as a medicinal preparation. About the former, the broadside boasts: "One table spoonful of the Syrup in a Tumbler of Water, furnishes a Superior Lemonade at one-twelfth the cost of Lemonade commonly made at Hotels." Its medicinal use was as an aid for digestion. A later description of Lemon Syrup states, "It is suitable to all stomach diseases; is excellent in sickness."[2]

As it turned out, the removal and conservation of the broadsides was only the beginning of the storage box's yield of treasures. The next layer of paper was newsprint, and even after the passage of almost two centuries, Tom was able to see that it was dated 1807 without having to remove it. This discovery naturally piqued our curiosity, and the joint decision was made to proceed with dismantling the box, layer by layer—a process comparable to uncovering the layers, or stratigraphy, of an archeological site. While this decision was not easy to arrive at, it was our belief that the potential value of the layers of the box's history outweighed its present value as a historical artifact.

The next layers of paper that were uncovered, and then removed, were a series of hymn sheets that subsequent analysis has shown are likely the first known examples of Shaker printing.[3] Printed around 1810—probably at New Lebanon but possibly at Hancock—these sheets allowed for the easy distribution of the growing number of Shaker hymn texts among the members. A letter written by Elder Jethro Turner at Watervliet, New York, to the Ministry at New Lebanon, dated 17 October 1810, describes in plain terms the need for these printed sheets: "I send here inclosed two hymns corrected for the press, one of which was over look'd when the rest were sent. . . . If it was convenient for the Elder Brother to send us a few printed copies we should be thankful for them, it would be clever to have one copy to a room. . . . It is truly much more convenient for the Brethren and Sisters to learn hymns from printed copies then from written ones: besides it is a considerable labour to write copies enough to supply the whole, especially when they come so plenty as they have latterly."[4]

A subsequent letter sent from Watervliet, New York, to Father David Darrow at Union Village, Ohio, dated 21 November 1811 describes the genesis of the project that resulted in the first Shaker hymnal: "Our brethren at Hancock lately provided themselves with a printing press and types and . . . they have undertaken to print our most useful hymns, for the use of Believers only."[5] At the time these fragments were found in the Andrewses' broadside box they were the only examples known of the first generation of Shaker printing. Subsequently, three bound gatherings of these sheets have been located at the Shaker Library, Sabbathday Lake, Maine, and the Stetson Library, Williams College, Williamstown, Massachusetts.

The next layers found after the printed hymn sheets were several long and narrow pieces of old, high rag-content paper with hand-written poems on them. On the back of one of these papers is written in manuscript: "Hulda Bracketts little note." Sister Brackett was born on 28 February 1770. She entered the East or Hill Family at New Lebanon at the age of seventeen with her mother and two sisters—among the earliest converts and founding members—and signed the covenant there in 1826. She died in the faith on 20 August 1853. The other two poems, each written by a different hand, were not signed and their authors are unknown.

As the conservator worked toward the outside surface, there were more sheets of newsprint, seven in all, with the latest one dating 1821. This means that unless older newspapers were stored and used fourteen years later—an unlikely occurrence—the box was constructed over many years. Adding weight to this latter supposition is the fact that the Lemon Syrup broadsides could not have been added before 1861. Most of the newspapers came from Albany, New York, but an 1810 sheet was from the Pittsfield (Massachusetts) Sun. There was even one newspaper from Philadelphia. Interleafed with the various printed and

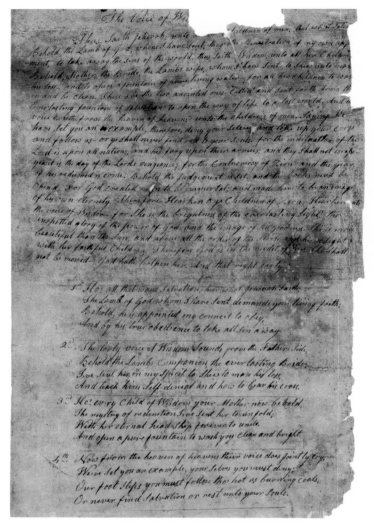

Manuscript hymn text entitled "The Voice of Wisdom"
Collection of David D. Newell

handwritten materials were additional layers of blank heavy papers and coarse fabrics. These added rigidity and weight.

A solid wooden mold in the collection of Hancock Shaker Village offers a clue to how the box was constructed. While the origins of this mold are uncertain—it may have been intended for use in basket making, since most large baskets were constructed using such molds—its size happened to conform to the size of the storage box. One further assumption: the absence of wear on the inner, broadside-lined surface indicates that if the box was used at all it probably stored soft materials, such as clothing or other fabrics.

The tale of this one modest object touches on several aspects of Shaker history and culture: one short-lived commercial enterprise, several private poetic writings that were apparently not intended to be seen by non-Shakers, and a cache of very early printed hymnal "trial" sheets. It also speaks to the value that the Shakers placed on thrift; written and printed materials that were no longer of use to them became lining for a box. If there is a lesson to be learned from examining this simple storage box it may be no more than this: humble objects have as much to tell us as major, iconic ones—we simply need to listen to the former more carefully.

Notes *for this section are found immediately following* **Notes for Object Captions**.

Box, Mount Lebanon, N.Y. ca. 1850
8 ⁷⁄₈" x 12 ¹⁄₂"

*Another excellent example of the accidental preservation
of Shaker printing is this pasted-up box covered entirely in
broadsides advertising Sarsaparilla, Phthisis Eradicating
Syrup, and Vegetable Pulmonary Pills. The contents of
the box when it was found by the Andrewses included a
sister's net cap and shoe, a section of peg-rail, palm leaf
bonnet braiding, a duster handle, and spool. Boxes such
as this, sometimes referred to as "make-do," are instances
of the Shakers' eminent practicality in reusing materials.*

Collection of Edward D. Andrews II

Case of Drawers, Community Unknown, late 19th century
8 ⅞" x 19" x 8 ¾"

*This unusual piece has a wooden case and drawers constructed entirely
of cardboard and decorative papers that have been pasted together.
The pulls are porcelain balls threaded through the drawer fronts.*

Andrews Collection, Hancock Shaker Village 1962.082

Writing Box, Mount Lebanon, N.Y. 1847
6 ¼" x 20 ¾" x 15"

Table top writing boxes were made in a variety of forms by the Shakers. Most were made of very thin pine boards and dovetailed. This example has a slanted top with applied moldings that close over the side walls. An exquisitely joined drawer opens from the lower right side. The piece is finished in chrome yellow over the exterior and much of the interior save the front divisions of the drawer, which is painted blue. A brass escutcheon frames the key-hole. "1847" is stamped into the bottom. **Shaker Furniture** *plate 38.*

Andrews Collection, Hancock Shaker Village 1962.157

Writing Box, Mount Lebanon, N.Y. ca. 1830
4 ¾" x 16 ⅝" x 11"

This writing box is pine and finished with a chrome yellow wash (inside), red wash (case sides), and clear varnish (top). Unlike the other examples it does not have a drawer for an inkwell or any internal divisions. "Angeline Cook" is written in script on the underside of the lid and along the top edge of the back of the case. She was admitted at Mount Lebanon on July 5, 1865. Shaker records indicate that she came from Watervliet to evade her father. Brother Isaac Newton Youngs recorded the construction of a number of writing boxes in the Church Family's Domestic Journal:

"March 1836 One dozen writing boxes were brot into the house, made & lately finished by Nicholas Bennet. They are well made, and Nicholas says they are worth $6.00 apiece, & that he has been near 6 days apiece making them. He began them some where about the 20th of January. The boxes were mostly for young Sisters, writers, &c."[57]

This box may be one of Brother Nicholas's, but could also have been made by Brother Orren Haskins or Brother Elisha D'Alembert Blakeman, both of whom are known to have constructed writing boxes.

Collection of the Family of David V. and Phyllis C. Andrews

Writing Box, Mount Lebanon, N.Y.
ca. 1830
4 ¹/₂" x 19" x 12"

*A unique feature of this writing
box is the paper-tray that lifts
automatically when the lid is raised.
A small drawer for an ink-well opens
from the upper right corner of the
case. Andrews family provenance
that accompanies this piece states
that it was acquired from Sister
Emma Neale, who had received
it from Sister Polly Lewis who
attributed it to her cousin, Brother
Orren Haskins. This piece is
illustrated on page 32 of*
Religion in Wood.

**Collection of Dr. John R. Ribic
and Dr. Carla Kingsley**

Chest, Unknown Community, ca. 1840
11 ¼" x 25 ½" x 11 ½"

This dovetailed pine chest, including the lidded till, is lined with deep blue "sugar paper." Its original use and community of origin are unknown.

Andrews Collection, Hancock Shaker Village 1963.1265

Chest, Unknown Community, ca. 1810
14 ⅝" x 54 ⅜" x 12"

The H-hinges and primitive wooden handles bespeak the early date of this long red-painted chest. It is made of pine and butt-jointed. The Andrewses collected a handful of early chests like this one. Faith Andrews recalled one such discovery in a 1973 interview:

> "In one of the rooms under the eaves, [at the 1786 Hancock Meetinghouse] there was a long chest, filled with copies of a book, leatherbound and Shaker printed, entitled Millennial Praises. We bought the chest with books."[58]

Andrews Collection, Hancock Shaker Village 1962.531

Box, possibly Enfield, Conn. ca. 1870
5 ¼" x 7 ⅞" x 7 ⅞"

This square box is typical of ones made at Enfield, Connecticut later in the 19th century in that it is finely dovetailed, uses walnut (others also use "white walnut" or butternut), and the interior is lined and bordered with fancy papers. The bottom is pine and the finish is a clear varnish. These were made in a variety of shapes and sizes, with or without lids.

Collection of Miriam R. and M. Stephen Miller

Box, Mount Lebanon, N.Y. ca. 1840
4 ½" x 12 ½" x 5"

This utility box is pine with brass hinges, lockset and key, and a bone escutcheon. It is finished in a clear varnish. The maker carefully joined it with eight dovetails in each corner— assuring it would be dimensionally stable. The interior bottom is lined is lined with later 19th century wallpaper. The box was a gift from Faith Andrews to her daughter Ann in 1961.

Collection of Miriam R. and M. Stephen Miller

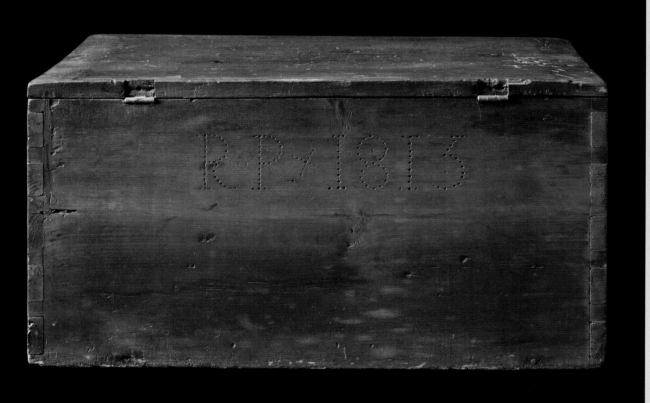

Chest, Mount Lebanon, N.Y. ca. 1815
10 ½" x 20" x 12"

This fully dovetailed pine chest has a label affixed to the front center reading "Poplar bark./Populus tremuloides." Also known as Quaking Aspen, this medicinal bark was used as a vermifuge on animals. The following is pricked into the back "R.P. x 1815." The exterior of this chest is finished in a dark red wash.

Andrews Collection, Hancock Shaker Village 1962.685

Box, Mount Lebanon, N.Y. ca. 1830
3 ¾" x 9 ½" x 5"

This colorful lidded box was given by Sister Sadie Neale to Ted Andrews during a visit to New Lebanon. Ted later gave it to his daughter Ann. It is finely dovetailed and the bottom is attached to the sides with tiny screws. The edges of the bottom are finished in a delicate quarter-round molding. The lid has breadboard moldings on the ends, each with a "lip." This is the same feature seen on many full size Mount Lebanon blanket chests (see page 162). In several ways this small box is a miniature version of those full size chests. Constructed of pine, it is finished in chrome yellow (top and sides), salmon (probably red lead), with blue paper inside.

Collection of Bob and Aileen Hamilton

Candle Box, Mount Lebanon, N.Y. ca. 1820
3 ⁷/₈" x 12" x 3 ³/₄"

*This pine candle box is finished in a blue-green
paint. The case is fully dovetailed and the lid
has a quarter-round molding to the edge.
Small boxes such as this one were used for many
purposes in Shaker dwellings and shops.*

Collection of Dr. Thomas and Jan Pavlovic

Pipe Boxes, Mount Lebanon or Watervliet, N.Y. ca. 1820
3 ⁵/₈" x 20" x 5⁵/₈", 3 ³/₄" x 21" x 3¹/₂"

Pipes have a central place in Shaker life and lore. While Mother Ann was being held in a stone prison in Manchester, England, she received nourishment in the form of "wine and milk, poured into the bowl of [a] pipe."⁵⁹ Many of the early Shakers, both men and women, smoked pipes. The Shakers at Mount Lebanon and Watervliet, New York. manufactured clay pipe bowls and stems for their own use and for sale to "the World." These dovetailed pine boxes were made to store smoking paraphernalia. The interior of the example at bottom is divided into one short compartment (for pipe bowls) and one long compartment (for stems). The initials under the lid, "A.M." are believed to be those of Elder Archibald Meacham (1779-1845). Br. Archibald was sent west to found the community of West Union, at Busro, Indiana, where he served as Ministry Elder. His later years were spent at his original home community of Watervliet, New York. The Andrewses acquired the box from Sister Sadie Neale in the early 1930s. (Sr. Sadie came to New Lebanon from Watervliet, New York.) Finished in a red wash, it was photographed by Noel Vincentini for The Index of American Design in 1935.

Andrews Collection, Hancock Shaker Village 1962.754 (above)
Collection of Miriam R. and M. Stephen Miller (below)

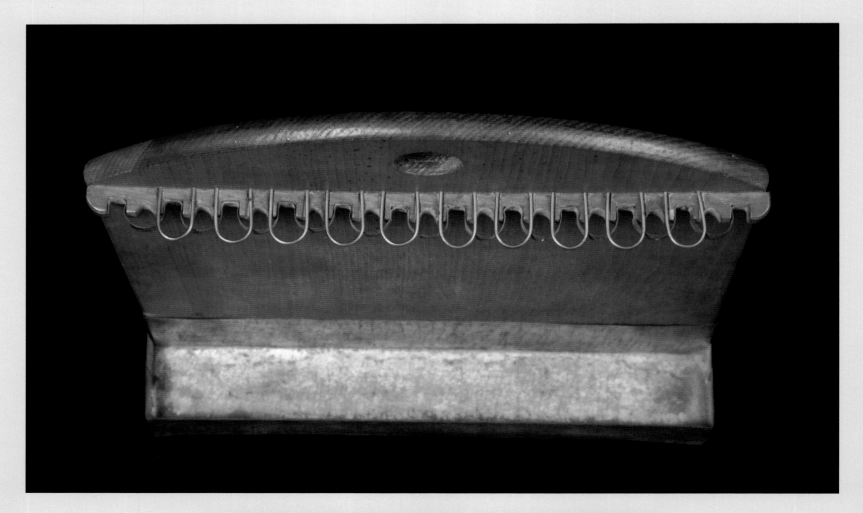

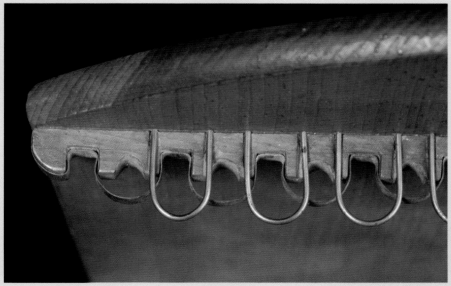

Pipe Rack, Watervliet, N.Y. ca. 1830
13" x 11 ¹⁄₂" x 2 ¹⁄₈"

Rocking Chair, Mount Lebanon or
Watervliet, N.Y. ca. 1810
46" x 22 ¹⁄₄" x 25 ¹⁄₂"

*This meticulously crafted pipe rack is one
of the finest objects in the Andrews
Collection at Hancock Shaker Village.
Constructed of pine, tin, and wire, it was
designed to be hung from a peg. The top
edge of the back is carefully rounded. The
framework for the rack has been carefully
cut and lined with a strip of tin and wire
loops. The tin well at the bottom is
tacked to the back. The photo at right is
an homage to William Winter's photograph for Plate 14 in* **Shaker Furniture.**
*The rocking chair was collected by the
Andrewses from the Shaker community
at Hancock. However, there is no
evidence that chairs were ever manufactured at Hancock, and this chair's style
suggests it was made at New Lebanon
or Watervliet, New York. It was not
uncommon for Shaker families to buy
and sell their products between different
communities. This sort of commerce offers
one possibility for how this New York
chair ended up in Massachusetts. Made
of cherry and maple (with replaced
cotton seating) the strong features of the
chair, especially the unusually large rocker
blades, mushroom handholds, and heavily
turned finials are all hallmarks of its
early construction. This image was shot
in the northwest attic of the 1830 Brick
Dwelling at Hancock, Massachusetts.*

Andrews Collection, Hancock Shaker Village
1962.600 (pipe rack),
1962.012 (rocking chair)

Arm Chair, Mount Lebanon or Watervliet, N.Y. ca. 1810
46 $^7/_8$" x 22 $^1/_8$" x 16"

This arm chair is similar in virtually every respect to the rocker illustrated on page 203. The main difference is that the finials, or "pommels" as the Shakers called them, are slightly more pointed. The chair is finished in a red wash and retains its original woven-splint seat. Note the prominent "mushroom" handholds found on these early Shaker chairs.

Collection of Dr. Thomas and Jan Pavlovic

Arm Chair, Mount Lebanon or Watervliet, N.Y. ca. 1810
46 ½" x 21 ³/₈" x 16"

This nearly identical example to the one illustrated on the page
opposite is finished in a dark stain. The seat has been replaced with
newer tape. The front posts taper from the seat upwards to where
they expand to receive the arm and "mushroom" handhold. The
arched slats with beveled top edges are found on chairs from
both Mount Lebanon and Watervliet, making it difficult
to definitively attribute these examples to either community.

Collection of Dr. Thomas and Jan Pavlovic

Side Chair, Watervliet, N.Y. ca. 1830
36 ½" x 18 ¼" x 13 ¼"

*Elder Freegift Wells was a prolific chairmaker at
the Watervliet community before he was called
west to administer Union Village, Ohio in 1839.
His characteristic "FW" cartouche is often found
embossed on the front posts of his work. The back
slats of this example exhibit the typical graduation
in height from lowest to highest, as well as the
beveled top edge. This chair retains its original
red wash and woven-splint seat, carefully joined
on the underside with a hook and notch. The
Andrewses acquired this chair from the South
Family at Watervliet, New York.*

Collection of J. Richard and E. Barbara Pierce

Side Chair, Mount Lebanon, N.Y. ca. 1840
40" x 18 ½" x 13 ½"

This side chair is typical of those made for use within the community at Mount Lebanon in the 1830s and 1840s. The top slat of this example is reinforced where it is mortised and pegged into the posts. "Girls 13." is written on the reverse of the top slat. The tape seat has been replaced.

Collection of the Family of David V. and Phyllis C. Andrews

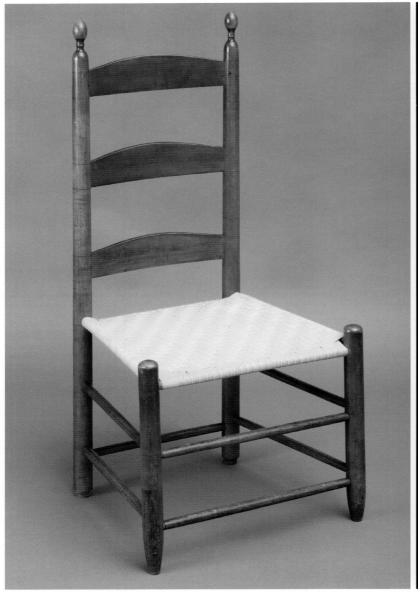

Side Chair, Mount Lebanon, N.Y. ca. 1840
38" x 18 ½" x 14"

This side chair with wooden tilters exhibits a form of ring turning below the pommel commonly found on chairs of this period. This low-seated chair was designed for a sister's use. This example sat in Faith Andrews's Whittier Avenue house in Pittsfield for many years until she gave it as a gift in 1989. The tape seat has been replaced.

Collection of Miriam R. and M. Stephen Miller

Side Chair, Watervliet, N.Y. ca. 1840
38 ½" x 18 ⅝" x 13 ¾"

Graduated, arched back slats (with beveled top edges), and large pommels with graduated, ring-turned collars beginning at the tops of the rear posts are typical of Watervliet chairs of this period. This chair retains its original splint seat.

Andrews Collection, Hancock Shaker Village 1962.493

Side Chair, Mount Lebanon, N.Y. ca. 1850
37 ³/₈" x 18" x 13 ³/₈"

*Brother George O. Donnell famously patented the
brass chair tilter in 1852. Around that time a number
of side chairs built of beautifully figured woods were
produced featuring this new innovation. The present
example is made of flame birch, tiger maple, and
maple. The back slats have all been cut from the same
piece of wood, creating a stunning visual effect.
The tilter is formed of a ferrule, ball, and foot. This
accommodation to the human tendency to rock
backwards in a chair seems surprising for a sect as
regulated as the Shakers. However, the tilter in its
wooden form was commonly used on community
chairs before and after Brother George's
patented innovation.*

Collection of Dr. Thomas and Jan Pavlovic

Rocking Chair, Mount Lebanon, N.Y. ca. 1800
45 ¼" x 21" x 14 ⅝"

The unrefined side-scroll arms and turned bottom on the posts point to the relatively early construction date of this rocker. The "mushroom" style hand-holds seen on other examples similar to this are not present here. Instead, the arms show a move towards the shape of those found on later rockers. "01" is either written, or affixed on a heavily finished label, on the center of the reverse of the top slat. The meaning of this is unknown. The finish is a red paint and the tape seat has been replaced. **Shaker Furniture** *plate 16.*

Collection of the Family of David V. and Phyllis C. Andrews

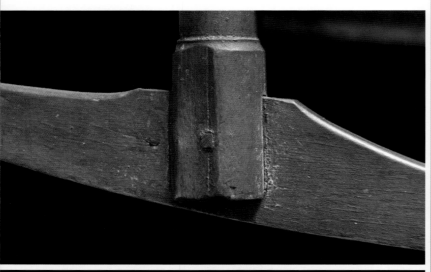

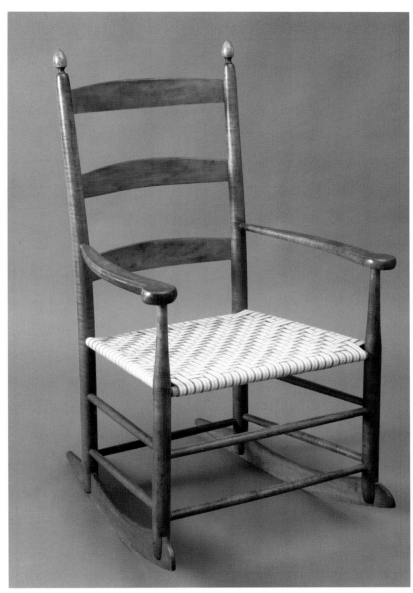

Rocking Chairs, Mount Lebanon, N.Y.
ca. 1870 (left), 39" x 21" x 23"
ca. 1850 (right), 42 ½" x 17 ¾" x 13 ⅜"

These two rockers date from the period when the commercial mass production of chairs was beginning at Mount Lebanon. The side scroll arms have assumed the elegant form associated with the finest chairs made for use within the community. The "acorn" pommels on the chair at left are characteristic of those used on chairs made for sale to the world throughout the late nineteenth and into the early twentieth century. The rocker at right is unusual in that the posts taper at the bottom and enter the top of the rocker blades with a dowelled end, rather than saddling the blades as shown at left. It was likely made for use within the community. **Shaker Furniture** *plate 30 (right).*

Collection of Gene and Karen Faul
Andrews Collection, Hancock Shaker Village 1962.156

Rocking Chair, Mount Lebanon, N.Y. ca. 1875
44" x 17" x 17 ¾"

The gently arched back slats and vase turnings to the front post distinguished the classic form of late nineteenth century rockers mass-produced at Mount Lebanon. Although this example was made for use within the community, chairs made for the outside world were nearly identical in form. Sale chairs were typically marked with a numeral—"0" to "7"— indicating the size on the center of one of the back slats, and, after 1876, a gold trademark decal applied to the inside of a rear post, rocker blade, or back slat. This rocker has the numeral "3" stamped in the middle of the top slat. The 1932 Berkshire Museum exhibit label is adhered to the underside of the original tape seat.

Andrews Collection, Hancock Shaker Village 1962.157.0003

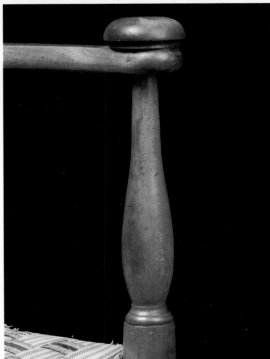

Children's Chairs

Watervliet, N.Y. ca. 1850 (left)
27 ½" x 16 ⅛" x 12 ½"

Mount Lebanon, N.Y. ca. 1865 (right)
26 ⅝" x 14" x 11 ¼"

The same principles and design characteristics used on chairs for adults were also used on chairs for children. In nineteenth-century Shaker communities children were under the care of a Deacon (for boys) or Deaconess (for girls), and usually lived apart from the adult population. The chair at left exhibits the arched, beveled back slat typical of Watervliet chairs. A detail photo shows the wooden ball-and-socket tilter used on the rear posts. A leather thong was pegged into a hole drilled into the chair post, then fed through the wooden ball and tied off at the bottom (note small hole in the bottom of the tilter). The 1932 Berkshire Museum label is visible on the inside of the chair post. The example at right retains its original taped seat. Shaker Furniture plate 18.

Andrews Collection, Hancock Shaker Village 1962.054, 1962.072

Work Chair, Mount Lebanon, N.Y. ca. 1820
38 ½" x 23 ½" x 14 ¼"

Chair Back Extender, Mount Lebanon, N.Y. mid-19th century
15 ⅜" x 14 ½" x 1 ½"

This unusually wide chair is seated in two planks which are screwed into the stretchers. The device attached to the top slat in the detail was used to extend the height of a chair back. **Shaker Furniture** *plate 11.*

Andrews Collection, Hancock Shaker Village 1962.483 (chair),
1962.635 (extender)

Dining Chairs, Mount Lebanon, N.Y. ca. 1850
25 ³/₄" x 16 ³/₄" x 14 ¹/₄" (left)
26" x 18 ³/₄" x 14 ¹/₄" (right)

These low-back chairs were used in the communal dining rooms of Shaker dwelling houses. The example at left has one slat and a nipple turning to the tops of the rear posts. The top posts of the two-slat example at right are flat with rounded edges. The two-slat chair also has wooden tilters. Both examples retain their original splint seats. Ted Andrews speculated that these chairs were made at Hancock, but subsequent research has uncovered no evidence of large-scale chair manufacturing at Hancock. It is more reasonable to assume that these chairs were made at Mount Lebanon and then purchased by the Hancock Shakers from their brethren who were a mere four miles away. **Shaker Furniture** *plate 3.*

Andrews Collection, Hancock Shaker Village 1962.192 (left), 1962.011 (right)

High Shop Chairs, Mount Lebanon, N.Y. ca. 1840 36 $^3/_8$" x 17 $^3/_4$" x 14 $^1/_2$" (left)
and possibly Hancock, Mass. ca. 1820 42 $^1/_2$" x 18 $^3/_4$" x 13 $^1/_2$" (right)

The posts on the slat-back chair at left have beveled edges and rounded tops. The rear posts are canted backwards above the seat to accommodate the back of the sitter. Based on the construction and design of a recently documented loom bench signed by Brother Orren Haskins (see pages 218-219) this chair can be attributed to him as well. The stretchers on this example are through-mortised. The tape seat has been replaced. The chair at right is a very unusual example due to the turnings at the bottom of the posts. The Andrewses purchased this chair from Hancock in 1929.[60] *Due to the lack of any documentation concerning chair manufacturing at Hancock, this one is just unusual enough to make it possible that it was made there for a special use. It retains its original splint seat.* **Shaker Furniture** *plate 46 (left) and plate 30 (right).*

Andrews Collection, Hancock Shaker Village 1962.013 (left), 1962.656 (right)

Revolving Shop Stool, Mount Lebanon, N.Y. ca. 1860
43 ½" x 14" x 16 ½"

This stool is easily the most tragic piece in the Andrews Collection. The heavy turnings on the posts and stretchers, and the unusually shaped seat and slat back, make it an unusual form. It is finished in a dark stain. In the early 1960s, after it had been donated to Hancock Shaker Village, Inc., a worker there was replacing the worn out leather seat. He uncovered the poem at right hidden under the seat. The manuscript is very badly faded due to the leaching of tannic acid into the paper, but the sad tale of Brother Charles Brown is just legible through the damage of the years. The stool was photographed in the northwest attic of the 1830 Brick Dwelling at Hancock. **Shaker Furniture** *plate 48.*

Andrews Collection, Hancock Shaker Village 1962.676 (chair)
Courtesy, The Winterthur Library: The Edward Deming Andrews
Memorial Shaker Collection, No. SA 992

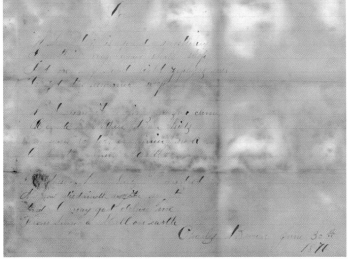

To the Finder. Remember me.

When this is found most likely
I within my grave shall sleep
And ore my head light zephyrs lull
To [make] the mourner weep.
But may it be in some far clime
Remote from these Bare hills
In some lo[w] del or shining nook
Or by the running Rills.
For these Bare hills I have a dred
My soul disdaineth myrth
And O may god deliver me
From living a Hell on earth.

Charles Brown
June 30, 1871

Loom Bench, Mount Lebanon, N.Y. 1839
34 ³/₈" x 17" x 9 ³/₄"

This loom bench was completed by Brother Orren Haskins at Mount Lebanon's Church Family on "Feb 19th 1839." His distinctively florid initials "O H" and the date are inscribed on the bottom in pencil. This, and the slat-backed loom benches illustrated on the next page, can all be attributed to Brother Orren, who also built looms. The present example has a plain wooden seat. The rear posts have beveled edges, rounded tops, and are screwed into the back of the sides. The unusual projection to the rear of the legs undoubtedly helped stabilize the chair. This loom bench was given as a gift by Faith Andrews to a friend whose husband complained of back problems.

Gift of Mrs. Jean Bousquet, Hancock Shaker Village 2007.016

Loom Bench, Mount Lebanon, N.Y. ca, 1840
21 ⁵/₈" x 18" x 11 ⁵/₈"

The seat of this example is curved to accommodate the weaver. The entire piece is finished in a red wash. It, and the two examples below were "found in loom rooms at the Mt. Lebanon Church." [61]

Collection of the Family of David V. and Phyllis C. Andrews

Loom Benches, Mount Lebanon, N.Y. ca. 1840
35 ⁵/₈" x 18 ³/₄" x 12" (left)
40" x 20 ¹/₄" x 13" (right)

These two loom benches vary only slightly from the previous example. The one at left has plain board sides (legs) and a stuffed leather seat. The example at right has a drawer under the seat. The unusually shaped legs allowed it to be pulled very close to the loom.

Andrews Collection, Hancock Shaker Village 1962.532.0002 (left), 1962.532.0001 (right)

Letter, Attributed to Father James Whittaker, Ashfield, Mass. 1782

This manuscript is one of the earliest extant documents relating to the Shakers. It was "found with a number of miscellaneous papers in a box at Hancock."[62] The letter was preserved in an envelope bearing the handwriting of Shaker antiquarian Brother Alonzo Hollister.[63] Ted Andrews attributed it to Father James Whittaker, who accompanied Mother Ann Lee from England to America in 1774. The letter is dated February 25th and was sent from the site of the Shaker leadership's winter quarters at Ashfield, Massachusetts. It is a stern exhortation to Josiah Tallcott, who had been recently converted at Hancock, Massachusetts. It reads in part:

Thou art idle and slothful, whereby thy land lays unimproved and pretty much waste; from whence arises want, and is a great burden to the poor man that dwells in the house not far from thee. This is abominable in the Sight of God, and will surely bring upon thee want and poverty, as well as the wrath of God in hell. . . Thy women with thee are also idle, hatchers of cockatrice eggs and breeders of lust and abominable filthiness, as well as covenant breakers. . . Make your women turn out and mortify their lusts, and they will find health as well to their bodies as to their souls.

Brother Josiah heeded the advice of Father James— consecrating his land for what would become the West Family of the Hancock Shaker community.

*In 1938 students of Carl Purington Rollins, who oversaw the printing of **Shaker Furniture**, printed the letter as a limited edition pamphlet entitled **The Shaker Shaken**.*

The Shaker Shaken reproduced courtesy of The Berkshire Athenaeum, Pittsfield, Mass.
Andrews Collection, Hancock Shaker Village 2208ab

THE

Shaker Shaken;

OR,

GOD's *Warning* to Josiah Talcott, as denounced in a Letter from James Whittaker, one of the *United Society of Believers in Christ's Second Appearing*, (vulgarly known as *Shakers*).

From an Original Manuscript.

NEW-HAVEN:
Printed at the BIBLIOGRAPHICAL PRESS, over against *Linonia & Brothers.* 1938.

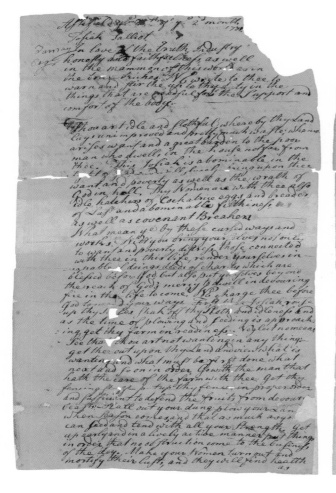

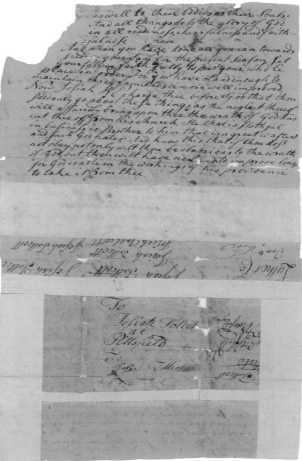

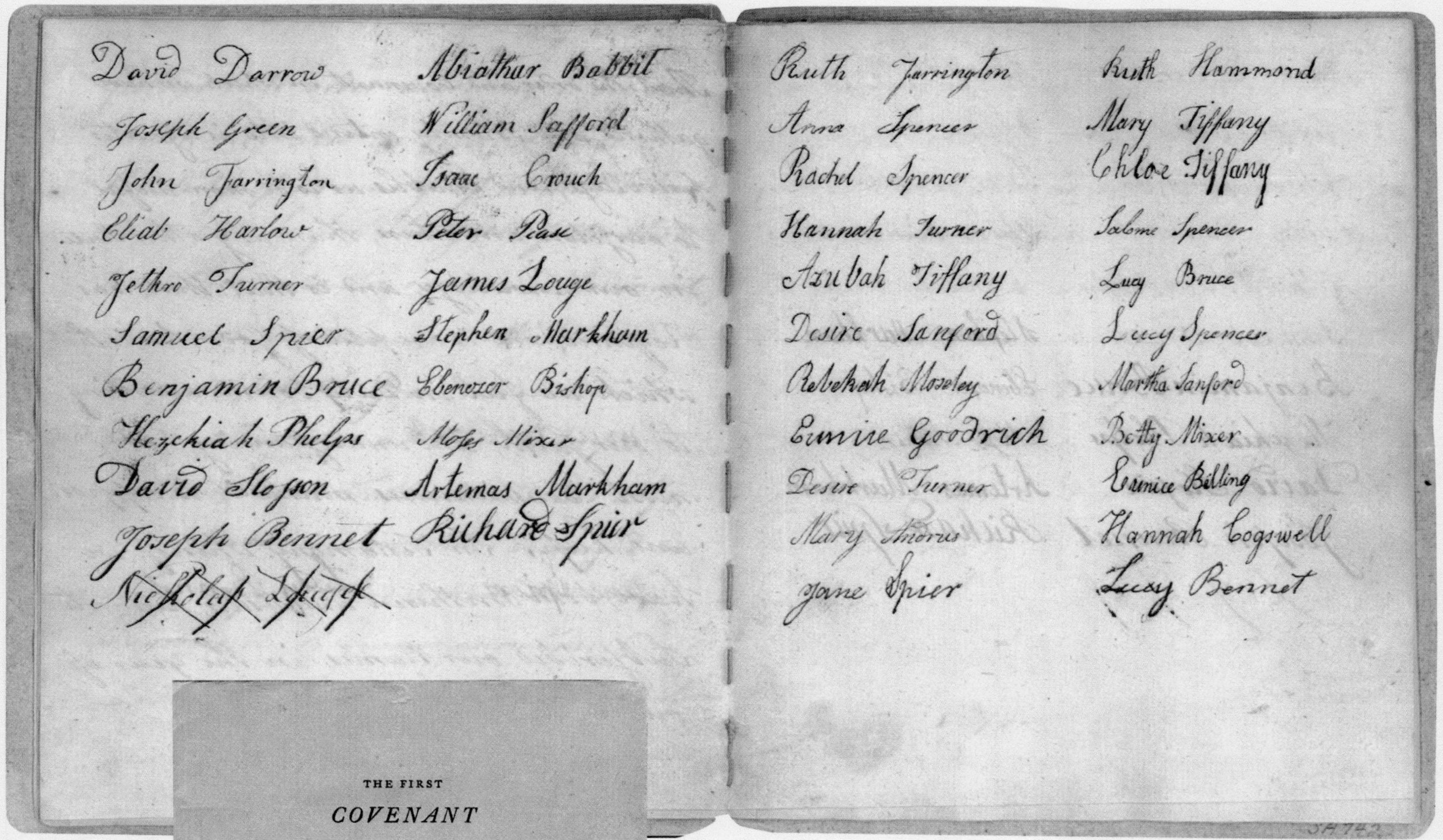

David Darrow	Abiathar Babbit	Ruth Farrington	Ruth Hammond
Joseph Green	William Safford	Anna Spencer	Mary Tiffany
John Farrington	Isaac Crouch	Rachel Spencer	Chloe Tiffany
Eliab Harlow	Peter Pease	Hannah Turner	Salome Spencer
Jethro Turner	James Louge	Azubah Tiffany	Lucy Bruce
Samuel Spier	Stephen Markham	Desire Sanford	Lucy Spencer
Benjamin Bruce	Ebenezer Bishop	Rebekah Moseley	Martha Sanford
Hezekiah Phelps	Moses Mixer	Eunice Goodrich	Betty Mixer
David Slosson	Artemas Markham	Desire Turner	Eunice Belling
Joseph Bennet	Richard Spier	Mary Andrus	Hannah Cogswell
Nicholas Bennet		Jane Spier	Lucy Bennet

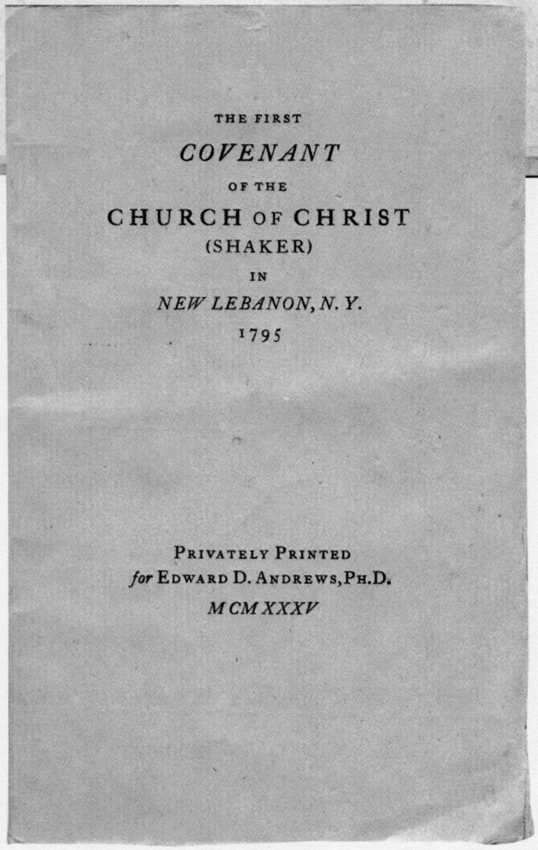

THE FIRST

COVENANT

OF THE

CHURCH OF CHRIST

(SHAKER)

IN

NEW LEBANON, N. Y.

1795

PRIVATELY PRINTED

for EDWARD D. ANDREWS, PH.D.

M CM XXXV

Covenant, Church Family, Mount Lebanon, 1795

This is one of the most important manuscripts collected by the Andrewses. It is the first written form of the covenant legally binding a Shaker family into "gospel order." Sister Sadie Neale entrusted it to the Andrewses, as they recalled in **Fruits of the Shaker Tree of Life.**

Often we talked with Sadie about the doctrines of the Shakers and the principles of their temporal economy, and through her instrumentality we acquired a considerable part of our library. One day, as we were discussing such matters, she became strangely quiet and distracted, then told us she had a document which she wanted us to have. Going over to a box by her bedside in which she kept farm accounts, memorabilia and other papers, she extracted, after some search, a manuscript booklet with a faded blue cover. It was the original Shaker covenant, signed in 1795 by the founders of the New Lebanon Church![64]

This foundation document was also printed privately for the Andrewses in a limited edition in 1935.

Courtesy, The Winterthur Library: The Edward Deming Andrews Memorial Shaker Collection, ASC 721
The First Covenant (pamphlet), Andrews Collection, Hancock Shaker Village 7697

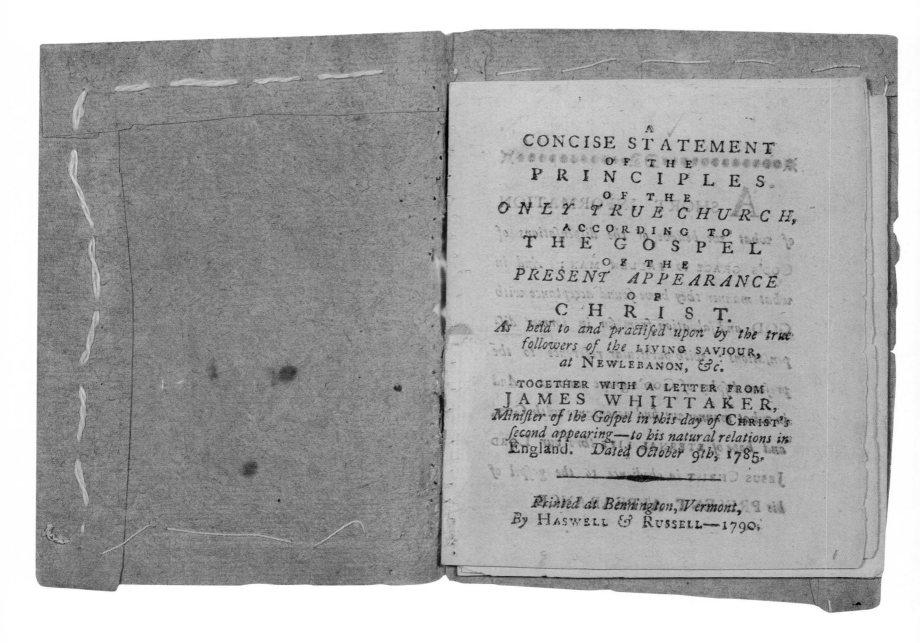

A Concise Statement of the Priniciples of the Only True Church. . . Bennington, Vt. 1790

The first printed publication issued by the Shakers was this statement of beliefs attributed to Father Joseph Meacham. Around ten copies of this imprint survive today. In an unpublished reminiscence on collecting Shaker imprints Ted Andrews wrote that: "The exceedingly rare Bennington pamphlet was found with some other pamphlets in the drawer of a shop piece in New Lebanon." [65]

Courtesy, The Winterthur Library: The Edward Deming Andrews Memorial Shaker Collection, ASC 333

Journal, Benjamin Seth Youngs, 1805

*This is the original journal kept by Elder
Benjamin Seth Youngs on his epic
journey, undertaken along with Brothers
Issachar Bates and David Meacham, to
bring the Shaker gospel to Kentucky and
Ohio. The three missionaries left Mount
Lebanon on January 1, 1805, at three in
the morning. They arrived at Malcolm
Worley's house at Turtle Creek, Ohio, on
March 22. In his "Autobiographical
Memoir," a copy of which was also
collected by the Andrewses, Issachar
Bates recorded that at Worley's the
missionaries "found the first rest for the
souls of our feet, having traveled 1223
miles in two months (58) and 22 days."[66]
Worley was soon converted to the new
faith and lead the missionaries to the
house of his near neighbor, Presbyterian
preacher Richard McNemar. The detail
photograph shows Youngs's entry for
March 23rd which records his first visit
to McNemar. After a period of intense
spiritual struggle Richard McNemar
converted to this new faith and became
one of the most important leaders in the
western Shaker communities. The
Andrewses discovered this manuscript
"tucked away in a chest" in an anteroom
of a New Lebanon dwelling house.[67]*

**Courtesy, The Winterthur Library: The
Edward Deming Andrews Memorial
Shaker Collection, ASC 859**

Bound Manuscripts, Mount Lebanon, N.Y. 19th century

The Andrewses' library of Shaker imprints and manuscripts ultimately came to be their most prized possession. In an unpublished writing on collecting books and manuscripts Ted Andrews wrote:

Gathering up printed and manuscript matter in Shaker buildings— in lofts, store-rooms, schools, meeting houses, shops, even barns— was the inevitable accompaniment of the zest to collect everything relating to the life and work of this religious society. Our first interest was in furniture, the craftsmanship of the sect, and afterwards tools, domestic utensils and products of the shop. When we came to the point of documenting our finds, however, we realized the importance of the printed and written word, and it was not long before we were picking up every scrap of evidence, in the way of journals, day books, letters and records of all kinds, along with printed literature, that we could find. Our experience, over some thirty years, has been the not uncommon one that every item has a value, useful in some piece of writing.[68]

All of the manuscripts pictured here are from Mount Lebanon, and include receipt books, day books, account books and ledgers.

Andrews Collection, Hancock Shaker Village

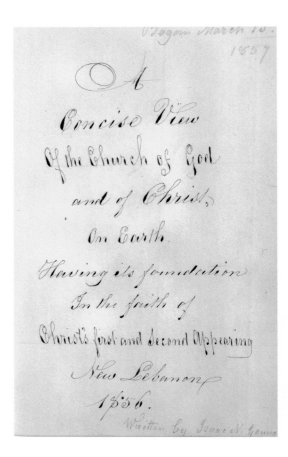

A Concise View of the Church of God and of Christ on Earth,
Mount Lebanon, N.Y. 1856

Day-Book B Kept by the Trustees of the CHURCH, Mount Lebanon, N.Y. 1836-1850

Brother Isaac Newton Youngs of Mount Lebanon was a notable polymath whose skills included clockmaking, cabinetmaking, building, painting, roofing, tailoring, writing music, and serving as scribe, or record-keeper, for the Church Family. A Concise View of the Church of God is one of the most important Shaker manuscripts in existence. It provides detailed information on the history of the Church at Mount Lebanon, as well as information on many Shaker industries. Brother Isaac was a meticulous record keeper with a scientific sense of documentation. His map of the Church Family in 1860 is a wonderful example of his documentary skills. Reproduced at lower right is his distinctive monogram, found in a number of manuscripts which he authored.

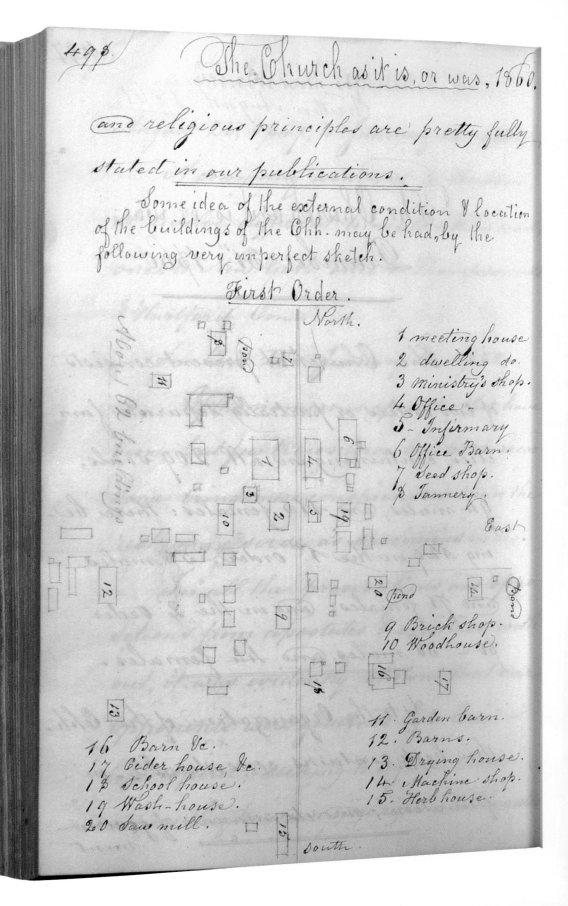

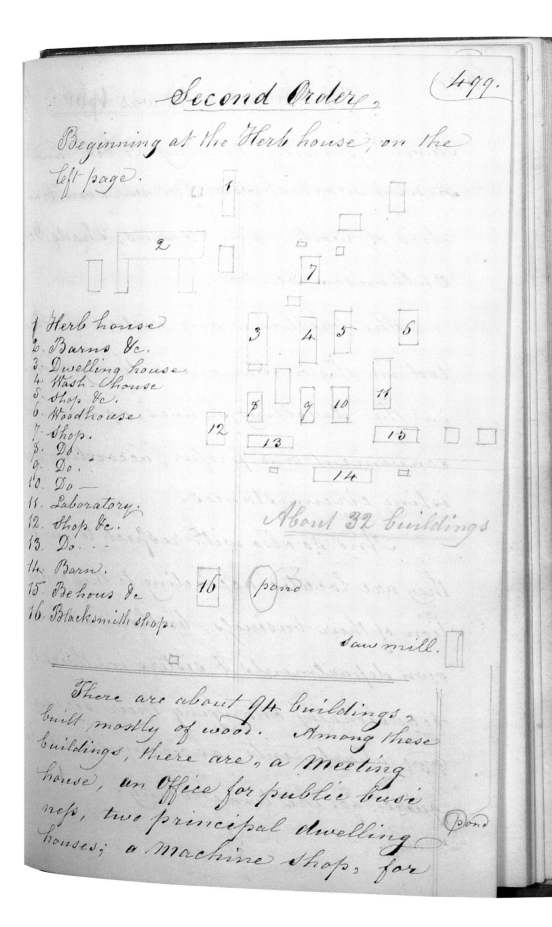

Second Order,

Beginning at the Herb house; on the
left page.

1. Herb house
2. Barns &c.
3. Dwelling house
4. Wash-house
5. Shop &c.
6. Woodhouse
7. Shop.
8. Do.
9. Do.
10. Do —
11. Laboratory.
12. Shop &c.
13. Do. -
14. Barn.
15. Pe house &c
16. Blacksmith shop.

About 32 buildings

Saw mill.

There are about 94 buildings,
built mostly of wood. Among these
buildings, there are, a Meeting
house, an Office for public busi
ness, two principal dwelling
houses; a Machine shop, for

Day-Book **B.**
Kept by the Trustees of the
CHURCH
at New-Lebanon.

This Closes the Accounts
of the year 1850
And with it too this book has run its race & done
And in a new one you must look, For 1851.

Music Manuscripts, Watervliet and Mount Lebanon, N.Y. ca. 1830-1840

The Andrewses were keenly interested in the music of the Shakers. The first scholarly study of Shaker music entitled **The Gift to Be Simple** *was published by the couple in 1940. The pages reproduced here are (clockwise from the upper left): Brother David Austin Buckingham of Watervliet employed the worldly "shape note" system of notation for his 1830 hymnbook; this "gift song," enclosed in a leaf, dates from near the beginning of the intense spiritual revival among the Shakers which scholars have come to call "The Era of Manifestations," or "Mother's Work," it was noted down by Sister Mary Hazard at Mount Lebanon in 1839; also from Sister Mary's hymnal is the song "Request from Mother Ann" written in the system of small letteral notation (without staff-lines) that became standard in Shaker musical notation beginning in the mid-1840s.*

Music Manuscripts, Courtesy, The Winterthur Library: The Edward Deming Andrews Memorial Shaker Collection, ASC 876 and 896.

Architectural Drawing, Mount Lebanon, N.Y. ca. 1863

*The Andrewses acquired a body of architectural drawings from Mount Lebanon. Most have remained unidentified to the present day.
However, researchers Julie Nicoletta, and more recently Lauren Stiles, have discovered that a number of these drawings relate to the
proposed construction of the Center Family Dwelling at Mount Lebanon, which was erected during 1867. The entire corpus of drawings
has been attributed to Brother George Wickersham. The elevation drawing reproduced above was the first proposed design for the
structure, which was to be built in stone and brick. The dwelling was eventually constructed as a wooden frame and clapboard
building in an effort to save money.[69]*

Andrews Collection, Hancock Shaker Village 1978.005.0001

Views of the Three Shaker Families at Alfred, Maine, Attributed to Joshua H. Bussell ca. 1880

Elder Joshua H. Bussell documented the Shaker communities of Maine and New Hampshire over a fifty year period in wonderfully naive "village views." The drawing reproduced above is from his later period when he embraced perspective techniques gleaned from "bird's eye view" illustrations made of towns throughout New England. Scholar Robert Emlen has studied Bussell's work extensively and documented his evolution as an artist in multiple articles and the book Shaker Village Views. This watercolor is especially important since the Church Family Dwelling, Meeting House, and Ministry Shop it shows were destroyed in a devastating fire at the Alfred Church Family in August of 1901.

Courtesy, The Winterthur Library: The Edward Deming Andrews Memorial Shaker Collection, SA 1534

Watercolor Illustrations by Benson John Lossing 1856

In September of 1937 the Andrewses went to the trouble of tracking down Helen Lossing Johnson, daughter of Benson John Lossing. Lossing was a noted author and artist whose 1857 article about the Shakers in **Harper's New Monthly Magazine** *is one of the best contemporary journalistic accounts of the Shakers. The Andrewses must have been extremely gratified to find that Lossing's daughter still retained some of her father's original watercolor sketches:*

Dear Mr. Andrews: Your letter of Sep 21st has been received. I have in my possession my father's private papers and correspondence . . . I have three of the original drawings made by my father at the time he visited the Shakers at Lebanon, viz. <u>Interior of the Meeting House</u>, <u>The herb house</u>, and <u>The Tannery</u>. All of these drawings were engraved on the wood, and published in the article, as you will see . . .

My father often told me of his visit with the Shakers, and the friendly courtesy which was shown him by the people of the Community in helping him get his material for his article.

Our home was in the hills of Duchess County, near Millbrook, and I remember, when a child, going to New York City with my father on the Harlem Rail Road, and meeting Elder Evans, the Shaker, who was going to the City by the "Pittsfield Express." His demeanor and dress seemed very sweet and quaint to a child.

My father always kept one of the Shaker herb remedies for a cold called 'Composition,' in our medicine chest, which he had received from time to time through Elder Evans.[70]

The Andrewses subsequently acquired the three drawings named above. These water color sketches are valuable documents in that they present colored views of Mount Lebanon prior to the advent of color photography. Additionally, scholar Glendyne Wergland believes that the bald man seated in the Meetinghouse is likely Brother Isaac Newton Youngs, who served as Lossing's guide for much of his time at Mount Lebanon. Many other watercolors made by Lossing on his visit are in the collection of the Huntington Library, San Marino, California. A complete edition of these drawings, along with the original text of the article. was published as **An Early View of the Shakers** *by Don Gifford and June Sprigg.*

"The Herbalists Frame building," Andrews Collection, Hancock Shaker Village 1988.005.0001.1
"Interior of the meeting house," Courtesy, The Winterthur Library: The Edward Deming Andrews Memorial Shaker Collection, 1438
Tannery, Andrews Collection, Hancock Shaker Village 1988.005.0001.2

Fresh Herbs, Enfield, Conn. ca. 1850 22 ¾" x 17 ⅞"
Printing Block, Mount Lebanon, N.Y. ca. 1860 1 ⅞" x 2 ½" x ⅞"
Garden Seeds, Enfield, Conn. ca. 1850 20 ¾" x 13 ½"

The Shakers were the first to commercially package gardens seeds for sale. Additionally, they were renowned for the medicinal herbs grown at many of the communities which were dried and pressed for sale in "bricks." These broadsides advertise seeds and herbs available from the Enfield, Connecticut community sold under the auspices of Trustee Jefferson White. The smaller example states "For sale by James Kilvin, Seedsman, COLUMBUS, GEO." The Enfield Shakers sold seeds throughout the South before the Civil War. The collapse of this market hastened the decline of that community. The printing block was used to mark seed packages for **Shakers' Brown Dutch Lettuce** *at Mount Lebanon's Second Family.*

Andrews Collection, Hancock Shaker Village *(clockwise from top left)*
1962.484.0002, 1972.241, 1962.484.0001

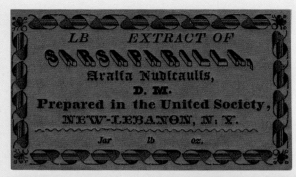

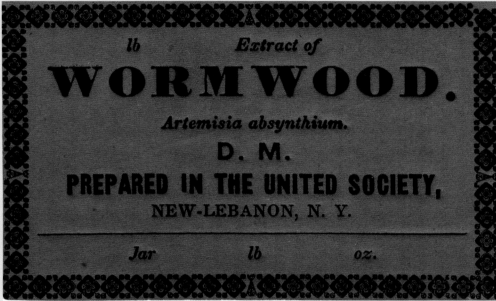

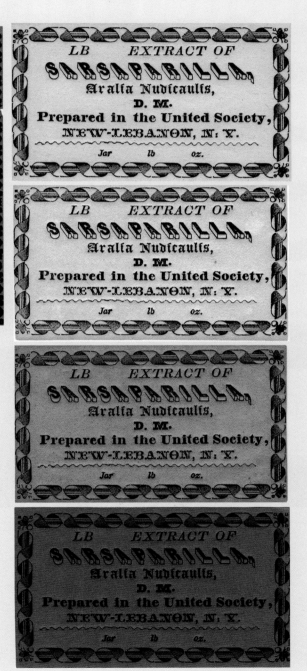

Herbal Preparation Labels, Mount Lebanon, N.Y. ca. 1850

The Andrewses preserved thousands of labels from the herbal extract industries at Watervliet and Mount Lebanon, New York. Benson Lossing described the process that resulted in the extracts for which these labels were made:

The Extract House, in which is the laboratory, for the preparation of juices for medical purposes, is a large frame building, thirty-six by one hundred feet. It was erected in 1850. It is supplied with the most perfect apparatus, and managed by James Long, a skillful chemist, and a member of the Society. In the principal room of the laboratory the chief operations of cracking, steaming, and pressing the roots and herbs are carried on, together with the boiling of the juices thus extracted. In one corner is a large boiler, into which the herbs or roots are placed and steam introduced. From this boiler the steamed herbs are conveyed to grated cylinders and subjected to immense pressure. The juices are then put in copper pans, inclosed in iron jackets, in such a manner that steam is introduced between the jackets and the pans, and the liquid boiled down to the proper consistency for use. Some juices, in order to avoid the destruction or modification of their medicinal properties, are conveyed to an upper room, and there boiled in a huge copper vacuum pan, from which, as its name implies, the air has been exhausted. This allows the liquid to boil at a much lower temperature than it would in the open air.[71]

Andrews Collection, Hancock Shaker Village

Herbal Preparation Labels, Mount Lebanon, N.Y. 1840-1860

While this group of labels was found by the Andrewses at Mount Lebanon, both that community and the community at Watervliet, New York used identical labels for their herbal preparations. These labels, measuring approximately 1" x 3", were likely printed at either one or both of those communities. They were placed on both the bottles containing the preparations, and the cardboard cylinders used to package the bottles. These groups remain in their original string-tied bundles, just as the Andrewses found them. Collector M. Stephen Miller was told by Faith Andrews that they "swept bundles of these labels into shopping bags at the medicine shop at New Lebanon."

Collection of Miriam R. and M. Stephen Miller

Extract Label Cupboard and Labels, Canterbury, N.Y. ca. 1850
27 ¾" x 48 ¼" x 2 ¼"

This bi-fold utilitarian cupboard contains pockets for sorting 216 different labels that were affixed to the wrappers of a tremendous variety of herbs, in different preparations and quantities, available from the Canterbury Shakers. Printed on bright yellow (and sometimes pink) paper, these labels were probably made by Elder Henry Blinn who printed many different works at Canterbury from the early 1840s until his death in 1905.

Andrews Collection, Hancock Shaker Village 1962.474

Apple Sauce Label and Printing Block,
Mount Lebanon N.Y. ca. 1880
7 ¼" x 7" x ½" (printing block)

Many Shaker communities produced apple sauce, both for their own consumption and for sale to the outside world. This label, printed on brilliant blue paper in gold ink, would have been trimmed and affixed to the top of an apple sauce firkin. The printing block used to make these labels has a hole in the center to allow for the name of the Trustee in charge of the business to be changed.

Andrews Collection, Hancock Shaker Village 6248 (label) and 1962.469 (printing block)

Apple Sauce Firkin, used at Canterbury, N.H. ca. 1880
7 ¾" x 8 ¼"

The Shakers did not manufacture their own firkins for apple sauce, but had them made by the firm of George F. Lane & Son of East Swanzey, New Hampshire. Scholar and collector of Shaker ephemera M. Stephen Miller has documented that Lane made apple sauce firkins for the Shaker communities at Mount Lebanon, New York; Shirley, Massachusetts; Enfield, New Hampshire; and Enfield, Connecticut.[72] This pail is missing its bottom hoop.

Andrews Collection, Hancock Shaker Village 1962.454.0002ab

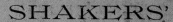

SHAKERS'

TRADE MARK.

MT. LEBANON, N. Y.

The above Trade-Mark will be attached to every genuine Shaker Chair, and none others are of our make, notwithstanding any claims to the contrary.

NOTICE.

All persons are hereby cautioned not to use or counterfeit our Trade-Mark.

ILLUSTRATED CATALOGUE

AND

PRICE LIST

OF

Shakers' Chairs.

MANUFACTURED BY THE

SOCIETY OF SHAKERS.

R. M. WAGAN & CO.,

MOUNT LEBANON, N. Y.

Shaker Chair Catalog and Printing Block, Mount Lebanon, N.Y. ca. 1880
1 ⅝" x 2 ¾" x ¾" (printing block)

The Shakers are more famous for their chairs than for any of the other products manufactured by the United Society over their long history. This chair catalog lists for sale the large variety of chairs produced by the South Family around 1880. Chairs were available in six sizes (0, 1, 3, 4, 6, 7), with or without rockers, arms, or pommels (a cushion rail could be substituted). Fully upholstered chairs could be custom ordered, but most were seated in cotton tape. The backs could either have wooden slats or woven cotton tape. The printing block was used to illustrate two upholstered chairs and stools in this catalog. The detail of the manuscript account book shows the Shakers' sales of chairs to the noted Chicago department store Marshall Field & Co.

Andrews Collection, Hancock Shaker Village 2473 (catalog), 1962.646 (printing block), 390 (manuscript)

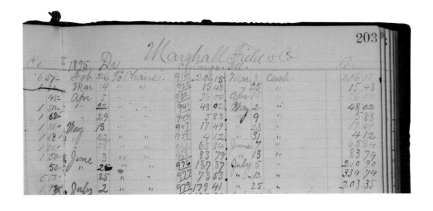

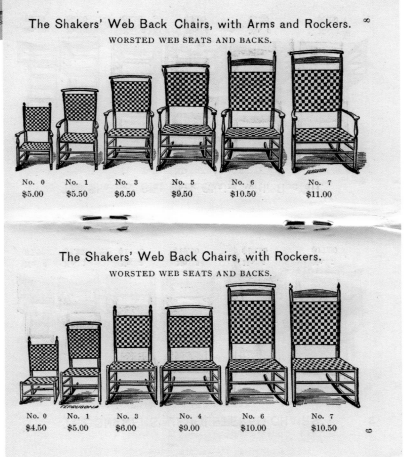

The Shakers' Web Back Chairs, with Arms and Rockers.
WORSTED WEB SEATS AND BACKS.

No. 0	No. 1	No. 3	No. 5	No. 6	No. 7
$5.00	$5.50	$6.50	$9.50	$10.50	$11.00

The Shakers' Web Back Chairs, with Rockers.
WORSTED WEB SEATS AND BACKS.

No. 0	No. 1	No. 3	No. 4	No. 6	No. 7
$4.50	$5.00	$6.00	$9.00	$10.00	$10.50

The Tree of Life
Hannah Cohoon, Hancock, Mass. 1854
Ink and watercolor; 18 ¹/₈" x 23 ⁵/₁₆"

The gift drawings collected by the Andrewses are among the greatest treasures of American folk art. These drawings are discussed extensively on pages 24-27 and 77-79. Sister Hannah Cohoon's "The Tree of Life" is the most widely known Shaker gift drawing, although the text, presumably of great importance to Sister Hannah, is rarely reproduced.[73] Written in ink below the tree, the text reads:

City of Peace Monday July, 3ʳᵈ 1854. I received a draft of a beautiful Tree pencil'd on a large sheet of white paper bearing ripe fruit. I saw it plainly; it looked very singular to me. I have since learned that this tree grows in the Spirit Land. Afterwards the spirit show'd me plainly the branches, leaves and fruit, painted or drawn upon paper. The leaves were check'd or cross'd and the same colours you see here. I entreated Mother Ann to tell me the name of this tree; which she did Oct. 1ˢᵗ 4ᵗʰ hour P.M. by moving the hand of a medium to write twice over Your Tree is The Tree of Life. Seen and painted by, Hannah Cohoon. Age 66.

Andrews Collection, Hancock Shaker Village 1963.117

The Tree of Light or Blazing Tree
Hannah Cohoon, Hancock, Mass. 1845
Ink and watercolor; 18 1/8" x 22 9/32"

From an 1816 account of early Shakers, we have the story of a vision given to Father James Whittaker while they were still in England:

When we were in England, some of us had to go twenty miles to meeting; and we travelled anights on account of persecution. One saturday night, while on our journey, we sat down by the side of the road, to eat some victuals. While I was sitting there I saw a vision of America, and I saw a large tree, and every leaf thereof shone with such brightness as made it appear like a burning torch, representing the Church of Christ, which will yet be established in this land. After my company had refreshed themselves, they travelled on, and led me a considerable distance before my vision ceased.[74]

Sister Hannah Cohoon executed this vision in 1845. Her inscription reads:

The Tree of Light or Blazing Tree. Oct 9th 1845. The bright silver color'd blaze streaming from the edges of each green leaf, resembles so many **bright** torches. N.B. I saw the whole Tree as the Angel held it before me as distinctly as I ever saw a natural tree. I felt very cautious when I took hold of it lest the blaze should touch my hand. Seen and received by Hannah Cohoon in the City of Peace Sabbath Oct 9th 10th hour A.M. 1845. drawn and painted by the same hand.

Andrews Collection, Hancock Shaker Village 1963.129

A Bower of Mulberry Trees
Hannah Cohoon, Hancock, Mass. 1854
Ink and watercolor; 18 ⅛" x 23 ¹/₁₆"

*Shaker apostate David Rich Lamson lived at Hancock, Massachusetts during the spiritually turbulent years of the 1840s. He published a memoir of those years entitled **Two Years' Experience Among the Shakers**. In describing the spring Passover celebration held by the Shakers on Mount Sinai (their holy mountain located just north of the Church Family) he described a spiritual feast like the one depicted by Sister Hannah in this drawing:*

Two rows of benches are arranged for seats, a few feet apart, upon which the brethren, and sisters, seat themselves, facing inward, and imagine a table before them. The seats are literal, but the table, and furniture, are all imaginary, or spiritual.

Those persons who have been anointed to be prophets, and prophetesses, (this anointing has already been described) are sent forth to gather food for the table. So they go out a little distance from the table, the anointed brethren in one direction, and the anointed sisters in another. The brethren shake the trees, and gather the fruit, in baskets, and bring it in upon their shoulders. The trees, and the fruit, and the baskets, are all imaginary ; but all the motions are made as if every thing were literal. You may see them stand pulling, and shaking, as though they had hold of a small tree, shaking off the fruit; and now stooping to gather up the fruit, and placing it in the basket, and then tugging at the basket to place it upon the shoulder, and staggering off with it towards the tables, and then distributing it on the tables. Thus they gather apples, pears, lemons, oranges, mellons, &c. All in the month of May, and in this northern climate. But all is spiritual. The sisters also, in their department, prepare and bring on various dishes. Turkey, chicken, pudding, pies, green corn, and beans, &c. &c. And they lean over to place the various dishes upon the table. And now see them eat. They seem to use knives and forks, chew and swallow, pass the food from one to the other. And the inspired ones pretended that they could positively see, and taste the different articles of fruit, and food, as really as if they were literal food. They had wine also; and some mimicked the drunken man. There was not the best of order about this feast, notwithstanding, it was directed by inspiration. And the anointed ones waited upon the table.[75]

Andrews Collection, Hancock Shaker Village 1963.118

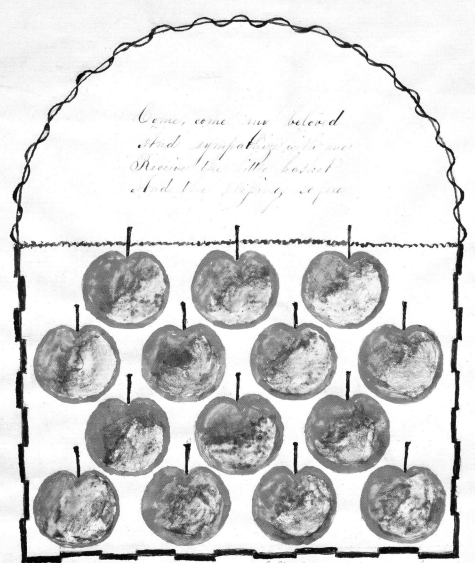

A little Basket full of Beautiful Apples
Hannah Cohoon, Hancock, Mass. 1856
Ink and watercolor; 10 ¹/₈" x 8 ³/₁₆"

The fourth of four extant drawings attributed to Hannah Cohoon, the basket of apples was executed when she was sixty-eight years old. Like her other drawings, it came to her as a full-blown vision and combines references to the Bible, in this case, to The Song of Solomon, and to past and present Shakers. Sister Hannah was careful to draw each upright apple stem, even as she had detailed the grass in the Bower of Mulberry Trees or the flames on the leaves of the Blazing Tree.

**Andrews Collection,
Hancock Shaker Village 1963.111**

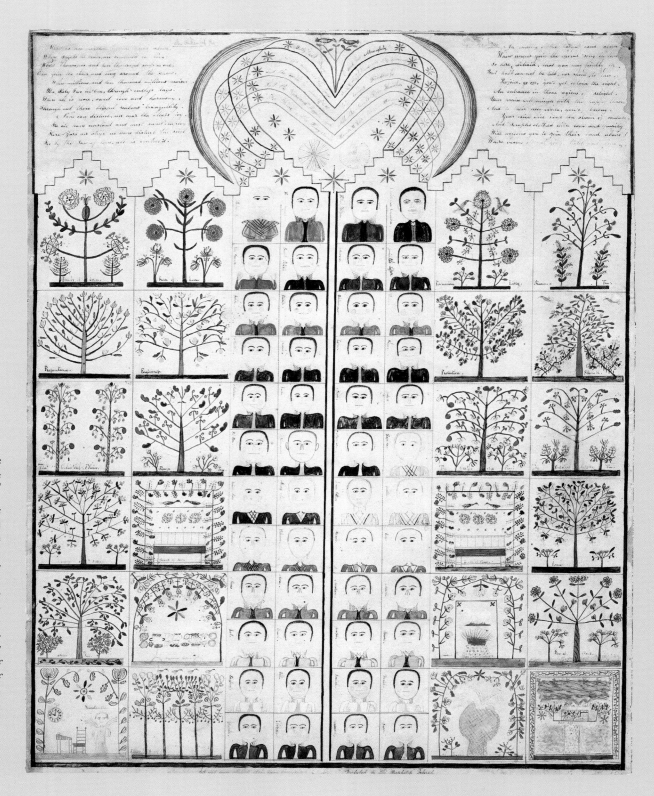

An Emblem of the Heavenly Sphere
Polly Collins, Hancock, Mass. 1854
Ink and watercolor; 23 ³/₄" x 18 ⁵/₈"

Like Hannah Cohoon, Polly Collins lived in the Hancock community. In this drawing, biblical figures from both the Old and New Testaments, and ranging from Adam to Jude and from Eve to Mary Magdalene, join Mother Ann, the Savior [Jesus Christ], and Christopher Columbus to extol the Shaker success in America and in heaven. A song of rejoicing embellishes the hearts, star, and rainbow center image at the top of the drawing while the side panels of trees and heavenly plants display the fruits of Shaker belief. This is the first drawing the Andrewses claimed to have seen.

**Andrews Collection,
Hancock Shaker Village 1963.113**

Wreath brought by Mother's little dove
Polly Collins, Hancock, Mass. 1853
Ink and watercolor; 12 1/16" x 11 15/16"

Polly Collins was forty-five when she prepared this drawing for the Ministry at Hancock, a fact that reminds the viewer that Shaker artists were often mature women, however untutored their skills were. To read the central text which is a poem of encouragement, the drawing must be turned around and around and, indeed, twirled like a Shaker dance to garner its message.

Andrews Collection, Hancock Shaker Village 1963.107

A Tree of Love, a Tree of Life
Polly Collins, Hancock, Mass. 1857
Ink and watercolor; 9 7/16" x 9 3/16"

This gift drawing to fellow Hancock believer, Sister Nancy Oaks, may contain a sly pun since the fruits of this tree are apparently three large acorns.

Andrews Collection, Hancock Shaker Village 1963.110

The Gospel Union, fruit bearing Tree
Polly Collins, Hancock, Mass. 1855
Ink and watercolor; 23 ⁵/₁₆" x 18 ¹/₁₈"

*Like other Christian sects, the Shakers
claimed they would be known by their
fruits, whether they meant their believers,
their fervency, or the righteousness of
their beliefs. Like Hannah Cohoon's
Bower of Mulberry Trees, this drawing
attests to an abundant feast to which
sincere believers are invited. It is possible
that Polly Collins and Hannah Cohoon
collaborated on some of the images in
their drawings.*

**Andrews Collection,
Hancock Shaker Village 1963.112**

A Type of Mother Hannah's Pocket Handkerchief
Polly Jane Reed, Mount Lebanon, N.Y. 1851
Ink and watercolor; 14 1/8" x 17 1/16"

Shaker Brother Calvin Green records a remarkable story of Polly Jane Reed's decision, approved by her parents, to join the Shakers when she was only seven years old. She was a faithful believer until her death over fifty years later in 1881 when she was a member of the Parent Ministry. Sally Promey has written extensively on this drawing, but even a casual viewer can see in this image that the exuberance and abundance of the Shaker vision begins with the central commitment to celibacy, illustrated by the white "Lamb of Innocence."[76]

Andrews Collection, Hancock Shaker Village 1963.126

[heart shaped cutout for] Sarah Ann Standish
Polly Jane Reed, Mount Lebanon, N.Y. 1844
Ink; 4" x 4 1/16"

Twenty-two extant heart cutouts are attributed to Sister Polly Jane Reed. There were likely many more made that were distributed to members of the Church Family at Mount Lebanon in June of 1844. Here Sarah Ann Standish is identified as a "fair virgin in Israel" and offered "a seal of sweet love, From thy Holy Father" and the chance to "dwell with thy Mother <u>in Heaven</u>."

Andrews Collection, Hancock Shaker Village 1963.123

[heart shaped cutout for] Rufus Bishop
Polly Jane Reed, Mount Lebanon, N.Y. 1844
Ink; 3 15/16" x 4"

Rufus Bishop was a long-time member of the Parent Ministry, and this heart cutout recognizes him, in the words of the Heavenly Father, as "A man of wisdom and child of God, upon whom I have place [sic] my Anointing oil, and into whose hands I have given the keys of my Kingdom."

Andrews Collection, Hancock Shaker Village 1963.121

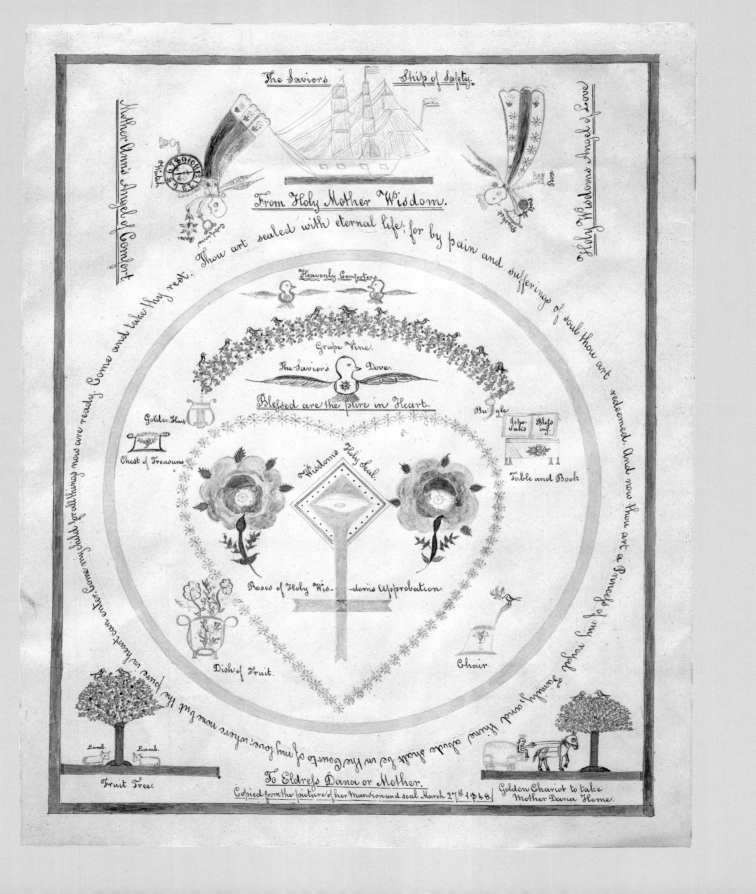

Family Sand Mar

Golden Chariot to take
Mother Dana Home.

$48.

From Holy Mother Wisdom . . . To Eldress Dana or Mother.
Miranda Barber, Mount Lebanon, N.Y. 1848
Ink and watercolor; 9 ¾" x 7 ¾"

When Miranda Barber composed this gift drawing for Eldress Dana Goodrich, she encapsulated a number of remarkable elements germane to Shaker theology and religious practice. In 1848, the Shakers were emerging from an intense time of spirit manifestations, a time when believers sought to revive their spiritual roots, to instruct a new generation distant from the first members, and to explore new paths of ritual and expression. In a society dedicated to simplicity and opposed to worldly art, the artists of the Era of Manifestations created images of almost lavish dimensions and did so, as this example shows, under the guise of heavenly instruction or as means of spiritual recognition to encourage continued faithfulness.

The richness of this document with hearts, flowers, and angels (albeit bald angels) is also orchestrated with borders and a balanced order. It could serve as a passport for the aged and ailing Cassadana Goodrich on her way to heaven for she is offered comfort, love, safety, fruit, a chair, and a golden chariot to take her home. The drawing is dated 27 March 1848, and Eldress Dana would pass away in June at the age of seventy-nine.

That the document comes from and bears the seal of Holy Mother Wisdom takes the viewer into the depths of Shaker theology where the Heavenly Father was joined by the female figure of Wisdom, a union Shakers referred to as the Everlasting Two. Miranda Barber was an established medium, or instrument, for visits by Holy Mother Wisdom during the height of the visionary era. Sister Miranda also employed the central image of a cross with the all-seeing eye of god in the golden diamond, surrounded by roses of approbation, in several other gift drawings. She consistently identified this complex image as the Seal of Holy Mother Wisdom to be sought after and awarded to worthy believers.

It is surprising that so few gift drawings employ images of a cross since Shakers always viewed Mother Ann Lee as a Christ-like figure parallel with Jesus of Nazareth. While theological interpretations of this association and function varied widely over time, Mother Ann brought the teachings of Jesus on celibacy into immediate practice and guided the Shakers into the millennial fulfillment of his first teachings.

Eldress Dana could travel safely to her Mansion in heaven, carrying a certificate of Shaker love and sealed already by Holy Mother Wisdom, by way of the visionary hand of Sister Miranda Barber.

Andrews Collection, Hancock Shaker Village 1963.108

Sampler, Mount Lebanon, N.Y. 1865
7" x 7 ½"

Faith Andrews's recounting of the acquisition of this sampler speaks for itself:

We had the most interesting word that we found Sadie developed for us in our semi-weekly trips over there. We found that out in one of the halls in the corner there was either a basket or maybe a big box without a cover. It could be anything and it was filled with odds and ends. Well of course odds and ends attracted us very much. So one time as we came by it we saw sticking out of the top a little china plate, a very beautiful majolica kind of a flower. And so we said to Sadie "What are the things in here? Every time we come we see a box like this filled with odds and ends." "Why," she said "that's trumpery." So she said "You may look through it." She said "I gather them up on my trips through the halls and rooms and I throw then away." But from then on she never threw another box away without we had a chance to go through it. And from then on we never failed to find something very great. We found the little cross-stitched sampler of Correnah Bishop's in there. The most fascinating thing. That was what Sadie considered trumpery.[77]

Collection of Dr. John R. Ribic and Dr. Carla Kingsley

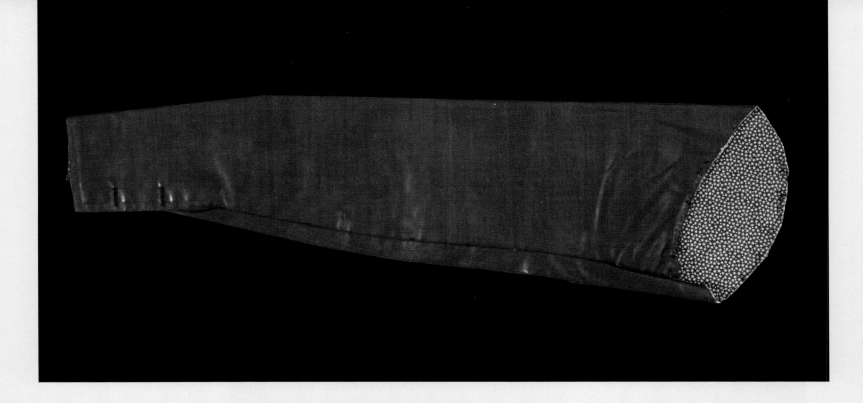

Dress Sleeve, Community Unknown, n.d.
24" x 7"
"Piece of Mother Ann's Dress," Enfield, Conn. n.d.
5" x 2"

The Andrewses were frequent visitors at the South Family of Watervliet, New York where they became great friends with Eldress Anna Case. In time, Eldress Anna bestowed on them a most remarkable gift. "And when Eldress Anna Case. . . gave us one of her choicest possessions, a piece of Mother Ann's dress, she gave us her confidence, her affection, an unfading memory." [78] *This precious fragment of cloth woven from linen and wool (or linsey-woolsey) was presented to the Andrewses in the paper envelope shown. A note was attached reading:*

> This little piece of cloth is a choice relic, a piece of our dear Mother Ann Lee's dress. Many of our older people testified to the same: indeed it has diminished considerably as our good Eldress Harriet Storer has given a mite to those who could not be satisfied any other way— we think it now small enough to remain in our home as a precious little memento of our dear Mother Ann Lee. Shaker Station Conn.

The butternut colored wool dress sleeve illustrated at top is also supposed to have come from a dress owned by Mother Ann. However, it appears to be more typical of a Shaker sister's dress of the mid-19th century.

Andrews Collection, Hancock Shaker Village
1963.260.0001 (top), 1980.074.0001 (bottom)

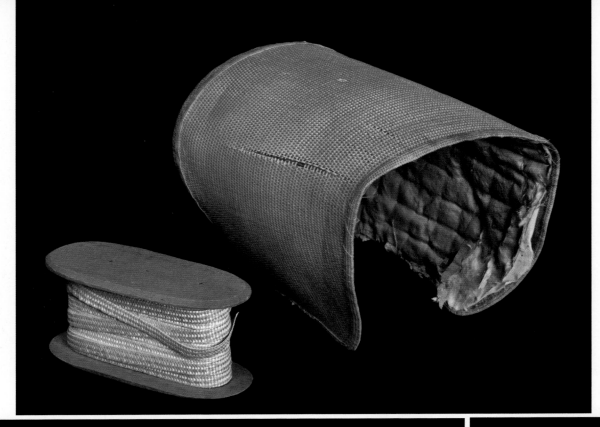

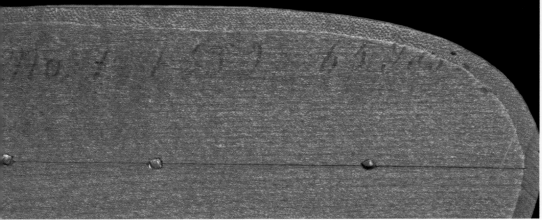

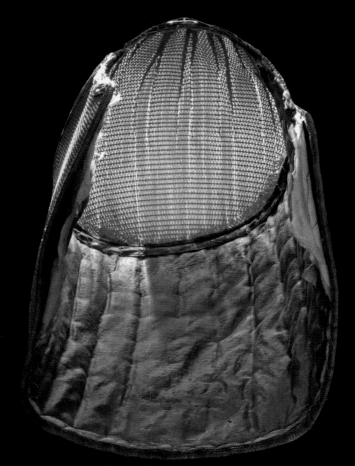

Straw Tape, Unknown Community, 1856   3 ³/₁₆" x 7" x 2 ³/₄"
Bonnet, Unknown Community, ca. 1840   8" x 7" x 12"

Shaker Sisters wore lighter bonnets woven from palm or straw in the summer months. This example is palm, and has three layers of lining: fine cotton cloth, wool batting, and an iridescent green silk. The wooden spool marked "No. 1 1852 65 yds" is wound with straw tape that was applied to the edges of bonnets.

Andrews Collection, Hancock Shaker Village 1962.322 (tape) and 1963.297 (bonnet)

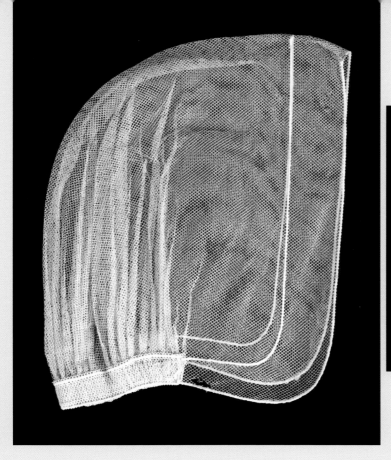

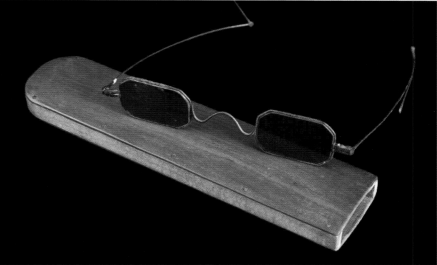

Cap, Unknown Community, ca. 1840 9 ¾" x 7 ½"
Glasses and Case, Unknown Community, mid 19th century 1" x 4 ½" x 4 ½" (case)
Winter Bonnet, Unknown Community, ca. 1860 13" x 6" x 7"

This type of white net cap was worn by Shaker Sisters beneath their
bonnets in all seasons. Sisters wore their hair pulled tightly back
beneath the cap, which has a pleated back to insure a snug fit. This
pair of glasses was collected from the Shakers, but is of the same
style as those worn in the outside world at the time. However, the
neatly constructed case, made in three sections of bent hardwoods
and finished with copper tacks, is distinctly Shaker in form. The
bonnet is of the type worn in the winter. The exterior is constructed
of a blue/grey silk, including the cape and ribbon ties. The inside
is lined with wool batting for warmth.

Andrews Collection, Hancock Shaker Village
1963.217 (cap), 1963.205 (bonnet),
1962.086.0001 (glasses and case)

Dress, Unknown Community, ca. 1860-1880
55" long

This brown cotton dress is of the type worn by Shaker sisters in the summer. The heavily pleated skirt and lower waistline indicates that it dates from later in the nineteenth century. The bodice is lined in brown cloth, and a pocket, lined in pink and green check cloth, is sewn inside the left side of the skirt.

Andrews Collection, Hancock Shaker Village
1963.219

Dress, Unknown Community, ca. 1860-1880
49 ⅞" long

Another example of a brown cotton dress for summer use. This dress has a dark brown tape binding at the wrist and neck, and a black tape binding at the hem. A pocket hidden inside the right side of the skirt is lined with a lighter brown cotton.

Andrews Collection, Hancock Shaker Village 1963.215

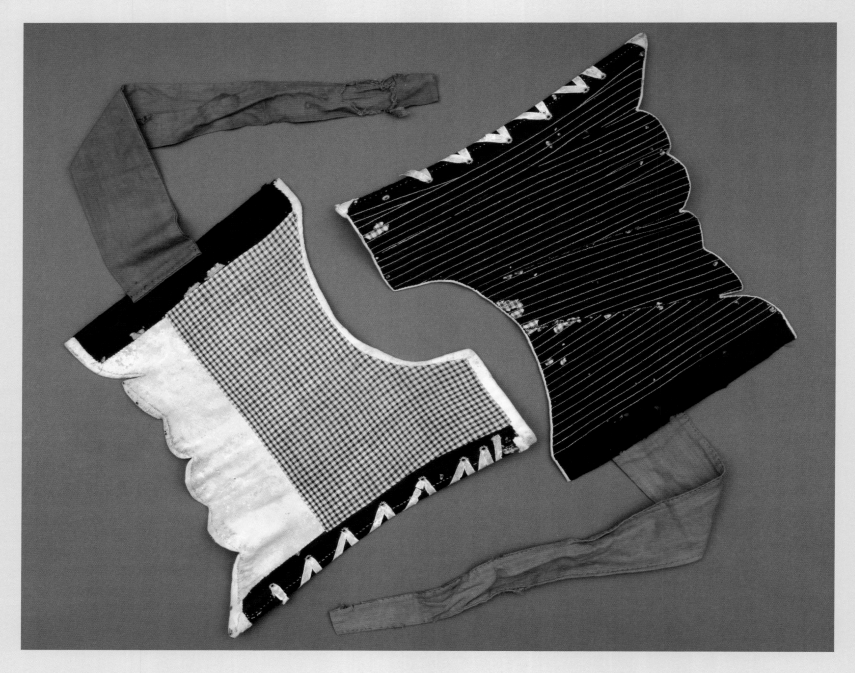

Corset, Unknown Community, ca. 1840
12" x 11 ¾"

This rare example of a Shaker corset is constructed of indigo and white-striped wool on the front, and lined with checked linen. The bottom third of the inside, as well as the top and bottom edges, are lined with white suede. There are bone stays between the layers. The corset was tied in the rear with the two brown ribbons. The front was laced tight through the eyelets with a string (now missing). The scalloped edge of the bottom accommodated the hips of the wearer. The entire garment is hand sewn, helping us to date it earlier than the 1850s, when many Shaker communities acquired sewing machines.

Andrews Collection, Hancock Shaker Village 1963.266

Pockets, Unknown Community,
ca. 1820
13 ½" x 12",
17 ½" x 14"

Shaker Sisters, like women in the outside world, often wore pockets to hold small implements necessary in their household work. The pocket at left is constructed of a sheet of linen woven in brown and white pin stripes. It has been folded in half and stitched at one side and the bottom. A linen tape, for tying it to the skirt, is attached at the upper right edge. "M" is cross-stitched on the front and the entire pocket is hand stitched. The pocket at right is also linen. The front is constructed of double-warped cloth of indigo, light brown, and natural and white linen. The whole pocket is edged in blue and white striped linen. "HM" is cross-stitched in the front and the entire pocket is handstitched.

**Andrews Collection,
Hancock Shaker Village
1963.277.0008,
1963.277.0010**

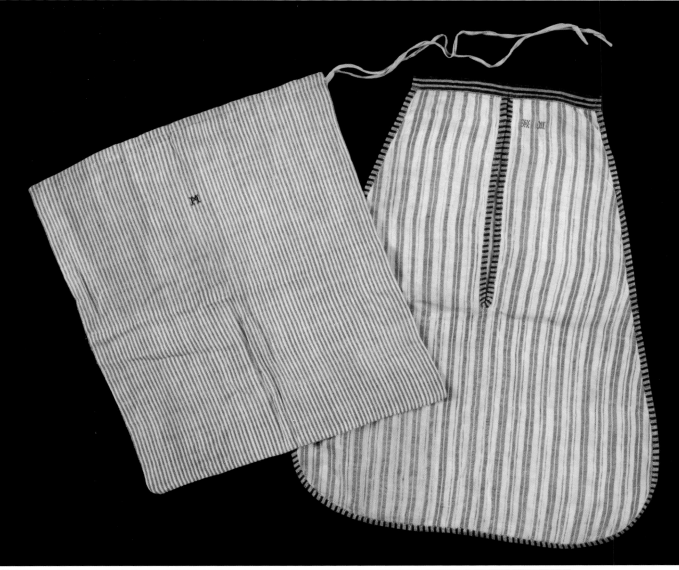

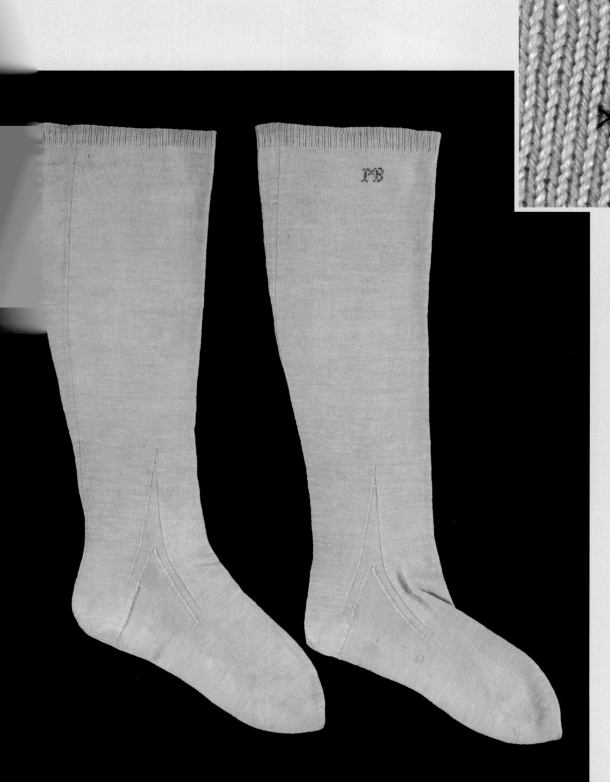

Stockings, Unknown Community, ca. 1820
23 ½" x 8"

These stockings are knit from linen or cotton with an "MB" cross-stitched at the top. The tops are reinforced with a 5/8" ribbing and a gusset provides flexibility at the ankle.

Andrews Collection, Hancock Shaker Village 1963.306ab

Shoe, Unknown Community, ca. 1840
9 ½" x 3" x 3 ¼"

Journalist Benson John Lossing described the shoes worn by Shaker Sisters in his 1857 article for **Harper's**: *"Their shoes, sharp-toed and high-heeled, according to the fashion of the day when the Society was formed, were made of prunella, of a brilliant ultramarine blue." This blue silk shoe has eyelets for laces, but this is the only accommodation to nineteenth century style, as it could have otherwise been made in the eighteenth century. The heel is pegged, and the leather sole is hand sewn to the body.*

Andrews Collection, Hancock Shaker Village 1963.304

Gloves, Unknown Community, ca. 1840
9 " x 5", 4 ½" x 5 ½"

These wool gloves were hand-knit. The pair at top, marked "DR," may have belonged to Deborah Robinson at Hancock, Massachusetts. They are knit from madder red and indigo dyed wool. The pair of half-mittens at bottom are butternut dyed brown wool and have "HW" cross-stitched above the wrist in blue thread.

Andrews Collection, Hancock Shaker Village
1963.529.0007ab (top), 1963.315ab (bottom)

Sister's Costume, Unknown Community, mid-19th century

The Andrewses directed the dressing of a mannequin in a full Shaker Sister's costume for installation in The American Museum in Britain. The garments used were a brown cotton dress, white linen collar, blue silk collar band, white linen chemise, and one blue silk shoe. The dress is made of "changeable" (as the Shakers called it) cotton cloth woven from red and blue threads.

Reproduced courtesy of The American Museum in Britain (Bath, UK), 1959.56.2a-e,g,h

Coat, Unknown Community, ca. 1840
38" long

This dark blue wool Brother's coat is marked "AB" on the inside. An orange and blue wool tape has been used to line the neck.

**Andrews Collection,
Hancock Shaker Village 1963.201**

Coat, Unknown Community, ca. 1850
39" long

This buff colored wool coat is marked "EJ 51" in blue thread cross-stitched inside the back. The six buttons on the front, and two in the back, are covered in brown silk. A pocket inside the left breast has a tan silk and cotton lining, and the two side pockets lined in brown cotton. A paper label affixed to this coat reads "Earl Jefferson. Died 87 years old."

Andrews Collection, Hancock Shaker Village 1963.223

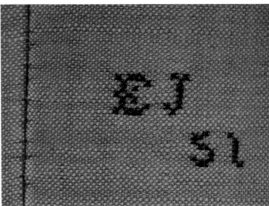

Vest, Unknown Community, ca. 1840
21" x 16"

This polished cotton vest is of the type worn by Shaker brethren to Sunday meeting. The five buttons on the front are turned from horn. There are two pockets on the front. What separates this vest from those typically worn by men in the outside world at that time is that the back is fully finished. This makes sense given that both sides of the vest were visible to public attendees at Shaker worship services. The inside is lined in blue cotton.

Andrews Collection, Hancock Shaker Village 1963.224

Pants, Unknown Community, ca. 1850
37" long

These wool pants have been treated with a process where zinc chloride was steamed into the fabric to make them wrinkle and water resistant. The buttons are made of gutta percha, a tropical tree resin used for this purpose beginning in the 1850s. The pants have been let out in the back (note the laces), perhaps Brother "JB" "Shakered his plate" once too often.

Andrews Collection, Hancock Shaker Village 1963.226

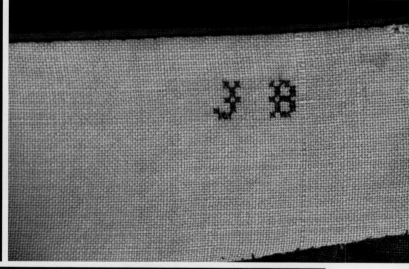

Collars, Unknown
Communities, 19th century
All measure 14 ½" x 2"

*These colorful collars belie the
notion that Shaker brethren
were dour in their dress. The
materials vary from one to the
next, but the first six examples
are primarily silk on the outside
with a cotton lining. The bottom
two are made of white linen.*

**Andrews Collection,
Hancock Shaker Village
1963.272.0006,7,1,9,3,10,15,16**

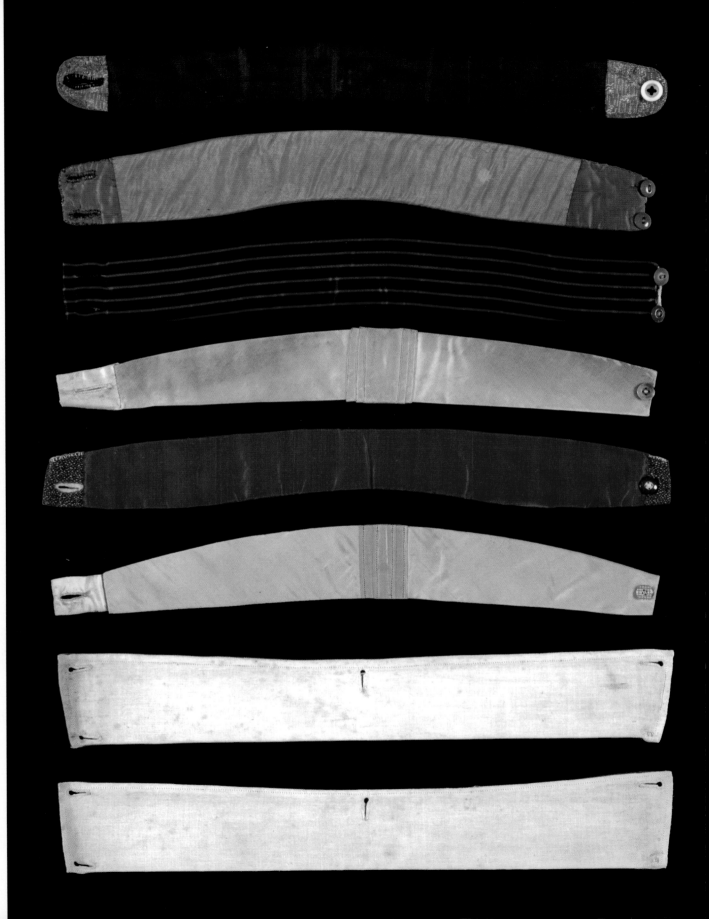

Brother's Costume, Unknown Community,
mid-19th century

*The Andrewses directed the dressing of a
mannequin in a full Shaker Brother's costume
for installation in The American Museum in
Britain. The garments used were brown cotton
trousers, frock coat and neckerchief, white linen
shirt and collar, blue cotton waistcoat, grey felt
hat, and a pair of black leather shoes.*

**Reproduced courtesy of The American Museum
in Britain (Bath, UK), 1959.56.a-h**

Shroud, Unknown Community,
19th century
55 ½"

*A newspaper report on the burial
of Eldress Antionette Doolittle
published in* **The Pittsfield Sun** *on
July 1, 1897 contains the following
description of the burial garment:
"a linen shroud of snowy whiteness
marvelously pleated." That shroud
was likely similar to the one depicted
here. It has linen ties at the wrists
and waist, and is coated in a zinc
chloride solution used to render it
wrinkle and water resistant. The
initial "M" is found in pencil on the
inside of the right wrist.*

**Andrews Collection,
Hancock Shaker Village 1963.264**

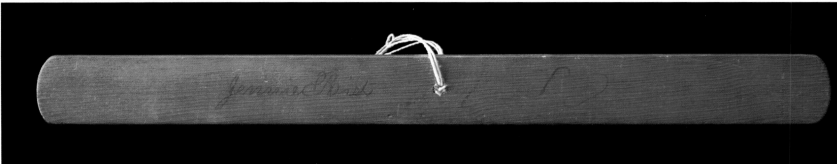

Hangers, Mount Lebanon, N.Y. ca. 1850
16 ½" x 3" (top), 18" x 18" (middle), 11 ⁹/₁₆" x 11 ¹⁵/₁₆" (bottom)

The Shakers made hangers in many different forms. The plain pine example at top is finished in a red wash and marked "Jennie Rist." The double hanger is also pine and was constructed with steel screws and copper tacks. It has been designed to hang from a peg. The example at bottom is delicately crafted from mahogany and bears the ownership label of Amy Reed.

Collection of Dr. Thomas and Jan Pavlovic (top)
Andrews Collection, Hancock Shaker Village 1962.499 (middle)
Courtesy, Winterthur Museum 1961.0350 (bottom)

270 |

Pillow Cases
probably Mount Lebanon, N.Y.
mid-19th century
37 ½" x 15 ⅜", 36" x 16"

The breadth of the Andrews collection is truly remarkable. In their concerted effort to document every aspect of Shaker culture they even acquired objects such as these hand-woven linen pillow cases. The example at left is marked "IIF 4" in tan thread, this may refer to a room in the Second Family dwelling house. The example at right is marked "CHH 8" in blue thread, likely indicating its home location in the Church Family dwelling.

**Andrews Collection,
Hancock Shaker Village
1962.372, 1962.178**

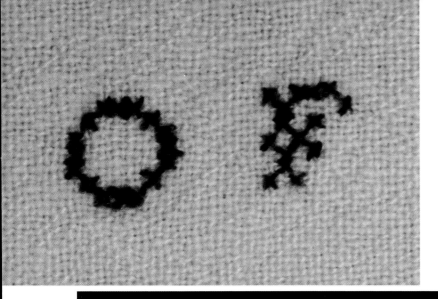

Blanket, Unknown Community, mid-19th century
94" x 76 ½"

This wool blanket is constructed of two pieces of woven cloth hand sewn together in the middle. It is marked "OF" in blue cross-stitching. This may have indicated its use in the Shaker Trustees' Office building at Mount Lebanon or Hancock.

Andrews Collection, Hancock Shaker Village 1962.331

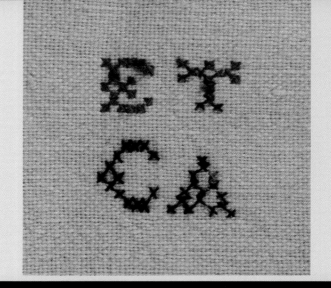

Towel, Unknown Community, mid-19th century
45 ¼" x 32 ⅝"

*This plainwoven cotton towel is marked "ET" and "CA" The two sides are selvedged,
forming a finished edge by virtue of the weft threads doubling back on themselves.*

Andrews Collection, Hancock Shaker Village 1963.280

Kerchief, Kentucky or Ohio Shaker community, mid-19th century
45 ¼" x 32 ⅝"

Silk was cultivated by the Shaker communities in Ohio, Kentucky, and briefly at Enfield, Connecticut, beginning in the early nineteenth century. This kerchief is made of a "changeable" silk. The warp is eight threads of a dark brown stripe. The weft is four threads of a gold stripe. The resulting effect is a high bronze/gold sheen which changes in the light. A tan satin ribbon is affixed for hanging.

Andrews Collection, Hancock Shaker Village 1963.245

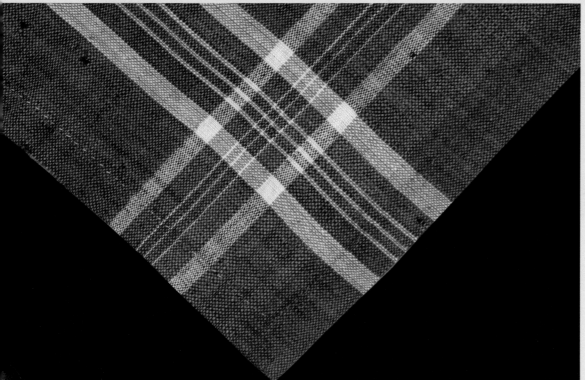

Kerchief, Unknown Community, mid-19th century
28 ½" x 50"

*This plainwoven triangular wool kerchief is another
example of a "changeable" Shaker textile. The blue warp
and red weft make the garment appear orange. The
border is executed in white stripes and it is marked
"BH" in blue thread. The detail photo of the damaged
area allows one to see the fineness of the weave.*

Andrews Collection, Hancock Shaker Village 1964.097

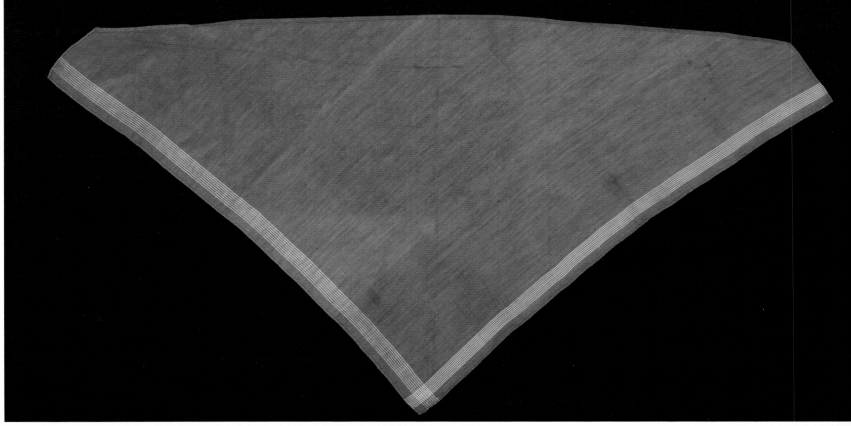

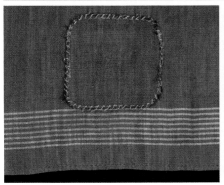

Kerchief, Unknown Community,
mid-19th century
47 ¼" x 25 ⅛"

*Another triangular kerchief, this time in blue
and red silk. The damaged area has been
patched with very similar cloth. This
garment would have been worn folded
around a Shaker Sister's shoulders and
pinned across the breast.*

**Andrews Collection, Hancock Shaker Village
1964.093**

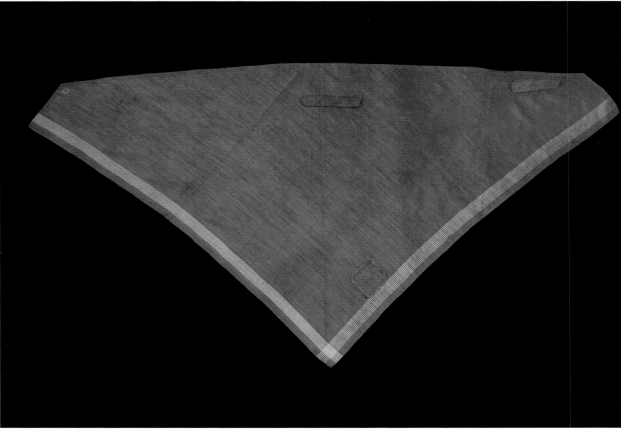

Kerchief, Kentucky or Ohio Shaker community,
mid-19th century
35" x 35"

*Among the most stunning Shaker textiles are the silk
kerchiefs produced by the western Societies. They were
worn within Shaker communities and also sold to the
outside world. This example has a white weft and rose
warp, giving it a "changeable" iridescence in light. The
borders are executed in black thread that appears
blue due to the density of the color around it.*

Andrews Collection, Hancock Shaker Village 1964.091

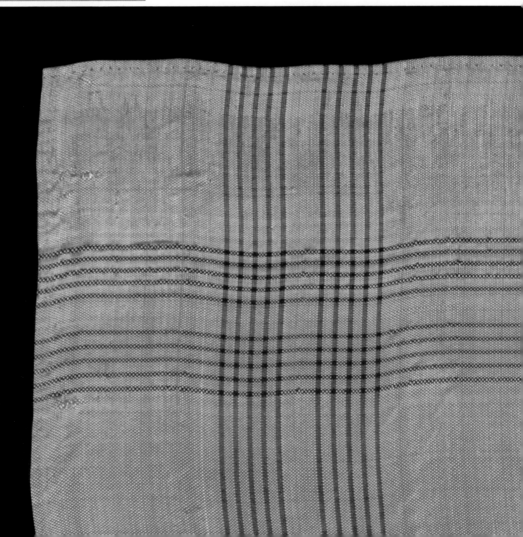

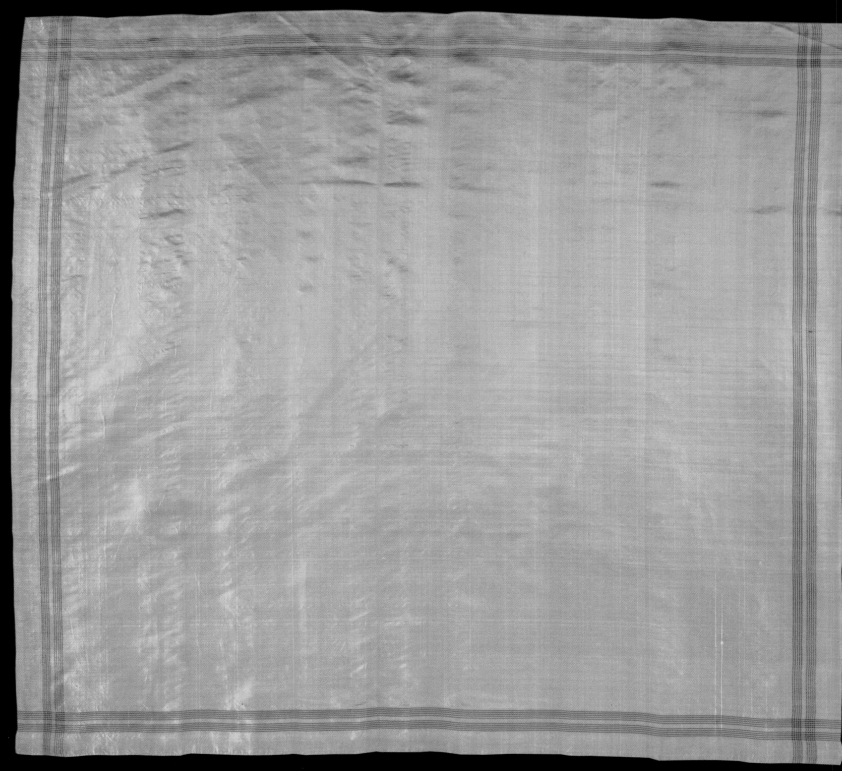

Kerchief, Unknown Community,
mid-19th century
35 ½" x 35 ½"

*This white cotton neckerchief is so finely
woven that when lofted into the air it
slowly settles to the ground, rather than
falling quickly. The border stripes on
this all-white garment are achieved by
grouping threads to make raised stripes.
It is marked "MB" in dark blue
cross-stitching.*

**Andrews Collection, Hancock Shaker
Village 1963.242**

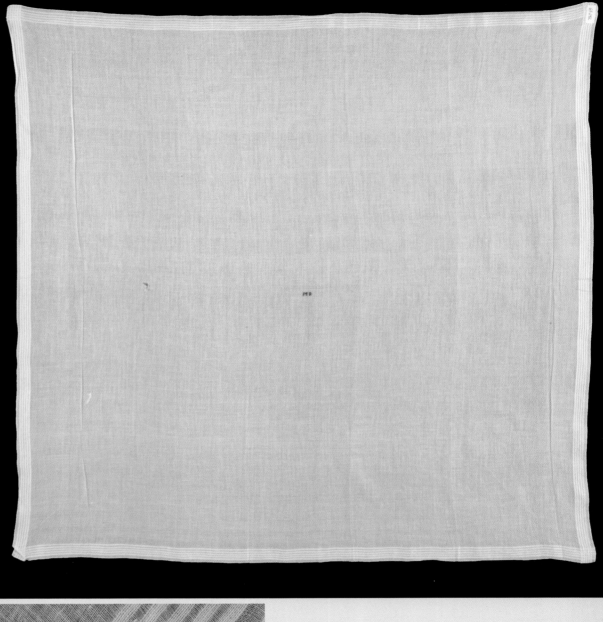

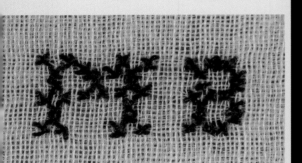

Towel, Unknown Community, mid-19th century
20 3/8" x 26"

This plainwoven white linen towel is notable for its ownership marking: "Ministry" is cross-stitched into the center of the top in blue thread. It was probably used by the Ministry at Mount Lebanon.

Andrews Collection, Hancock Shaker Village 1963.343

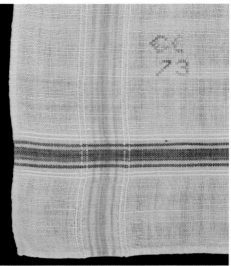

Kerchief, Unknown Community, mid-19th century
22" x 22"

*The border of this plainwoven white linen kerchief
is more complex than those typically found on
Shaker kerchiefs. It consists of two raised doubled
white threads, three blue, twelve blue, three blue,
and then two more raised doubled white. It is
marked "GC 73" in blue thread.*

**Andrews Collection, Hancock Shaker Village
1962.518.0003**

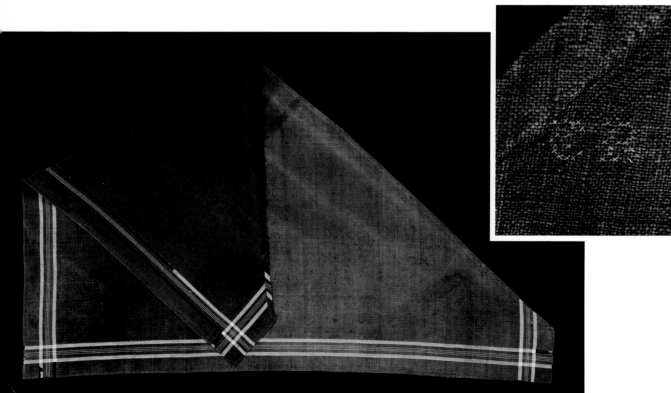

Kerchief, Unknown Community,
mid-19th century
27 ½" x 50"

*This deep blue linen kerchief was
probably dyed with indigo. It has
a white border and is marked
"ER." It has faded badly in places
due to light exposure. The fade
lines clearly show where it had
been folded and then left in the
sun for years.*

**Andrews Collection, Hancock
Shaker Village 1964.100**

Kerchiefs, Unknown Communities, mid-19th century
61" x 24 ¹/₂" (top), 37" x 38 ³/₈"(middle), 39 ³/₄" x 41 ¹/₂" (bottom)

The green and white checked kerchiefs at top and bottom are made of cotton. The example on top is marked "GA 61" and the one at bottom (shown in the detail) "AB. 50." in red thread. The silk example in the middle is made of pink and tan/gold threads that produce a dull sheen in the light. It is marked "JD" in white thread.

Andrews Collection, Hancock Shaker Village 1964.098 (top), 1962.518.0004 (middle), 1962.518.0002 (bottom)

Kerchief
Unknown Community,
mid-19th century
27 ¹/₂" x 50 ¹/₂"

A triangular kerchief made of indigo-dyed cotton woven in a white grid pattern.

Andrews Collection, Hancock Shaker Village 1962.518

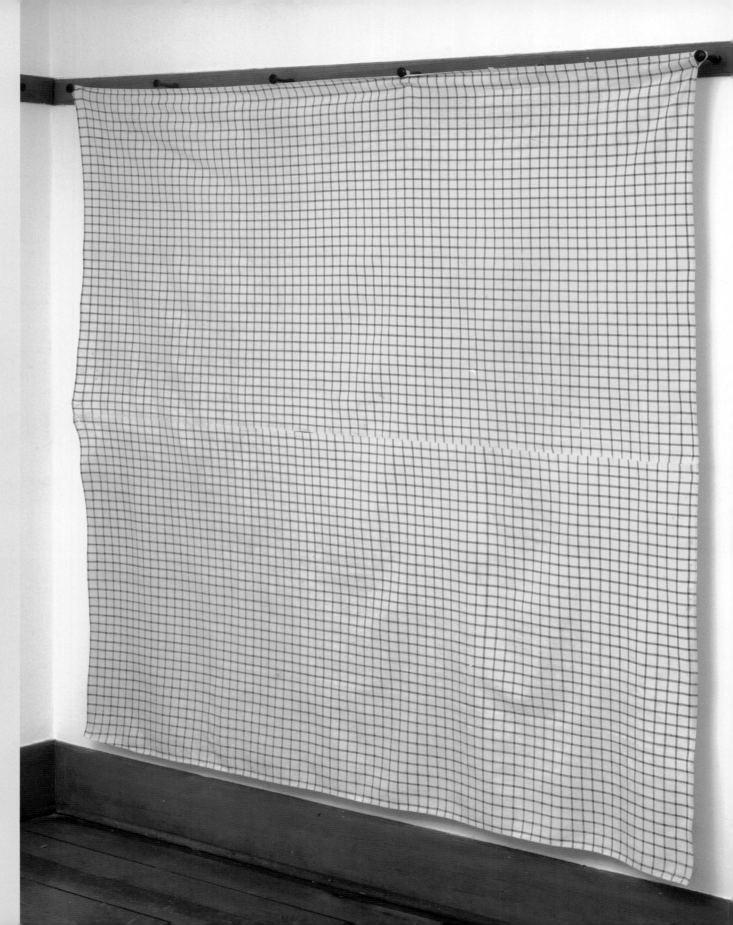

Wall Curtain
Unknown Community,
mid-19th century
72" x 69"

*Wall curtains were used in
retiring rooms in Shaker
dwelling houses to keep down
drafts and provide a small
amount of insulation for
the occupants. This cotton
example is made of two
commercially woven panels
sewn together in the middle.
At the top, twill tapes have
been affixed for hanging.*

**Andrews Collection,
Hancock Shaker Village
1962.177**

Grain Bag, Mount Lebanon, N.Y. mid-19th century
35 ½" x 22 ⅛"

*It is often overlooked that the Shakers were, and are, farmers.
This rare surviving piece is a white linen grain bag from
Mount Lebanon. It is stencilled "Mt. Lebanon 1ˢᵗ O. CHH
Farm" for the farm of the First Order of the Church Family.
"Dx" is cross-stitched in black thread above the stencil.
The bag is machine sewn.*

Andrews Collection, Hancock Shaker Village 1963.278

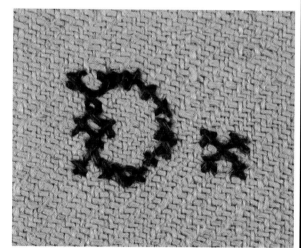

Chair Tape, Mount Lebanon, N.Y. 19th century

This assortment of chair tape is representative of the wide variety of colors used by the Shakers to seat chairs both for themselves and for sale to the outside world. The Shakers used both cotton and wool tape. They initially wove it for themselves, but began purchasing it from commercial manufacturers by the mid-nineteenth century.

Andrews Collection, Hancock Shaker Village 1979.082

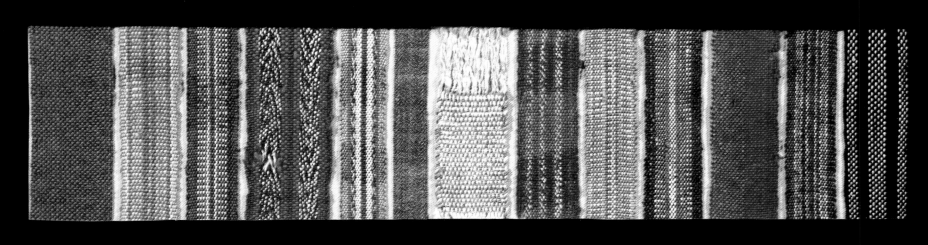

Chair Tape, Mount Lebanon, N.Y. 19th century

A framed assortment of fragments of handwoven chair tape further illustrates the variety of colors and styles made by Shaker Sisters.

Andrews Collection, Hancock Shaker Village 1979.082

Chair Cushion, Mount Lebanon, ca. 1880
20" x 14"

This hooked wool chair cushion, executed in bright purple and green, would have been stuffed and used to pad the seat of a Shaker chair. The bottom panel of the inside is constructed of assorted colors of chair tape: gray, brown, purple and tan. The outside bottom is lined with brown and white cotton. Brown cloth tapes are present and would have been used to tie it to the rear posts of the chair.

Andrews Collection, Hancock Shaker Village 1963.411

Rug, Unknown Community, mid-19th century (right)
61" x 26"

The warp of this colorful rug is cotton. The weft consists of a half-inch wide strip of yellow wool, and then many rows of plied rag strips in indigo, pink, off-white, white, and gray.

Andrews Collection, Hancock Shaker Village 1962.083

Rug, Unknown Community, late 19th century
(opposite, top)
10 ½" x 27"

This rug is formed of rows of braided wool and cotton cloth that have been sewn together in an elliptical form.

Andrews Collection, Hancock Shaker Village 1963.350

Rug, Unknown Community, mid-19th century
(opposite, bottom)
208" x 45"

This extremely long rug was used as a hall runner. The warp is indigo dyed wool cloth. The weft consists of black wool; white cotton plied with white and blue wool; white cotton plied with six strands of madder wool; and blue wool. The end is finished in a linen warp binding.

Andrews Collection, Hancock Shaker Village 1962.165

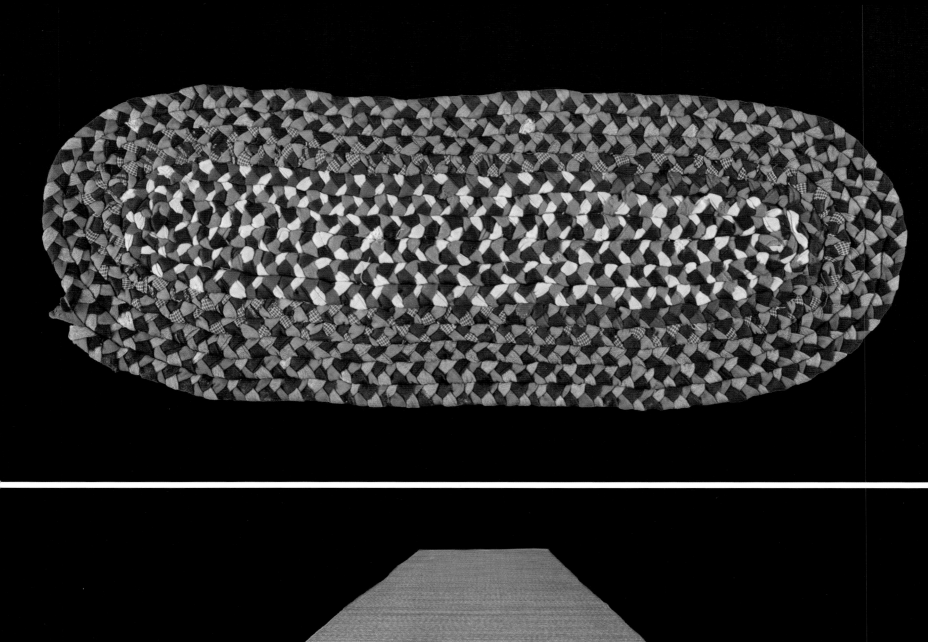

Needle Cases, Unknown Community, late 19th or early 20th century
Pin Cushions, Unknown Community, late 19th or early 20th century
Strawberry Emery, Unknown Community, late 19th or early 20th century
15" x 5", 13 ³⁄₈" x 4 ¹⁄₂" (needle cases), 6 ³⁄₈" (pin cushion diameter)

*As the numbers of Brothers declined in Shaker communities the economic
burden to support the communities fell more heavily to the Sisters.
Shaker Sisters at the northeastern communities manufactured and sold
"fancy goods" at upper class summer resorts beginning in the 1890s and
continuing into the mid-twentieth century. These velvet pin cushions and
needle cases are typical of the products made and sold. Strawberry emeries
were often affixed to the inside of sewing carriers as an accessory. They
were made by taking a small piece of satin, stitched into a cone shape, and
then setting this in a wooden form to be filled with emery powder.
This was then sewn shut and a green cloth top with loop was attached.
These diminutive items were used for sharpening needles.*

**Andrews Collection, Hancock Shaker Village 1963.277.0001, 1963.277.0002,
(needle cases), 1963.300, 1963.299 (pin cushions), 1963.299 (emery)**

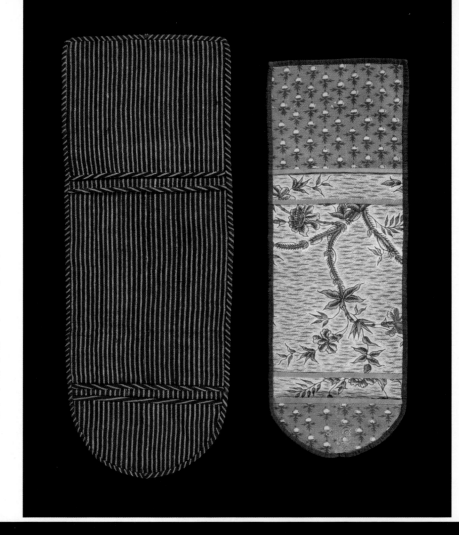

Potholders, Unknown Community
mid-20th century
6 ³/₄" (dia.), 5 ¹/₂" x 4 ¹/₂", 6 ¹/₄" x 5 ³/₈", 6" (dia.)
6 ¹/₄" (dia.), 10" x 10"

*Crocheted potholders were produced by the
Canterbury Shakers in the mid-20th century for
sale in their gift shop and as gifts for friends of
the family. Those who contend that the Andrewses
glorify only the early history and productions of
the Shakers are likely unaware of the large
collections of late nineteenth and early twentieth
century Shaker textiles assembled by the couple.*

**Andrews Collection, Hancock Shaker Village
(clockwise from upper left, center object last)
1963.265.0008, 1, 5, 7, 3, 4.**

Potholder, Unknown Community
mid-20th century
9 ⁵/₈" (dia.)

Needle Folders, Unknown Community,
mid-20th century
3 ⁵/₈" (length of mitten needle folders)
3 ¹/₄" (dia. round needle folder)

*This knitted potholder has a chain-stitched crocheted
edging. The mitten shaped needle folders are made of
layers of felt stitched together and tied with satin
ribbons. The black and orange example has a faux
leather back. The orange needle folder is composed of
a crocheted top and bottom with felt discs edged
in orange thread between.*

**Andrews Collection, Hancock Shaker Village
1963.265.0006 (potholder), 22 and 23 (mitten
needle folders), 18 (orange needle folder).**

Foot Rest, Hancock, Mass.
ca. 1820
5 ½" x 10" x 6 ½"

Foot rests were used by Shaker Sisters when doing lap-work such as knitting and sewing. This example is finished in brilliant chrome yellow and red lead paint. The legs are splayed for stability, but the half-round cutouts on the ends were consciously cut parallel to the floor. The edges of the skirt and top are molded. The bottom of this piece bears the inscription in pencil "Hancock Mass. ED Andrews" as well as a tag from the 1932 Berkshire Museum exhibition. **Shaker Furniture** *plate 7.*

**Andrews Collection,
Hancock Shaker Village 1962.071**

Foot Rest, Canterbury, N.H. 1860
11" x 15 ³/₈" x 9 ⁷/₈"

The following inscription is written in pencil on the underside of this pine foot rest: "This bench was made for Sister Annie J. Baker in 1860." The initials "A.J.B." are also on the bottom. The top is hinged and opens to reveal an interior compartment for storing personal and sewing effects.[79]

Collection of the Family of David V. and Phyllis C. Andrews

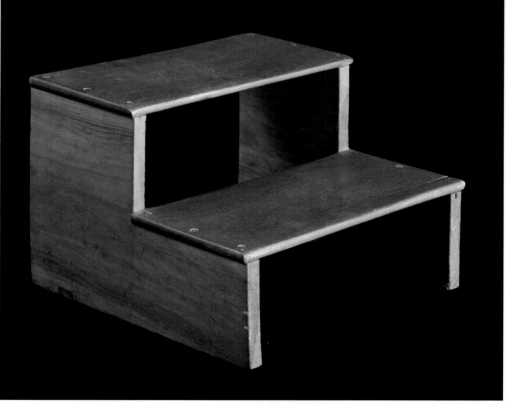

Foot Rest, Mount Lebanon, N.Y. 1836
8 3/8" x 11 5/8" x 11"

The cherry steps on this foot rest are screwed into the side walls, which have been cut from single pieces of pine. It is fitted with a dovetail brace that stretches between the side walls at the bottom. The following is inked into the underside of the top "Lx. 1836." **Shaker Furniture** *plate 27.*

Andrews Collections, Hancock Shaker Village 1962.159

Foot Rest, Mount Lebanon, N.Y. 1851
7 3/4" x 8 1/4" x 7 7/8"

This humble foot rest bears one of the most amusing inscriptions found on any piece of Shaker furniture in the form of a humorous poem. It is made from pine and white ash, and also bears the initials "ES" and the date "Dec 26 1851."

Courtesy, Winterthur Museum 1967.1687

The things of time are perishing / even I old stool have seen my / best days when boxes or any / heavy pressure falls on me I shrink / beneath the weight of my burden / and need a physician to set my bones / are you not a good one?

Gout Stool, Unknown Community, ca. 1850
13" x 19 ⅛" x 16"

This folding stool is joined by three dowelled stretchers and finished in a bright yellow paint. The cloth top has been replaced. The Andrewses referred to this item as a gout stool. It was probably acquired from Mount Lebanon and was used to comfortably elevate and support the foot of an ailing Shaker. The chamfering on the legs is similar to other high shop stools made at Mount Lebanon.

Collection of J. Richard and E. Barbara Pierce

Foot Rest, Unknown Community, ca. 1880
6 ½" x 12 ⅛" x 6 ¼"

This felt topped foot rest is an example of the Shakers' embrace of the Victorian aesthetic. The maple base is varnished and bears the inscription "C. B." in red pencil. The legs, which resemble Shaker pegs or "wheel fingers," are dowelled into the base and splay outwards. **Shaker Furniture** *plate 15.*

Andrews Collections, Hancock Shaker Village 1962.182

Step Stool, Hancock, Mass. ca. 1840
25 ¼" x 15 ⅞" x 11 ⅝"

Ted Andrews called this pine step stool "an especially good example, as it is both dove-tailed and molded." [80] *The front edges of the steps are screwed onto the frame where a molding visually unites the two components.* **Shaker Furniture** *plate 22.*

Andrews Collections, Hancock Shaker Village 1962.014

Step Stool, Hancock, Mass. ca. 1840
25 ¼" x 17 ½" x 13 ¾"

Ted Andrews remarked that this three-step stool "came from Hancock, where the finer ones seem to have been made. The bracings are mortised." [81] *These front bracings (under the treads), and the cross-braces on the back, have beaded edges. The sides cant progressively backwards, allowing more clearance for the foot. The treads have carefully rounded edges on three sides to prevent splitting. Preserved on the bottom are traces of the bright yellow paint that once covered this piece which was exhibited at the Berkshire Museum in 1932.* **Shaker Furniture** *plate 26.*

Reproduced courtesy of The American Museum in Britain (Bath, UK), 1959.71

Round Stools, Mount Lebanon, N.Y. ca. 1830
12 ½" x 9 ¾", 12 ½" x 10 ¼"

The turned legs and bottom (on the example at right) distinguish these stools from other examples. The legs are dowelled into the bottom and splay outwards to provide stability. The leather seats replace earlier ones that were largely worn away. These stools were probably used for milking. The example at left was illustrated in the January 1933 issue of The Magazine **Antiques. Shaker Furniture** *plate 7 (right).*

Andrews Collections, Hancock Shaker Village 1962.632, 1972.209

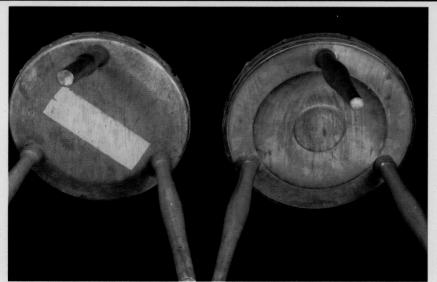

Poplar Baskets, Mount Lebanon, N.Y. second half 19th century
(clockwise from top left) 3 ½" x 4", 2" x 4 ½", 1 ½" x 3" x 1 ½", 1" x 1 ½"

Shaker Sisters at Mount Lebanon began weaving "popple" (as they called it), or poplar, baskets after about 1850. They were sold as fancy work to visitors from the outside world. Poplar wood was soaked and then cut into strips even narrower than those made from ash wood. The splints used to weave these baskets are quite fine and delicate.

Reproduced courtesy of The American Museum in Britain (Bath, UK), 1959.61

Basket Molds and Splint Cutter, Mount Lebanon, N.Y. 19th century
(top row from left) 4 ⅛" x 10 ⅛" x 4 ⅝", 3 ½" x 9 ¾" x 5 ¼", 2 ⅞" x 10" x 4", 5 ¾" x 7 ⅞" (dia.),
(bottom row from left) 2 ¾" x 2 ⅜" x 3 ⅜", 2 ¾" x 2 ⅜" x 2 ⅜", 2 ¼" x 5" x 3 ¼", 2 ¼" x 4 ¼" x 3 ⅜", 11 ¼" x 5 ³⁄₁₆" x 4 ½"

These molds are a small sampling of the huge variety used to make baskets at Mount Lebanon during the nineteenth and early twentieth centuries. The mold at top right is a cat head mold for making a handled apple basket. The trapezoidal molds would have been used to build the forms for poplar ware, a fancy good created from woven strips of poplar cloth. The molds at lower left were used to create corners. The form with applied wooden braces was used to mold the rims of small baskets. At lower right is a splint cutter used to cut the rings of a poplar tree into weaveable strands. A number of tiny blades are set into the crossbar.

Andrews Collections, Hancock Shaker Village (top row from left) 1962.496.0002, 1972.313, 1962.505.0004, 1962.496, (bottom row from left) 1962.701, 1962.701.0002, 1963.1246, 1962.505.0003, 1962.297.

Basket, Mount Lebanon, N.Y. 19th century
16 3/8" x 18" x 14 1/2"

This leather lined basket was used for carrying woodchips. The leather lining is made of three panels sewn together. It is stitched to the splint along the top edge. The handle is notched to the outside rim and has a "Ph" stamped into the top.

Andrews Collections, Hancock Shaker Village 1972.315.0008

Winnowing Basket, Unknown Community, 19th century
12" x 20" x 34"

This large basket was used to loft grain into the air, allowing the chaff, and pests, such as weevils, to be blown away— leaving only the grain. There is little, other than the Andrews provenance, that separates this Shaker winnowing basket from worldly examples.

Andrews Collections, Hancock Shaker Village 1962.561

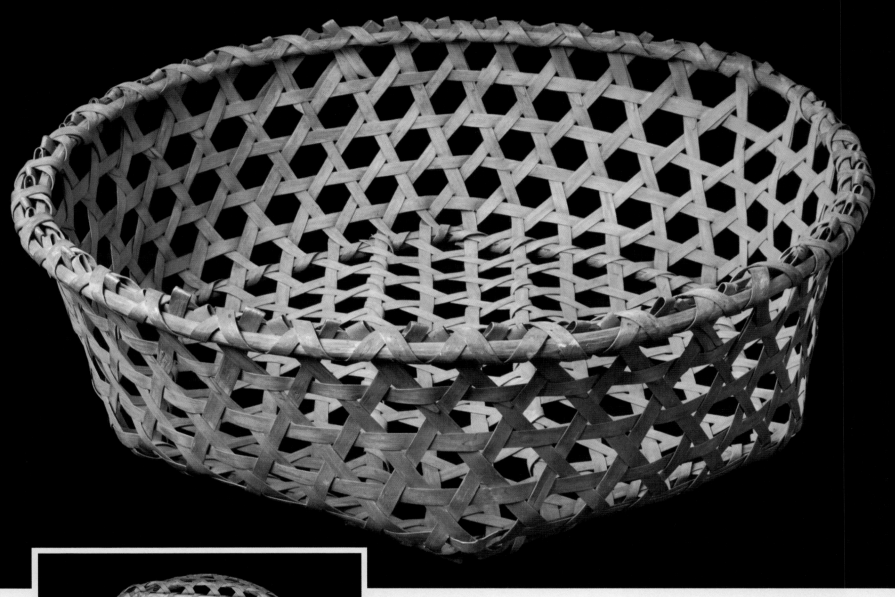

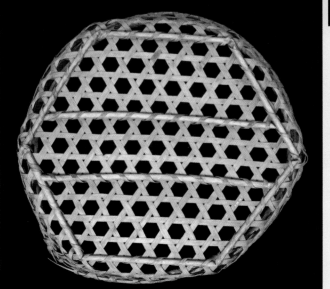

Cheese Basket, Unknown Community, 19th century
9 ¹/₂" x 28 ¹/₂"

This type of open weave basket allowed the whey to drain off of a cheese as it cured.

Andrews Collections, Hancock Shaker Village 1972.315.0003

Basket, Unknown Community, 19th century
22" x 25"

This black ash basket has a double-lashed rim. The handles are notched into the rim on the outside and taper in thickness as they are engaged by the weavers.

Andrews Collections, Hancock Shaker Village 1962.394

Baskets, Native American, 19th century
6 7/8" x 11" x 8", 7" x 13" x 9 1/2"

The Shakers learned from, and employed, Native American basket makers. Brother Isaac Newton Youngs noted the following in the Mount Lebanon Church Family's Domestic Journal in December 1837: "An indian by the name of William Henry, having worked on our mountain some at making baskets & 5 days at chopping wood, went from there down into our cabin in the interval[e]." [82] The baskets shown here are made of poplar. The example at left has diamond and circle stamped decorations and is varnished. The example at right has red, blue, and green painted weavers. These baskets were collected from the Shakers by the Andrewses. In **The Community Industries of the Shakers** *Ted Andrews wrote: "In the early days traveling groups of Indians made and sold baskets to the Shakers. Several of these have been found in the settlements, decorated in quaintly formal patterns with berry juice." [83]*

Andrews Collections, Hancock Shaker Village 1972.315.0027, 1962.427.0002

Baskets, Unknown Community, 19th century
3 ½" x 26 ½" x 21" (top), 5 ⅛" x 11 ½" x 8" (bottom)

The large black ash basket at top has a single-lashed rim and handles notched to the outside. The smaller basket at bottom is double-lashed and has a finely crafted, deeply-notched hardwood handle.

Andrews Collections, Hancock Shaker Village
1962.427.0002, 1972.315.0021

Basket Lid, Unknown Community,
19th century 1 ½"x 12 ⅝"
Lidded Basket, Unknown Community,
19th century 6" x 3"
Basket Lid, Unknown Community,
19th century 5" x 6"

*An interesting decorative effect has been
achieved by leaving the spokes wide where
they intersect on the round lid. The small
poplar basket with lid may have been made
later in the nineteenth century for sale to the
outside world as a "fancy basket." The small
twill-woven lid at bottom is similar to the
lids on the example illustrated on page 304.*

**Andrews Collections, Hancock Shaker Village
1972.315.0031 (round lid), 1962.181.0003
(lidded basket), 1965.185 (basket lid)**

Basket, Unknown Community, 19th century
14 ⅜ x 9 ½ x 9 ½

*This round basket has a square bottom. The
initials "E.L." are painted in chrome yellow on
the bottom. The rim is double lashed and the
bottom is cathead style.*

**Andrews Collections, Hancock Shaker Village
1962.427.0002**

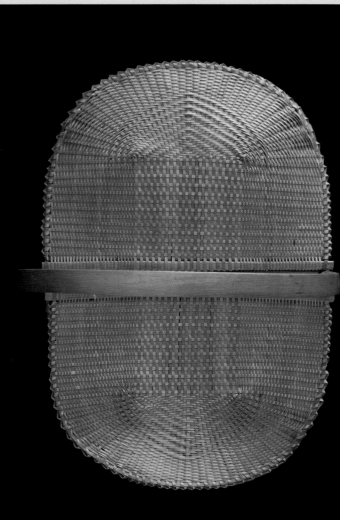

Fancy Basket, Mount Lebanon, N.Y. ca. 1860
9" x 10" x 6"

This example of a lidded fancy basket is made of unusually fine black ash splint. The lids are woven in a twill pattern and finished with a sawtooth edge. The lids are hinged to the center stretcher of the basket by copper wires. The rim is double-lashed and the handle is notched to the inside of the rim.

Andrews Collection, Hancock Shaker Village 1962.181.0002

Oval Boxes and Oval Box Molds, Mount Lebanon, N.Y. ca. 1840

14" x 11 ¼" x 7 ¾" (block mold), 4 ⅝" x 10 ½" x 7 ⅛" (box at right), ¾" x 10" x 6 ¾" (mold at right), 1 ⁷⁄₁₆" x 4 ½" x 3" (box at center),
¼" x 4 ³⁄₁₆" x 2 ¾" (small mold at center), 3" x 5 ¼" x 3 ³⁄₁₆" (box at left), ¼" x 5" x 3" (small mold at left)

*Brother Isaac Newton Youngs described the oval box industry at Mount Lebanon in his 1856 **Concise View:***

These have been manufactured almost or quite yearly, since perhaps the year 1800. This has been a very good little branch of business, tho' not so extensive as some. A great improvement has been made in this line. Formerly the rims were sawed out in a common saw mill, which did the work slowly and imperfectly. The heading & rims were planed by hand. But about the year 1830 the sawing was done by a buz saw, and the heading planed by water. And shortly after a planning machine was erected, (say in 1832) to plane the rims, which performed the work admirably. Since there has been considerable done for sale yearly.[84]

Oval boxes are among the best known Shaker products. This photograph shows three different sizes, along with molds that were used to form them. The sides were generally made of maple which was soaked in hot water and then bent around a form such as the one shown at center. The tops, or "headers" as the Shakers called them, were typically made of clear pine. Oval boxes were joined with iron or copper tacks at the fingers, and wooden pegs or iron points where the headers attach to the sides. They were finished in paints (both opaque and washes) and varnishes (pigmented and clear). The box at right is finished in a chrome yellow wash, at center in a varnish, and at left in a red lead wash.

Andrews Collection, Hancock Shaker Village 1962.298 (block mold), 1962.026 (box at right), 1962.337.0003 (box at center), 1962.030 (box at left), 1964.110.0004 (medium lid mold), 1962.713 (small lid molds)

Oval Boxes, Mount Lebanon, N.Y. ca. 1840
(clockwise from top left) 2" x 5 ½", 1 ¼" x 4 ⅝", 1 ⅜" x 3 ⅝", 2 ⅛" x 5 ½"

The Shakers used oval boxes for a wide variety of purposes. Three of these examples still have their original contents: copper tacks (used in box manufacturing), wooden pegs (used in cobbling), and "Irish Glue" (an animal glue dried in flakes). The box containing the wooden pegs bears an interesting inscription on the underside of the lid: "$1.10 The latter part of 1854 I came to the wash house being then 23 [illegible] was in the year 1855" and the name "Louisa." The "Irish Glue" box has the initials "I.Y" incised on the underside of the lid, presumably for Brother Isaac Newton Youngs.

Collection of the Family of David V. and Phyllis C. Andrews

Oval Boxes, Mount Lebanon, N.Y. ca. 1840
4 ½" x 11 ½" x 8 ½", 7 ½" x 14 ¾" x 10 ¾"

These examples in green and yellow are typical of the oval boxes produced at Mount Lebanon. The green box is painted all over, even on the bottom, and bears the inscription "J.D.K. 1836" on the underside of the lid in ink. The larger box is finished in a chrome yellow wash. The fingers on it are particularly fine, displaying a beveled edge that slowly flattens as the finger thins. Both of these boxes were exhibited in 1932 at The Berkshire Museum.

Reproduced courtesy of The American Museum in Britain (Bath, UK), 1959.59.5, 1959.59.7

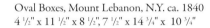

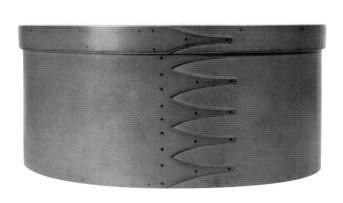

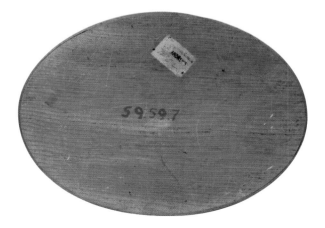

Oval Boxes, Mount Lebanon, N.Y. ca. 1840
2 ³⁄₈" x 6 ¹⁄₄", 2 ¹⁄₂" x 5 ¹⁄₄", 2 ¹⁄₄" x 6 ¹⁄₈"

These boxes bear labels for "CREAM TARTAR." and "Gum Mastich." The box at bottom bears a lengthy gift inscription from one Shaker Sister to another: "Presented/By Betsy Crosman/to Sarah Crother/June 30 1874/Truely I love the Giver/her life is one of/sweet Contentment."

Collection of the Family of David V. and Phyllis C. Andrews

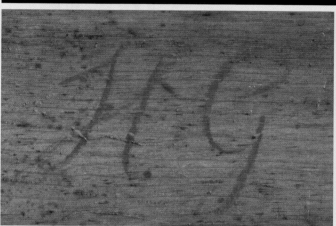

Oval Boxes, Mount Lebanon, N.Y. and Canterbury, N.H. ca. 1840
(top to bottom) 1 $^7/_{16}$" x 4 $^1/_2$" x 3", 3" x 5 $^1/_4$" x 3 $^3/_{16}$", 3" x 7 $^1/_2$" x 5",
3 $^3/_{16}$" x 6 $^1/_8$" x 2 $^9/_{16}$", 3 $^3/_{16}$" x 6 $^1/_8$" x 2 $^9/_{16}$", 5 $^1/_8$" x 13 $^3/_8$" x 9 $^1/_4$"

*Oval boxes made at Canterbury, New Hampshire, tend to have the tacks
spaced closely on either side of the finger-notches. The boxes second and
fourth from the bottom in this stack display that characteristic. The
box second from the bottom has "HG" written on the bottom in red
crayon. The one fourth from the bottom has the letters "NF" imprinted
in the bottom. The box second from the top was exhibited at the
Berkshire Museum in 1932.*

Andrews Collection, Hancock Shaker (top to bottom)
1962.337.0003, 1962.030, 1962.024, 1962.025, 1967.094

Oval Box, Mount Lebanon, N.Y. ca. 1840
3 ¾" x 10 ¼" x 7 ¾"

*This box was painted twice, first in a deep green,
and later in a similar green on the lid and bottom.
The paint on the lower half is opaque and hides the
copper tacks, whereas the paint on the rim has
been worn due to handling, revealing the tacks.*

Collection of J. Richard and E. Barbara Pierce

Oval Box, Mount Lebanon, N.Y. ca. 1840
3 ³⁄₁₆" x 6 ⅛" x 2 ⁹⁄₁₆"

This chrome yellow box was lined with the title page of an 1886 issue of the Shakers' monthly periodical
The Manifesto. *It also bears a handwritten label affixed to the side which reads "Variety of Tools." The
box was painted with the lid on, leaving an unpainted band along the top edge of the side.*

Andrews Collection, Hancock Shaker Village 1962.025

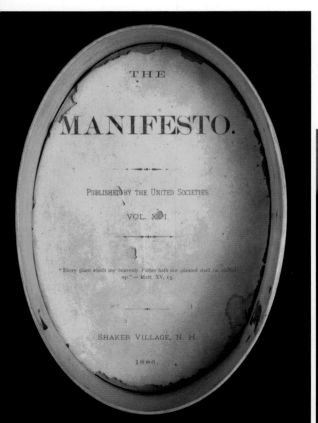

Oval Boxes, Mount Lebanon, N.Y. ca. 1840
4 ⁷/₈" x 11 ⁹/₁₆" x 8 ½", 5" x 12" x 8 ½"

Two fine examples in chrome yellow and blue/green. The upper finger on the side of the yellow box
split at some time in the past and was repaired by the Shakers. The paint on the blue example is
thin and ropey, it may have been applied over a varnish coat causing a resistance effect.

Andrews Collection, Hancock Shaker Village 1962.029, 1962.028

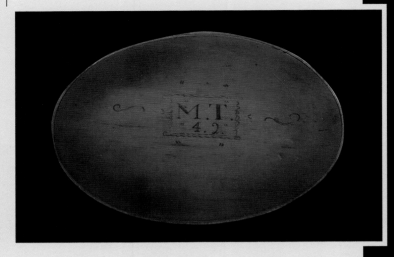

Oval Box, Mount Lebanon, N.Y. ca. 1840 3 ½" x 8 ¾" x 6" (top)
Oval Box, Canterbury, N.H. ca. 1840 3 ³⁄₁₆" x 6 ⅛" x 2 ⁹⁄₁₆" (bottom)

*The lid of the box on top has a decorative cartouche containing the inscription
"M.T./4.2." It is filled with quartz crystals probably collected by Sister
Marguerite Frost who gathered stones as souvenirs of her visits to other Shaker
communities. The green box at bottom has a paper label affixed to the side
reading "Spools of Winding Silk." The inside of the lid bears the following
inscription: "George Hodgson's Box May 1827 I came among Believers."*

Collection of Dr. John R. Ribic and Dr. Carla Kingsley

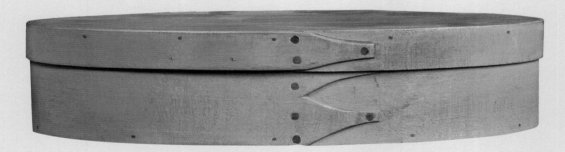

Oval Box, Mount Lebanon, N.Y. ca. 1840
2 ⅜" x 10 ¼" x 7 ⅛"

*This unusually short box was owned by
William Winter who photographed all of
the plates in **Shaker Furniture.***

**Collection of Dr. John R. Ribic and
Dr. Carla Kingsley**

Oval Box, Mount Lebanon, N.Y. ca. 1840
5 ½" x 13 ½"

*The finish on this box has changed color over time. Lifting the lid reveals the
light orange wash that covers the entire box, but has faded on exposed surfaces.
This orange was probably made using red lead, a fugitive pigment that fades due
to light. A fragmentary printed label reading "White T" is affixed to the side.*

Collection of Bob and Aileen Hamilton

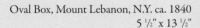

Oval Boxes, Mount Lebanon, N.Y. and Canterbury, N.H. ca. 1840

This colorful stack of boxes in the collection of the American Museum in Britain amply demonstrates the tremendous array of colors and sizes manufactured by the Shakers. The tacking pattern of the box fourth from the bottom is characteristic of boxes made at Canterbury, New Hampshire.

Reproduced courtesy of The American Museum in Britain (Bath, UK)

Brother Isaac Newton Youngs recorded the astonishing number of oval boxes manufactured at the Mount Lebanon society in the Church Family's Domestic Journal at the end of the year 1836:

Oval Box Makers Department
There have been made this year 3560 boxes.
Review of boxes made for 15 years past.
In 1822- 895
1823- 935
1824- 790
1825- 1226
1826- 1170
1827- 1258
1828- 1334
1829- 1300?
1830- 1308
1831- 2034
1832- 1554
1833- 1944
1834- 2094
1835- 2848
1836- 3560
Whole number for 15 years 24250.[85]

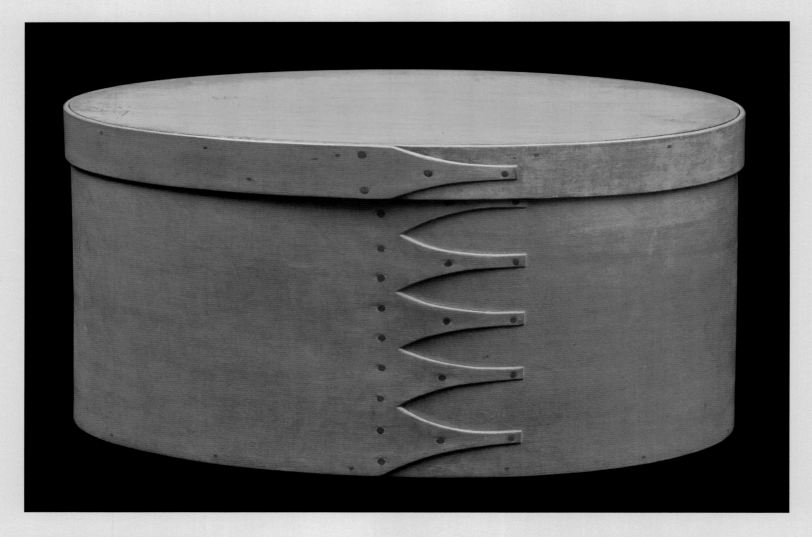

Oval Box, Mount Lebanon, N.Y. ca. 1840
7 ½" x 14 ⁷/₁₆" x 11"

The exceptionally well crafted fingers and regularly spaced tacks make this box an outstanding example. It is finished in a chrome yellow wash. This size is close to the largest that was commonly made by the Shakers, it may have been used to store a bonnet.

Andrews Collection, Hancock Shaker Village 1962.032.0001ab

Oval Box, Mount Lebanon, N.Y. ca. 1820
4 ⅛" x 9 ⅜" x 7"

The Andrewses had many, many oval boxes in their collection. A manuscript inventory of boxes in their collection dated August 12, 1932 records that they already had seventy-three by that date.[86] This one is an early example that has tiny wooden pegs, rather than iron points, to secure the top and bottom to the sides. It was never finished, but shows the mellow patina of age. The scribe line that the maker used to lay out his tacks is visible. This box has a partial paper label (New Lebanon or Watervliet, New York) at one end that reads: Balm of Gilead Buds. A photograph of Dr. Andrews sitting in the couple's Richmond farm house includes several books, a double candle sconce and a similar oval box atop a the school desk illustrated on page 124 of this book. The photograph was published in **Look** *magazine, March, 1954, p. 76. (The image was later used for cover illustrations on* **Religion in Wood** *(1966) and* **Shaker Furniture** *(1964 reprint).*

Collection of Miriam R. and M. Stephen Miller

Leading Shaker authority Edward D. Andrews sits at early schoolroom desk, one of the pieces in his documented collection which is recognized as the largest in the world.

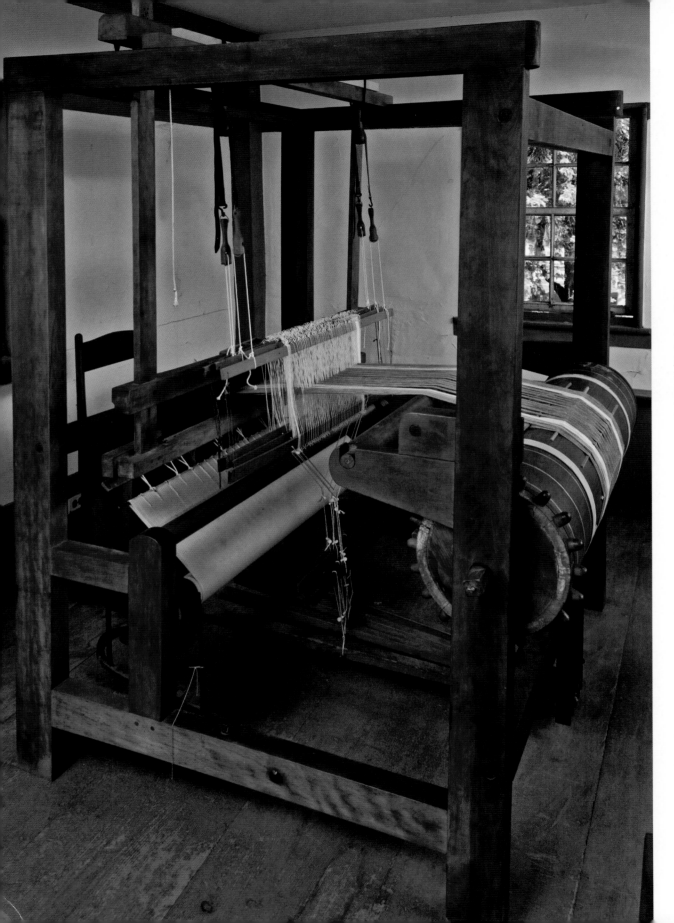

Loom, Mount Lebanon, N.Y. 1834
80 ⅝" x 64" x 60"

Brother Henry DeWitt was a multi-talented craftsman at Mount Lebanon's Church Family practicing the trades of bookbinder, printer, nail maker, cobbler, reel and wheelwright, basket maker, and cabinetmaker. Jerry Grant and Douglas R. Allen discovered the following references in DeWitt's journal for March 1834:

> The two past weeks, after my days work at making cloth shoes; I have employed myself at making a loom; or began to make one. It is to replace the loom that was bought, it proved nothing at all. In the morning I commenced working on my loom and expect to continue. I have been working at said loom the past week... I finished said loom. It was stain'd yesterday.

[and later in the month]

> I have been about 4 weeks making this spring shuttle loom. I took my new loom over to the spinshop and set it up for weaving. Beamed on about 30 yards of course linen. Betsy Crossman wove some & it went well.[87]

Brother Henry inscribed the following on the inside of the top front beam: "H.D. March 1834." Today this loom is on display in the weave loft of the Sisters' Shop and Dairy at Hancock Shaker Village, where it still used for weaving reproduction Shaker textiles.

Andrews Collection, Hancock Shaker Village 1962.520

Reels, first half of the 19th century
(left to right)
Hancock, Mass. 44 ⁷/₈" x 25"
Sabbathday Lake, Me. 38 ⁷/₈" x 25 ³/₈"
Mount Lebanon, N.Y. 35 ¹/₈" x 17"
Enfield, Conn. 42 ⁷/₈" x 25 ³/₄"

*Reels for winding yarn were made in almost
all Shaker communities. At Mount Lebanon
they were made for sale to "the world." These
examples display the wide variety of forms
made by the Shakers. The reel at far left from
Hancock is a "clock reel." It has a dial that
allows the user to keep track of the number of
revolutions the reel has made. The bright
orange "snap reel" is finished in brilliant red
lead paint. A similar example is illustrated
in the Andrewes' book* **The Community
Industries of The Shakers** *on page 155. This
"snap reel" is missing the long wooden trigger
formerly attached to the base which "snapped"
when the reel had made forty revolutions.
The next example from Mount Lebanon has
an unusual base that resembles a primitive
stand of similar form also from that community. The post has a subtle swelled turning
before terminating in a ball finial like those
found on Mount Lebanon "great" or "walking"
wheels. The Enfield, Connecticut reel is the
most finely constructed of this group. The
Queen Anne legs are very much like those
found on stands from the Hancock Bishopric.
The crossbar attached to the spoke at top in
the photo displays the rounded off end (as
opposed to rimmed end) that allowed the
weaver to remove a skein of wound yarn from
the reel.* **Shaker Furniture** *plate 24 (except
second from left).*

**Andrews Collection, Hancock Shaker Village
1962.526.0008, 1962.526.0007,
1962.526.0005, 1962.526.0004**

Reel, Hancock, Mass. first half of the 19th century

This detail shows the numbered dial impressed into the face of the "clock reel." **Shaker Furniture** *plate 24.*

Andrews Collection, Hancock Shaker Village
1962.526.0008

Reel, Mount Lebanon, N.Y. first half of the 19th century

The ball finial at the top of the post on this reel is incised with: "57". The finely turned hub and spokes are visible in this detail photograph. **Shaker Furniture** *plate 24.*

Andrews Collection, Hancock Shaker Village 1962.526.0005

Reel, Enfield, Conn. first half of the 19th century

The careful dovetailing of the crossbars, rounded ends of the frame, and carefully turned spokes and post on this reel carry it out of the realm of the purely functional. It appears to have been made by a fine cabinetmaker, almost certainly one who was also making tripod stands. **Shaker Furniture** *plate 24.*

Andrews Collection, Hancock Shaker Village 1962.526.0004

Reel, Sabbathday Lake, Me. first half of the 19th century

The finely cut wooden gear, rounded posts and crossbars, and screw all bespeak the careful craftsmanship that went into the making of this utilitarian implement. The red lead paint finish remains remarkably vibrant.

Andrews Collection, Hancock Shaker Village 1962.526.0007

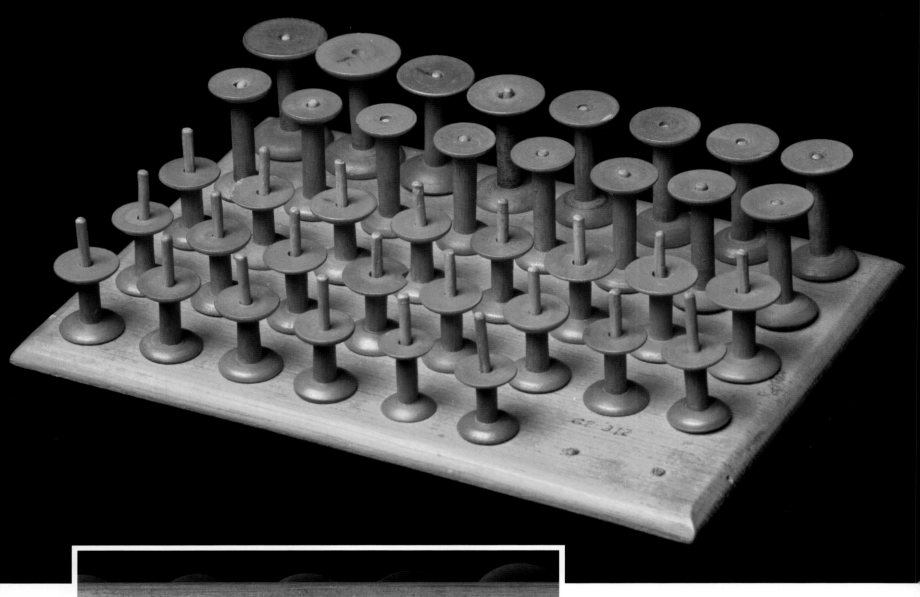

Spool Rack, Mount Lebanon, N.Y. ca. 1870
7" x 5"

*Crafted from a thin piece of pine and finished in chrome
yellow, this spool rack would have been used by a Shaker
Sister to keep her thread in order. The edges are carefully
rounded off and forty uprights are dowelled into the base.
"Levi Shaw made this" is written in pencil on the bottom.
Brother Levi lived at Mount Lebanon until his death
in 1908.*

Andrews Collection, Hancock Shaker Village 1962.312

Lap Board, Mount Lebanon, N.Y. ca. 1850 11 ¼" x 21 ⅛"
Lap Board, Mount Lebanon, N.Y. 1865 11 ¼" x 24 ¾"
Folding Scissors, Mount Lebanon, N.Y. ca. 1840 2 ⅞" x ⅞"

These lap boards were used by Shaker Sisters as a surface for textile work while seated. Sometimes they were used in conjunction with sewing desks that have under-hung support rods that extend from the front. The example at top is backed with blue fabric (cotton or linen) and stained yellow on the front. It is made of pine with chestnut breadboard ends to prevent warping. A printed ownership label on the back reads "Nancy." The other lap board is made of the same materials, but is slightly longer. It bears the inscription "C.B. 1865." The folding scissors were acquired by the Andrewses at Mount Lebanon. It is not known if they are of Shaker manufacture.

Collection of Dr. Thomas and Jan Pavlovic

Mitten and Stocking Forms,
Unknown Community, 19th century
14" x 10 ½" x 2 ½" (stocking forms),
10 ⅜" x 3 ⅜" (mitten form with thumb),
12 ½" x 3 ¾" (mitten form with handle),
12 ⅜" x 3 ⅞" (detail at bottom)

Shaker Sisters used these forms to stretch, or block, wool yarn. This process shrinks the yarn making for a more weather proof final product. The Andrewses collected many examples of these types of forms at Mount Lebanon and Hancock. The form with the removal thumb piece bears the faint initials "T.G." and the date "1850." The next form has "1837" impressed into the handle, through which a hole has been drilled. The detail photo at bottom shows the initials "GT" found on another form (which is not fully illustrated here). The stocking forms are each shaped from a single block of wood and painted red.

Andrews Collection, Hancock Shaker Village 1962.579.0002ab, 1962.623.0001ab, 1962.716.0002, 1962.716.0002

Hatchel
Unknown Community,
19th century
18 ¹/₈" x 4 ¹/₈"

Also known as a hackle, heckle, and hetchel, this tool was used to comb and separate flax fibers as part of the process of making linen cloth. This example, marked "CHH." for the Church Family, was screwed to a table top for ease of use.

Andrews Collection, Hancock Shaker Village 1962.530.0002

Wheel Finger, Unknown Community, 19th century
8 ³/₄" x 4 ¹/₈"

This birch finger is turned in a similar manner to Shaker pegs. It was used by Shaker Sisters to turn the "great" or "walking" wheels.

Andrews Collection, Hancock Shaker Village 1962.448

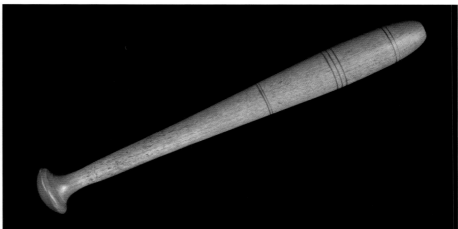

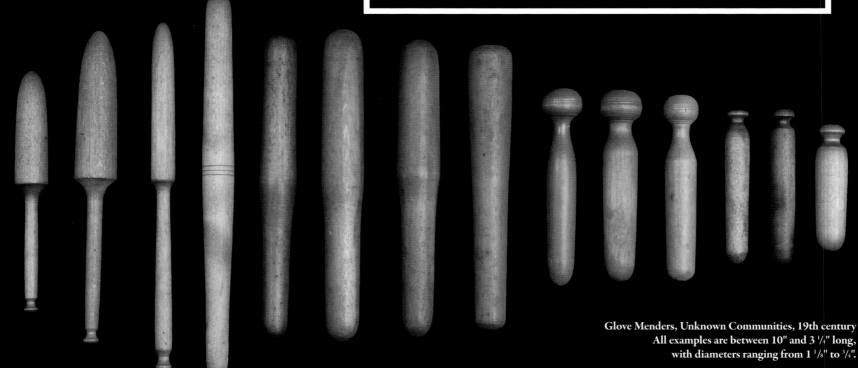

**Glove Menders, Unknown Communities, 19th century
All examples are between 10" and 3 ¹/₄" long,
with diameters ranging from 1 ¹/₈" to ³/₄".**

The Andrewses collected a large number of these small textile tools. Two possible uses for them have been proposed. They may have been inserted into the finger of a glove so it could be mended, or else they could have been used to turn the fingers of finished gloves inside out after they were knitted.

Andrews Collection, Hancock Shaker Village (left to right, all are 1962.715) .0010, .0005, .0006, .0009, .0003, .0001, .0002, .0004, .0011, .0010, .0015, .0012, .0014, .0013

Tailor's Measure, Unknown Community, mid 19th century 36" x 3 ½" x ¼"
Compass, Unknown Community, 1827 15" x 4 ¼"
Square, Unknown Community, 1857 24" x 2"
Tailor's Measure, Unknown Community, 1851 36" x 3 ⅝" x ¼"

The curved edges of the tailor's measures at top and bottom (detail) were used in drawing patterns for clothing. The measure at bottom has a large hole in it, allowing it to be hung from a Shaker peg. It is stamped "1851" and has traces of a red lead painted finish. The compass is made from maple, fastened with copper tacks, and stamped "1827". The finely marked maple square is fastened with copper tacks. It is dated "1857" and bears the initials "H.S." in ink.

Andrews Collection, Hancock Shaker Village 1962.510.0007 (tailor's measure at top), 1962.510.0005 (square), 1962.510.0003 (tailor's measure at bottom), 1962.612 (compass)

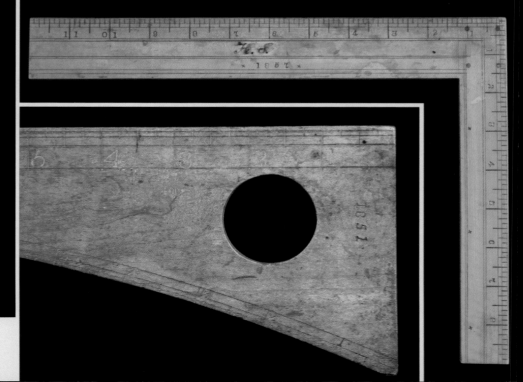

Dustpan or Scoop, Unknown Community, 19th century
18" x 9 ⅛"

This scoop is marked "Wash House." It may have been used for dry soap. The turned handle is similar to those found on Shaker dippers. The bentwood side was made using the same technique as used in making oval boxes, and is tacked into the bottom along the edges. The front scooping edge is protected with a tacked-on tin strip.

Andrews Collection, Hancock Shaker Village 1962.389

Chalk Line Safe, Mount Lebanon, N.Y. ca. 1860
3" x 3"

This colorful device was made for sale to the world at Mount Lebanon. A printed label with a decorative border on the front reads: "CHALK LINE SAFE." Another affixed to the back reads "ALSO FOR LADIES FLOWER BEDS OR ROOM LINE, FOR HANGING SMALL ARTICLES TO DRY." Other examples collected by the Andrewses contain red chalk dust, used to "snap" lines.

Andrews Collection, Hancock Shaker Village 1962.730.0002

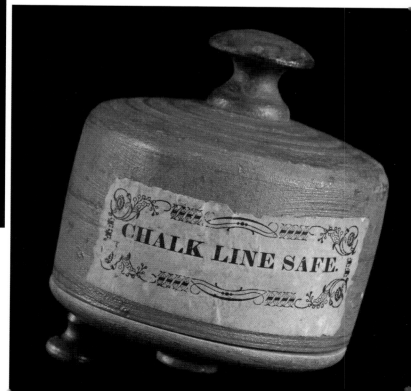

Iron and Weights, Unknown Community, 19th century
Weights range in height from 4" to 3 ¾" and
diameter from 2 ⅛" to 2"

The dressmaker's weights at right are turned from solid blocks of wood. The center of each is hollow and contains a lead weight. They were used to hold down cloth for garment making and ironing.

Collection of the Family of David V. and Phyllis C. Andrews

Draining Rack, Unknown Community, mid-19th century
5 ½" x 30 ½" x 19"

This rack was used to drain wet textiles after they had been washed, and then to carry them to the drying room. It is made of pine and an unknown hardwood. The angled corners of the basin are joined with dovetails, a remarkable use of complicated joinery for such a utilitarian object.

Andrews Collection, Hancock Shaker Village 1962.466.0001

Table, Enfield, Conn. ca. 1830
26 ½" x 57" x 33 ⅞"

"Found at the Enfield, Conn. settlement in 1929. Top in pine; base, ash. A strongly built piece, possibly for shop use. Stretchers are mortised into leg posts." [88] The top of this table consists of two pine boards with breadboard ends. The Andrewses stated in **Shaker Furniture** that this table was used as an ironing table at Enfield. This seems to conflict with the speculation in the unpublished notes transcribed above. Whatever its use, the sawbuck, or X-trestle, base of this table would have made for a sturdy work surface. **Shaker Furniture** plate 6.

Collection of the Family of David V. and Phyllis C. Andrews

The Shaker Washing Machine.

Washing Machine Model, Canterbury, N.H. ca. 1858
14" x 36" x 37"

"The carefully constructed model on which the patent was secured for the Shaker 'wash mill' evokes the figure of Sister Marguerite Frost and the quiet school room at Canterbury where we found it." [89] *This remarkable working model is a scale replica of the wash mill patented by its inventor Canterbury Shaker Trustee David Parker on January 26, 1858. The wash mill consists of two tubs which were filled with clothes, soap, and water. These tubs were agitated on a swing frame, and then the soapy water was wrung out using the levers on the sides. The Shakers sold this machine to hotels, hospitals, and colleges. Customers listed in an article about the machine published in the March 10, 1860 issue of* **Scientific American** *included hotels in Boston, New York, Philadelphia, and Washington D.C. This intricate model actually works. The iron crankshaft moves the agitators back and forth when turned, and the wringer arms can also be moved. The model is finished in red and black paint and a dark stain. Trustee David Parker advertised his machine on billheads used by the Canterbury Society. The small handwritten label photographed with the machine reads "581. Model of a Washing Machine made at Canterbury N.H."*

Andrews Collection, Hancock Shaker Village 1971.077

Rulers, Unknown Communities, mid-19th century
The longest measure is 36", the shortest are 12".
Tailor's Shoulder Measure, Unknown Community, mid-19th century
15" x 10"

Hundreds of rulers survive that were made in Shaker communities. They were made of a large variety of wood types and finished with paint, or varnish, or sometimes left unfinished. This small sampling of rulers in the Andrews Collection at Hancock Shaker Village gives a sense of the multiplicity of forms produced. The detail photo at right shows examples in flame birch (top), curly maple, and finished in chrome yellow. The tailor's measure could be hung from a peg. It also has a separate extendable tab slotted into the end shown at top.

Andrews Collection, Hancock Shaker Village 1962.510.0008ab (tailor's measure), (measures from top to bottom) 1962.062.0003, 1962.062.0008, 1962.062.0001, 1962.062.0002, 1962.756.0002, 1962.062.0004, 1962.062.0005, 1962.062.0009, 1962.062.0010, 1962.510.0001, 1962.510.0002, 1962.755.0001, 1962.755.0005, 1962.510.0006

Chandelier, Tyringham, Mass. ca. 1820
23" x 26 ¹/₂" x 24"

The Andrewses stated that this tin chandelier came from the Shaker Meetinghouse at Tyringham, Massachusetts.[90] In 1875 the community at Tyringham was the first Shaker village to be closed. The Meetinghouse there was eventually moved from its original site, and had been moved by the time that the Andrewses began collecting. It is not known if they acquired this chandelier directly out of the building, or from someone who told them its history. It is made of tin, and has six arms that are reinforced with wire and terminate in candleholders.

Andrews Collection, Hancock Shaker Village 1965.235

Wall Sconce, Unknown Community, ca. 1830
16" x 8 ³/₄" x 6 ³/₄"
Candlestick, Unknown Community, ca. 1830
7" x 3 ³/₄"

This wall sconce was designed to be hung from a Shaker peg. It is made of pine and finished in an orange stain which has faded over time. The edges have been carefully rounded off. The candlestick is of the "hogscraper" variety and was collected from a Shaker community, though it is unknown if this example was made by the Shakers. **Shaker Furniture** *plate 12.*

Reproduced courtesy of The American Museum in Britain (Bath, UK), 1959.68 (sconce), 1959.82.1 (candlestick)

Lillies, Unknown Community, ca. 1840
19 ¼" x 8" x 6" (left), 29 ¾" x 11 ¾" (right)
Wick Trimmers, Unknown Community, ca. 1840
6 ¹⁵/₁₆" x 2 ⅛" x 1 ½"

These tin lillies, which have been painted black, were used to conduct the fumes from an oil lamp into a flue so they could be vented through a chimney. The example at left has a circular lamp platform which is attached to the hood by a piece of wrought iron. These wick trimmers were collected by the Andrewses from the Shakers, but it is unknown whether they were made by the Shakers. In February of 1836 Isaac Newton Youngs carried out an experiment with some of the oil lamps at Mount Lebanon. He recorded the results in the Church Family's Domestic Journal: "s. 27 I have made an experiment this week past to see how much oil our meeting room lamps burn in a given time, & found the one burnt 4 ½ ozs. in 1 ¾ hour, & the other 3 ½ ozs."[91]

Andrews Collection, Hancock Shaker Village
1962.284 (left lilly), 1963.1258 (right lilly)
Collection of Dr. Thomas and Jan Pavlovic (wick trimmers)

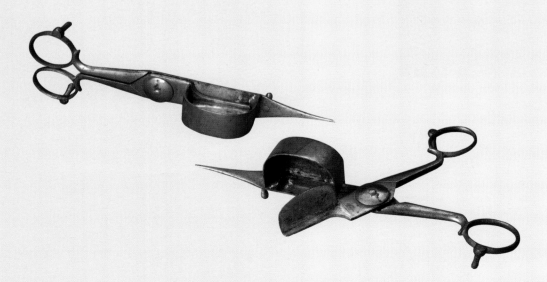

Wall Sconce, Hancock, Mass. early 19th century
19 ¼" x 6" x 5"

"The tin candle sconce (from Hancock) is provided with a rack for matches or matchbox." [92] *It has a scalloped top edge and would have been hung from a nail.* **Shaker Furniture** *plate 1 and plate 27.*

Collection of the Family of David V. and Phyllis C. Andrews

Wall Sconces, Unknown Communities, early 19th century
18" x 11" x 5 ¼" (wooden sconce), 11" x 3 ½" x 3 ⅛" (tin sconce),
Candle Holder and Snuffer, Unknown Community, early 19th century
4 ¼" x 7 ⅜" (candleholder)

*The wooden sconce at left was designed to be hung from a peg and hold two candlesticks.
The tin wall sconce at right was nailed to the wall through the small hole at top.
The candleholder and snuffer may or may not have been made by the Shakers.
The wooden sconce is illustrated in* **Shaker Furniture** *plate 33.*

Andrews Collection, Hancock Shaker Village 1962.016 (wooden sconce)
Collection of Miriam R. and M. Stephen Miller (tin sconce)
Collection of the Family of David V. and Phyllis C. Andrews (candleholder and snuffer)

Tea Pot, Mount Lebanon, N.Y. ca. 1820
8 ¼" x 13 ½"

This tea pot was one of Faith Andrews's favorite gifts from Sister Sadie Neale of the Mount Lebanon's Church Family. Faith carefully recorded its provenance on the small note depicted here. Silhouette artist Helen Laughon made the image of Faith below in 1981. The tea pot is shown, along with the tripod stand illustrated on page 181.

Collection of the Family of David V. and Phyllis C. Andrews (tea pot)
Gift of Gustave Nelson, Hancock Shaker Village (silhouette)

Early Shakers made
Tin and pewter tea pot.
Given to us by Sister
Sadie Neale, New
Lebanon, N.Y.
F.A.

Faith Andrews
Jan. 1981

Funnel, Unknown Community, 19th century
38" x 4 ½"(diameter)

The use of this long tin funnel is unknown.

Andrews Collection, Hancock Shaker Village
1962.1259

Pitcher and Lid, Mount Lebanon, N.Y.
mid-19th century
8 ½" x 7"

*A note in Faith Andrews's hand inside
this pitcher states: "Sadie Neale/Herb
Shop New Leb." The ceramic pitcher was
made by a non-Shaker potter, but the
carefully crafted lid was made by a
Shaker. It is carved from a single piece of
hardwood, and carefully rounded on the
top edges. The bottom has been relieved
to fit the pitcher, and a hardwood
knob is threaded into the top.*

**Collection of the Family of David V.
and Phyllis C. Andrews**

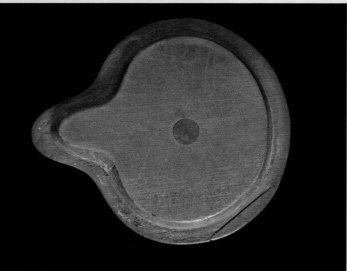

Tinware, Unknown Communities, 19th century

Identifying Shaker-made tinware is very difficult, as it often varies little in form and construction from tinware made in "the world." These pieces were all collected by the Andrewses at Shaker communities. However, that does not guarantee that they were Shaker made. Brother Isaac Newton Youngs summarized the Mount Lebanon Shakers' limited tinware manufacture in his 1856 Concise View:

Brass and Tin Work.
This business was followed in the beginning of the Chh. much as one branch of business. The tinkering, or tinman's department making and mending of tin ware &c. was on a small scale, and very limited, as to tools and fixtures, in comparison to the generality of tin shops. The work done in this line was chiefly for the Church's own use. A greater portion of the tin, brass or copper utensils needed or used in the Chh. were purchased, from the first to the present time.[93]

Among the objects illustrated here are measures, oil cans, tea pots, funnels, sugar molds, a dipper, and a lidded pail. The tallest object is the tea pot at far left (6 ¼").

Andrews Collection, Hancock Shaker Village (spiraling inward from upper left) 1962.268.0001, 1962.272.0001, 1962.171.0001, 1962.269.0002, 1962.269.0001, 1962.268.0002, 1962.267.0001ab, 1968.272.0002, (sugar molds collection, unnumbered), (lidded pail), 1962.041.0001ab, 1962.173.0001, 1962.269.0001

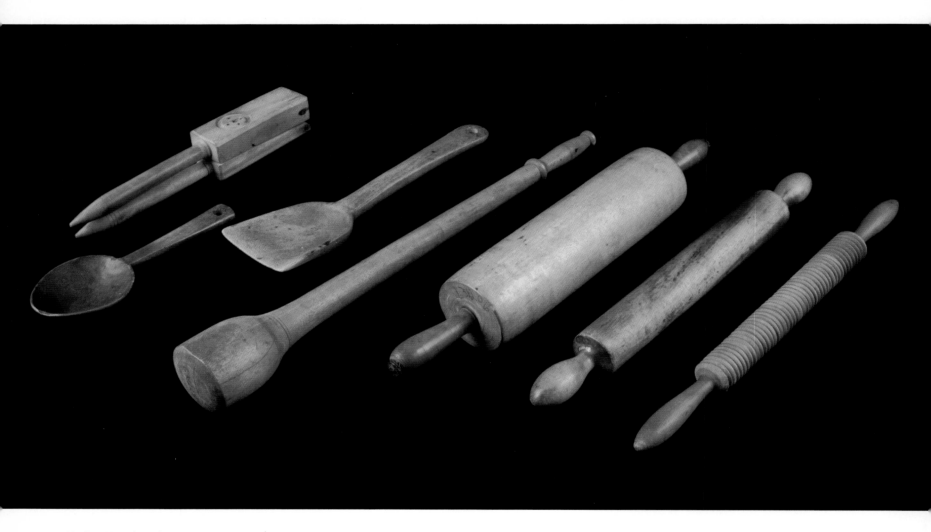

Kitchen Utensils, Unknown Community, 19th century

Overseen by Kitchen Deaconesses who supervised rotating groups of Sisters, Shaker kitchens prepared immense amount of food every day. This array of kitchen utensils is but a small sampling of what was collected by the Andrewses. These utensils are not necessarily all Shaker-made, but some certainly were (such as the rolling pins and masher). From left to right: lemon squeezer, spoon, scoop, masher, rolling pins (3), ash scraper, spatula, fork, and skimmers(3). The largest item shown here is the masher, which measures 23" long and has a diameter of 3" at the end. The scoop and masher are illustrated in plate 11 of **Shaker Furniture**.

Andrews Collection, Hancock Shaker Village (from left) 1963.1212.0001, 1963.365.0003, 1963.1226.0003, 1963.1224.0001, 1963.1206.0001, 1963.442.0003, 1963.1209.0001, 1962.397.0003, 1963.1227.0001, 1963.1225.0001, 1962.367.0001, 1962.1219.0001, 1962.1221.0001

Soap Dishes, Unknown Community, early 19th century
Plates, Unknown Community, early 19th century
Dipper, Unknown Community, early 19th century

The green painted soap dish at upper left was turned from one piece of wood. The other soap dish (just to the right) consists of a carefully turned base and lid. The wooden plates are all turned and have a lipped edge. The wooden dipper was also crafted from one piece of wood. It is painted chrome yellow on the outside and white inside. The handle is beautifully carved, ending in a pointed hook suitable for hanging on a bucket edge.

Andrews Collection, Hancock Shaker Village
1962.392.0001 (green soap dish),
1962.544.0001ab (small soap dish),
1962.366.0001a-f (plates)

Pie Board Rack, Unknown Community, early 19th century
Pie Boards, Unknown Community, early 19th century
31 ½" x 23 ¾" (pie rack), 8" x 8" x ¼" (pie boards)

"Second family, Mt. Lebanon. Pies were made in large quantities in the early days of the sect, and were eaten three times a day. In order to conserve tinware, the pies were transferred after baking to maple boards, which were scrubbed after using and placed between the rods of the rack to dry." [94] *Pies may not have actually been eaten three times a day by the early Shakers, but they certainly were a staple of their diet. This unique kitchen piece is made of a pine frame with hardwood rods doweled into the front. It is finished in an orange wash. Designed to hang from a peg, it held wooden cooling boards that were set under the numerous pies (both sweet and savory) baked daily in Shaker kitchens.*

**Andrews Collection, Hancock Shaker Village
1963.188.0001 (pie board rack), 1963.1204.0001-7 (pie boards)**

Pie Safe, Unknown Community,
early 19th century
20" x 30 ½" x 18 ½"

Keeping food safe from vermin was a constant job in nineteenth century homes. This finely crafted hanging pie safe is screened and painted red. It was hung from the ceiling by the four chamfered corner posts. A door allows access to the two shelves inside.

**Andrews Collection, Hancock Shaker Village
1963.1257.0001**

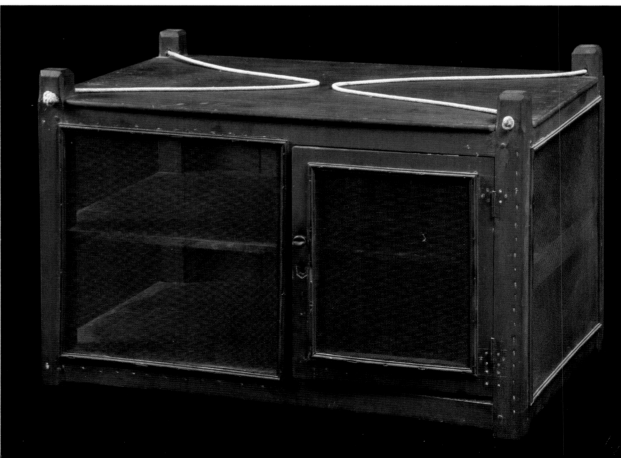

Apple Quarterer, Unknown Community,
early 19th century
25 1/4" x 8 1/4" x 1 1/8"

*A Shaker would sit on this device, straddling the
cutouts, and push apples through the cross-blades
at the end. A pail beneath would have caught
the quartered apples.*

**Andrews Collection, Hancock Shaker Village
1965.280.0001**

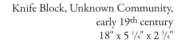

Knife Block, Unknown Community,
early 19th century
18" x 5 1/4" x 2 3/4"

*This knife block was designed to hang from a peg.
The knives in it were also collected by
the Andrewses.*

**Andrews Collection, Hancock Shaker Village
1963.185.0001**

Dough Bin, Unknown Community, early 19th century
40" x 20 1/2" x 10 3/4"

*This pine dough bin is carefully dovetailed at an angle.
The bottom is nailed on. Large quantities of dough
used in making bread and other baked goods were
set in bins like this to rise.*

**Andrews Collection, Hancock Shaker Village
1963.1202.0001**

Cutting Devices
Unknown Communities,
early 19th century
(clockwise from top left)
24" x 9" x 6 ½", 5 ⅞" x 3 ¾", 5 ⅝" x 5 ¼",
11 ¾" x 8 ⅜", 20 ⅜" x 5 ¼"

The slicer at left was probably used for cutting vegetables and apples. It stands on four legs and all edge surfaces on it have been chamfered. It is finished in a red wash. The other choppers all have finely turned handles. It cannot be known for certain if they were made by the Shakers, or just purchased by them, but they were all collected from the Shakers by the Andrewses.

Andrews Collection, Hancock Shaker Village (clockwise from top left) 1962.439.0001, 1963.1238.0001, 1963.1210.0006, 1963.1210.0001, 1963.1220.0001

Slicer, Mount Lebanon, N.Y. mid-19th century
12" x 20" x 6 ¼"

This intricately constructed slicer was designed for use at the edge of a table. The guillotine style blade is fixed within a moveable wooden frame that is held in place by the uprights screwed to the base. The handle screwed to the blade-frame moves up and down, enabling the user to slice herbs or vegetables passed through the blade. The whole implement is finished in a red wash and every edge on it has been carefully chamfered to avoid splits.

Andrews Collection, Hancock Shaker Village 1962.440.0001

Dust Pans, Mount Lebanon, N.Y. 19th century
10" x 9 ½", 9 ½" x 8"

The Shakers manufactured tin-plated iron dust pans. They are similar in form to those made in "the world," but the Shakers' use of iron, rather than flimsy tin sheeting, is one way to tell the two apart. Small rings for hanging are affixed to the handle ends.

Collection of Dr. Thomas and Jan Pavlovic

Box, Unknown Community, 19th century
14" x 13 ½" x 14"

This fully dovetailed box is divided down the middle. The rear wall is higher than the front wall and a hand-hold is cut from the center wall. It is finished in a dark stain.

**Andrews Collection, Hancock Shaker Village
1962.654.0001**

Tool Holder, Unknown Community, 19th century
10 ½" x 8 ½"

It is unclear exactly what this finely crafted object was used for. The base consists of two pieces, beautifully turned and held together with screws. Numerous square holes have been cut into the top with a fine chisel, presumably for holding small tools. An iron handle is set into the center.

Andrews Collection, Hancock Shaker Village 1962.729.0001

Brushes, Mount Lebanon, N.Y. mid-19th century
(left to right) 8 3/8" x 3 1/2", 11 3/4" x 3 1/2", 9 1/4" x 1 3/4", 10 5/8" x 1 1/4"

The Mount Lebanon Shakers made brushes both for their own use and for sale to "the world." The brush at left is a scrub brush with a leather handle. There are 119 bunches of animal bristle set into the wooden base with copper wire. The wire runs through the channels cut into the base. The next brush is a dust pan brush with a distinctive quarter-round head. The brush third from the left is a clothes brush. There are three different colors of horsehair wired into 65 bunches in this brush which is stamped "D.H." on the end for Second Family Trustee Daniel Hawkins. The brush handle at right is unfin-ished. The way that the holes are cut for the bristles shows the angle at which the bristles would splay, indicating it was probably going to be finished as a shop brush. Note the similarity in turning on the handles of all three brushes.

Andrews Collection, Hancock Shaker Village (left to right)
1962.666, 1962.664, 1962.665, 1962.668

Cheese Press, Unknown Community,
early 19th century
33 ½" x 33" x 24"

This "self acting" cheese press is similar to one in the
collection of the New York State Museum that was
collected from the South Family at Mount Lebanon.
The lever built into the base exerted pressure onto the
cheese curds within the hoops. The threaded uprights
were used to exert further pressure from the top.
There are traces of gray paint on this example.

Andrews Collection,
Hancock Shaker Village 1962.414

Stitching Vise, Unknown Community, early 19th century
23" x 12" x 3 ½"

This upright vise was used for stitching pieces of leather together. The clamp is adjusted by the threaded wooden screw fitted into the center of the uprights. It is finished in a gray paint.

Andrews Collection, Hancock Shaker Village 1962.717

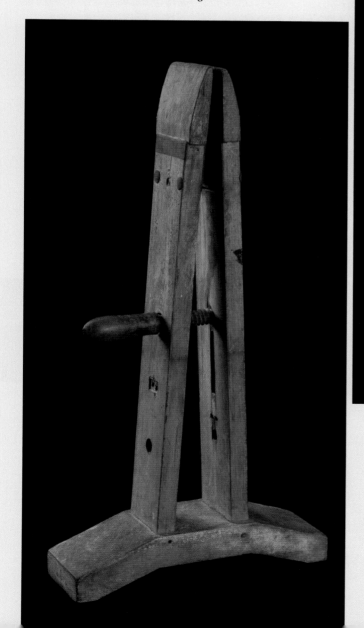

Press, Unknown Community, early 19th century
23" x 37 ¾" x 4"

This fully dovetailed press may have been used in conjunction with bookbinding, though the platen seems small for that use. It is fully dovetailed and finished in a dark varnish. The platen has a small metal receptacle fitted into the center where the screw presses into it. It is not known if the iron fittings for this press were made by the Shakers. Shown in the press is a copy of the 1810 edition of **The Testimony of Christ's Second Appearing.**

Andrews Collection, Hancock Shaker Village 1962.044

Sieves, Mount Lebanon, N.Y. ca. 1830
Sieve Binder, Mount Lebanon, N.Y. ca. 1830

The Second, South (which was a branch of the Second), and East Families at Mount Lebanon all produced sieves during the early and mid-nineteenth century. Second Family Trustee Daniel Hawkins traded the following products to the Church Family between 1828 and 1843: "hair sieves, cockle riddles, wheat riddles, brass sieves." East Family Trustee Joseph Allen also traded brass wire, hair, wire, and cockle sieves in nests, and riddles (large coarse sieves) to the Church Family.[95] The sieve binding frame shown was used to catch the woven mat between the two wooden hoops that bound the sieve together. The domed disc on top sits loosely on the three-legged platform, it can be lifted free and the woven mat placed underneath for binding. The collection sieves (mostly unfinished) displayed around it give an idea of the wide variety of sizes available from the Shakers. The sieve at top is outfitted with a handle and may have been used to sift flour in a kitchen. It is 9 ½" in diameter. The sieve shown at right is inscribed in ink: "E. Brother Asa/Shirley." This may refer to Elder Asa Brocklebank of the Shirley, Massachusetts, Shaker community. The Shakers at Shirley did make sieves, so this example could be from there, but its construction is very similar to Mount Lebanon examples. It is 5 ¾" in diameter.

Andrews Collection, Hancock Shaker Village 1962.726 (sieve binder), 1962.436 (handled sieve at top), 1962.328 ("E. Brother Asa" sieve), 1962.456.0004 (large sieve under sieve binder), 1962.456.0001 and 1962.456.0005 (stacked to the right of the sieve binder)

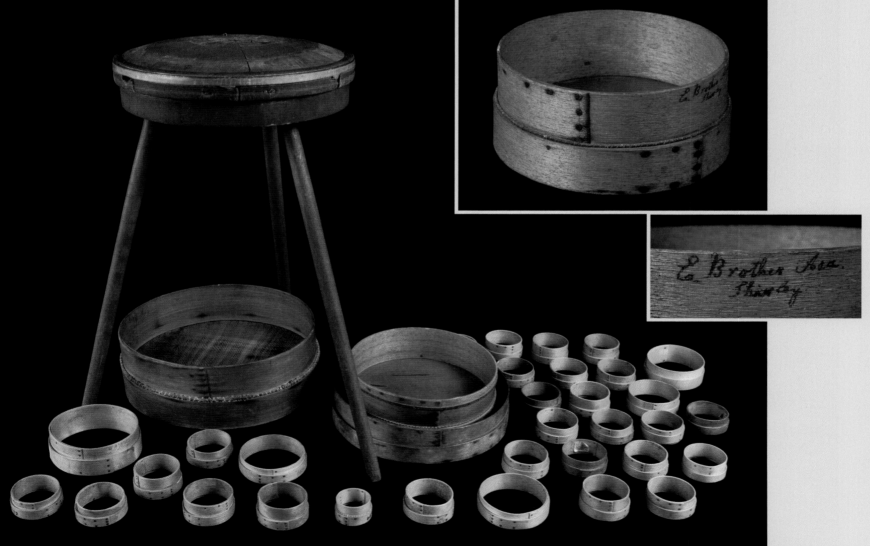

Shingle or Stave Bench, Unknown Community, early 19th century
35" x 63" x 21"

The exact use of this bench is not known, but it may have been used by a shingle or stave maker. The user would have sat on the end at left and depressed the foot pedal— thereby trapping wooden material beneath the head so it could be shaved with a draw knife. The upper part of this bench is hinged by a barrel-shaped axis at the right end of the bench. A thin piece of curved wood moves up and down with the upper part of the bench as it is raised and lowered. The whole piece is finished in a red wash.

Andrews Collection, Hancock Shaker Village 1962.677

Seed Riddles, Mount Lebanon, N.Y. mid-19th century 4 1/2" x 17", 4 1/2" x 17 7/8"
Tray, Mount Lebanon, N.Y. mid-19th century 2 3/4" x 27 1/4" x 14 1/2"

These large riddles, or coarse sieves, were used in a Shaker seed garden at Mount Lebanon. The example at left is marked "SEEDS 10m NO. 22", the one at right is stencilled "GARDEN NO 11." According to Sister Sadie Neale the tray at bottom "came from the old herb houses in New Lebanon. Sister Sadie Neale said the tray was used by the sisters to shell beans and empty them into a large bin." [96] *The underside is stencilled "MT LEBANON SEED GARDEN." The tray is made of pine.*

Andrews Collection, Hancock Shaker Village 1962.456.0003, 1962.456.0002 (riddles)
Courtesy, Winterthur Museum 1978.0014 (tray)

Printing Block, Unknown Community, late 19th century ³/₄" x 3 ¹/₄" x 2 ⁷/₈"
Dried Green Sweet Corn Can, Hancock, Mass. ca. 1860 6 ⁵/₈" x 4 ⁵/₈"
Corn Kernel Cutter, Unknown Community, 19th century 3" x 5 ¹/₂" x 8 ¹/₄"
Rake, Unknown Community, 19th century 40" x 15 ⁵/₈" x 6 ¹/₂"

The production of dried green sweet corn was a major industry in the late nineteenth century at Mount Lebanon, Hancock and Enfield, Connecticut. The cylindrical can was used by the Hancock Shakers to package and sell dried corn under the auspices of Trustee Isaac Augur. The small printing block illustrates one type of corn-cutting machine used by the Shakers. It might have been used in printing promotional or advertising literature for the product. The cast iron kernel cutter at right would have been clamped to the edge of a table and the ear of corn run across its blades. The small rake at bottom may have been used to rake out sweet corn as it dried on screens in buildings specially constructed for that purpose.

Andrews Collection, Hancock Shaker Village 1962.1248 (printing block), 1962.418 (can), 1962.417 (kernel cutter), 1962.450 (rake)

Cobbler's Bench, Mount Lebanon, N.Y. early 19th century
33 ¾" x 51" x 25 ¼"

The Andrewses discovered an abandoned cobbler's workroom in the brethrens' shop at Mount Lebanon's Second Family. In **Fruits of the Shaker Tree of Life** *they remembered: "One of the few brethren left at New Lebanon guided us to the loft of an old stone shop to show and sell us a shoemaker's bench, with little dovetailed tin bottom drawers and all its equipment including the Shaker asthma powder on which some cobbler once depended for relief."⁹⁷ This is the cobbler's bench found that day. It is made of pine and butternut. The case is finely dovetailed and the tin-bottomed drawers have delicately turned bone pulls. Some of them still hold their original contents such as the shoe pegs shown in the detail at right. The underhung drawer contains a handblown glass bottle used for blacking, as well as scraps of leather and a form used to make a Sister's shoe. A flat-paneled door secures the bench when closed. This door has a leather polishing strip and depressions filled with wax built into it. The work surface and seat are covered in leather.* **Shaker Furniture** *plate 47.*

Andrews Collection, Hancock Shaker Village 1962.573

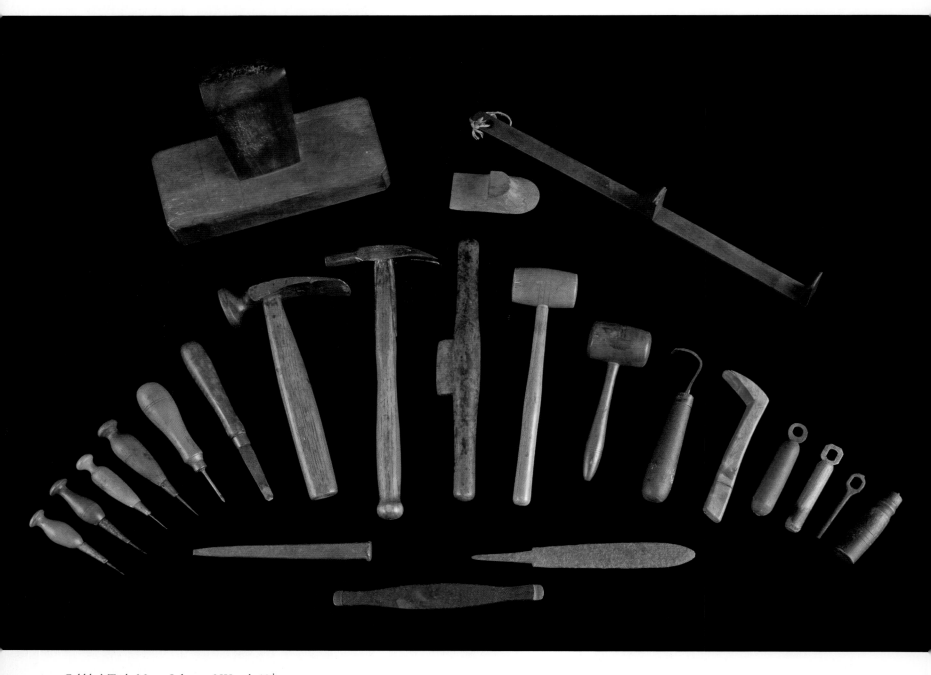

Cobbler's Tools, Mount Lebanon, N.Y. early 19th century

The Andrewses acquired a large collection of cobbler's tools from Mount Lebanon. Shown in the assemblage above (from left to right) in the top row are: last, heel, foot measure; second row: awls, hammers, slick, mallet, scraper, burnisher, wrenches; at bottom: punch, creasing stick, knife. The foot measure was not made by the Shakers. The Andrewses collected many awls with finely turned handles as shown above. The measure is 15 ¼" long.

Andrews Collection, Hancock Shaker Village 1962.719.0037 (last), 1962.573.0023 (heel), 1971.333.0002 (foot measure), 1962.719.0021 and 1962.573.0008 (awls), 1962.573.0006 (hammer), 1963.573.0007 (hammer), 1962.574.0008 (slick), 1962.310.0002 and 1962.310.0001 (mallets), 1962.573.0010 (scraper), 1962.719.0024 (burnisher), 1962.573.0014 and 1962.573.0020 (wrenches), 1962.573.0018 (punch), 1962.573.0017 (creaser), 1962.573.0005 (knife)

Cobbler's Last, Mount Lebanon, N.Y. early 19th century 7 ¼" x 3 ¼" x 2 ⅞"
Cobbler's Candlestand, Mount Lebanon, N.Y. early 19th century 32 ½" x 12 ½" x 6 ¾"

This adjustable last can be expanded by turning the screw fitted into the middle. The last is hinged on the bottom and finished in a red wash. The candlestand consists of a threaded maple shaft set into an oak base. It can be raised and lowered by turning the double candle-arm, and is painted with red lead. **Shaker Furniture** *plate 47 (candlestand).*

Andrews Collection, Hancock Shaker Village 1971.334 (last), 1962.575 (candlestand)

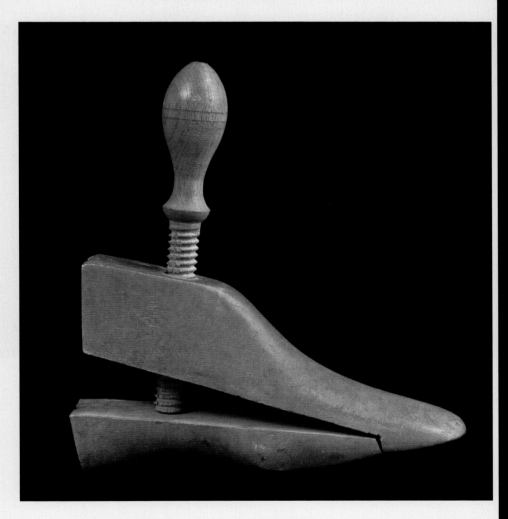

Hat Mold, Unknown Community, early 19th century 7" x 17"
Hatmaker's Form, Unknown Community, early 19th century 15 ½" x 14 ¼"
Hat Shaper, Unknown Community, early 19th century 13" x 2 ½"
Hat Brush, Unknown Community, early 19th century 16 ½" x 2 ½"
Hat Form, Unknown Community, early 19th century 4 ¼" x 5 ½"

The hat mold shown at top center has a crown formed of three sections. The adjustable form at bottom left has eight finely-turned wooden screws that press against a band of tin. The hat shaper consists of a metal head fitted on to a wooden handle. The hat brush has horsehair bristles and a delicately turned maple handle. The crown mold at bottom is made from one block of wood. The two Shaker hats illustrated are not in the Andrews Collection but are provided for context.

Andrews Collection, Hancock Shaker Village 1962.494.0003 (hat mold), 1962.498 (hatmaker's form), 1962.732 (shaper), 1962.663 (brush), 1962.299.0002 (form)

Leather Wallet, Mount Lebanon, N.Y. 1824 7 ³/₄" x 4 ¹/₂"
Graining Board, Unknown Community, early 19ᵗʰ century
3 ¹/₂" x 18" x 6 ¹/₂"

This leather wallet belonged to Shaker Deacon Stephen Munson. It is hand-stitched and can be closed using the leather strap attached to the top panel. It bears the stamped ownership mark of "Stephen Munson/ New Lebanon, 1824." Deacon Stephen conducted business for the community, sometimes traveling far from Mount Lebanon for that purpose. Although individual Shakers would not have kept personal wallets at this early date, it was appropriate for a Trustee or Deacon to have such a personal effect. When the Andrewses found this wallet it contained the Apple Jelly recipe shown below. The leather that the wallet is made from has been decoratively grained, a process whereby chemicals are introduced into the leather, probably by using a graining board as shown at right.

**Andrews Collection, Hancock Shaker Village
1962.043 (wallet), 1962.288 (graining board)**

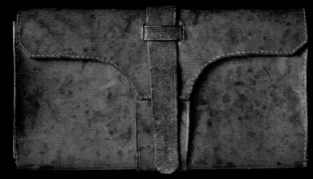

Herb Press, Watervliet or Mount Lebanon, N.Y. ca. 1840
36" x 24" x 18"

The Shakers at Mount Lebanon and Watervliet, New York used presses like this one to form dried herbs into small blocks. The blocks were then wrapped in paper, affixed with a label indicating the contents, and sold to the outside world. This press is constructed with a mortise and tenon frame. The cast-iron press is activated by turning the handle. The entire frame is finished in a red/orange wash.

Andrews Collection, Hancock Shaker Village 1962.480.0001ab

Patterns, Unknown Community, 19th century
(clockwise from top left) 2" x 22" x 16 ½", 2 ¾" x 8 ¼" x 7 ¾", 3 ¼" x 6 ½" x 19 ½", 2 ½" x 8"

The Shakers at Mount Lebanon's Second Family traded many cast iron products with the other families at that community. The Shakers may have done limited sand-casting of iron, but it appears that the majority of their cast iron was purchased from foundries outside of the community. These wooden patterns were models from which a foundry would have produced a finished product in iron. The pattern at upper left appears to have been made for a stove door. The two part pattern is for a bearing, and beneath it a mold for a double-bearing. At bottom is a beautifully crafted pattern for a clutch pulley made of tiger maple.

Andrews Collection, Hancock Shaker Village (clockwise from top left) 1962.721.0001, 1962.721.0004, 1962.721.0006, 1962.721.0003

Stove Patterns, Unknown Community, mid-19th century
(clockwise from top left) 35 ⅝" x 20" x ¾", 38 ⅛" x 15 ½" x ¾",
12" x 16 ½" x 33", 6" x 6" x ¾"

"November 1836: Samuel Turner is making a new kind of stove pattern, on a plan chiefly suggested by Hiram Rude." [98] *So wrote Brother Isaac Newton Youngs in the Mount Lebanon Church Family's Domestic Journal. It cannot be known if these are the stove patterns made by Brother Samuel, but they were certainly made to guide the casting and construction of a Shaker stove. The patterns at top were for different forms of the base, and are carefully rimmed along the edges with an applied wooden strip. Illustrated below are the stove chamber and a hinged door. The patterns are made of pine and finished with a dark stain.*

Andrews Collection, Hancock Shaker Village (clockwise from top left)
1962.747.0002, 1962.747.0001, 1962.747.0003, 1962.747.0004

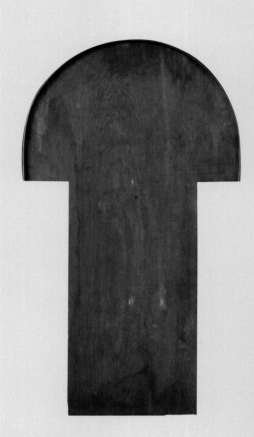

Stove, Unknown Community, mid-19th century
20" x 34" x 13 ¾"

This cast iron stove is typical of those designed by the Shakers in the mid-19th century. The stoves were cast in non-Shaker foundries. Generally each Shaker retiring and workshop room were outfitted with one of these small wood-burning stoves. This example has a wide curved apron attached to the front, and a door provided with a small draft door at bottom. The latch is finished with a polished wooden handle. The legs are finished in "penny feet" for extra stability.

Collection of Dr. Thomas and Jan Pavlovic

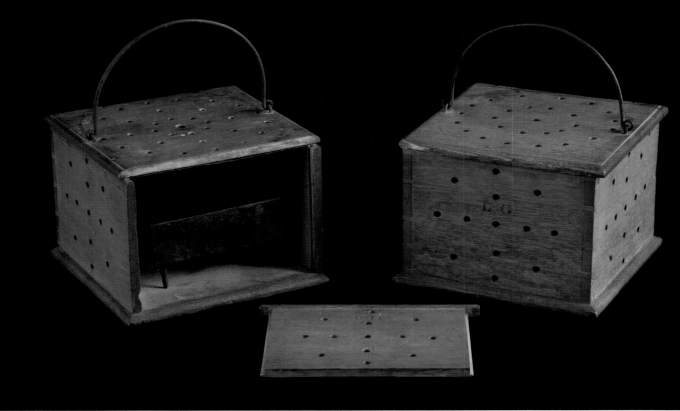

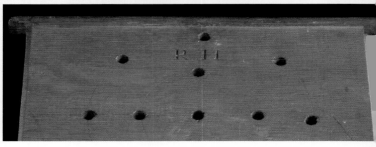

Canes, Unknown Communities, 19th century
41 ⅛", 43 ¾", 43 ¼", 38 ¼"

Foot Warmers, Hancock, Mass. early 19th century
6 ⅛" x 8 ⅛" x 8 ⅜", 8" x 8" x 7 ⅝"

These turned wooden canes taper in thickness from top to bottom. Each has a hole drilled through the top end to accommodate a string for hanging. The cane at right is finished in a bright red paint. The footwarmers are made of butternut and were acquired from Hancock.[99] They are small dovetailed boxes fitted out with a wrought-iron handle for carrying. The side walls and top have holes drilled in them to allow heat to radiate from coals held by a small metal tray within. Both are incised with the owner's initials: "R.H." (left) and "L.G." (right). Two grooved edges hold the door, which can be slid in and out to access the inside. These foot-warmers were finished in red lead, which has faded. **Shaker Furniture** *plate 20 (foot warmer).*

Andrews Collection, Hancock Shaker Village 1962.741.0001, 1962.741.0007, 1962.741.0009 (canes), 1962.503 and 1962.162 (footwarmers)
Collection of Edward D. Andrews II (red cane at right)

Mirror and Mirror Rack, Hancock, Mass. mid-19th century
12 ¼" x 16 ⅜"

"The mirror frame is veneered with curly maple on the front and sides, the side-strips forming a beveled edge around the frame. Made at Hancock." [100] *This mirror is hanging from blue-painted peg rail salvaged from the 1786 Meetinghouse at Hancock, Massachusetts (demolished in 1938).* **Shaker Furniture** *plate 30.*

Reproduced courtesy of The American Museum in Britain (Bath, UK), 1959.65

Herb Containers, Mount Lebanon, N.Y. mid-19th century

These cardboard containers were used to ship jars of herbal preparations made by the Mount Lebanon Shakers. The exteriors are covered in green paper. Labels identifying the contents are affixed to each, along with a label bearing the initials of Trustee David Meacham Sr.

Reproduced courtesy of The American Museum in Britain (Bath, UK), 1959.54.1-4

Adult Cradle, Unknown Community, early 19th century
24" x 24" x 66 ½"

*Shaker infirmaries were outfitted with these large cradles used to rock the infirm and elderly. This example is
made of butt-jointed pine, with iron brackets on the corners and hardwood rockers. It is finished in a red wash.*

Andrews Collection, Hancock Shaker Village 1962.570

Electrostatic Medical Device
Mount Lebanon, N.Y. ca. 1810
33" x 20 ½" x 14 ¼"

*"Second family, Mt. Lebanon. The
machine generated electricity, which
presumably was applied by means of the
pentodes to parts of the body affected by
disease. The wood-work is a choice
example of Shaker craftsmanship.
Found in 1926."* [101] *The two-part pine
case of this device is finished with a red
wash and finely dovetailed. Ted
Andrews cited the following reference
from a Ministry Sisters' Journal from
Mount Lebanon in his description of
the piece in* **Shaker Furniture:** *"the
first electrical machine made in the
church was put in operation.' on Dec. 17,
1808."* [102] **Shaker Furniture** *plate 39.*

**Andrews Collection,
Hancock Shaker Village 1962.068.0001**

Crock, Mount Lebanon, N.Y. ca. 1830
6 7/8" x 5 3/4"

Mortar and Pestle, Unknown Community, early 19th century
8 1/2" x 5 7/8"

Pill Roller, Unknown Community, mid-19th century
16 1/2" x 8 7/8" x 2"

*These objects were all associated with the apothecary, or medical
department, at a Shaker village. The crock at left was probably
not made by the Shakers, but it is stamped with the name of
the herbalist at Mount Lebanon: "G K. LAWRENCE/
NEW.LEBANON N.Y." The pestle has a porcelain head, and
was probably purchased by the Shakers, but the turned wooden
mortar was likely made within a Shaker community. The pill
roller was also probably commercially made, but the top part
of the implement is stamped with the initials "A•B" within a
decorative cartouche. Thin rolls of pill compound were laid
across the ridged metal cutting surface. When the top was
passed over the roll it was cut into individual pills.*

**Andrews Collection, Hancock Shaker Village
1962.435.0001ab (crock), 1962.444.0001ab (mortar and pestle),
1962.438.0001ab (pill roller)**

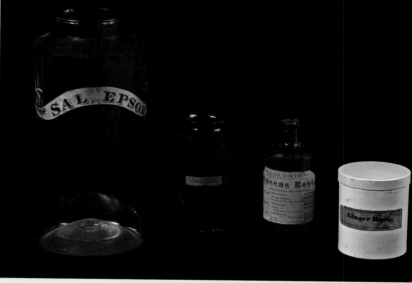

Herbal Preparation Jar, Mount Lebanon, N.Y. mid-19th century 3 1/8" x 2 7/8"
Lithographer's Stone, Mount Lebanon, N.Y. mid-19th century 2" x 6 3/4" x 4"
Jar, Unknown Community, 19th century 13 1/2" x 6 1/8"
Jar, Unknown Community, 19th century 7 1/4" x 3 1/2"
Herbal Preparation Jar, Mount Lebanon, N.Y. mid-19th century 7" x 2 3/4"
Herbal Preparation Jar, Canterbury, N.H. mid-19th century 4 3/4" x 3 5/8"
Glass Demijohns and Jars, Mount Lebanon, N.Y. early 19th century

The porcelain jar at upper left has a blue transferred label on it that reads "EXT. BUTTERNUT."
It was not made by the Shakers, but commercially made for the merchants "Bush & Hillyer" listed
on the bottom. The lithographer's stone was used to print the labels affixed to the outside of the
containers and jars that held herbal preparations. The first jar of the second group is decoratively
painted to read "SAL EPSOM", and the jar next to it has a paper label reading "COPPERAS".
The "Queens Root." jar bears a typical mid-nineteenth century Mount Lebanon label, while the
"Ginger Root." jar next to it is from Canterbury, New Hampshire. Pictured on the bench below
are a collection of hand-blown green glass demijohns and jars that were used
in the herb industry at Mount Lebanon.

Andrews Collection, Hancock Shaker Village *(clockwise from top left) 1962.095, 1962.487, 1962.477,*
1962.412.0008, 1962.106, 1962.097, 1962.412.0003, 1962.412.0015, 1962.412.0011,
1962.412.0012, 1962.412.0009, 1962.412.0013, 1962.412.0010, 1962.412.0014

Bench, Unknown Community, early 19ᵗʰ century
20 ¹/₂" x 29 ¹/₈" x 12 ¹/₂"

This simple bench has turned legs dowelled into the base and is chamfered along the lower edges. It is painted a deep red. **Shaker Furniture** *plate 25.*

Collection of the Family of David V. and Phyllis C. Andrews

Wash Bench, Mount Lebanon, N.Y. ca. 1820
22" x 11 ³/₄" x 7 ³/₄"

"Strengthened by a medial stretcher projecting and fastened beyond the end braces. From the Second Family, New Lebanon." [103] **Shaker Furniture** *plate 10.*

Andrews Collection, Hancock Shaker Village 1962.145

Sleigh Bench, Unknown Community, early 19ᵗʰ century 25" x 33" x 9 ¼"
Sleigh Bells, Unknown Community, early 19ᵗʰ century 23 ⅛" x 2 ¾" x 2", 14" x 2 ¾" x 2"

*This oak sleigh bench is mortised and pegged in place. It shows traces of a
yellow/green paint. The sleigh bells are probably not Shaker-made.*

Collection of the Family of David V. and Phyllis C. Andrews

Teaching Clock, Watervliet, N.Y. 1870
9 ¾" x 9 ¾" x 1"

This teaching clock was made at Watervliet, N.Y. It is decoratively painted on both sides and has cut tin hands. **Shaker Furniture** *plate 35.*

Andrews Collection, Hancock Shaker Village
1962.048

Trustees' Office sign, Unknown Community, ca. 1830
9 ¼" x 67 ⅜" x 1 ½"

This painted sign was hung outside of a Shaker Trustees's Office to indicate to visitors from the outside world where they should conduct their business. It was exhibited in 1932 at the Berkshire Museum.

**Andrews Collection, Hancock Shaker Village
1973.248**

Signs, Mount Lebanon, N.Y. 1842
36" x 36" x 2" and 94" x 5 ¼" x 4" (sign and post at left),
36" x 36" x 2" and 100" x 5" x 3 ½" (sign and post at right)

The "Confidential Journal Kept in the Elder's Lot. . . 1st Order" of Mount Lebanon's Church Family contains the following entry for July 25, 1842:

> There had been two wooden crosses prepared and painted white with writing upon them. They were by order of the Savior, each to be placed on a post, one just within the pickets fronting the Meeting House facing the road, the other, just within the fence fronting the Office facing the road. They were to be prepared by the Elders of the Second Order, and put up on the First day of May, the day of our first sacred and holy feast on the mount, and these crosses were to go up every Sabbath thro' the present season.[104]

These crosses are a physical remnant of the extreme manifestations exhibited in Shaker worship services during the late 1830s and early 1840s. During this period, known to scholars as "The Era of Manifestations," or "Mother's Work," Believers received spiritual gifts from the departed of all nations. Community members danced in the manner of Native Americans, Africans, slid like Eskimos, and moved to mimic other ethnic rituals under the operations of the spirits. It was decided by the Ministry at this time to cease welcoming the public to Shaker meetings on Sundays. These crosses were made to announce the closure. Edward Deming and Faith Andrews recalled how they first found these iconic crosses in **Fruits of the Shaker Tree of Life:**

> We had read that crosses had been erected at New Lebanon with a proclamation warning the world away, but supposed that these had long since been destroyed. It came as a surprise then, to find, stacked away in a corner of the top loft of the barrel-roofed meeting house, another proof that these fantastic rituals had once been observed. When the public meetings were reopened in 1845 the crosses, set on long posts, had been stored to await, perhaps, another awakening that never occurred. We photographed the crosses. But some years later, when the Shaker property changed hands, we looked in vain for them. In vain until one day, in the course of planning a project on Shaker architecture, we had occasion to make a survey of the brethren's brick shop at the Church family, a building long disused. In the cellar there was a mass of miscellaneous discarded material— stair rails, window frames, broken down cupboards and drawers, baskets, coopersware, machine and shop tools— a tangled mass, a mess. But in the half-light two lines of white caught our attention, revealing themselves on closer inspection, as the upright and cross piece of one of the crosses. There it lay in the midst of clutter, but with its message bravely surviving the hand of indifferent men.[105]

The Andrewses later arranged the acquisition of these crosses for Hancock Shaker Village, Inc. The cross at left bears the inscription: "Enter not within these gates, for this is my Holy Sanctuary saith the Lord. But pass ye by, and disturb not the peace of the quiet, upon my Holy Sabbath." It was placed outside the Meetinghouse. The cross at left was placed outside the Trustee's Office. It reads: "This is a place of trade and public business, therefore we open it not on the Sabbath. So let none contrive evil against my people saith the Lord, lest with my hand, I bring evil upon them." The photograph at center was made by Noel Vincentini in 1935 for the Index of American Design. It shows the Meetinghouse cross where the Andrewses first saw it in the attic of the 1824 Meetinghouse at Mount Lebanon, New York.

Andrews Collection, Hancock Shaker Village 1966.211.0001 (Meetinghouse cross), 1966.211.0002 (Trustees' Office cross), 1966.211.0003 (Meetinghouse post), 1966.211.0004 (Trustees' Office post)

The story of how the Andrewses rescued the interior of the 1786 Hancock Meetinghouse (below) is told on pages 85-87. Illustrated opposite are drawings and a watercolor made by architect H.M. Seaver at the behest of the Andrewses before the building was torn down in 1938. The latch is from one of the original pair of south doors (shown at right). The raised-panel doors are very similar in design and construction to late Georgian style doors used on houses throughout New England. These doors are now in the Andrews Collection at Hancock Shaker Village.

Meetinghouse, Hancock, Mass. ca. 1880
Andrews Collection, Hancock Shaker Village 909

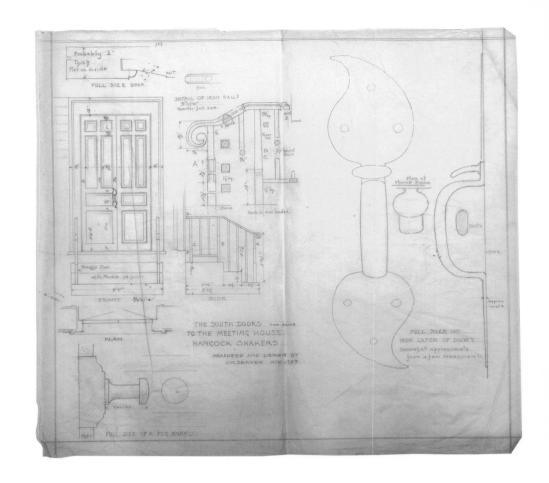

Watercolor and pencil drawings courtesy, The Winterthur Library:
The Edward Deming Andrews Memorial Shaker Collection,
No. SA 1290 (drawing), SA 1702.3 (watercolor).

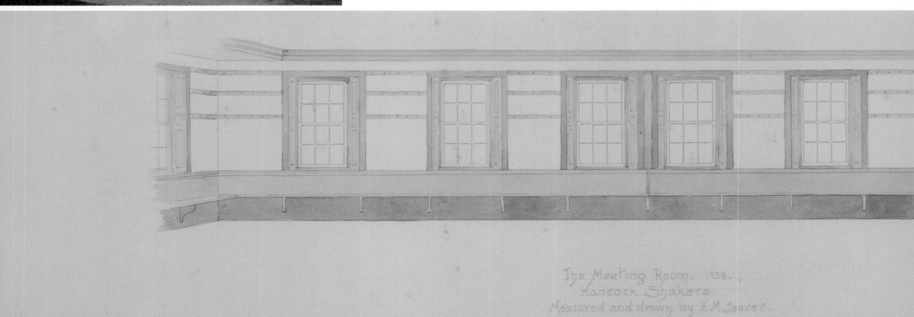

The western set of south doors of the 1786
Hancock Meetinghouse, shown from the
inside. The light blue paint visible on most
of the woodwork was applied after the
mid-19th century when many Shaker
communities repainted the interiors of their
Meetinghouses. The original dark Prussian
blue paint is visible beneath the ghosts of a
box lock and slide bolt (both still extant in
the Andrews Collection at Hancock). The
bottom portion of a door surround shows
the red baseboard, also seen on the bottoms
of the doors, that was painted around the
perimeter of the room. Just above that red
band is another undisturbed patch of
Prussian blue. The strap hinges are nailed
into the door and fitted with leather
washers that have survived.

Andrews Collection, Hancock Shaker Village
1962.048

Notes

Endnotes for the object captions continue in the same bibliographic style established in the notes to the essays by De Pillis and Goodwillie. Short form citations used below can be fully identified by searching in the notes for the essays.

1   Isaac Newton Youngs, "A Concise View of the Church of God" (1856), New Lebanon, New York, 255-256, Andrews Shaker Collection, 861. Edward Deming Andrews Memorial Shaker Collection, Winterthur Museum, Garden, and Library, Winterthur, Delaware (hereafter EDAMSC).

2   Margaret Hall, *The Aristocratic Journey ... 1827-1828*, ed. Una Pope-Hennessy (New York: G. P. Putnam's Sons / Knickerbocker Press, 1931), 39-43.

3   Harriet Martineau, *Society in America*, 3rd ed (New York: Saunders and Otley, 1837), Vol. 1, pt. 2:309-15.

4   H. "The Shakers." *National Intelligencer*, April 1, 1837.

5   Youngs, "Concise View," 256-257.

6   Isaac Newton Youngs, "A Domestic Journal of Daily Occurances: Kept By Isaac N. Youngs. Beginning at January, 1834. New Lebanon," New Lebanon, New York, [unpaginated], New York State Library, reel 10.

7   Youngs, "A Domestic Journal," unpaginated.

8   The reference to this kindling carrier is found in Jerry Grant and Douglas R. Allen, *Shaker Furniture Makers* (Hanover: University Press of New England, 1989), 38.

9   Youngs, "A Domestic Journal," unpaginated.

10 Youngs, "Concise View," 229-230.

11 Andrews and Andrews, *Shaker Furniture,* 114.

12 For more information on Brother Isaac's clockmaking see Grant and Allen, Shaker Furniture Makers, 42-48, and the extensive discussion in Glendyne Wergland, *One Shaker Life: Isaac Newton Youngs, 1793-1865* (Amherst: University of Massacusetts Press, 2006), 64-78.

13 Edward Deming Andrews, "Descriptive Catalogue of Shaker furniture collection . . . In possession of Mr. & Mrs. E. D. Andrews . . . Pittsfield, Mass. c. 1937," SA 1715, EDAMSC. Item #44 on the list.

14 Andrews and Andrews, *Fruits,* 66-69.

15 Grant and Allen, *Shaker Furniture Makers,* 39.

16 EDAMSC SA 1715. Item #45 on the list.

17 EDAMSC SA 1715. Item # 39 on the list.

18 Andrews and Andrews, *Fruits,* 139.

19 See Babara Isherwood, "A Special Tailoring Counter," *American in Britain* Vol. XXIX, 2 (1991): 8-11.

20 EDAMSC SA 1715. Item #10 on the list.

21 Youngs, "A Domestic Journal," unpaginated.

22 Andrews and Andrews, *Shaker Furniture*, 72.

23 EDAMSC SA 1715. Item #12 on the list.

24 Edward Deming Andrews, "Descriptive Catalogue of the Edward Deming and Faith Andrews Shaker Collection at Hancock (Mass.) Village," restricted archives, EDAMSC. Item #12 on the list.

25 Andrews and Andrews, *Fruits,* 139.

26 Written provenance in the possession of Richard J. and E. Barbara Pierce.

27 Timothy D. Rieman and Jean Burks, *The Encyclopedia of Shaker Furniture* (Arglen, PA: Schiffer Publishing, Ltd., 2003), 34.

28 EDAMSC, [miscellaneous notes], SA 1711. Item #28 on the list.

29 EDAMSC, [miscellaneous notes], SA 1711. Item #21 on the list.

30 John Kassay, *The Book of Shaker Furniture* (Amherst: University of Massachusetts Press, 1980), 211.

31 EDAMSC, "Descriptive Catalogue," restricted archives. Item #19 on the list.

32 Edward Deming Andrews, [miscellaneous notes written on yellow legal paper], box 8, Folder SA 1711 (#1018), EDAMSC. Item #30 on the list.

33 Emerich, *Shaker Furniture*, 53.

34 EDAMSC, "Descriptive Catalogue," restricted archives. Item #2 on the list.

35 EDAMSC, [miscellaneous notes], SA 1711. Item #24 on the list.

36 EDAMSC, [miscellaneous notes], SA 1711. Item #54 on the list.

37 EDAMSC, [miscellaneous notes], SA 1711. Item #27 on the list.

38 Andrews and Andrews, *Shaker Furniture*, 46.

39 EDAMSC SA 1715. Item #2 on the list.

40 Andrews and Andrews, *Fruits*, 25.

41 Youngs, "A Domestic Journal," unpaginated.

42 Andrews and Andrews, *Shaker Furniture,* 73.

43 Andrews and Andrews, *Fruits*, 65.

44 Emerich, *Shaker Furniture*, 66.

45 Andrews and Andrews, *Fruits*, 63.

46 Andrews and Andrews, *Fruits*, 64.

47 EDA to Dallas Pratt, May 3, 1959, Archives of The American Museum in Britain, Bath, U.K.

48 Dallas Pratt, [unpublished memoirs], Archives of The American Museum in Britain, Bath, U.K.

49 EDA to Dallas Pratt, May 3, 1959, Archives of The American Museum in Britain, Bath, U.K.

50 Flo Morse, "Creating a Shaker Room," *America in Britain,* Vol. XXXVI (1998), 4-11.

51 Rieman and Burks, *Encyclopedia*, 308.

52 EDAMSC, [miscellaneous notes], SA 1711, 22.

53 EDAMSC SA 1715. Item # 31 on the list.

54 [Grove Wright], Diary (1860), Andrews Shaker Collection, 822. EDAMSC.

55 Andrews and Andrews, *Shaker Furniture,* 90-91.

56 Andrews and Andrews, *Fruits*, 89.

57 Youngs, "A Domestic Journal," unpaginated.

58 Emerich, *Shaker Furniture*, 25.

59 [Rufus Bishop], *Testimonies of the Life of the life, character, revelations and doctrines of our ever blessed Mother Ann Lee* (Hancock [Mass.]: Printed by J. Tallcott & J,. Deming, Junrs., 1816), 51.

60 EDAMSC SA 1715. Item #60 on the list.

61 EDAMSC SA 1715. Items #93a and 93b on the list.

62 Andrews and Andrews, *Fruits*, 123.

63 This envelope is now among the uncataloged items in the Andrews Archives at Winterthur.

64 Andrews and Andrews, *Fruits*, 91.

65 Edward Deming Andrews, "A Personal Note," uncataloged in restricted archives, EDAMSC.

66 Issachar Bates, "A Sketch of the Life and Experience of Issachar Bates," *The Shaker Quarterly,* (Volume 1 Number 4 (Winter 1961), 156.

67 Andrews and Andrews, *Fruits*, 122.

68 Edward Deming Andrews, "A Personal Note," uncataloged in restricted archives, EDAMSC

69 For further discussion of these drawings see Julie Nicoletta, "Structures for Communal Life: Shaker Dwelling Houses at Mount Lebanon, New York" (PhD diss., Yale University, 1993) and Lauren Stiles, "The Mythical Structure is Created: Planning and Construction of the Center Family Dwelling House, Mount Lebanon, 1856-1868," in *The American Communal Societies Quarterly*, vol. 2, no. 1 (January 2008).

70 EDAMSC, Box 5, SA 1381 (#743).

71 Benson John Lossing, as quoted in Don Gifford and June Sprigg, *An Early View of the Shakers*, (Hanover [N.H.]: University Press of New England, 1989), 50.

72 M. Stephen Miller, *From Shaker Lands and Shaker Hands*, (Hanover [N.H.]: University Press of New England, 2007), 100.

73 For a further discussion of Hannah Cohoon's life and work see Jane F. Crosthwaite, "The Spirit Drawings of Hannah Cohoon: Window on the Shakers and Their Folk Art," *Communal Societies* 7 (1987): 1-15.

[74] [Rufus Bishop and Seth Y. Wells], eds. *Testimonies of the Life, Character, Revelations and Doctrines of Our Ever Blessed Mother Ann Lee, and the Elders with Her* (Hancock: Printed by J. Tallcott & J. Deming, Junrs., 1816), 66.

[75] David Rich Lamson, *Two Years' Experience Among the Shakers* (West Boylston [Mass.]: Published by the Author, 1848), 64-66.

[76] Sally M. Promey, *Spiritual Spectacles: Vision and Image in Mid-Nineteenth-Century Shakerism* (Bloomington: Indiana U. Press, 1993), 143-47; 151-152.

[77] Andrews, interview by Brown, 75.

[78] Andrews and Andrews, *Fruits*, 139.

[79] EDAMSC SA 1715. Item #77b on the list.

[80] EDAMSC SA 1715. Item #75 on the list.

[81] EDAMSC SA 1715. Item #76 on the list.

[82] Youngs, "A Domestic Journal," unpaginated.

[83] Edward Deming Andrews, *The Community Industries of the Shakers* (Albany: University of the State of New York, 1933), 164.

[84] Youngs, "Concise View," 256-257.

[85] Youngs, "A Domestic Journal," unpaginated.

[86] Edward Deming Andrews, "Inventory of oval boxes. . . Aug, 12, 1932," SA 1711, EDAMSC.

[87] Grant and Allen, *Shaker Furniture Makers*, 74.

[88] EDAMSC SA 1715. Item #5 on the list.

[89] Andrews and Andrews, *Fruits*, 139.

[90] Andrews and Andrews, *Fruits*, 220.

[91] Youngs, "A Domestic Journal," unpaginated.

[92] Andrews and Andrews, *Shaker Furniture*, 67.

[93] Youngs, "Concise View," 233-234.

[94] EDAMSC SA 1715. Item #91 on the list.

[95] New Lebanon Church Family Account Book 1828--1843, Hancock Shaker Village, Acc. 360.

[96] Information from Object Report on file in Curatorial Records, Winterthur, Del.

[97] Andrews and Andrews, *Fruits*, 138.

[98] Youngs, "A Domestic Journal," unpaginated.

[99] EDAMSC SA 1715. Item #94 on the list.

[100] Andrews and Andrews, *Shaker Furniture*, 85.

[101] EDAMSC SA 1715. Item #86 on the list.

[102] Andrews and Andrews, *Shaker Furniture*, 93.

[103] EDAMSC, "Descriptive Catalogue," restricted archives. Item #15 on the list.

[104] "A "Confidential Journal Kept in the Elder's Lot. . . 1st Order," Mount Lebanon, N.Y., V:B-136, Western Reserve Historical Society, Cleveland, Oh.

[105] Andrews and Andrews, *Fruits*, 49-50.

Notes: Layers of Evidence

[1] "Ministry Journals," New Lebanon, N.Y., NN, mss. no. 4, March 26–April 27, 1861, Shaker Collection, New York Public Library, New York.

[2] *Shaker Manifesto* 11.4 (April 1881): 91.

[3] I am deeply indebted to Christian Goodwillie, curator of Hancock Shaker Village, where these hymn sheets currently reside, for his generous and insightful help with this section. The University of Massachusetts Press published his and co-author Jane Crosthwaite's recent book, *Millennial Praises: A Shaker Hymnal* (2008).

[4] Correspondence, Watervliet, N.Y., f. 77, Western Reserve Historical Society (WRHS), 4:A-77.

[5] Correspondence, Mt. Lebanon, N.Y., f. 32, WRHS 4:A-32.

APPENDIX ONE:
Catalog Raisonné

Compiled by Michael Vogt

This listing accounts for all known objects donated by the Andrewses to Hancock Shaker Village, Inc.

1962.007.0001 – Desk, Double
1962.008.0001 – Candlestand
1962.009.0001 – Candlestand
1962.011.0001 – Chair, Dining
1962.012.0001 – Chair, Rocking
1962.013.0001 – Chair, Straight
1962.014.0001 – Stool, Step
1962.015.0001 – Stand, Sewing
1962.016.0001 – Sconce
1962.017.0001 – Box, Spit
1962.018.0001 – Box, Rectangular with Handle
1962.019.0001 – Chair, Rocking
1962.020.0001 – Stove
1962.021.0001ab – Carrier, Oval with Handle and Lid
1962.022.0001 – Box, Round
1962.022.0002 – Box, Oval
1962.023.0001 – Box, Oval
1962.024.0001ab – Box, Oval
1962.025.0001ab – Box, Oval
1962.026.0001ab – Box, Oval
1962.027.0001 – Box, Oval
1962.028.0001ab – Box, Oval
1962.029.0001ab – Box, Oval
1962.030.0001ab – Box, Oval
1962.031.0001 – Box, Oval
1962.032.0001ab – Box, Oval
1962.034.0001ab – Box, Oval
1962.036.0001ab – Box, Cardboard
1962.037.0001 – Box, Letter
1962.038.0001ab – Box, Round
1962.039.0001ab – Box, Round
1962.040.0001 – Cane, Walking
1962.041.0001ab – Teapot, Tin
1962.042.0001 – Book, Account
1962.043.0001 – Wallet
1962.044.0001 – Press, Bookbinding
1962.045.0001 – Table
1962.046.0001 – Desk, School
1962.047.0001 – Bench, School
1962.048.0001 – Device, School Clock
1962.054.0001 – Chair, Child's Side
1962.055.0001 – Chair, #1 Rocking
1962.059.0001-4 – Slate
1962.060.0001 – Blackboard
1962.062.0001-8 – Ruler, 1-Foot
1962.062.0009-10 – Ruler, 16"
1962.063.0001 – Chart, Anatomical
1962.064.0001 – Map
1962.066.0001 – Candlestand

1962.067.0001 – Stove
1962.068.0001 – Machine, Electrostatic
1962.069.0001 – Rack, Towel
1962.070.0001 – Platform
1962.071.0001 – Footstool
1962.072.0001 – Chair, #1 Rocking
1962.074.0001 – Warmer, Foot
1962.075.0001ab – Crutches
1962.076.0001ab – Pot, Chamber
1962.077.0001 – Rack, Towel
1962.078.0001 – Head, Phrenological
1962.079.0001 – Stool
1962.080.0001ab – Box, Rectangular with Lid
1962.081.0001 – Carrier, Coals
1962.082.0001 – Drawers, Portable
1962.083.0001 – Rug, Woven
1962.084.0001 – Bonnet
1962.085.0001 – Soapstone
1962.086.0001 – Spectacles
1962.086.0002 – Spectacles
1962.087.0001 – Coverlet
1962.088.0001 – Coverlet
1962.089.0001 – Towel, Linen
1962.090.0001 – Towel, Linen
1962.091.0001 – Curtain, Wall
1962.092.0001 – Curtain, Wall
1962.093.0001 – Pillowcase, Linen
1962.094.0001 – Glass, Blister
1962.095.0001 – Jar, Ceramic
1962.096.0001 – Container, China
1962.097.0001ab – Jar, Ceramic
1962.098.0001 – Box, Cardboard
1962.099.0001 – Box, Cardboard
1962.100.0001 – Container, Tin
1962.100.0002 – Container, Tin
1962.101.0001-2 – Vial, Glass Measuring
1962.102.0001-25 – Spool, Wooden
1962.103.0001 – Jar, Glass
1962.104.0001 – Jar, Glass
1962.105.0001 – Bottle, Glass
1962.106.0001 – Bottle, Glass
1962.108.0001-2 – Container, Asthma Cure
1962.119.0001 – Settee
1962.121.0001 – Footstool
1962.125.0001 – Basket, Wood Chip Carrying
1962.128.0001 – Print
1962.129.0001 – Print
1962.130.0001 – Print
1962.131.0001 – Print
1962.132.0001 – Print
1962.135.0001 – Stove
1962.136.0001 – Shovel
1962.136.0002 – Tongs
1962.137.0001 – Bench, Spindle Back
1962.138.0001 – Bench
1962.140.0001 – Portrait, Framed
1962.141.0001 – Portrait, Framed
1962.142.0001 – Portrait, Framed
1962.143.0001 – Portrait, Framed
1962.144.0001 – Portrait, Framed
1962.145.0001 – Bench, Wash
1962.146.0001 – Stove, Double Decker
1962.147.0001 – Basket, Melon
1962.147.0002 – Mat, Round Table
1962.147.0003 – Holder, Whiskbroom

1962.147.0004 – Basket, Round
1962.147.0005 – Basket, Oblong with 2 Side Handles
1962.147.0006 – Poplar, Woven
1962.147.0007 – Basket, Round
1962.147.0008 – Basket, Round Open Work
1962.147.0009 – Basket, Tub with 2 Side Handles
1962.147.0010 – Basket, Round with Handles
1962.147.0011 – Cover, Basket
1962.148.0001 – Gauge
1962.149.0001 – Gauge
1962.150.0001 – Shears
1962.152.0001 – Rack, Towel
1962.154.0001 – Cupboard, Wall
1962.155.0001 – Stool, Revolver
1962.156.0001 – Chair, Rocking
1962.157.0001 – Desk, Lap
1962.157.0002 – Cabinet, Sewing
1962.157.0003 – Chair, #3 Rocking
1962.158.0001 – Stove
1962.159.0001 – Footstool
1962.160.0001 – Mirror with Holder
1962.162.0001 – Warmer, Foot
1962.163.0001 – Tray, Sewing
1962.165.0001 – Rug, Runner
1962.166.0001a-bbb – Case, Knitting Needle
1962.167.0001 – Pincushion
1962.168.0001 – Shears
1962.169.0001ab – Spectacles and Case
1962.171.0001 – Can, Kerosene
1962.172.0001 – Can, Hot Water
1962.173.0001 – Measure, 1/2 Pint
1962.174.0001 – Broom, Whisk
1962.174.0002 – Brush, Whisk
1962.175.0001 – Box, Oval with Lid
1962.176.0001 – Towel, Hand
1962.176.0002 – Towel, Hand
1962.177.0001 – Curtain, Wall
1962.178.0001 – Pillowcase
1962.178.0002 – Pillowcase
1962.179.0001 – Sheet
1962.180.0001 – Curtain, Wall
1962.181.0001 – Basket, Round with Handle
1962.181.0002 – Basket, Oblong with Handle
1962.181.0003 – Basket, Round
1962.182.0001 – Footstool
1962.191.0001 – Desk
1962.192.0001 – Chair, Dining
1962.193.0001 – Rack, Hanging
1962.194.0001 – Candlestand
1962.199.0001 – Box, Oval
1962.225.0001-3 – Form, Basket
1962.226.0001 – Presser, Pleat
1962.227.0001 – Form, Basket
1962.228.0001 – Form, Basket
1962.230.0001 – Sieve
1962.232.0001 – Comb, Curry
1962.233.0001 – Tongs
1962.233.0002 – Tongs
1962.234.0001 – Rod, Ash
1962.242.0001 – Poster, Framed
1962.252.0001 – Brace
1962.253.0001 – Shave, Spoke
1962.254.0001 – Plane

1962.255.0001 – Brush, Dustpan
1962.256.0001-2 – Mallet
1962.257.0001-2 – Shears
1962.258.0001-2 – Hammer
1962.259.0001 – Saw, Pruning and Chisel
1962.260.0001 – Pliers
1962.261.0001-2 – Knife
1962.262.0001 – Awl
1962.262.0002 – Remnants, Cloth
1962.264.0001 – Chair, Dining
1962.266.0001-2 – Mop
1962.266.0003 – Brush
1962.267.0001ab – Teakettle, Tin
1962.268.0001-2 – Measure, Tin
1962.269.0001-2 – Funnel
1962.270.0001 – Strainer, Tin
1962.271.0001 – Scoop, Perforated
1962.272.0001 – Dipper, Tin
1962.273.0001 – Pitcher, Tin
1962.274.0001 – Dustpan, Tin
1962.275.0001 – Carrier, Coals
1962.276.0001 – Pail, Covered
1962.277.0001-9 – Mold, Maple Sugar
1962.278.0001-2 – Cutter, Cookie
1962.279.0001 – Sprinkler, Tin Laundry
1962.280.0001-2 – Ladle, Perforated
1962.280.0003 – Carrier, Basket
1962.281.0001 – Ladle, Copper
1962.282.0001 – Cover, Tin
1962.283.0001ab – Colander
1962.284.0001 – Lily, Tin
1962.285.0001 – Plane, Beading
1962.285.0002 – Plane, Beading
1962.286.0001 – Saw, Turning
1962.288.0001 – Board, Graining
1962.289.0001-5 – Plane, Smoothing
1962.291.0001-2 – Whetstone
1962.292.0001 – Plane, Long Jointer
1962.293.0001 – Plane, Short Jointer
1962.294.0001-7 – Plane, Molding
1962.295.0001-3 – Plane, Special Purpose
1962.296.0001-2 – Tool, Glass in Wooden Handle
1962.297.0001 – Stripper
1962.298.0001 – Form, Box
1962.298.0002 – Form, Box
1962.299.0001 – Form, Hat
1962.299.0002 – Form, Hat
1962.308.0001-2 – Kit, Sewing
1962.312.0001 – Stand, Spool
1962.313.0001 – Stand, Spool
1962.314.0001 – Stand, Spool
1962.318.0001-2 – Broom, Whisk
1962.319.0001 – Box, Round
1962.320.0001 – Scarne
1962.320.0002-7 – Spool, Wooden
1962.322.0001 – Tape, Straw
1962.323.0001 – Pincushion
1962.324.0001 – Case, Cloth
1962.325.0001-38 – Tool, Bone or Ivory
1962.325.0039 – Tool, Horn
1962.326.0001-5 – Brush, Clothes
1962.327.0001 – Brush, Scrub
1962.328.0001 – Sieve, Silk
1962.330.0001 – Shaker, Sand
1962.331.0001 – Mold, Round Basket

1962.331.0002 – Mold, Round Basket
1962.331.0003 – Mold, Oblong Basket
1962.331.0004-5 – Mold, Round Basket
1962.331.0006-7 – Mold, Oblong Basket
1962.332.0001 – Measure, Dry
1962.333.0001 – Box, Pine
1962.334.0001 – Presser, Pleat
1962.335.0001 – Pliers
1962.336.0001 – Weight, Wooden
1962.337.0001 – Box, Oval
1962.337.0002 – Box, Oval
1962.337.0003 – Box, Oval
1962.337.0004 – Box, Oval
1962.337.0005 – Box, Oval
1962.341.0001 – Portrait, Framed
1962.342.0001 – Portrait, Framed
1962.344.0001 – Hanger, Clothes
1962.347.0001 – Bench
1962.348.0001 – Bench
1962.357.0001 – Table, Trestle
1962.358.0001 – Bench
1962.359.0001 – Bench
1962.360.0001 – Stove
1962.361.0001 – Box, Wood
1962.363.0001 – Chest, Storage
1962.363.0002abcd – Knives and Forks
1962.365.0001-3 – Spoon, Wooden
1962.366.0001 – Plate, Wooden
1962.366.0002 – Plate, Wooden
1962.366.0003 – Plate, Wooden
1962.366.0004 – Plate, Wooden
1962.366.0005 – Plate, Wooden
1962.366.0006 – Plate, Wooden
1962.367.0001 – Skimmer, Brass
1962.376.0001 – Rack, Hanging
1962.378.0001 – Tub, Draining
1962.379.0001 – Tub, Draining
1962.382.0001 – Barrel
1962.383.0001 – Barrel with Cover
1962.384.0003 – Rack, Draining
1962.384.0004 – Carrier, Laundry
1962.385.0001 – Cart
1962.386.0001 – Pail, Wooden
1962.386.0002-5 – Bucket, Wooden with Wooden Bail
1962.386.0006 – Pail, Wooden
1962.386.0007 – Bucket, Wooden with Wooden Bail
1962.387.0001 – Dipper, Wooden
1962.388.0001-2 – Paddle
1962.389.0001 – Scoop, Dry Soap
1962.390.0001 – Funnel, Wooden
1962.391.0001 – Carrier with Handle
1962.392.0001 – Dish, Soap
1962.394.0001 – Basket, Round
1962.395.0001 – Basket, Clothes
1962.396.0001 – Shovel
1962.396.0002 – Shovel
1962.397.0001 – Tool, Ash Cleaning
1962.397.0002 – Tool, Ash Cleaning
1962.397.0003 – Tool, Ash Cleaning
1962.402.0001 – Cloth
1962.403.0001 – Bellows, Hand
1962.403.0002 – Bellows, Embossed Leather
1962.403.0003 – Bellows

1962.404.0001 – Shovel, Wooden
1962.405.0001-2 – Crane
1962.406.0001 – Kettle
1962.410.0001 – Portrait, Framed
1962.411.0001 – Cupboard, Herb
1962.412.0001-6 – Jar, Blown Glass
1962.412.0007 – Bottle, Glass
1962.412.0008-9 – Jar, Blown Glass
1962.412.0010 – Bottle, Wide Mouth
1962.412.0011-15 – Flask, Blown Glass
1962.412.0016 – Bottle, Glass
1962.413.0001 – Bowl, Garden
1962.413.0002 – Bowl, Garden
1962.414.0001a-c – Press, Cheese
1962.415.0001 – Basket, Cheese
1962.417.0001 – Device, Three-Bladed
1962.418.0001 – Container, Green Sweet Corn
1962.419.0001 – Poster, Colored
1962.420.0001-8 – Can, Summer Savory
1962.423.0001 – Jar, Candy
1962.426.0001 – Kettle
1962.427.0001 – Basket, Rectangular with Handles
1962.427.0002 – Basket, Rectangular
1962.427.0003 – Basket, Rectangular with Handles
1962.427.0004-5 – Basket
1962.435.0001ab – Jar, Brown Crockery with Lid
1962.436.0001 – Sieve with Handle
1962.437.0001-2 – Knife, Asparagus Cutting
1962.438.0001ab – Roller, Pill
1962.439.0001 – Slicer, Vegetable
1962.440.0001 – Knife on Frame
1962.443.0001 – Stand, Iron with Arms
1962.444.0001ab – Mortar and Pestle
1962.445.0001 – Mortar
1962.445.0002 – Pestle
1962.447.0001 – Bottle, Salepsom
1962.447.0002 – Bottle, Glass with Stopper
1962.447.0003 – Bottle, Glass
1962.447.0004 – Jar, Glass
1962.448.0001-6 – Finger, Wheel
1962.449.0001 – Rack, Herb Drying
1962.450.0001 – Rake
1962.451.0001 – Barrel, Sap or Molasses
1962.454.0001 – Bucket, Wooden
1962.454.0002ab – Bucket, Wooden with Lid
1962.454.0003ab – Bucket, Wooden with Lid
1962.455.0001-3 – Box, Berry
1962.456.0001 – Sieve, Wire
1962.456.0002 – Sieve, Wire
1962.456.0003 – Sieve, Wire
1962.456.0004 – Sieve, Wire
1962.456.0005 – Sieve, Horse Hair
1962.456.0006 – Sieve, Silk
1962.457.0001-9 – Box, Round
1962.457.0009 – Box, Round
1962.457.0010 – Box, Round
1962.457.0011 – Box, Round
1962.457.0012 – Box, Round
1962.457.0013 – Box, Round
1962.457.0014 – Box, Round
1962.458.0001-6 – Box, Round
1962.459.0001 – Carrier
1962.460.0001 – Pail, Wooden
1962.460.0002 – Box, Round
1962.460.0003 – Box, Round

1962.461.0001 – Pail, Milk or "Calf"
1962.462.0001 – Box, Round
1962.463.0001ab – Bucket, Wooden with Lid
1962.464.0001 – Pail, Covered
1962.465.0001ab – Box, Round
1962.466.0001 – Carrier, Bottle
1962.466.0002 – Rack, Draining
1962.467.0001 – Knife, Herb Cutting
1962.468.0001ab – Firkin
1962.469.0001 – Block, Electrotype
1962.470.0001 – Rack, Herb Drying
1962.471.0001 – Box, Dust
1962.472.0001 – Shelves, Flight
1962.473.0001 – Cupboard, Herb Label
1962.474.0001 – Cupboard, Herb Label
1962.475.0001 – Stool, Revolving
1962.476.0001 – Label, Apple Sauce
1962.480.0001ab – Press, Herb
1962.483.0001 – Chair, High Shop
1962.484.0001-2 – Broadside, Framed
1962.487.0001 – Stone, Lithographers
1962.490.0001 – Bench, Pine
1962.491.0001 – "Throne"
1962.492.0001 – Steps, Sewing
1962.493.0001 – Chair, Side
1962.494.0003 – Mold, Hat
1962.496.0001-2 – Mold, Basket
1962.497.0001 – Mold, Oval Box
1962.498.0001 – Stretcher, Hat
1962.498.0002 – Stretcher, Hat
1962.499.0001 – Hanger, Clothes
1962.500.0001 – Stove, Shop
1962.502.0001-2 – Board, Shirt
1962.502.0003-5 – Board, Clothes
1962.503.0001 – Warmer, Foot
1962.505.0001 – Mold, Round Basket
1962.505.0002-3 – Mold, Basket
1962.507.0001 – Remnant, Cloth
1962.508.0001-2 – Board, Sleeve
1962.510.0001 – Ruler
1962.510.0002 – Square, Tailor's
1962.510.0003 – Measure, Tailor's
1962.510.0004 – Measure, Tailor's
1962.510.0005 – Square, Tailor's
1962.510.0006 – Ruler
1962.510.0007 – Measure, Tailor's
1962.510.0008ab – Measure, Shoulder
1962.510.0009 – Measure, Tailor's
1962.513.0001 – Sample, Flannel
1962.513.0002 – Sample, Flannel
1962.516.0001 – Stand, Iron
1962.518.0001-5 – Kerchief
1962.520.0001 – Loom, Weaver's Bench
1962.521.0001 – Loom, Tape
1962.523.0001 – Wheel, Wool
1962.523.0002 – Batshead
1962.524.0001 – Winder, Quill
1962.525.0001 – Wheel, Flax
1962.526.0004 – Reel, Clock
1962.526.0005 – Reel, Clock
1962.526.0008 – Reel, Clock
1962.527.0001 – Frame, Warping
1962.528.0001 – Scarne
1962.528.0002-30 – Spool, Wooden
1962.529.0001 – Scarne

1962.530.0002 – Hackle, Flax
1962.531.0001 – Box, Loom Reed Storage
1962.531.0002-31 – Reed, Loom
1962.531.0032 – Box, Loom Reed Storage
1962.531.0033-40 – Harnesses, Loom
1962.533.0001 – Stand, Loom
1962.536.0001-28 – Spool, Wooden
1962.536.0029 – Basket of Spindles
1962.538.0001 – Sink, Dry
1962.539.0001 – Stove, Shop
1962.540.0001 – Box, Wood
1962.542.0001-8 – Container, Medicine
1962.543.0001 – Boonder
1962.544.0001ab – Dish, Soap with Cover
1962.545.0001 – Pail, Water
1962.546.0001 – Mirror
1962.547.0001-2 – Box, Match
1962.561.0001 – Basket, Winnowing
1962.562.0001 – Rack, Coffin Carrying
1962.563.0001 – Rake
1962.569.0001ab – Wheel, Wool with Batshead
1962.570.0001 – Cradle, Adult
1962.573.0001 – Bench, Cobbler's
1962.573.0002 – Block, Cobbler's Beeswax
1962.573.0003 – Awl, Leather Sewing
1962.573.0004 – Creaser and Burnisher,
         Combination
1962.573.0005 – Knife, Cobbler's
1962.573.0006 – Hammer, Cobbler's
1962.573.0007 – Hammer, Cobbler's
1962.573.0008 – Awl, Leather Sewing
1962.573.0009 – Container, Shoe Tack
1962.573.0010 – Tool, Cobbler's Scraping
1962.573.0011 – Awl, Leather Sewing
1962.573.0012 – Punch, Cobbler's
1962.573.0013 – Gimlet
1962.573.0014 – Wrench, Cobbler's
1962.573.0015 – Wrench, Cobbler's
1962.573.0016 – Awl, Leather Sewing
1962.573.0017 – Stick, Double Creaser
1962.573.0018 – Punch, Cobbler's
1962.573.0019 – Awl, Leather Sewing
1962.573.0020 – Wrench, Cobbler's
1962.573.0021 – Slick, Cobbler's
1962.573.0022 – Last, Heel
1962.573.0023 – Last, Heel
1962.573.0024 – Last, Heel
1962.575.0001 – Candlestand, Cobbler's Floor
1962.578.0001 – Rack, Shoe Last
1962.579.0001 – Last, Boot
1962.579.0002ab – Last, Boot
1962.579.0003 – Last, Boot
1962.580.0001-2 – Jack, Boot
1962.583.0001ab – Gaiters, Leather
1962.584.0001 – Smock, Linen
1962.590.0001 – Clock, Wall
1962.593.0001 – Stool, High Shop
1962.594.0001 – Box, Spit
1962.596.0001 – Sieve
1962.597.0001 – Whip Lash, Braided
1962.598.0001 – Molds, Plaster
1962.599.0001-4 – Pin, Clothes
1962.600.0001 – Rack, Pipe
1962.600.0002ab – Pipe
1962.600.0003ab – Pipe

1962.600.0004ab – Pipe
1962.601.0001ab – Mold, Pewter Pipe
1962.601.0002ab – Mold, Pewter Pipe
1962.602.0001 – Plane, Pipe-stem
1962.603.0001-9 – Box, Oval
1962.604.0001 – Box, Round with Lappers
1962.605.0001 – Ruler
1962.605.0002 – Ruler
1962.606.0001-4 – Tool, Small
1962.607.0001 – Comb, Horn
1962.610.0001 – Bench
1962.612.0001 – Compass
1962.616.0001 – Stretcher, Hat
1962.618.0001 – Fork, Long Handled
1962.619.0001 – Sauce or Bowl
1962.620.0001-3 – Hanger, Coat
1962.621.0001 – Tool, Bonnet Pressing
1962.623.0001ab – Mender, Mitten
1962.624.0001 – Measure, Tailor's
1962.625.0001 – Tool, Turning
1962.631.0001 – Bench, High
1962.632.0001 – Stool
1962.633.0001 – Seat, Double Wagon
1962.635.0001 – Heightening Tool, Chair
1962.638.0001 – Board
1962.640.0001 – Anvil
1962.641.0001 – Box, Spit
1962.643.0001-2 – Catalogue, Chair
1962.644.0001 – Medal, Bronze
1962.645.0001 – Lithograph
1962.646.0001 – Block, Electrotype
1962.647.0001 – Sample, Chair Tape
1962.648.0001 – Stand, Bonnet Form
1962.651.0001 – Vise
1962.652.0001 – Thread, Broom
1962.654.0001 – Box
1962.655.0001 – Clamp
1962.656.0001 – Chair, Shop
1962.658.0001 – Broom
1962.659.0001 – Box, Spit
1962.660.0001 – Print, Glossy
1962.661.0001-3 – Broom, Whisk
1962.662.0001 – Brush
1962.663.0001 – Brush
1962.663.0002 – Brush
1962.664.0001 – Brush, Dustpan
1962.665.0001-3 – Brush, Clothes
1962.666.0001-3 – Brush, Scrub
1962.667.0001 – Boonder
1962.668.0001 – Handle, Brush
1962.669.0001 – Duster
1962.670.0001-5 – Mop
1962.671.0001 – Brush, Floor
1962.672.0001-3 – Tool, Floor Waxing
1962.676.0001 – Chair, Revolver / Swivel
1962.677.0001 – Bench
1962.678.0001 – Stool, Shop
1962.679.0001 – Tub-foot, Tin
1962.680.0001 – Froe
1962.680.0002 – Froe
1962.681.0001-2 – Knife, Draw
1962.682.0001 – Shovel, Wooden
1962.683.0001 – Shovel, Tin and Iron
1962.684.0001 – Box, Pine
1962.685.0001 – Box, Pine

1962.686.0001 – Broom, Ceiling
1962.687.0001 – Box
1962.692.0001 – Bracket, Wall
1962.694.0001-2 – Can or Pot
1962.695.0001 – Skimmer
1962.698.0001 – Stock, Bit
1962.699.0001-34 – Rings, Sieve
1962.700.0001-19 – Measure, Dry
1962.700.0020 – Box, Wooden
1962.700.0021 – Measure, Dry
1962.700.0022 – Box, Round
1962.701.0001 – Mold, Basket
1962.701.0002 – Mold, Basket
1962.702.0001 – Box, Spit
1962.703.0001 – Tool, Round
1962.704.0001 – Header, Nail
1962.705.0001 – Tongs
1962.706.0001 – Anvil
1962.707.0001-2 – Bellows
1962.708.0001 – Keeler
1962.711.0001-2 – Form, Oval Box
1962.712.0001ab – Box, Oval
1962.712.0002ab – Box, Oval
1962.713.0001-49 – Template, Oval Box
1962.714.0001 – Rim, Oval Box
1962.714.0002 – Glovemender
1962.715.0001-17 – Glovemender
1962.716.0001-6 – Mender, Mitten
1962.716.0007-12 – Mender, Mitten - Thumb
1962.717.0001 – Vise
1962.718.0001-3 – Rack, Mirror
1962.719.021 – Awl, Leather Sewing
1962.719.024 – Burnisher, Leather
1962.719.037 – Last, Cobbler's
1962.721.0001 – Patterns, Wood
1962.721.0002 – Patterns, Wood
1962.721.0003 – Patterns, Wood
1962.721.0004ab – Patterns, Wood
1962.721.0005ab – Patterns, Wood
1962.721.0006ab – Patterns, Wood
1962.724.0001 – Hook, Hand Weeding
1962.725.0001 – Mallet, Heavy
1962.726.0001 – Binder, Sieve
1962.729.0001 – Chisel
1962.729.0002 – Tap
1962.729.0003 – Gouge
1962.729.0004 – Needle, Harness Maker's
1962.730.0001 – Safe, Chalk Line
1962.730.0002 – Safe, Chalk Line
1962.731.0001 – Rake
1962.732.0001 – Shaper, Hat
1962.733.0001 – Tool, Book Binders'
1962.733.0002 – Tool, Book Binders'
1962.734.0001 – Saw, Planemaker's
1962.737.0001 – Anvil
1962.738.0001 – Bench, Low Shop
1962.739.0001 – Square, Carpenter's
1962.741.0001-2 – Cane, Walking
1962.741.0004-9 – Cane, Walking
1962.742.0001 – Board, Pressing
1962.743.0001 – Box, Candle
1962.745.0001 – Box, Candle-small
1962.746.0001 – Dustpan
1962.747.0001 – Pattern, Stove
1962.747.0002 – Pattern, Stove

1962.747.0003 – Pattern, Stove
1962.747.0004 – Pattern, Stove
1962.748.0001 – Tool, Marking
1962.749.0001 – Helve, Axe
1962.752.0001 – Stand, Iron
1962.753.0001-3 – Shovel, Fire
1962.754.0001 – Box, Pipe Stem
1962.755.0001-7 – Yardstick
1962.756.0001-2 – Ruler, 1-Foot
1962.757.0001 – Stick
1962.758.0001 – Stick, Measuring
1962.759.0001-2 – Carrier, Oval with Handle
1962.760.0001 – Measure
1962.761.0001 – Bucket, Wooden
1962.765.0001 – Box
1962.776.0001 – Box, Hat
1962.793.0001 – Pipe
1962.796.0001-7 – Form or Mold
1962.797.0001 – Board, Ironing
1962.810.0001 – Stand, Reading
1962.813.0001 – Rack, Book
1962.815.0001 – Measure, Dry
1962.841.0001 – Bench
1963.107.0001 – Drawing, Gift
1963.108.0001 – Drawing, Gift
1963.110.0001 – Drawing, Gift
1963.111.0001 – Drawing, Gift
1963.112.0001 – Drawing, Gift
1963.113.0001 – Drawing, Gift
1963.114.0001 – Drawing, Gift
1963.117.0001 – Drawing, Gift
1963.118.0001 – Drawing, Gift
1963.119.0001 – Drawing, Gift
1963.121.0001 – Drawing, Gift
1963.122.0001 – Drawing, Gift
1963.123.0001 – Drawing, Gift
1963.124.0001 – Drawing, Gift
1963.125.0001 – Drawing, Gift
1963.126.0001 – Drawing, Gift
1963.129.0001 – Drawing, Gift
1963.185.0001 – Rack, Knife
1963.185.0002 – Knife, Kitchen
1963.185.0003 – Knife, Kitchen
1963.186.0001 – Ruler
1963.188.0001 – Rack, Trivet
1963.189.0001 – Board, Meat
1963.190.0001 – Table, Bread
1963.191.0001 – Board, Bread
1963.192.0001 – Cutter, Iron Breadknife
1963.195.0001 – Box, Drain
1963.197.0001 – Cutter, Curd
1963.198.0001 – Pitter, Cherry
1963.199.0001 – Box, Spice Grater
1963.200.0001 – Kerchief, Silk
1963.201.0001 – Coat, Wool
1963.202.0001 – Bonnet, Quilted
1963.203.0001 – Bonnet, Quilted
1963.204.0001 – Bonnet, Quilted
1963.205.0001 – Bonnet, Quilted
1963.206.0001 – Bonnet, Silk Covered Straw
1963.207.0001 – Bonnet, Straw
1963.208.0001 – Dress, Wool
1963.209.0001 – Dress, Wool
1963.210.0001 – Cape, Cloak
1963.211.0001 – Cape, Shoulder

1963.212.0001 – Dress, Cotton
1963.213.0001 – Dress, Cotton
1963.214.0001 – Dress, Glazed Wool
1963.215.0001 – Dress, Cotton
1963.216.0001 – Cape, Cotton
1963.217.0001 – Cap, Net
1963.218.0001 – Pouch, Leather
1963.219.0001 – Dress, Cotton
1963.220.0001 – Kerchief, Silk
1963.221.0001 – Towel
1963.222.0001 – Front, Shirt
1963.223.0001 – Coat, Wool
1963.224.0001 – Vest, Cotton
1963.225.0001 – Shirt, Cotton
1963.226.0001 – Pants, Cotton
1963.227.0001ab – Socks, Men's Wool
1963.228.0001 – Cloth, Wool
1963.229.0001 – Bonnet, Net
1963.230.0001 – Kerchief, Silk
1963.231.0001 – Smock
1963.232.0001 – Shirt, Cotton
1963.233.0001 – Pants, Wool
1963.234.0001 – Cap, Net
1963.235.0001 – Form, Bonnet
1963.236.0001 – Cape, Cloak
1963.237.0001 – Cape, Cloak
1963.238.0001 – Blanket, Wool
1963.239.0001 – Cape, Cloak
1963.240.0001 – Kerchief, Cotton
1963.241.0001 – Kerchief
1963.242.0001 – Kerchief, Cotton
1963.243.0001 – Kerchief, Silk
1963.244.0001 – Kerchief, Cotton
1963.245.0001 – Kerchief, Silk
1963.246.0001 – Kerchief, Cotton
1963.247.0001 – Cap, Net
1963.248.0001 – Form, Bonnet
1963.249.0001 – Capelet
1963.250.0001 – Dress, Cotton
1963.251.0001 – Smock, Gardener's
1963.252.0001 – Dress, Cotton
1963.253.0001 – Sack
1963.254.0001-5 – Yarn, Wool
1963.255.0001 – Cloth, Cotton
1963.256.0001 – Cloth, Cotton
1963.257.0001 – Cloth, Wool
1963.258.0001 – Cloth, Wool
1963.259.0001 – Cloth, Cotton
1963.260.0001 – Sleeve, Mother Ann's Dress
1963.261.0001 – Cloth, Wool
1963.262.0001 – Remnants, Cloth
1963.263.0001 – Leather
1963.264.0001 – Shroud
1963.265.0001-2 – Potholder, Cloth
1963.265.0003-5 – Potholder, Crocheted
1963.265.0006 – Potholder, Knitted
1963.265.0007-8 – Potholder, Crocheted
1963.265.0009 – Wiper, Pen
1963.265.0010-11 – Emery
1963.265.0012 – Beeswax
1963.265.0013 – Purse
1963.265.0014 – Case, Spool and Needle Folder
1963.265.0015 – Shoe, Doll's High-Heeled
1963.265.0016 – Case, Needle
1963.265.0017-18 – Folder, Needle

1963.265.0019 – Case, Needle
1963.265.0020 – Book, Needle
1963.265.0021-23 – Case, Needle
1963.265.0024-25 – Bag, Drawstring
1963.266.0001 – Corset
1963.267.0001 – Pincushion
1963.268.0001 – Bolt, Binding Tape
1963.269.0001 – Cloak, Hooded
1963.270.0001 – Bag, Small Wool
1963.270.0002 – Pad, Cloth Remnant
1963.270.0003-4 – Remnant, Cloth
1963.270.0005 – Remnant, Wool
1963.270.0006 – Remnant, Flannel
1963.270.0007 – Remnant, Cloth
1963.270.0008-10 – Remnant, Wool
1963.270.0011-12 – Remnant, Cotton
1963.270.0013-15 – Remnant, Wool
1963.270.0016 – Ribbon, Satin
1963.270.0017 – Tape, Wool
1963.270.0018 – Remnant, Wool
1963.271.0001-4 – Remnant, Wool
1963.272.0001 – Collar, Silk
1963.272.0002 – Collar, Silk
1963.272.0003 – Collar, Silk
1963.272.0004 – Collar, Silk
1963.272.0005 – Collar, Silk
1963.272.0006 – Collar, Silk
1963.272.0007 – Collar, Silk
1963.272.0008 – Collar, Silk
1963.272.0009 – Collar, Silk
1963.272.0010 – Collar, Silk
1963.272.0011 – Cuff, Cotton
1963.272.0012 – Collar, White
1963.272.0013 – Collar, White
1963.272.0014 – Collar, White
1963.272.0015 – Collar, White
1963.272.0016 – Collar, White
1963.272.0017-36 – Collar, White
1963.273.0001ab – Socks, Pair
1963.275.0001ab – Stockings, White Pair
1963.277.0001-2 – Case, Sewing
1963.277.0003ab – Fragments, Wedding Dress
1963.277.0004-5 – Pouch, Drawstring
1963.277.0006 – Bag, Linen
1963.277.0007 – Bag, Cotton
1963.277.0008 – Bag, Linen
1963.277.0009 – Bag, Linen Drawstring
1963.277.0010 – Pocket
1963.277.0011 – Pocket
1963.277.0012 – Bag, Drawstring
1963.277.0013-19 – Bag, Cotton Canvas
1963.277.0020-21 – Pouch, Canvas
1963.278.0001 – Bag, Grain
1963.279.0001 – Towel
1963.280.0001 – Towel
1963.281.0001 – Stocking, Women's
1963.282.0001 – Curtain, Infirmary
1963.283.0001 – Curtain, Infirmary
1963.284.0001 – Towel
1963.285.0001 – Curtain, Infirmary
1963.286.0001 – Towel
1963.287.0001 – Bag, Apron
1963.288.0001 – Bag, Laundry
1963.289.0001-2 – Towel
1963.290.0001 – Pants, Cotton

1963.291.0001 – Pants, Cotton
1963.292.0001 – Pants, Cotton
1963.293.0001 – Pants, Cotton
1963.294.0001 – Cape, Cloak
1963.295.0001 – Form, Bonnet
1963.296.0001 – Bonnet
1963.297.0001 – Bonnet, Straw
1963.298.0001 – Bonnet, Straw
1963.299.0001 – Pincushion
1963.300.0001 – Pincushion
1963.301.0001 – Rug, Woven
1963.302.0001ab – Stockings, White Pair
1963.303.0001 – Tray, Zinc-Lined
1963.304.0001 – Shoe, Women's
1963.305.0001 – Shoes, Pair
1963.306.0001ab – Stockings, White Pair
1963.307.0001ab – Stockings, Pair Wool
1963.310.0001 – Cloak, Hooded
1963.311.0001 – Cloak, Hooded
1963.312.0001 – Cape, Cotton
1963.314.0001 – Bag, Treated Cotton Work
1963.315.0001ab – Mitts, Pair Half
1963.316.0001 – Pincushion
1963.317.0001 – Rug, Braided
1963.318.0001 – Rug, Woven
1963.319.0001 – Kerchief, Linen
1963.320.0001 – Towel
1963.321.0001 – Towel
1963.322.0001 – Towel, Linen
1963.323.0001 – Tablecloth
1963.324.0001 – Case, Thread Holding
1963.325.0001 – Dress, Cotton
1963.326.0001 – Dress, Cotton
1963.327.0001 – Blanket, Wool
1963.328.0001 – Cloth, Cotton
1963.329.0001 – Sheet, Linen
1963.330.0001 – Sheet, Linen
1963.331.0001 – Blanket, Wool
1963.332.0001 – Coverlet
1963.333.0001 – Rug, Woven
1963.334.0001 – Sheet, Crib
1963.335.0001 – Sheet, Cotton
1963.336.0001 – Sheet, Crib
1963.337.0001 – Rug, Woven
1963.337.0002 – Rug, Woven
1963.339.0001 – Cover, Chair
1963.340.0001-26 – Remnants, Cloth
1963.341.0001a-hh – Tape, Fabric
1963.342.0001 – Material, Dress
1963.343.0001 – Towel, Linen
1963.344.0001 – Cloth, Cotton
1963.345.0001 – Kerchief, Cotton
1963.346.0001 – Kerchief, Cotton
1963.347.0001 – Bonnet
1963.348.0001 – Form, Bonnet
1963.349.0001 – Coverlet
1963.350.0001 – Rug, Braided
1963.352.0001 – Kerchief, Cotton
1963.372.0001 – Pillowcase
1963.394.0001 – Dress, Cotton
1963.395.0001 – Kerchief, Checked
1963.396.0001 – Pants
1963.397.0001 – Coat, Wool

1963.411.0001 – Cushion, Chair Seat
1963.412.0001 – Cushion, Chair Seat
1963.413.0001 – Cover, Chair Seat
1963.414.0001 – Cover, Chair Seat
1963.415.0001 – Cover, Chair Seat
1963.416.0001 – Sample, Hooked Wool
1963.417.0001 – Cover, Chair Seat
1963.418.0001-2 – Cover, Chair Seat
1963.419.0001 – Sample, Cloth
1963.529 – no record
1963.529.0001ab – Gloves, Pair
1963.529.0002ab – Gloves, Pair
1963.529.0003ab – Gloves, Pair
1963.529.0004ab – Gloves, Pair
1963.529.0005ab – Gloves, Pair
1963.529.0006ab – Gloves, Pair
1963.529.0007ab – Gloves, Pair
1963.570.0001 – Box, Dust
1963.1201.0001 – Box, Knife
1963.1201.0002-4 – Knife
1963.1202.0001 – Trough, Wooden Dough
1963.1203.0001 – Mallet
1963.1204.0001 – Trivet
1963.1204.0002 – Trivet
1963.1204.0003 – Trivet
1963.1204.0004 – Trivet
1963.1204.0005 – Trivet
1963.1204.0006 – Trivet
1963.1204.0007 – Trivet
1963.1204.0008 – Trivet
1963.1204.0009 – Trivet
1963.1204.0010 – Trivet
1963.1205.0001-2 – Sconce, Wall
1963.1206.0001 – Pin, Wooden Rolling
1963.1207.0001 – Pin, Wooden Rolling
1963.1209.0001 – Pin, Wooden Rolling
1963.1210.0001-7 – Chopper
1963.1211.0001-2 – Scrubber
1963.1212.0001-2 – Lemon Squeezer, Wooden
1963.1213.0001-6 – Paddle, Wooden
1963.1214.0001 – Mallet
1963.1216.0001-2 – Corer, Apple
1963.1217.0001 – Knife, Butter
1963.1218.0001 – Plate, Wooden
1963.1219.0001 – Strainer
1963.1220.0001 – Cutter, Cheese
1963.1221.0001 – Skimmer
1963.1221.0002 – Skimmer
1963.1221.0003 – Skimmer
1963.1221.0004 – Skimmer
1963.1222.0001 – Masher, Wooden
1963.1222.0002 – Masher, Wooden
1963.1223.0001 – Grate, Wrought Iron
1963.1224.0001 – Masher
1963.1225.0001 – Fork, Long Handled
1963.1226.0001 – Scoop
1963.1226.0002 – Scoop
1963.1226.0003 – Scoop
1963.1226.0004 – Scoop
1963.1227.0001 – Spatula
1963.1228.0001-2 – Knife, Coring
1963.1229.0001 – Spoon, Wooden
1963.1230.0001 – Rack, Draining

1963.1231.0001 – Rack, Wooden
1963.1232.0001 – Scoop
1963.1233.0001 – Lid, Wooden
1963.1234.0001-2 – Knife, Butter
1963.1235.0001 – Handle, Wooden
1963.1236.0001 – Scoop
1963.1237.0001 – Scraper
1963.1238.0001 – Cutter
1963.1240.0001 – Puller, Asparagus
1963.1241.0001 – Handle, Wooden
1963.1242.0001 – Cappadocia
1963.1243.0001 – Mop
1963.1244.0001-2 – Mop
1963.1245.0001 – Caster, Bed
1963.1246.0001 – Form, Basket
1963.1247.0001 – Bracket, Wall
1963.1248.0001 – Electrotype
1963.1249.0001 – Press, Butter
1963.1250.0001 – Bracket, Wall
1963.1251.0001 – Iron, Pleating
1963.1251.0002 – Iron, Pleating
1963.1252.0001ab – Box, Rectangular
1963.1253.0001 – Lamp, Glass Oil
1963.1255.0001 – Skillet, Iron
1963.1256.0001 – Bracket, Long Arm
1963.1257.0001 – Cage, Food
1963.1258.0001 – Lily, Tin
1963.1259.0001 – Funnel, Tin
1963.1265.0001 – Chest
1963.1268.0001 – Box, Spice Grater
1964.009.0001 – Dipper
1964.010.0001 – Scoop
1964.018.0001 – Strainer
1964.089.0001ab – Gloves, Pair Sheepskin
1964.091.0001 – Kerchief, Silk
1964.093.0001 – Kerchief, Silk
1964.094.0001 – Kerchief, Silk
1964.095.0001 – Kerchief, Cotton
1964.096.0001 – Kerchief, Cotton
1964.097.0001 – Kerchief, Wool
1964.098.0001 – Kerchief, Cotton
1964.099.0001 – Kerchief
1964.100.0001 – Kerchief, Cotton
1964.101.0001 – Kerchief, Cotton
1964.283.0001 – Scraper, Toothed
1964.319.0001 – Chair, Dining
1965.176.0001 – Basket, Fine
1965.177.0001 – Basket, Fine
1965.178.0001 – Basket, Fine
1965.179.0001 – Basket, Fine
1965.180.0001 – Basket, Fine
1965.181.0001 – Basket, Fine
1965.182.0001 – Basket, Fine
1965.183.0001 – Tube of Fine Basketry
1965.184.0001 – Pad of Fine Basketry
1965.185.0001 – Lid of Fine Basketry
1965.186.0001 – Piece of Fine Basketry
1965.235.0001 – Candelabra, Tin
1965.280.0001 – Device, Apple Quartering
1965.281.0001-3 – Corer, Apple
1966.200.0001 – Table, Double Drop Leaf
1967.113.0001 – Candlestick
1968.015.0001 – Mallet, Small

1968.033.0001 – Funnel, Glass
1968.034.0001 – Bottle, Aqua Glass
1968.039.0001 – Graduate, Glass
1968.050.0001 – Map, Columbia County, NY
1971.077.0001 – Model, Washing Machine
1971.083.0001ab – Shoes, Pair Men's
1971.083.0002 – Plane
1971.085.0001ab – Mortar and Pestle
1971.177.0001 – Reel, Warping
1971.245.0001 – Clock, Wall
1971.327.0001 – Beater, Rug
1971.333.0001 – Stick, Foot Measuring
1971.333.0002 – Stick, Foot Measuring
1971.334.0001 – Last, Cobbler's
1972.024.0001 – Carrier, Bottle
1972.074.0001 – Ladle, Tin
1972.304.0001 – Cabinet, Storage
1972.310.0001 – Mold, Basket
1972.310.0002 – Implement, Basket
1972.311.0001 – Mallet
1972.313.0001-2 – Mold, Basket
1972.315.0001 – Basket, Egg
1972.315.0002 – Basket, Utility
1972.315.0003 – Basket, Cheese
1972.315.0004 – Basket
1972.315.0005 – Basket, Rectangular
1972.315.0006 – Basket, Utility
1972.315.0007 – Basket
1972.315.0008 – Basket, Wood Chip Carrying
1972.315.0009 – Basket, Round
1972.315.0010 – Basket
1972.315.0011 – Basket
1972.315.0012 – Basket, Vegetable
1972.315.0013 – Basket, Fruit
1972.315.0014 – Basket, Egg
1972.315.0015 – Basket, Egg
1972.315.0016 – Basket, Tray
1972.315.0017 – Basket, Tray
1972.315.0018 – Basket, Utility
1972.315.0019 – Basket
1972.315.0020 – Basket, Utility
1972.315.0021 – Basket
1972.315.0022 – Basket, Utility
1972.315.0023 – Basket, Utility
1972.315.0024 – Basket, Vegetable
1972.315.0025 – Basket, Tray
1972.315.0026 – Basket, Utility
1972.315.0027 – Basket
1972.315.0028 – Basket, Egg
1972.315.0029 – Basket, Vegetable
1972.315.0030 – Basket, Sewing
1972.315.0031 – Basket, Dish Shaped
1973.005.0001 – Jack, Boot
1973.006.0001 – Chair, Side
1973.134.0001 – Loom, Tape
1975.135.0001 – Scale
1978.005.0001-4 – Drawing, Architectural
1979.082.0001-116 – Tape, Chair
1980.074.0001 – Fragment, Mother Ann's Dress
1982.021.0001-4 – Page from Tailor's System
1993.002.0001 – Unidentified Garment

APPENDIX TWO:

The Andrews Gift Agreement

This agreement made this 18th day of November, 1960, between Edward Deming Andrews and Faith Y. Andrews, husband and wife, both of New Haven, New Haven County, Connecticut, hereinafter called the Donors, and Shaker Community, Inc., a Massachusetts nonprofit corporation having its principal office in Pittsfield, Berkshire County, Massachusetts, hereinafter called the Donee.

1. In consideration of the solicitation for funds being conducted by the Donee and of the contributions made and to be made to it, and in further consideration of the Donee's undertakings set forth herein and its borrowing of funds to pay part of the purchase price of premises to be used for housing the property hereby conveyed, the Donors do hereby grant, transfer and convey to the Donee the Donor's collection of Shaker articles of every kind, whether furniture, artifacts, books, manuscripts, drawings, other library and pictorial materials, and other items, wherever now situated, principally located both in storage and on premises of the Donors in said New Haven and in Richmond, Berkshire County, Massachusetts; to have and to hold said collection to the Donee, its successors and assigns, to their own use and behoof forever, except as otherwise provided herein.

2. The Donors hereby covenant with the Donee that to the best of their knowledge and belief they are the lawful owners of said collection, it is free from all encumbrances, and they have good right to convey the same as aforesaid.

3. Said collection shall be delivered to the Donee and the Donee shall remove same from its present location or locations at its own expense as soon hereafter as may be practical and convenient to both the Donors and the Donee.

4. Said collection shall be used, exhibited, displayed and maintained by the Donee, its successors and assigns, under the direction of the Donors, at all times consistently with the nonprofit educational purposes of the Donee.

5. If said collection shall at any time after receipt by the Donee cease to be used as aforesaid (except during periods of preparation for exhibition, repair and the like), the same shall upon demand be surrendered to and become the property of the Donors or the survivor of them or the executors, administrators, legatees or assigns of such survivor; it being the intent of the Donors hereby to avert the diversion of any part of said collection to private use or profit.

6. This agreement shall be binding upon and shall enure to the benefit of the parties hereto and their respective executors, administrators, legatees, successors and assigns.

7. This is a Massachusetts agreement, made in that Commonwealth, and the interpretation and performance of all of its provisions shall be governed by the laws thereof.

In witness whereof, we, Edward Deming Andrews and Faith Y. Andrews, have set our hands and seals to this instrument and to another instrument of like tenor, and Shaker Community, Inc. has caused said instruments to be signed, sealed with its corporate seal and delivered in its name and behalf by Amy Bess Williams Miller, its President, hereunto duly authorized, on the day and year first above written.

APPENDIX THREE:

A Statement by the Donors

[Edward Deming Andrews and Faith Andrews]

On January 25, 1963, the donors received a letter from the president of this corporation saying in part that "Several of the officers and Trustees have suggested that. . . it would seem appropriate that this items in the (Andrews) collection which have not yet been received should now be brought to the village in Hancock and made available for exhibition and study as soon as possible, including the library and any remaining pictorial and other materials and furnishings. . . In order that we may make the necessary arrangements for transferring the various materials, please let me know during the next week as to just what date and time will be most convenient for you."

Since there existed this concern on the part of the board, on February 15 the donors wrote to the president requesting, in the hope that any misunderstandings could be clarified, that the matter be brought to the attention of the entire board. Previous attempts to settle the issue involved have not been successful.

The donors would remind the board that for 35 years they have been engaged in collecting, documenting and publishing Shakeriana. It has been their life work, in which they have worked as a team. They have an established reputation in this field of American history. The collection which they have assembled has been the result of a joint effort, a long and precious friendship with many Shaker sisters and brethren built on a foundation of good will and mutual understanding. The collection was assembled only because the Shakers respected our motives, and because they believed they were transmitting to us a trust and we would project, in our use of the materials, the heritage which, as a dwindling order, had to be placed in the minds and hearts of others. The donors accepted this charge, working together. One without the other could not have done what they have done. It is not their intention that this combination will be broken up.

The importance of such a collaboration was recognized when the contract was drawn up, in 1960, between the donors and Shaker Community, Inc., the donee. In the contract it was stated that the collection "shall be used, exhibited, displayed and maintained by the Donee, its successors and assigns, under the direction of the Donors, at all times consistently with non-profit educational purposes of the Donee."

The donors feel that attempts have been made to make ineffective this essential collaboration in the development of what could be, and still can be, a unique museum enterprise. In the beginning there was recognition of the fact that only through close cooperation between the donors and the donee could the project succeed. There was respect for the qualifications of the donors, their knowledge, and the prestige they brought to the undertaking. On the donors' part, there was the faith that through this organization their vision of a restoration memorializing the Shaker heritage would be realized, and that the work they had done would be projected into the future. There was a mutually acknowledged friendship, going back many years, between the donors and the president of this corporation. All seemed to feel as the donors did, agreeing with the principles they expressed in the prospectus prepared before the project got under way. In that pamphlet the donors emphasized the importance of preserving values as well as artifacts, of educating people in the unique contributions inherent in the Shaker culture. The Shakers were idealists, and <u>we all</u> accepted the responsibility of presenting their "gifts" to the world.

In those early days it was to be expected that there would be differences in opinion on certain matters. With this in mind the donors suggested regular staff meetings to discuss procedures and arrive at satisfactory agreements. However, little opportunity was given them in the early days and none in the last year to discuss and work out what should be mutual problems. They overlooked much in the hope that as knowledge of the project increased there would come increasing cooperation in working out the principles to which we all were committed. This has not happened, and in its place has come resentment and hostility to suggestions for developing the project in the true Shaker tradition.

The donors have made repeated attempts to correct the situation. Last summer, on their initiative, a closed meeting was held, attended by the president, the director, two board members and the donors. One problem on which there was misunderstanding was the library. In the course of the meeting it was clearly demonstrated that under present conditions it was not "practical and convenient" to transfer the library to the village; that there was no protection for it; that no provision had been made for its care, maintenance and use as an educational instrument. This priceless material, which represents the heart and spirit of Shaker culture, was entrusted to the donors by the Shakers on the understanding that it would always be carefully safeguarded. Yet despite the facts brought out at this meeting the donors were ordered by the president to release this irreplaceable property this spring.

On two other occasions one of the donors has appealed to have the opportunity of discussing problems with the president of the corporation, but in neither case has the request been honored. One cannot avoid the conclusion, from what has just been mentioned, and what happened at the last meeting of this board, that there is an attempt to remove one of the donors from all directional rights in the project.

How distressing such lack of understanding and cooperation has been to the donors, they hope this board will realize. It has meant, for instance, that the persons most qualified to direct certain installations have not been able to do so, even though it was originally agreed that all exhibits or displays should be set up under their direction. This was true in the retiring-rooms, and particularly in the costume room, which was opened against their wishes— with the result that the public, they feel, receive a false impression of the Shaker quality. It will be true of other areas such as the kitchen or cook-room, where the donors had many meals and good talks with the sisterhood. This area was, and is, a woman's province, like the retiring rooms and all areas of housekeeping. Restoration and installation of such areas should be under the direction of knowledgeable persons.

To all intents and purposes a collaboration which has produced four authoritative books, some 40 articles and monographs, and permanent installations here and abroad has been seriously challenged. How can this project succeed if the foundation principles are dishonored?

Another result of the breach has been the creation of a climate in which it is difficult to do creative writing and research, which were an important function of one of the donors. There has not been the peace of mind which is conducive to his best efforts.

To return briefly to the contractual agreement that the collection shall be "used, exhibited, displayed and maintained under the direction of the donors." one more example of the nullification of that right should be cited. Upon returning from his vacation in February, one of the donors found in the kitchen a large amount of material obtained from the cellar of, and purchased from, an Albany collector. No mention of this acquisition, now being catalogued, has been made to that donor. Much of the material is inferior and non-Shaker, and if retained and installed will vitiate the standards set by the community. Acquisitions such as this are desecrations which will debase the standards set by such fine collections as the Newton, Parsons and Andrews ones.

As the donors see it, there is only one solution to an impasse which is handicapping the development of the village, and that is a revival of the spirit of selfless dedication and mutual respect in which the project was undertaken three years ago. This can be accomplished, and when it is the future of the village will be assured.

APPENDIX FOUR:

Resignation of the Chief Donors to Shaker Community, Inc.

When we, the principal donors of furniture, industrial artifacts, inspirational paintings, etc. to the newly established community museum at Hancock, Mass., made the donation in 1960, we believed that the work of interpreting Shaker culture and craftsmanship, which had been our concern for thirty-five years, would be continued, with expert knowledge and integrity, under our active consultancy. We saw the Community as an educational enterprise, one that would educate the public, the "world," in the principles of Shakerism and the many ways in which these principles found expression in the work of Shaker hands. The gift was an act of faith. The Community, we trusted, would be truly a community of mind and spirit dedicated to a single purpose.

Since the gift was made, influences alien to such an ideal have so affected the operation at Hancock that its high purpose has been obscured if not subverted. It is not the aim of the present statement to detail the mistakes that have been made. Suffice it to say that though the original agreement specified that the donors should direct the use of what they gave, the administration has often seen fit to ignore advice and pursue an independent course violating both the latter and spirit of the agreement. The shortcomings of the project at Hancock are particularly evident when one compares it with the carefully planned Shaker installations, the professional guidance services and the distinguished sponsorship of such institutions as the Henry du Pont museum at Winterthur, Delaware, and the American Museum in Britain. Both of these museums are dedicated, by the spirit animating their enlightened directorship, to projecting the truth of the Shaker heritage.

Man's ideals, it is said, often exceed his grasp. We, the donors, reluctantly confess that— through no fault of our own— we have been unable to realize our cherished ideals for Hancock. Though we feel that we must therefore resign from the board of trustees of Shaker Community, Inc., we leave with best wishes for its future and the hope that, as long as the village lasts, what we have given will teach to others, in good measure, those lessons the Collection taught when it was in our hands.

E.D.A.

F.A.

1963

Index